THE WANING OF MAJOR WAR

The Waning of Major War is a systematic effort by leading international scholars to map the trends in major-power warfare and to explore whether it is waxing or waning. Although the main point of departure is that major-power war as a historical institution is in decline, this does not mean that wars between states are, in general, disappearing. While there is some convergence in the conclusions reached by individual authors in this volume, they are by no means unanimous about the trend. The essays presented here explore different causes and correlates of the declining trend in major-power warfare, including the impact of the international structure, nuclear weapons, international law, multilateral institutions, sovereignty and value changes.

This book will be of considerable interest to advanced undergraduate and postgraduate students in international relations, security studies and war studies.

Raimo Väyrynen is President of the Academy of Finland. He has been Professor of Political Science at the University of Notre Dame, Indiana, USA, and at the University of Helsinki, Finland. He has also been Director of the Helsinki Collegium for Advanced Studies, University of Helsinki. He is author or editor of six books on international relations and conflict.

CONTEMPORARY SECURITY
STUDIES SERIES

THE WANING OF MAJOR WAR

Theories and Debates

Edited by
Raimo Väyrynen

Routledge
Taylor & Francis Group

LONDON AND NEW YORK

First published 2006
by Routledge
2 Park Square, Milton Park, Abingdon, Oxon OX14 4RN

Simultaneously published in the USA and Canada
by Routledge
270 Madison Ave, New York, NY 10016

Routledge is an imprint of the Taylor & Francis Group

Selection and editorial material © 2006 Raimo Väyrynen;
individual chapters © the contributors

Typeset in Times New Roman
by Keystroke, Jacaranda Lodge, Wolverhampton
Printed and bound in Great Britain
by TJ International Ltd, Padstow, Cornwall

British Library Cataloguing in Publication Data
A catalogue record for this book is available from the British Library

Library of Congress Cataloging in Publication Data
A catalog record for this book has been requested

ISBN 0–714–65723–9 (hbk)
ISBN 0–714–68588–7 (pbk)

CONTENTS

CONTRIBUTORS

Martin van Creveld is one of the leading experts on military history and strategy, world-wide. Professor van Creveld has been a faculty member at the History Department, the Hebrew University, since 1971. He has authored seventeen books, the most important of which are *Supplying War* (1978), *Command in War* (1985), *The Transformation of War* (1991), and *The Rise and Decline of the State* (1999).

Marie T. Henehan, Ph.D. Rutgers University, is Research Associate and Senior Lecturer at Colgate University. She is the author of *Foreign Policy and Congress: An International Relations Perspective*, published by the University of Michigan Press, and co-editor of *The Scientific Study of Peace and War: A Text-Reader*, published by Lexington Books. She also does research on gender and international relations and her research has appeared in the *Journal of Peace Research* and in various book chapters.

Kalevi J. Holsti is University Killam Professor of Political Science (emeritus) and Research Associate at the Centre for International Relations at the University of British Columbia in Vancouver, Canada. He received his Ph.D. from Stanford University. He has been editor of the *International Studies Quarterly* and the *Canadian Journal of Political Science*. Holsti is the author of eight books, and many chapters in edited volumes and articles in leading journals of International Relations and Political Science. His most recent book, *Taming the Sovereigns: Institutional Change in International Politics*, was published in 2004.

Patrick M. Morgan is Professor of Political Science and holder of the Tierney Chair in Peace and Conflict Studies at the University of California, Irvine. He is a specialist in national and international security affairs with particular interests in deterrence and arms control, East Asian security affairs (particularly US–Korean relations) and US–European relations. His latest book, *Deterrence Now*, was published in 2003.

John Mueller is Woody Hayes Chair of National Security Studies, Mershon Center, and Professor of Political Science at Ohio State University where he teaches courses in international relations. His most recent books are *Capitalism,*

Democracy, and Ralph's Pretty Good Grocery (1999) and *The Remnants of War* (2004). He is currently working on terrorism and particularly on the reactions (or over-reactions) it often inspires.

T. V. Paul is James McGill Professor of International Relations in the Department of Political Science at McGill University, Montreal, Canada, where he has been teaching since 1991. He specializes and teaches courses in international relations, especially international security, international conflict and conflict resolution, regional security and South Asia. Paul is the author or co-author of many books, articles and chapters, including *Asymmetric Conflicts: War Initiation by Weaker Powers* (1994), *The Absolute Weapon Revisited: Nuclear Arms and the Emerging International Order* (1998/2000), *International Order and the Future of World Politics* (1999–2003), *Power versus Prudence: Why Nations Forgo Nuclear Weapons* (2000), *India in the World Order: Searching for Major Power Status* (2002), *The Nation-State in Question* (2003), *Balance of Power: Theory and Practice in the 21st Century* (co-editor, 2004), and *The India–Pakistan Dispute: An Enduring Conflict* (editor, forthcoming).

Paul W. Schroeder is Professor Emeritus of History and Political Science at the University of Illinois (Urbana-Champaign). He is the author or co-editor of six books and many articles primarily on the history and theory of European international relations, including *The Transformation of European Politics, 1763–1848* (1994/1996) and *Systems, Stability and Statecraft: Essays in the International History of Modern Europe*, edited by David Wetzel, Robert Jervis and Jack S. Levy (2004).

Hendrik Spruyt is Norman Dwight Harris Professor of International Relations at Northwestern University. He is the author of *The Sovereign State and Its Competitors* (1994), which won the J. David Greenstone Award. His latest book *Ending Empire: Contested Sovereignty and Territorial Partition* (2005) is a comparative analysis of various instances of imperial dissolution as well as of the Arab–Israeli conflict. He is currently working on a co-authored book dealing with how states divide and contract different forms of sovereign authority.

William R. Thompson is Professor of Political Science at Indiana University, Bloomington and President at the International Studies Association (2005–2006). He is the co-author most recently of *Growth, Trade and Systemic Leadership* (2004) and *Puzzles of the Democratic Peace* (2005).

John Vasquez holds the Harvey Picker Chair in International Relations at Colgate University. He has published over a dozen books including *The War Puzzle, The Power of Power Politics*, and *What Do We Know About War?* His articles have appeared in *International Studies Quarterly, American Political Science Review, British Political Science Review, Journal of Peace Research, World Politics, IO*, and *Security Studies*, among others. He is a former President of the International Studies Association and the Peace Science Society (International).

Raimo Väyrynen is President of the Academy of Finland. He has been Professor of Political Science at the University of Notre Dame, Indiana, USA, and at the University of Helsinki, Finland. He has also been Director of the Helsinki Collegium for Advanced Studies, University of Helsinki. He is author or editor of six books on international relations and conflict.

Peter Wallensteen has held the Dag Hammarskjöld Chair in Peace and Conflict Research at Uppsala University, Sweden, since 1985. He leads the Uppsala Conflict Data Program which presents annual updates on armed conflicts in the world. The program regularly publishes in the *Journal of Peace Research* and the SIPRI Yearbooks. Peter Wallensteen has most recently published *International Sanctions: Between Words and Wars in the Global System* (ed. with Carina Staibano, 2005), *Making Targeted Sanctions Effective: Guidelines for the Implementation of UN Policy Options* (with C. Staibano and M. Eriksson, 2003), *Alva Myrdal in International Affairs* (ed., 2003) and *Understanding Conflict Resolution: War, Peace and the Global System* (2002).

PREFACE

This volume has a long history in at least two senses. First, all authors have a long track record in doing research on issues of war and peace from various historical, empirical, and normative points of view. Second, the preparation of this volume has taken a while, primarily because of my moving from one job to another: first from Notre Dame to the University of Helsinki, and then from there to the Academy of Finland. Because of the willingness of the contributors to revise their chapters on several occasions, I am sure, though, that the contents of the volume are up to date and have also improved in the process.

The first versions of the chapters were presented to a conference organized and funded by the Joan B. Kroc Institute for International Peace Studies at the University of Notre Dame in May 2001. As mentioned, the chapters have been revised several times since then. One reason for doing so is that in the last several years the international political and military context of warfare has changed significantly. The growing use of military means in responding to new threats, in particular terrorism, has given credence to the argument that war and violence are on the rise again.

This view is not without foundation, as we are indeed witnessing new forms and waves of violence and counter-violence. The waning of violence as such is not, however, the main theme of this book which rather suggests that wars between major powers have become less and less likely. Moreover, it is difficult to imagine that such a war would break out in the future. As the editor, I stand behind this argument which is not necessarily shared by all the authors of this volume.

As the editor and former employee of the Institute, I would like to thank the Kroc Institute, and especially its John M. Regan Director, Professor Scott Appleby, for the generous support for the conference. The commitment of the Institute to fund the expenses helped us to bring to Notre Dame world-class scholars dealing with the history, the present state, and the future of warfare. The conference also greatly benefited from a Henkels grant provided by Notre Dame's Graduate School and a similar grant from the University's Nanovic Institute for European Studies.

Others who helped greatly in the organization of the conference include Linda Brady (White), Hal Culbertson, and Midge Holleman of the Kroc Institute. In addition, the international and US students of the Institute's graduate peace studies program were pivotal for the success of the conference. In Helsinki, Tuomas Tammilehto has been of great help in the editorial process which we have tried to finalize in the middle of other responsibilities.

Helsinki, March 2005
Raimo Väyrynen
Professor
President, Academy of Finland

INTRODUCTION

Contending views

Raimo Väyrynen

Introduction

In public discussion, the claim that the major interstate war is waning as an international institution is heard more and more often. One thinks of the statement of retired Marine General, Charles Krulak, in the Congressional testimony that 'the days of armed conflict between nation-states are ending.'[1] The mostly peaceful end of the Cold War generated a public expectation that the Damocles sword of international war would finally be lifted from humankind. The breakdown of bipolarity and the growing integration of the major powers in the world economy are ushering in a new historical period of stable peace or, at a minimum, of non-war.

The anticipation of a long era of interstate peace ahead of us is neither new nor should it be left unqualified. Several authors have argued the contrary case that warfare is either built in the nature of societies or human minds, or that wars follow a temporal or structural pattern, recurring at certain intervals and in certain contexts. In a related manner, it has been suggested that a particular international configuration of power tends to be more war-prone than another pattern.

Rapoport makes a distinction between political and cataclysmic models of war. In the former, Clausewitzian model, war is a rational military instrument used by governments for political purposes. On the other hand, in the cataclysmic version, wars are due to historical or structural forces that are largely beyond human control and hence prone to escalation.[2] This distinction is an important one; in the political model, human instrumentality matters, while, in the cataclysmic view, laws of society and culture shape the timing and nature of hostilities between human communities.

Obviously, if war is a natural phenomenon, peace is, then, unnatural. On the other hand, if war is made by human beings, then they can also avert it by building and maintaining peace. There is an equivalence between war and peace:

> the preservation of peace requires active effort, planning, the expenditure
> of resources, just as war does. In the modern world especially the sense

1

that peace is natural and war an aberration has led to a failure in peacetime to consider the possibility of another war, which, in turn, has prevented efforts needed to preserve the peace.[3]

Thus, neither peace nor war are natural conditions, but they can be both initiated and ended.

Therefore, neither rational calculation by decision-makers nor impersonal historical or structural forces can alone provide an adequate explanation for the frequency and intensity of interstate wars. The causes of war have been and will continue to be an imperfectly understood problem; we have been able to come up at best with 'islands of findings' about its correlates and causes, but we are still far from a general theory of war.[4]

This chapter aims to assess whether the major interstate war is waning or not as a policy practice. This thesis relies on the extrapolation of the fact that, with regard to war between great powers, the world has been living in peace for the past half century. In the case of Europe, Luard gives a lot of weight to this fact: 'this is a change of spectacular proportions: perhaps the single most striking discontinuity that the history of warfare has anywhere provided.'[5] This 'striking discontinuity' has been captured by the theory of 'long peace' that has prevailed in East–West relations since World War II.[6]

Over time, the number of wars per year turns out to be lowest in 1945–95 compared with previous periods. On the other hand, the costs of great-power wars have increased, presumably because of the growing power of the state, material resources generated by industrialization, and the development of new technologies of destruction. The escalation of the destructiveness of wars may have helped to erode, since at least World War I, its political legitimacy. Thus, the growing chasm between the costs and benefits of major wars may have contributed to the gradual pacification of interstate relations.[7]

The historical contextualization of the post-World War II 'discontinuity' can be criticized on at least two different grounds. One possibility is to deny the existence of any historical trends in the frequency of major-power wars and consider the latest non-war decades an exception that is hardly going to last.[8] Another historical argument against the waning-of-major-war proposition is that the frequency of great-power wars is cyclical in nature; they alternately wax and wane rather than decline. The roots of this fluctuation are usually assumed to be structural; a great-power war is a means to settle the problem of systemic hegemony, it reflects national and international economic dynamics, or war tends to break out at the inflection points of the national power cycles.[9]

From eternal peace to obsolescent war?

The ancestor of all peace optimists is obviously Immanuel Kant, whose *Idee zu einer allgemeinen Geschichte weltbürgerlicher Absicht* (1784) and *Zum ewigen Frieden. Ein philosophischer Entwurf* (1795) outlined a road toward an eternal peace by means of six 'preliminary articles' and three 'definitive articles.' The latter articles stipulate that international interaction should be free and safe ('universal hospitality'), the law of nations should be based on their 'pacific union' (*foedus pacificum*), and the constitution of each state should be 'republican' in nature. If translated into the current terminology, the modern Kantian would say that the eternal peace can be achieved if free trade, the rule of international law, and democracy become the guiding, and preferably enforceable, principles of international relations.

The scholars working in the realist tradition have regarded the Kantian premises of the universalist peace tradition, as opposed to the Hobbesian rivalry among states for survival. However, the duality of the Kantian thinking between universalism and particularism has made his appropriation by any particular school of thought difficult. Yet, not only liberals but also realists have made repeated efforts to capture Kant to their own camp.[10]

Kant was definitely a liberal as he abhorred international anarchy; wars created by it are both immoral and destructive. International anarchy and war also form a huge obstacle to the realization of the rights and freedoms of individuals in an orderly and moral society. Genuine individual freedom and social justice are possible only if interstate war can be eliminated as an international institution. Peace starts from the people, especially in the republican countries; because they know the deprivations of war, they do not want to start one.[11]

Kant's distaste for anarchy is, however, ethical rather than empirical in nature. It has been suggested that Kant agreed with Hobbes on the existence of the state of nature in international relations, but considered optimistically that it could be ameliorated to bring an end to continuous and destructive war by developing a set of principles by which this goal could be achieved. Yet, this does not mean that the ideas by Hobbes and Kant can be compared without qualification; on the contrary, Tuck, while underlining many of their similarities, speaks about the three kinds of 'Hobbesianisms of Kant.'[12]

Kant's universalism has been often misinterpreted as an ideological precursor for a global political system. In reality, he was opposed both to a hierarchical international state as an impractical proposition and the cosmopolitan federation of people. It seems that, ultimately, Kant was more of a statist than a communitarian thinker, as he saw autonomous states as the key actors of international relations.

Kant believed that *foedus pacificum* should be formed in a gradual manner by free, republican states whose democratic form makes it possible to set up a voluntary union or confederation (*Staatenbund*). Such a union could be formed only by republican states, but in a manner that there would be an enforcement mechanism above them.[13] In Kant's own words, the

> union is not directed toward the securing of some additional power of the state, but merely toward maintaining and making secure the freedom of each state by and for itself and at the same time of the other states thus allied with each other. And yet, these states will not subject themselves (as do men in the state of nature) to laws and the enforcement of such laws.

Thus, Kant believed that the road to a peace union starts from a cooperative arrangement between like-minded republican states, possibly under the influence of the strongest state of this kind.[14]

Kant has been criticized for setting too high a threshold for the attainment of a cosmopolitan order. Despite incomplete democratization of its member states, such a global order is, in the view of Habermas, already in existence. Particularly with regard to human rights, the United Nations has already moved beyond the requirements of *foedus pacificum*. In other words, Kant failed, by giving priority to sovereign states, to seriously consider the possibility of world citizenship and the international rights of individuals.[15] Kant can be saved, however, from this criticism by noting that he did not necessarily mean that only republican members can join the federation of states. As his highest goal was to end international anarchy, the federation should include also non-republican states as long as they subscribe to the principle of collective security.[16]

In sum, Kant's idea about the coming of the eternal peace is neither very radical nor utopian. He believes that the aggressiveness of states and individuals can be best contained by creating first a legal framework for rights and justice within states. The *Rechtstaat* then spills over to interstate relations, in which states agree on the rules of their political cooperation and economic interdependence. The republican *Staatenbund* creates the need for the non-members to emulate its political form by democratizing their own systems. Kant argues that the gradual enlargement of the republican community from the national to the regional and, ultimately, to the global level is a key to the overcoming of war. This process to strengthen the rule of law mitigates the adverse effects of the international anarchy.[17]

Thus, the Kantian theory recognizes the centrality of state actors and of their mutual competition, but also the importance of their socialization. The adverse effects of rivalry can be overcome only gradually through the moral development of individuals and the constitutional evolution of states, which both contribute to the socialization process. This development may also be contradictory and suffer from backtracking. In fact, in the Kantian thinking, the bar for the permanent peace is so high that the combination of all three factors – i.e. democratic constitution, respect for international law, and economic interdependence – is needed to sustain liberal peace.[18]

For this reason, most people think that we have not yet reached the Kantian *foedus pacificum* in its mature form. Even authors who are sympathetic to the Kantian ideas, and Deutsch's theory of security communities, readily acknowledge that we are far away from a global system of common security.[19] This is understandable, especially if we accept the interpretation that the Kantian peace process is a form of evolutionary social learning through which collectivities become gradually more democratic and learn to live in peace with each other. There is also empirical evidence that this learning process has reduced the probability of violence in the democratic dyads of states, although democracy alone cannot assure this development.[20]

To conclude, the Kantian argument is centered on the assumption that a combination of moral improvement, domestic political transformation, and the establishment of international rules will help to bring about the end to warfare. The democratization and pacification of international relations, composed of autonomous state actors, are the key elements of this development. In assessing this argument, the main dispute is whether we still live in an international anarchy or whether the relations between states have become so well regulated by norms of sovereignty, non-aggression, and cooperation that we have moved beyond the state of anarchy.

Those who answer affirmatively, tend to believe that a kind of 'code of peace,' however rudimentary in nature, has emerged. In tracing the history of this change, Jones times the origins of this code to the political and legal changes that started before World War I and continued in the 1920s.[21] The 'code' refers to various restraints and regulations between sovereign states pushing them from a national toward an international society. A similar, but a more sophisticated idea underlies Jackson's 'global covenant,' which is based on procedural and prudential norms that aim to manage the diversity and imperfections of human communities. Jackson's covenant stresses the importance of complying with the rules of the law of war, but it does not advocate a norm banning the resort to war. Thus, the covenant is not an instrument to eliminate war, but rather to promote moderation in warfare and stress the responsibility of great powers.[22]

Kant's theory is evolutionary, but only in a limited sense because the progress towards a permanent peace depends upon a number of conditions, such as individual rights and a republican constitution. A more evolutionary idea of the peace process, which is difficult to reverse, has been developed by Elias. He discerns in human development a 'civilizing process' that gradually strengthens the management of emotions and thus creates internal and external constraints on individual and collective aggressive behavior. As a result, pacified spaces expand from families and local communities to nation states and entire world regions.

In a contemporary formulation, Senghaas has suggested that the civilizing process integrates mutually supportive projects, such as democratic participation, economic interdependence, social justice, and constructive conflict culture. In that way, it becomes cumulative and difficult to reverse.[23] Behind the focus on the civilizing process there is the idea that modernity sheds violence and helps societies to internalize peaceful culture. This theory is largely unilinear, as Elias does not consider the possibility that states and other pacified spaces can be reversed by a 'decivilizing process' and slide back to violence and warfare.[24]

The optimism of Kant, Elias, and other authors about the feasibility of the gradual realization of permanent peace has been criticized and even ridiculed by a large group of skeptics who consider such a peace unattainable. They include authors who regard the evil human nature and the constant of international anarchy as causes of war as well as economic determinists.

These determinists fall into two categories: those who consider commercial rivalries to be the normal reasons for going to war and those who stress scarcity as the source of war. Various theories of imperialism focus usually on capitalists, great powers, and other mischief-makers competing with each other for the profit-producing resources of dependent areas. To secure the conquest, profits, and loot, the rivals may try to settle their scores by means of an imperialist war.[25]

Another view considers the amount of resources to be rather constant; as a result, when the number of nations and companies increases and they expand in the market, they face the condition of scarcity and clash with each other. In this mode of thinking, 'the cause of war is as permanent as hunger itself; since both spring from the same source, the law of decreasing returns.' The struggle for the constant or even shrinking pie does not need to be military. It can be also economic in nature: 'war of the most deadly character, war which ruins states and crushes nations is waged without firing a shot.'[26]

All the theories discussed above focus on long-term secular trends that alter the probability of peace and war. A different view is adopted by those authors who identify turning points in historical development; once such a point has been passed, the probability of major war starts to decrease in a big way. This kind of explanation usually postulates that, beyond the turning point, war becomes an arcane and even counterproductive social institution. This aspect of peace history cannot be tackled without a reference to Angell's *The Great Illusion*.

The book sets out to refute the standard pacifist argument about the immorality of war; it is 'not due to evil intention; is not made by wicked men knowing themselves to be wrong.' The book also denies the economic justification of war; due to their high costs, all wars tend to be futile. Angell takes seriously both the people's economic needs and the obstacles to economic cooperation among states. He argues, though, that these problems can be solved by the international exchange of goods which creates common interests, while war destroys them. Therefore, any efforts to acquire wealth by military means would turn out to be counterproductive.

In the years preceding World War I, the 'new world' of economic complexity and interdependence was taking over the 'old politics' of securing economic gains by military means. The new interdependent world economy and politically conscious human communities could not be governed any more by coercion. Instead, one needs international political cooperation which should be hampered by war only for pressing national reasons.[27] Angell's argument reflects the theory of commercial peace that has a long pedigree, especially in British liberal thinking.[28]

The commercial peace theory preceded the current view that economic globalization paves the way for peace and thus contributes to the waning of major war. In the contemporary scholarship, Rosecrance has been perhaps the most vocal advocate of the thesis that wars are waged by territorial states and not by trading states whose interests are in the expansion of market share rather than in territories. Trading states do not need the control of territory and its resources, but they can enrich themselves by developing international networks of economic relations. According to Rosecrance, 'the whole trend of international politics in the past half century moves against the notion of perpetual conflict.' Some regions, like the Middle East and Sub-Saharan Africa, continue to be afflicted by military conflicts, but a typical struggle is increasingly for the control of business networks rather than territorial power.[29]

The thesis that the major interstate war is waning is not novel at all, but it has gained new currency since the 1980s. The decline of the Cold War fostered the idea that peace may be possible. The changing political atmosphere also made it easier to discern alternative paths of development. The recent popularity of the Kantian philosophy and the democratic peace theory are manifestations of this reorientation.[30]

In modern political science and military studies, John Mueller and Martin van Creveld have, in addition to Rosecrance, been the main advocates of the thesis concerning the decline of the major-power war. Mueller considers the prolonged condition of peace a result of the historical process due to the emergence of a new political psychology. In his view, major-power war is becoming obsolescent in the same way as the institutions of dueling and slavery did in the past; people find such practices increasingly repulsive and obnoxious, and they start growing out of such socially malignant action.

Therefore, writes Mueller, 'like dueling and slavery, war does not appear to be one of life's necessities . . . one can live without it, quite well in fact. War may be a social affliction, but in important respects it is also a social affectation that can be shrugged off.' According to this view, the decline of interstate warfare reflects a deep attitudinal change and cultural transformation.[31] Such a transformation requires, however, a strong catalyst to break through the wall of resistance and ignorance. In the case of the decline of major war, this catalyst has usually been traced back to the 'Great War' of 1914–18, whose long duration, physical devastation, and cruelty made the war 'to become enemy'.[32]

Mueller concludes that a major war has become 'subrationally unthinkable'; even without its formal denunciation and renunciation, such war becomes increasingly inconceivable as a coherent political option. In his view, major war is replaced neither by a new moral equivalent nor an alternative international political structure. Among the developed countries, at least, it simply seems to have become an outdated and irrelevant institution. Yet, the demise of an institution is not necessarily permanent and the possibility remains that war may break out between major powers.[33]

Black also lends support to this interpretation by noting in Western societies 'a shift away from bellicosity,' which has led them to perceive war increasingly as an 'aberration.' The key reason for the institutionalization of peace is the 'demilitarization of civil society,' which deprives war of its political oxygen. Black points out that the preponderance of nuclear weapons contradicts only in appearance the cultural–intellectual shift from war to peace. In fact, nuclear weapons may have, by constraining the use of conventional military force, created a condition for the decline of militarism in everyday life.[34]

Ultimately, as Shaw argues, the decline of militarism as a popular ideology means that a transition to a 'post-military society' is taking place. In such a society, the military and even militarism may continue to exist, not as an autonomous force, but as a 'technologically determined "armament" element in mass consumer culture.' This means that the 'young specialists of violence,' to whom Howard refers, are tamed, and, without independent and aggressive political leadership, they have become mere technicians of war. However, the post-military society is not necessarily a pacific one – it is only a step in this direction – as the government may still decide to use military force to serve specific national or collective political ends.[35]

A certain problem in all of these accounts of emerging peace is their unproblematic treatment of World War I. Its horrors no doubt fortified the determination of many people not to experience them again. This commitment did not, of course, alone assure peace, because others drew a different conclusion; the injustices of the Versailles peace had to be rectified. A new war was possible, because the postwar settlement failed to create adequate international institutions to assure peace.[36]

The focus on the post-World War I politics overlooks, however, that the original reason for the outbreak of the 'Great War' was the failure of politics. I find much sense in the following observation about the origins of the war: it 'was not the continuation of politics by other means. It was the abandonment of politics to the military and to the streets. The mere existence of nation-states and their general staffs, not their irreconcilable differences, had given rise to the war.'[37] If properly interpreted, this observation allows the possibility that the roots of the long-term trend toward major-power peace extend to the period preceding World War I.

This conclusion does not suggest that the role of military power is about to vanish in international relations; nor does the waning-of-major-war theory contain such an implication. The change has taken place, as Rosecrance argues, in the objectives of the states and the means that are used to pursue them. Today, among the developed countries, the lust for territories, dynastic succession, the protection of religious rights, and colonial competition do not figure in any prominent way in the political agenda.[38]

In fact, the reduction in the relative economic value of land and the fear of the escalation of territorial disputes into a general war, which have given rise to the 'territorial integrity norm,' may be an important factor keeping major wars in check. The emphasis given to the norm has been a counterreaction to the territorial aggrandizement that was an integral part of both world wars. For this very reason, the norm has become increasingly respected; it has served well the interests of states to uphold their sovereignty and integrity.[39] In sum, this and other developments have tended to make military power less consequential in international relations, making them whirl increasingly around political and economic factors.[40]

The analyses by Mueller and other like-minded authors stress the importance of domestic changes, in particular those taking place in political culture. They associate the declining risk of major war with a cultural shift and its impact on the minds of people, providing thus an antidote to neorealist claims about the systemic roots of interstate warfare. The neorealist theory continues to insist that the distribution of international power is the only valid way to explain 'war's dismal occurrence through the millennia.' A bipolar distribution of power is the best guarantee of peace, while multipolarity, especially its unbalanced variant, is the most risky structure.[41]

Various versions of political realism provide their own explanations for the amount, nature, and functions of international warfare. For instance, the supporters of the unipolar view of the contemporary world see it as peaceful: 'the current unipolarity is prone to peace . . . unipolarity is durable and peaceful and the chief threat is the U.S. failure to do enough.'[42] In this thinking, peace is considered a public good that the dominant state provides for the world.

Thus, there is a disagreement in the realist camp on whether unipolarity or bipolarity is more conducive to peace. However, all realists of different hues consider the structure of international relations to be the key determinant of the frequency and intensity of interstate war. As long as international relations are 'anarchic' in nature, major-power war is a distinct possibility and, over a long term, perhaps even inevitable.[43] One may witness in realism, however, a certain return to the basics in which the practice of politics has become appreciated again.[44]

As to the key conclusion, van Creveld has also noted that, in the historical perspective, the major-power war is fading. In his view, 'large-scale, conventional war – war as understood by today's principal military powers – may indeed be at its last gasp; however, war itself, war as such, is alive and kicking and about to enter a new epoch.'[45] Van Creveld's explanation pays less attention to cultural changes and puts, instead, the premium on institutional transformation, in which the role of the state as the main war-making entity declines. The fragmentation of power fosters, instead, low-level violence, especially terrorism, with which the states require new institutional and practical responses to cope.[46]

Technology: peaceful or warlike?

Another major historical interpretation of the decline of major interstate war has focused on the self-deterrence created by increasingly destructive weapons technologies. The story starts from the revolution in military affairs (RMA) brought about by the invention of gunpowder and it continues through other similar revolutions, up to the invention and use of nuclear weapons. Such revolutions do not involve only the development and deployment of new weapons, but also broad economic and political transformations that change the ways in which military organizations and their instruments of war operate.[47]

The idea that military technology has reached such gigantic destructive capacity that no sensible leader will use it has a long pedigree. Toynbee was one of those who were afraid that the growing destructiveness of war would deliver a deathblow to Western civilization as had happened earlier in the history of some twenty-odd civilizations. In this pessimism, Toynbee was not by any means alone.[48] Victor Hugo thought that balloons had made air warfare so destructive that it had to be banned. In reality balloons and dirigible airships turned out to be so vulnerable and difficult to navigate that bombardment from them was prohibited in the Hague Peace Conference in 1899. Instead of heralding a new positive era, as its advocates hoped, the new 'aerial age' turned out to be very destructive. Bombs were dropped in 1911 on the civilians of Tripoli, and the bombing campaigns before World

War I were punitive colonial raids in North Africa and South Asia.[49] Only in World War II did air war become an integral part of major-power warfare.

Postwar surveys indicated that strategic bombing had had a more limited impact than had been anticipated. This might have limited the investment of resources in strategic air power had not a new weapon been developed that could be delivered to remote targets: the atomic bomb. The very destructiveness of this explosive, especially after the development of intercontinental missiles, created a major constraint on its employment in warfare. Nuclear weapons challenged in a fundamental way the Clausewitzian logic of war, in which available military tools are used to serve political ends. Now these tools became unusable, except for in the most extreme circumstances. Nuclear weapons internalized (self-)deterrence in a manner that was alien to the core of the Clausewitzian thinking.

Thus, there is only limited historical evidence that the fear of the destructive consequences of new military technologies has restrained their use in war. On the other hand, there is a strand of thinking which points to the adverse military and political consequences of new technologies. These arguments do not need to be of the pacifist or humanitarian variety, but they can be anchored, for instance, in the theory of offense–defense balance.

This balance has fluctuated over time, which means that the amount of war, fueled by the offensive predominance, is also historically variable. According to van Evera's operationalization, defensive technology favored peace in 1816–56, 1871–90, and again from 1945 onward.[50] Obviously, his results do not prove that a new era of major-power peace has been necessarily inaugurated since 1945, but neither does it deny that possibility. Some scholars have expressed doubts that the technological versions of the offense–defense balance have overstated the explanatory power of the theory and its political impact on decisions taken.[51]

Studies on the impact of the offense–defense balance on the probability of war point to the importance of the potential discrepancy between the 'real' and the 'perceived' balance. In addition, they show that there is only a scant concern about the ethical aspects of the offense–defense relationship. One would think that the benefits of defense could also be argued on ethical and not just on military or technical grounds. This is perhaps an aspect of the more general tendency to interpret the changing patterns of warfare as reflections of RMAs and other technological developments rather than results of political, economic, or cultural changes.[52]

Before World War I, it was commonly thought that offense had the military advantage, an idea which materialized in the 'cult of the offensive,' while in reality defense had many strengths that were underappreciated. This was pointed out by Ivan Bloch, a Polish banker, in his six-volume study, *Guerre Future* (1898), which argued that the defensive preponderance of the infantry has significantly undermined the chances of success by any offensive military operation. Bloch also observed that the growing duration of wars made them economically unsustainable and that they were also eroded by the spread of peaceful civilizational dynamics.[53]

These considerations led Bloch to suggest, in a rather prescient manner, as Engels had done already in the 1880s, that the next war would likely lead to a military stalemate and would, therefore, be long and bloody. Bloch did not deny the possibility of such a war, but regarded the decision of any government to start one as political folly and economic suicide. These views had some resonance among the military specialists, but, rather than adopting Bloch's pacifist remedies, they started to develop alternative military solutions to the dilemma, though with limited immediate success.[54]

Contrary to Bloch's ideas, it has been more common to suggest that new technological opportunities and their materialization have made war more likely or, should it break out, more destructive than previous wars. New technologies have also created new military uncertainties whose control has required their bureaucratization and industrialization reducing the chances of the political control of the military. At least in modern RMAs, the armies have become more autonomous and less subject to democratic control.[55] More generally, it has been argued that the constant (r)evolution in military technologies has reduced the role of human agency, creating a machine culture in which wars have become almost unstoppable.[56]

These views lead, however, too easily to technological determinism, in which impersonal forces mold societies and people's minds. For instance, Mumford sees a close connection between the development of capitalism and militarism, which both, in turn, strengthen the surveillance power of the state and its ruling class. The organizational model provided by the army served the emerging capitalism by teaching it the virtues of regimentation and standardization. Mumford did not like this trend, as it restricted the individual behavior to a military pattern and also encouraged rough-actions in the military sphere. Yet, he did not see an alternative to this historical dynamic driven by the development of technology and capitalism.[57]

Of course, not all authors agree that the risk of war is driven by technology. Initially, it may shape the organization and strategies of the military, but usually armies have adjusted, albeit slowly, to RMAs. Over time, the military absorbs the new technologies into its standard operating procedures. Thus, van Creveld insists that technology has not changed the essential functions of warfare; on the contrary, 'the logic of conflict, that logic which in turn dictates the essential principles of its conduct, is immutable and immune to any amount of technology that is applied to or used for it.'[58]

On that basis, he suggests further that the 'underlying logic of war . . . [is] paradoxical.' More specifically, 'technology and war operate on a logic which is not only different but actually opposed.'[59] The efforts to push technology in ever more destructive directions may not deter the use of military force altogether, but it gives rise to countervailing tendencies, as wars cannot be successfully waged by technological principles alone. In the nuclear age, this has become more obvious than ever. Similarly, following the theorists of commercial peace, one can argue that economic changes may not entirely eliminate war, but they lead to changes in the nature of warfare, thus ruling out wars of territorial conquest as a prudent national strategy.

The rest of this chapter focuses on the reasons why the major interstate war may be waning. It suggests several perspectives to account for this tendency, including the rise and decline of the state, the structural characteristics of the international system, the role of nuclear weapons and deterrence, multilateral norms and institutions, ethical and legal constraints, economic growth and integration, and democratic values and practices. The point is that the waning of major war requires some fundamental changes in societies and international relations. It therefore refutes the idea that international war can disappear in the absence of major changes in underlying human and social conditions.[60]

The rise and decline of major-power war

For centuries, war has been a central international institution. Its nature, frequency, and consequences have had major implications for the theory and practice of international relations. In the sixteenth and seventeenth centuries, a system of sovereign nation states emerged from the crucible of wars among various state and non-state units. The consolidation of the power of states over mercantile companies, pirates, feudal actors, and other private units was a long and complex and by no means a preordained development.[61]

The need to meet the financial, technological, and disciplinary requirements of the expanding warfare was an important motive for building up states and promoting national and cultural coherence. State machinery was needed to collect taxes, discipline the members of society, and invest resources in the development of new military technologies which all required the growing size of states.[62]

The impact of warfare on state-building has been uniform neither in Europe nor elsewhere on the globe. Yet, one can defend the general argument that the rise of the state has been linked with the development of modern war.[63] One of those links concerns the economic basis of war; the strengthening of state capabilities has fostered public order, which, in turn, has paved the way for a more robust economic growth and thus more resources for use in military competition with other states.[64] Conversely, it may be that the recent relative decline and transformation of the state may be associated with the declining relevance of the conventional interstate war. Modern states are welfare states rather than warfare states.[65]

The consolidation of states and their ability to monopolize violence have historically transformed the nature of warfare. The expansion of state power, economic growth, and the mass production of weapons all contributed to total war that included protracted fighting and massive human and material loss. The complexity of our subject matter is revealed by the fact that, while many authors consider modern technology and industry as harbingers of mass killings others see them ultimately as factors of progress and peace.

By the eighteenth and nineteenth centuries, the control of state power and the industrial capacity came increasingly to define the nation's position in the international war system. In addition, state interests, both offensive and defensive, were routinely used by governments to justify the resort to arms. States could not, however, fight wars without nations, but the people had to be mobilized extensively for the war effort. Instead of using elite units or mercenaries, modern battles pitched mass armies against each other. First in the US Civil War and subsequently in the two world wars, the mass armies suffered grievously from the use of the new military technologies and strategies.[66]

This chapter rests on the assumption that the waning of the major interstate war is due to the culmination of a profound historical process. The duration and intensity of wars have fluctuated over the centuries, although there seems to be a secular trend towards shorter, but more destructive wars.[67] Today, an international war between major powers has become a statistical rarity and perhaps soon an anachronism. In this process, technological, economic, institutional, and ethical forces may start converging into a durable interstate peace system, in which a major use of military force between states is increasingly unlikely.[68]

This argument is intellectually akin to the accounts that profess the spread of international security communities. Thus, anarchy becomes embedded in an increasingly multi- and plurilateral international society, in which its direct impact on political outcomes is reduced. In this development, material, political, and cultural factors conducive to peace are reinforcing each other and thus mitigating the military competition among states. It seems that the opportunity for an interstate peace has been more readily perceived by social constructivist authors. This may be due to their methodological preference for acknowledging the existence of multiple social realities and the possibility of their reconstruction as opposed to more deterministic neorealist schemes.[69]

The thesis about the decline of major interstate war is obviously controversial and it has been contested both on ideological and empirical grounds. Obviously, it is impossible to clarify the problem without defining the key concepts of the inquiry. In definitional terms, *a major interstate war occurs between the leading global powers or two or more dominant regional powers*. This definition includes not only wars between the great or major powers, but it also considers major regional wars.

The ranking of states on the basis of their material capabilities and political power is a notoriously difficult task. The concept of major power should be treated separately from war to avoid the tautology in which, for instance, A.J.P. Taylor becomes trapped when he defines great powers by their ability to wage war. If that definition is followed, and, if interstate war is waning, then there will soon be no great powers left! Wight makes more subtle distinctions between dominant powers, operating as world powers, great powers, medium powers, and minor powers. Historically, there have been great powers, such as Germany and Japan, which have not been genuine world powers. On the other hand, all world powers have been great and even dominant powers.[70]

Today, there is one dominant power, the United States, and seven great powers: China, France, Germany, India, Japan, Russia, and the UK, none of which is a world power. This list may look too long and include middle rather than great powers, and this objection is, to a certain degree, true. For instance, India has only recently graduated to this club and one can ask whether all European powers really belong to it. I prefer, however, a rather expansive definition as it makes the test of the hypothesis and speculation about its future validity more interesting.

In the post-World War II period, two major interstate wars at most have taken place. The first one was the Korean War, in which China and the US were involved as parties. In the Vietnam War, China and the Soviet Union provided extensive military support to North Vietnam, but their troops did not participate in fighting, unlike the Chinese forces did in Korea. In 1962, China and India waged a brief border war against each other. One may query, though, whether China and/or India were genuine great powers in the 1950s and the 1960s, and the answer is probably no. As both the Korean and Vietnam Wars are borderline cases, there seems to be rather strong evidence to support the thesis that major interstate war has become a rare event.

In regional systems, major interstate wars are fought between their leading members, who stand out from the rest of the states on the basis of their capabilities and political purposes. Moreover, such regional wars should have international consequences that affect the policies of the global great powers even to the point that a regional war prompts them to initiate a political or military intervention in the conflict. The possibility of regional wars, their causes, and the opportunities for their management depend obviously upon the structure, compatibility, and legitimacy of the regional systems. Miller argues that regional wars usually result from local causes and, particularly in stable regions, the impact of great powers is limited. In unstable and war-prone regions, the great powers may either provoke war or restrain it by their own actions.[71]

For instance, in a unipolar regional system, such as Southern Africa, there is no possibility of a major regional war because there is no counterpart to South Africa's capabilities. A regional war is most likely in an incompatible bipolar system that has a history of intra-regional conflict. I would include in this category the following regions: the Southern Cone (Argentina vs. Brazil), the Persian Gulf (Iran vs. Iraq), South Asia (India vs. Pakistan), and East Asia (especially the Korean Peninsula). The Middle East can be operationalized either as a bipolar or multipolar regional system, depending upon the criteria used.

If the hypothesis of the waning of major-power war is valid on the regional level, then such interstate wars should be rare and their risk declining. In assessing the evidence, we can neglect some cases in which the states are too inconsequential to be considered regional powers, even though they may have rivalries with each other. Thus, one can exclude the wars between Ecuador and Peru, Ethiopia and Eritrea (even though it was quite bloody), Armenia and Azerbaijan over Nagorno Karabakh, and the war in Bosnia. On similar grounds, one can leave out unilateral military operations such as the Tanzanian intervention in Uganda and the Vietnamese intervention in Cambodia in the late 1970s.

Yet, there have been regional interstate wars that cannot be discarded.[72] First of all, there have been three wars between India and Pakistan, and a fourth is not entirely impossible. Similarly, the three wars between Israel and the Arab countries have all affected international relations beyond the Middle East. The destructive war between Iraq and Iran in the 1980s for regional hegemony came close to a major war. On the other hand, the Chinese attack on Vietnam in 1979 was hardly a major war, as Beijing's intention was only to 'teach a lesson' to Hanoi. In sum, although regional interstate wars have been waged, they have been rather infrequent. Moreover, some regions – especially the Southern Cone, Southeast Asia, and the Korean Peninsula – have been saved from such wars.

There have been, of course, interventions by great powers into the affairs of small states. The United States has sent its forces to Vietnam, Afghanistan, and Iraq, not to speak of the Dominican Republic, Grenada, and Panama. Soviet troops intervened in Hungary, Czechoslovakia, and Afghanistan. Today, the pattern of great-power interference has changed; unilateral interventions to topple governments and eliminate local resistance have been replaced by collective operations that have been, as a rule, sanctioned by multilateral organizations. This happened in the Gulf in 1990–91, Kosovo in 1999, and Afghanistan in 2001, but not in Iraq in 2003. It is difficult to define these cases as interstate wars; in fact, they were enforcement operations resulting from the violation of the sovereignty of another state (Iraq vs. Kuwait), ethnic cleansing (Kosovo), and the support of terrorist activities (Afghanistan).

Thus, the argument that major interstate wars have become less likely has at least some face validity, although in recent decades there have been exceptions to it. In addition to empirical criticism, one can develop various general theoretical and practical arguments against the thesis. It has been said, for example, that the lack of internal strength and legitimacy of states continues to fuel warfare – though primarily, civil wars – which undermines, in turn, the capacity for peacemaking. This problem is seen also to persist in interstate relations, as the decline of the state increases the risk of war and reduces the restraints on limited and fragmented war.[73]

One way of solving the difference between these two schools, which argue, respectively, that major wars are waning and that such wars continue to be an available option for states, is to note the changing nature of warfare. It has been transformed from pitched battles between organized forces into a more fragmented, uncontrolled, and indeterminate series of military events. As a result, violence has become fractured and privatized and now serves different political interests than before; new forms of violence seem to be multiplying and spreading.[74] Thus, the diminishing risk of major interstate wars does not need to mean that other forms of violence are disappearing or even decreasing.

In any case, one has to be open to contrary evidence about the decline of major war. For instance, it has been argued that the persistence of war as a human institution is due to its ability to become culturally 'self-replicating' which obviously means that its eradication will be an uphill struggle.[75] The empirical and ideological challenges to the thesis on the decline of major war can also be countered by saying that, instead of being a universal institution, war has become increasingly place-specific.

For instance, it may be that war has returned to its rural roots; most civil wars take place in agricultural settings. The concepts of urban guerrilla warfare, which had some popularity in the early 1970s, have little relevance today (although one may say that terrorism is the current form of urban warfare). Today's rural wars rely upon primitive modes of combat and are waged by simple weapons. This can be contrasted with the omnipresence, sophistication, and speed of missiles, satellites, and other modern weapons that have a global reach.[76] Precision-guided munitions and unmanned flying vehicles are the contemporary rage. Global militarism is expensive, but local militarism costs human lives.

International system structure

The most common structural approaches to accounting for the causes of major wars, or, for that matter, of peace, focus on the structure of the international system and on conventional and nuclear weapons. Yet, the results concerning their role in the outbreaks of major wars are less than robust. For instance, scholars have reached no consensus on how hegemony, bipolarity, and multipolarity, as static international structures, are related to peace and war. There is equally little consensus on the impact of dynamic structural processes on the probability of interstate war.

Neorealists usually swear by balance of power and bipolarity as the best safeguards of peace. They tend to argue that 'unbalanced power, whoever wields it, is a potential danger to others,' who, therefore, aim to balance the situation by countervailing power. In practice, this means that to preserve peace, the dominant contemporary power, the United States, must contain its expansionism, while the second-tier major powers should pursue balancing policies.[77]

The supporters of the unipolar view part from the neorealist analysis in that they see the United States as so dominant a power that no one can even think of matching it. These authors are convinced that the unipolar international system, dominated by the US, is a key to stability and peace.[78] Another school of thought is less confident about the robustness of the US unipolarity and considers its hegemony 'hollow.' International peace and stability can be assured only if the international system makes a managed transition to multipolarity.[79]

The exclusive focus of the Waltzian approach on the gross structures of power in accounting for war has been criticized even by other realists. For instance, a plea has been made that, in the effort to trace the causes of war, one should also study the 'fine-grained structure of power,' which is created by political and material opportunities. This plea intends to bring back to the study of war decision-makers' perceptions, political strategies, first-mover advantages, and windows of opportunity. This turn does not mean that such structural factors as the offense–defense balance should be overlooked, but it underlines the need to examine also the micro factors of peace and war.[80]

The structural analyses of the causes of war are often static in nature. However, one has to keep in mind that not only do international structures change, but that the processes of change are not linear and they display various phases, cycles, and discontinuities. Cyclical explanations can focus on hegemonic power or leadership cycles, the rise and decline of leading technology sectors, or long-term economic fluctuations. A common feature of these approaches is that major wars are neither waning nor waxing, but fluctuating; such wars tend to recur as the political, economic, or technological cycles mature.[81]

Theories of power cycles and power transitions indicate that some phases of global power dynamics are more prone to warfare than others. A common element of these theories is that the use of military force becomes more likely if the expanding states clash at the intersections of their power trajectories or the rising and declining states are locked in a hegemonic competition. In both of these cases, the material power dynamics and its political perceptions are supposed to critically affect decision-making and, thus, the likelihood of war. The 'lateral pressure' theory places economic, technological, and demographic expansion and their impact on territorial competition in the key position. The theory has dynamic qualities, as it also considers interconnections and feedback mechanisms.[82]

In the power transition models, change is the constant. During the Cold War, it looked as though the Soviet Union would be able to overtake the United States, which went into a period of relative decline in the 1960s when the Soviet economy was still vibrant. Despite efforts at domestic reforms, the institutional and political inertia of the Soviet system foiled its trajectory. Now the same thing, *mutatis mutandis*, seems to have happened to Japan. This has permitted the US to retain its international leadership.[83] A remarkable thing in this development has been that the end of the Cold War happened peacefully; no major war was needed to clarify the new power relations that now heavily favor the United States.

Most explorations and speculations regarding the future predict either the continuation of US dominance, perhaps at the head of an international concert, or the long-term rise of China to challenge the US leadership. If that challenge is not managed carefully, the risk of a major-power war might arise again, thus re-enacting the hegemonic cycle in international relations.

The peaceful end of the Cold War happened because the US chose to be restrained in its victory, partly because of the pressures by its European allies, and because Russia remained committed to domestic reforms and international cooperation. The existing international institutions signaled the credibility of the commitments to restraint and further cooperation that have continued in the post-Cold War world through the enlargement of old institutions and the establishment of new ones.[84] In addition, the decision of the Gorbachev administration not to use military force against its former allies defecting from the socialist model and the Warsaw Pact was of central importance for the peaceful outcome of the transition.

In sum, there was in 1989–91 no power in the system that was so dissatisfied with the prevailing political arrangement, and yet strong enough, that it felt the need to embark upon revisionist or resistance policies. In all, this outcome can be explained either by serendipity, the happy concurrence of factors conducive to peace, or the notion that the net benefits derived by the major states from the international economic and political order have increased to such an extent that the decision to challenge peace requires extraordinary grievances.

Nuclear weapons

Among the military factors most frequently mentioned as explanations for the 'long peace' is the deterrent effect of nuclear weapons and the underlying dominance of offense over defense, which puts in jeopardy the existence of nuclear-weapon powers locked in competition with each other. Moreover, the high economic costs of war and occupation, compared with their diminishing benefits, have been additional reasons for discouraging territorial expansionism by means of war (which is, in fact, an economic version of the defense dominance). This reasoning leads to two simple propositions: that nuclear weapons and the defense dominance are contributing to peace.

According to the deterrence theory, the strategic range of nuclear weapons and the threat of their employment have prevented the outbreak of major wars and brought about the 'long peace'. The emphasis on nuclear weapons is usually complemented by reference to systemic bipolarity as another factor discouraging major war.[85] The relationship between nuclear weapons and bipolarity is not obvious. One can argue both that nuclear weapons were the key element of military power that constituted bipolarity or that bipolarity contributed to credible nuclear deterrence.

On the other side, nuclear weapons have been considered 'essentially irrelevant' in safeguarding peace among the great powers. In this view, their risk-averse leaders, recalling the horrors of the two world wars, were more comfortable with the status quo and avoided the explicit and active reliance on nuclear weapons to regulate their mutual relations. Such a policy would have also been politically inefficient, as the other party could have easily called the bluff, thus, nuclear weapons were politically sterilized.[86]

There are, however, limits to the argument that nuclear weapons have been essentially irrelevant in maintaining the great-power peace. The proliferation of nuclear weapons, especially in South Asia, keeps reminding us that their acquisition and use by major regional powers cannot be excluded altogether. Thus, while the nuclear weapons and deterrence provided by them were neither the main force of peace nor the catalyst of war in the US–Soviet confrontation, they can still be a source of instability and tensions. It may be, though, that the learning experiences associated with nuclear weapons and their destructive potential have paralyzed their active political role. It may even be that nuclear weapons have reinforced the effects of other peace factors, such as international institutions, and thus contributed contextually to the prevention of war.[87]

The structural explanations for major wars run the risk of becoming too mechanistic if one does not pay adequate attention to the substance of conflicts. Therefore, one has to consider the issues over which wars are waged and the stakes that various powers have in them. The nature of conflict-producing issues has changed significantly over the last centuries. Holsti has shown in a wide-ranging historical and empirical study that territorial and economic factors have become less central causes of warfare, while nation- and state-building, in conjunction with ideological and ideational factors, have retained their relevance as reasons for war.[88]

Institutions, norms, and values

Conclusions about the viability of the 'long peace' should not be based solely upon the possession and spread of nuclear weapons or the existence of specific international system structures. One of the remarkable developments in post-war international relations has been the strengthening of multilateral norms and institutions. While the United Nations has been, in most cases, unable to provide effectively for international safety, in recent decades a host of other international and regional security regimes have emerged. Some of them have clearly altered the regional landscapes of peace and war.

Multilateral regimes have not influenced national policies primarily by means of deterrence and prevention, but more so by establishing new normative standards, communication channels, and institutional practices.

Thus, new norms, patterns of consultation, transparency, interdependence, and learning opportunities, rather than specific constraints embedded in multilateral institutions, have modified the behavior of states, restricted the resort to arms, and thus contributed to the decline of both minor and major wars.[89] In sum, there appears now to be more political trust in major-power relations than ever since World War I. To that one has to add, though, that multilateral institutions are, as a rule, unable to cope with aggressive behavior among major powers. On the other hand, relative regional stability can also be attained, as has happened in East Asia, without elaborate institutional structures.[90]

Another way of tackling the problem is to suggest that institutions, instead of shaping national actions by their own independent influence or reflecting deeper material changes, are expressions of more fundamental changes in ideas, values, and norms concerning the use of military force. This argument is related to the earlier point on Elias's conception of the civilizing process. International law has, of course, contributed to this development by giving substance both to *jus ad bellum* and *jus in bello* to advise decision-makers when war is justifiable and by what rules it should be fought.

The Hague Peace Treaties of 1899 and 1907 formulated novel principles regarding the proper conduct of war. However, the legal profession in most countries remained deeply divided in its attitudes toward peace and war. This is clearly shown by the political fights and intellectual debates among the German international lawyers before and after World War I.[91] However, international law, while continuing to respect the principles of sovereignty and national self-defense, has grown more and more critical of the use of military force. It is still legally permitted, but under increasingly strict conditions.[92]

This may reflect a more general historical trend away from militarism and chauvinism as formative national attitudes towards what Ceadel calls 'defencism' and perhaps even 'pacific-ism.' 'Defencism' does not believe that war can be ever abolished or that international politics can ever resemble a society. However, it rejects the 'bellicist' view that wars are inevitable and believes that wars of aggression are becoming increasingly rare and the only legitimate type of war is defense against the attack. 'Pacific-ism' does not entirely condemn war, as real pacifists would do, but believes that by effective political actions its outbreaks can be prevented and that war can be abolished by appropriate national and international reforms.[93]

Changes in political ideas and values do not come out of the blue, but their sources and consequences must be contextualized in political, economic, and cultural terms. One way of doing this is to suggest that the alleged second coming of liberalism (the first one was in the late nineteenth century) has already had and will continue having real and lasting peaceful consequences. For instance, in contrast to the period preceding World War I, capitalists do not compete any more via states, but directly with each other in the global market. Such competition is more indeterminate, more profit-oriented, less politically loaded, and, hence, less violent in nature. Compared with military conflicts, commercial competition is less destructive, and potentially even rewarding, for the general public.[94]

Democracy and capitalism

The present Kantian moment is said to be located in the moral, political, and economic spheres of society, leading, respectively, to theories about cultural, democratic and capitalist peace. As all these types of peace have a modern ring, peace is, in this approach, associated with the strengthening of the political and economic aspects of modernity. On the other hand, as detailed above, it is also commonplace to think that modern economy, technology, and culture are conducive to war rather than peace. Especially in postmodern scholarship, their transformations are thought to often contribute to new imageries and rhetoric of war and disorder.[95]

An even more contrary argument is that democratic development *per se* has been fueling war. This was summarized, for instance, by Toynbee as follows: 'if industrialism provided the material resources for modern war, democracy fueled its dynamism.' He was puzzled why democracy was able to help to abolish slavery but seemed to aggravate the institution of war.[96]

Extensive theoretical and empirical work has shown that, historically, democratic states rarely fight each other, due to their domestic institutional constraints, common identities and values, and the mutual transparency and ease of communication.[97] While empirical evidence provides strong support for the democratic peace theory, the interpretation of its details is contested. It has been, for instance, pointed out that democracy and peace/war do not historically have any fixed meanings. Therefore, to understand the complexity of the relationship between democracy and peace, they have to be anchored in appropriate historical and spatial contexts.[98] Perhaps the ultimate test of the democratic peace theory is whether the democratization of all great powers, and their transition to the market system, will lead to the universal abolition of major war; if the theory is correct, it should.[99]

The ideas of liberal, i.e. democratic and capitalist, peace have been countered by historical evidence that the breakthroughs of capitalism and industrialism increased the destructiveness of war. The pivotal role of industry in the total war has been explained by the huge expansion of its production and the waves of technological

20

innovation. As new capabilities were made available for war, there was less need to choose between fighting and trading. Thus, in the nineteenth century, 'commerce ceased to work for peace after conditions of scarcity were replaced by conditions of abundance'; wars are related to wealth rather than scarcity.[100]

It is a part of conventional wisdom that, historically, warfare has been fueled by various illiberal ideologies, which have prevented the expression of the peaceful popular will by the civil society. Before both world wars, such illiberal ideologies tried to overcome the growing public resistance to war and convert it from a limited engagement to an existential struggle creating 'authentic' human beings. On the other hand, it has been shown that, in relation to war, liberalism and illiberalism are not necessarily polar opposites of each other and can have some of the same roots.[101] The global decline of authoritarian ideologies and the spread of liberal democracy in recent decades seem to have severed some of these connections and helped liberalism to 'purify' itself of the remnants of the past.

This observation also pertains to the economic variant of the liberal peace theory, which argues that war has been a remnant of the feudal society that has carried dynastic and aggressive habits over to the modern era. Only the spread of capitalist rationality, since the late nineteenth century, through the rise of industries and markets, has helped to overcome the feudal atavisms and pave the way for a new type of liberal peace. The political rationality and material benefits of war have been reduced by economic growth, social differentiation, and functional dependence within societies. In addition, the globalization of national economies has fostered, through transnational specialization and interdependence, peaceful relations between states.[102]

There is, indeed, empirical evidence to show that economic openness and integration reduce both inter- and intra-state violence and thus contribute to peace. The argument is not, of course, new, but it can be traced back to Montesquieu, Smith, and Kant, who all felt that commerce requires hospitality and promotes civility and peace. However, the empirical evidence regarding the relationship between globalization and peace is not very robust; it is beset by methodological problems, and the direction of causality is open to debate. There is also contrary evidence showing that, in some circumstances, foreign trade and investment can amplify conflicts.[103]

The standard critical response to the notion that global capitalism promotes peace is that the growth of economic resources and technology has made interstate wars much more destructive if they occur. Thus, the economic glass of peace is half empty, though it may also be half full, as the destructiveness of war may have helped to preserve peace by propping up (self-)deterrence. In any case, it is obvious that the relationship between economic change and peace is not a simple and unidirectional one. More often than not, it promotes peace, but, depending upon the nature of growth, it may also be conducive to war.[104]

Conclusion

The purpose of this introduction has not been to test the theory that the risk of major-power war is disappearing and the age of a long peace is in the offing. Rather, the intention has been to discuss the main arguments that have been put forward in favor of the transition toward a world in which a general war or even a bilateral war between great powers is unlikely. At the same time, care has been taken to also present the most important counterarguments. On both sides of the debate, there is an abundance of ideological convictions that cannot be swayed by any amount of evidence and logic.

In recent years, the mood has changed in many halls of power, accepting the view that wars of various kinds are a permanent element of politics. Naturally, the spread of terrorism and the US response to it have been key ingredients of this development. This shift does not undermine, however, the key thesis of this analysis for two reasons: first, war on terrorism is quite different from the historical institution of major-power war and second, the future of the shift depends on political choices made in domestic policies of leading powers.

In the light of history, one can safely say that there are peaceful periods, even long ones, in international relations, especially if peace is defined by the absence of major interstate war.[105] It is more controversial to argue that the fluctuations of the international system between major wars and periods of peace are now coming to an end and the interstate wars between major powers are fading into history. There are both theoretical and empirical reasons to propose that conclusion, and the statistical historical evidence lends support to this thesis. In fact, theoretical objections to the waning-of-major-war thesis can be stronger than the empirical ones, but the problem is that these theories are usually based on a single logic of international relations and border determinism. Our view gains some support from the fact that it can be sustained by several different kinds of theoretical arguments, i.e. it has a more pluralistic flavor.

If the hypothesis about the waning of major-power war is accepted, it has important consequences for the study of international relations. Wars have been assumed to be major engines of political, economic, and cultural change. Many theories of international relations will simply cease to exist if the thesis about the decline of major-power wars can be sustained. Moreover, historical international orders have been interpreted in many a research tradition, either as a cause or consequence of major-power wars. If wars do not determine the key changes in international life, one has to come up with alternative approaches relying on factors other than warfare.

Notes

1 See T. E. Ricks, 'U.S. Faces Defense Choices: Terminator, Peacekeeping Globocop or Combination', *The Wall Street Journal*, 12 November 1999.
2 A. Rapoport, 'Editor's Introduction', in C. von Clausewitz, *On War* (Harmondsworth: Pelican Books, 1968 [1832]), pp. 11–80.

3 D. Kagan, *On the Origins of War and the Preservation of Peace* (New York: Doubleday, 1995), p. 567.

4 J. A. Vasquez, 'What Do We Know About War?', in J. A. Vasquez (ed.), *What Do We Know About War?* (Lanham: Rowman & Littlefield, 2000), pp. 366–8.

5 E. Luard, *War in International Society: A Study in International Sociology* (New Haven: Yale University Press, 1986), p. 77.

6 This thesis was originally developed by J. L. Gaddis, *The Long Peace: Inquiries into the History of the Cold War* (New York: Oxford University Press, 1987). The idea has been discussed and assessed in C. W. Kegley, Jr (ed.), *The Long Postwar Peace: Contending Explanations and Projections* (New York: HarperCollins, 1991).

7 J. S. Levy, *War in the Modern Great-Power System, 1495–1975* (Lexington: University Press of Kentucky, 1983), pp. 112–49 and J. S. Levy, T. C. Walker and M. S. Edwards, 'Continuity and Change in the Evolution of Warfare', in Z. Maoz and A. Gat (eds), *War in a Changing World* (Ann Arbor: University of Michigan Press, 2001), pp. 16–19, 23–4.

8 J. D. Singer, 'Peace in the Global System: Displacement, Interregnum, or Transformation?', in C. W. Kegley, Jr (ed.), *The Long Postwar Peace: Contending Explanations and Projections* (New York: HarperCollins, 1991), pp. 56–84. In the present volume Henehan and Vasquez note that conclusions about the trends in interstate warfare depend on the research technique chosen. Their analysis shows that there has been a rather significant decline in the probability of interstate war in the post-1945 period. Luard's empirical exercise shows that the number of wars per year has fluctuated quite significantly among five historical periods in 1400–1984 and is also distributed very unevenly among individual countries; see E. Luard, *War in International Society*.

9 On these explanations, see, respectively, R. Gilpin, *War and Change in World Politics* (Cambridge: Cambridge University Press, 1981), W. R. Thompson, *On Global War: Historical-Structural Approaches to World Politics* (Columbia: University of South Carolina Press, 1988) and C. F. Doran, *Systems in Crisis: New Imperatives of High Politics at Century's End* (Cambridge: Cambridge University Press, 1991).

10 This is one way of reading K. N. Waltz, 'Kant, Liberalism, and War', *American Political Science Review*, 56, 2 (1962), pp. 331–40.

11 I am using here the translation of *Zum ewigen Frieden* included in C. Friedrich, *Inevitable Peace* (Cambridge: Harvard University Press, 1948), pp. 245–81.

12 R. Tuck, *The Rights of War and Peace: Political Thought and the International Order from Grotius to Kant* (Oxford: Oxford University Press, 1999), pp. 207–25.

13 This point is made with characteristic clarity by F. H. Hinsley, *Power and the Pursuit of Peace: Theory and Practice in the History of Relations between the States* (Cambridge: Cambridge University Press, 1963), pp. 62–80.

14 For more detailed analyses of Kant's peace theory, see A. Hurrell, 'Kant and the Kantian Paradigm in International Relations', *Review of International Studies*, 16, 3 (1990), pp. 182–205; M. W. Doyle, *Ways of War and Peace: Realism, Liberalism, Socialism* (New York: W.W. Norton, 1997), pp. 252–84; and C. Covell, *Kant and the Law of Peace: A Study in the Philosophy of International Law and International Relations* (New York: St Martin's, 1998). These studies indicate how controversial Kant's legacy has been in the study of war and peace; he has been appropriated both by liberals and realists, neither of whom have necessarily benefited from this in their theory-building efforts; on this, see M. F. N. Franke, *Global Limits: Immanuel Kant, International Relations, and Critique of World Politics* (Albany: State University of New York Press, 2001).

15 J. Habermas, 'Kant's Idea of Perpetual Peace, with the Benefit of Two Hundred Years' Hindsight', in J. Bohman and M. Lutz-Bachmann (eds), *Perpetual Peace. Essays on*

Kant's Cosmopolitan Ideal (Cambridge: MIT Press, 1997), pp. 113–53, esp. pp. 126–35.

16 This realist interpretation of Kant has been put forward by G. Cavallar, 'Kantian Perspectives on Democratic Peace: Alternatives to Doyle', *Review of International Studies*, 27, 2 (2001), pp. 243–7. The liberal case has been made in Doyle, *Ways of War and Peace*, pp. 277–84. See also Friedrich, *Inevitable Peace*, pp. 43–6 and Covell, *Kant and the Law of Peace*, pp. 124–41. Friedrich in particular rejects the view that non-republican states could be members of *foedus pacificum*.

17 W. L. Huntley, 'Kant's Third Image: Systemic Sources of the Liberal Peace', *International Studies Quarterly*, 40, 1 (1996), pp. 56–7. The impact of the democratic pressure emanating from an established union of states can be seen in the role of the EU and NATO in transforming the political and economic systems of Central and Eastern Europe in return for the promise of membership in these institutions.

18 Doyle, *Ways of War and Peace*, pp. 282–4. See also L.-E. Cederman, 'Back to Kant: Reinterpreting the Democratic Peace as a Macrohistorical Learning Process', *American Political Science Review*, 95, 1 (2001), pp. 16–17.

19 W.-D. Eberwein, 'The Future of International Warfare: Toward a Global Security Community?', *International Political Science Review*, 16, 4 (1996), pp. 341–60.

20 Cederman, 'Back to Kant', pp. 15–31. A contrary view to the Kantian one is provided by an empirical study which concludes that interstate war is rarest in the relations between developed socialist countries, while it is most common between developing socialist countries; see I. Oren and J. Hays, 'Democracies May Rarely Fight Each Other, but Developed Socialist States Rarely Fight At All', *Alternatives*, 22, 4 (1997), pp. 493–522.

21 D. V. Jones, *Code of Peace: Ethics and Security in the World of Warlord States* (Chicago: Chicago University Press, 1989).

22 R. Jackson, *The Global Covenant: Human Conduct in a World of States* (Oxford: Oxford University Press, 2000).

23 N. Elias, *The Civilizing Process: State Formation and Civilization* (Oxford: Basil Blackwell, 1982 [1939]); and D. Senghaas, 'Zivilisierung und Gewalt: Wie den Frieden gewinnen?', in W. R. Vogt (ed.), *Frieden als Zivilisierungsprojekt – Neue Herausforderungen an die Friedens- und Konfliktforschung* (Baden-Baden: Nomos, 1995), pp. 37–55.

24 The Elias theory is discussed in detail by J. Fletcher, *Violence and Civilization: An Introduction to the Work of Norbert Elias* (London: Polity Press, 1997).

25 Various economic and political theories of imperialism and expansion are discussed in N. Etherington, *Theories of Imperialism: War, Conquest and Capital* (London: Croom Helm, 1984).

26 E. V. D. Robinson, 'War and Economics in History and in Theory', *Political Science Quarterly*, 15, 4 (1900), pp. 581–627 (the quotations are on p. 622). Gilpin also considers the 'law of diminishing returns' a cause of the economic stagnation and political decline that increase the war propensity of status quo nations in their competition with rising powers; see R. Gilpin, *War and Change in World Politics*, pp. 78–84, 159–62. This kind of determinism is not shared by all authors. For instance, Robbins in his survey of the economic theories of war concludes that exclusive national sovereignty and monopolistic control of resources are more likely causes of war than the capitalist profit motive; see L. Robbins, *The Economic Causes of War* (New York: Macmillan, 1940).

27 N. Angell, *The Great Illusion* (New York: G.P. Putnam's Sons, 1933 [1909]). For a discussion of Angell's theory, see J. D. B. Miller, *Norman Angell and the Futility of War: Peace and the Public Mind* (London: Macmillan, 1986).

28 For histories of this intellectual tradition see, e.g., H. Caton, *The Politics of Progress: The Origins and Development of the Commercial Republic 1600–1835* (Gainesville:

University of Florida Press, 1988) and A. Howe, *Free Trade and Liberal England 1846–1946* (Oxford: Clarendon Press, 1997).

29   R. Rosecrance, *The Rise of the Trading State: Commerce and Conquest in the Modern World* (New York: Basic Books, 1986) and R. Rosecrance, *The Rise of the Virtual State: Wealth and Power in the Coming Century* (New York: Basic Books, 1999). For a similar, though less reflective analysis, see J. T. Matthews, 'Power Shift', *Foreign Affairs*, 76, 1 (1997), pp. 50–66.

30   One should remember, though, that the Kantian idea of peace has never completely lost its appeal; see in particular Friedrich, *Inevitable Peace*. One example of the new popularity of Kantian thinking is R. Wright, 'What Was War? In the Next Millennium, Peace Will Have a Chance', *The New York Times Magazine*, 15 December 1999, pp. 98–100.

31   J. Mueller, *Retreat from Doomsday: The Obsolescence of Major War* (New York: Basic Books, 1989), p. 13 (see also Mueller's Chapter 2 in the present volume). World War I left a deep cultural impact on many European nations, including the French, who found 'the war's meaning only by depriving it of meaning; nothing about the experience in the trenches makes any sense; and the war seems justified only by the hope that the war's very horror will make future conflicts unthinkable', see C. S. Brosman, *Visions of War in France: Fiction, Art, Ideology* (Baton Rouge: Louisiana State University Press, 1999), pp. 135–74 (the quotation is on p. 154). On the other hand, it was the fear of war that permitted the aggressive and expansionist policies of the National Socialists in Germany in the 1930s, who had in their service 'young specialists of violence: tank commanders, airmen, storm-troopers', see M. Howard, *The Invention of Peace: Reflections on War and International Order* (New Haven: Yale University Press, 2000), pp. 65–71.

32   Mueller, *Retreat from Doomsday*, pp. 53–61.

33   Ibid., pp. 240–4 and J. Mueller, *Quiet Cataclysm: Reflections on the Recent Transformation of World Politics* (New York: HarperCollins, 1995), pp. 125–53. See also E. A. Nadelman, 'Global Prohibition Regimes: The Evolution of Norms in International Society', *International Organization*, 44, 4 (1990), pp. 479–526.

34   J. Black, *Why Wars Happen* (New York: New York University Press, 1998), pp. 225–6, 231–3.

35   M. Shaw, *Post-Military Society: Militarism, Demilitarization and War at the End of the Twentieth Century* (Philadelphia: Temple University Press, 1991); the quotation is on p. 184. Howard, *The Invention of Peace*.

36   This is the key conclusion by G. J. Ikenberry, *After Victory: Institutions, Strategic Restraint and the Rebuilding of Order after Major Wars* (Princeton: Princeton University Press, 2001), pp. 117–62. See also C. W. Kegley, Jr and G. A. Raymond, *How Nations Make Peace* (New York: St Martin's, 1999), pp. 142–68.

37   J. Epstein, 'Always Time to Kill', *The New York Review of Books*, 46, 17 (1999), pp. 57–64 (the quotation is at p. 62). A similar general argument informs N. Ferguson, *The Pity of War: Explaining World War I* (New York: Basic Books, 1999).

38   Historically, these have been among the main causes of warfare, as has been shown by K. J. Holsti, *Peace and War: Armed Conflicts and International Order* (Cambridge: Cambridge University Press, 1991).

39   M. W. Zacher, 'The Territorial Integrity Norm: International Boundaries and the Use of Force', *International Organization*, 55, 2 (2001), pp. 215–50. In the present volume, both Holsti (Chapter 6) and Spruyt (Chapter 8) refer to the normative opposition to forceful territorial revisions and the strong defense of the territorial sovereignty.

40   The declining importance of military force has been suggested, for instance, by E. Luard, *The Blunted Sword: The Erosion of Military Power in Modern World Politics* (New York: New Amsterdam, 1988), pp. 7–24.

41   A succinct, orthodox formulation on the impact of system structure on the risk of major war is provided by J. J. Mearsheimer, *The Tragedy of Great Power Politics* (New York: W.W. Norton, 2001), pp. 334–47.

42   W. C. Wohlfort, 'The Stability of a Unipolar World', *International Security*, 24, 1 (1999), pp. 5–41; the quotations are on pp. 7–8.

43   K. N. Waltz, 'The Origins of War in Neorealist Theory', in R. I. Rotberg and T. K. Rabb (eds), *The Origin and Prevention of Major War* (Cambridge: Cambridge University Press, 1989), pp. 39–52; the quotation is on p. 44.

44   See S. van Evera, *Causes of War: Power and the Roots of Conflict* (Ithaca: Cornell University Press, 1999); and D. C. Copeland, *The Origins of Major War* (Ithaca: Cornell University Press, 2000).

45   M. van Creveld, *The Transformation of War* (New York: Free Press, 1991), p. 2.

46   Ibid., pp. 192–223.

47   For a brief account of military revolutions, see W. Murray and M. Knox, 'Thinking about Revolutions in Warfare', in M. Knox and W. Murray (eds), *The Dynamics of Military Revolution 1300–2050* (Cambridge: Cambridge University Press, 2001), pp. 1–14.

48   K. W. Thompson, *Toynbee's Philosophy of World History and Politics* (Baton Rouge: Louisiana State University Press, 1985), pp. 70–2.

49   S. Lindqvist, *Nu dog du: Bombernas århundrade* (Stockholm: Norstedts, 1999).

50   S. van Evera, 'Offense, Defense, and the Causes of War', *International Security*, 22, 4 (1998), pp. 5–43.

51   K. Lieber, 'Grasping the Technological Peace: The Offense–Defense Balance and International Security', *International Security*, 25, 1 (2000), pp. 71–104.

52   For technological explanations of arms races and wars, see W. H. McNeill, *The Pursuit of Power: Technology, Armed Force, and Society since A.D. 1000* (Chicago: University of Chicago Press, 1982); and M. Pearton, *Diplomacy, War and Technology since 1830* (Lawrence: University of Kansas Press, 1983). One may also place in this category M. Kaldor, *The Baroque Arsenal* (London: Abacus, 1983).

53   In 1998 a conference was organized in St Petersburg to commemorate and assess Bloch's contribution to the study of war; see G. Prins and H. Tromp (eds), *The Future of War* (The Hague: Kluwer Law International, 2000).

54   Ferguson, *The Pity of War*, pp. 8–11; and A. J. Echevarria II, *After Clausewitz: German Military Thinkers before the Great War* (Lawrence: University of Kansas Press, 2000), pp. 85–91. Echevarria portrays Bloch's analysis in a rather negative light; for a more positive assessment, see A. Gat, *The Development of Military Thought: The Nineteenth Century* (Oxford: Clarendon Press, 1992), pp. 108–13.

55   McNeill, *The Pursuit of Power*. On the impact of technology on strategy, see also M. Knox, 'Conclusion: Continuity and Revolution in the Making of Strategy', in W. Murray, M. Knox and A. Bernstein (eds), *The Making of Strategy: Rulers, States, and War* (Cambridge: Cambridge University Press, 1994), pp. 638–43.

56   D. Pick, *War Machine: The Rationalisation of Slaughter in the Modern Age* (New Haven: Yale University Press, 1995).

57   L. Mumford, *Technics and Civilization* (San Diego: Harcourt Brace Jovanovich, 1963 [1934]). See also L. Mumford, *The Pentagon of Power: The Myth of the Machine* (New York: Harcourt Brace Jovanovich, 1970).

58   M. van Creveld, *Technology and War from 2000 B.C. to the Present* (New York: The Free Press, 1989) (the quotation is on p. 314). See also R. L. O'Connell, *Of Arms and Men: A History of War, Weapons, and Aggression* (Oxford: Oxford University Press, 1989).

59   Van Creveld, *Technology and War from 2000 B.C. to the Present*, pp. 316, 319.

60   Mueller, *Retreat from Doomsday*, p. ix.

61 J. E. Thompson, *Mercenaries, Pirates, and Sovereigns: State-building and Extra-territorial Violence in Early Modern Europe* (Princeton: Princeton University Press, 1994); and H. Spruyt, *The Sovereign State and Its Competitors: An Analysis of Systems Change* (Princeton: Princeton University Press, 1994).

62 R. Bean, 'War and the Birth of the Nation State', *Journal of Economic History*, 33, 2 (1973), pp. 203–21.

63 B. D. Porter, *War and the Rise of State: The Military Foundations of Modern Politics* (New York: The Free Press, 1994); C. Tilly, *Coercion, Capital, and European States AD 990–1990* (Oxford: Blackwell, 1990); M. van Creveld, *The Rise and Decline of the State* (Cambridge: Cambridge University Press, 1999); and K. Jaggers, 'War and the Three Faces of Power: War Making and State Making in Europe and the Americas', *Comparative Political Studies*, 25, 1 (1992), pp. 26–62.

64 This argument is developed in more detail by E. L. Jones, *The European Miracle: Environments, Economies and Geopolitics in the History of Europe* (Cambridge: Cambridge University Press, 1981), pp. 127–49.

65 Van Creveld, *The Rise and Decline of the State*, pp. 337–54. See also N. Ferguson, *The Cash Nexus: Money and Power in the Modern World: 1700–2000* (New York: Basic Books, 2001), pp. 100–1 and *passim*. A reverse causality posits that the decline and various risks of fragmentation of the state results from the more benign international security environment of the post-Cold War era; see M. C. Desch, 'War and Strong States, Peace and Weak States', *International Organization*, 50, 2 (1996), pp. 237–68.

66 The phases in the historical transformations of war are discussed, for instance, in Black, *Why Wars Happen* and M. Howard, *War in European History* (Oxford: Oxford University Press, 1976).

67 The historical variation in the characteristics of warfare has been explored by Levy, *War in the Modern Great-Power System*; Luard, *War in International Society*; and G. Blainey, *The Causes of War* (New York: Free Press, 1973), esp. chs 12–15.

68 See, e.g., Mueller, *Retreat from Doomsday*; van Creveld, *The Transformation of War*; and R. L. O'Connell, *Ride of the Second Horseman: The Birth and Death of War* (New York: Oxford University Press, 1995).

69 See E. Adler and M. Barnett (eds), *Security Communities* (Cambridge: Cambridge University Press, 1998); A. Wendt, *Social Theory of World Politics* (Cambridge: Cambridge University Press, 1999), pp. 297–308; and A. M. Kacowicz (ed.), *Stable Peace among Nations* (Lanham: Rowman & Littlefield, 2000). It is, however, good to remember the point that 'there is no historical necessity, no guarantee, that the incentives for progressive change will overcome human weakness and the countervailing incentives to maintain the status quo' (Wendt, *Social Theory of World Politics*, p. 311).

70 M. Wight, *Power Politics* (ed. by H. Bull and C. Holbraad) (Harmondsworth: Penguin, 1978), chs 1–5. For a similar classification without world powers, see R. L. Tammen *et al.*, *Power Transitions. Strategies for the 21st Century* (New York: Chatham House, 2000), pp. 6–9. On the definition of great powers, see also Levy, *War in the Modern Great-Power System*, pp. 10–24.

71 For further elaboration, see B. Miller, 'Hot Wars, Cold Peace. An International–Regional Synthesis', in Z. Maoz and A. Gat (eds), *War in a Changing World* (Ann Arbor: University of Michigan Press, 2001), pp. 93–141; and B. Miller, 'The Global Sources of Regional Transitions from War to Peace', *Journal of Peace Research*, 38, 2 (2001), pp. 199–225.

72 Holsti uses (in this volume, Chapter 6) stricter criteria – participants must be great powers and war must produce at least one million victims – and comes to the conclusion that East Asia is the only area of tension where major war is even remotely possible.

73 F. Delmas, *The Rosy Future of War* (New York: Free Press, 1995).

27

74 Van Creveld, *The Transformation of War*. For a similar, but more modest statement, see J. J. Weltman, *World Politics and the Evolution of War* (Baltimore: Johns Hopkins University Press, 1995). The patterns of warfare are systematically examined by M. Kaldor, *New and Old Wars: Organized Violence in a Global Era* (Cambridge: Polity Press, 1999).

75 B. Ehrenreich, *Blood Rites: Origins and History of the Passions of War* (New York: Henry Holt, 1997).

76 P. Virilio, 'The Military Space', in J. D. Derian (ed.), *The Virilio Reader* (Oxford: Blackwell, 1998), pp. 22–8. O'Connell, *Ride of the Second Horseman*, also emphasizes the rural roots of contemporary warfare.

77 See K. N. Waltz, 'The Emerging Structure of International Politics', *International Security*, 18, 2 (1993), pp. 44–79 and K. N. Waltz, 'Structural Realism after the Cold War', *International Security*, 25, 1 (2000), pp. 5–41.

78 Wohlfort, 'The Stability of a Unipolar World'.

79 C. A. Kupchan, 'Hollow Hegemony or Stable Multipolarity?', in G. J. Ikenberry (ed.), *America Unrivaled: The Future of the Balance of Power* (Ithaca: Cornell University Press, 2002), pp. 68–97.

80 Van Evera, *Causes of War*; the quotation is on p. 256.

81 In addition to the literature mentioned in note 9 above, see C. F. Doran, 'Power Cycle Theory of Systems Structure and Stability: Commonalities and Complementarities', in M. Midlarsky (ed.), *Handbook of War Studies* (Ann Arbor: University of Michigan Press, 1989), pp. 83–110; Thompson, *On Global War*; G. Modelski and W. R. Thompson, 'Long Cycles and Global War', in M. Midlarsky (ed.), *Handbook of War Studies* (Ann Arbor: University of Michigan Press, 1989), pp. 23–54; and J. S. Levy, 'Long Cycles, Hegemonic Transitions, and the Long Peace', in C. W. Kegley (ed.), *The Long Postwar Peace: Contending Explanations and Projections* (New York: HarperCollins, 1991), pp. 147–76.

82 See N. Choucri and R. C. North, *Nations in Conflict: National Growth and International Violence* (San Francisco: W.H. Freeman, 1975); N. Choucri and R. C. North, 'Lateral Pressure in International Relations: Concept and Theory', in M. Midlarsky (ed.), *Handbook of War Studies* (Ann Arbor: University of Michigan Press, 1989), pp. 289–326; and R. K. Ashley, *The Political Economy of War and Peace* (London: Frances Pinter, 1980).

83 Doran, *Systems in Crisis*; and Tammen *et al.*, *Power Transitions*.

84 This is, in essence, the interpretation provided by Ikenberry, *After Victory*, pp. 215–56.

85 This proposition originates from Gaddis, *The Long Peace*. On the other hand, it is not uncommon to see statements that bipolarity was inconsequential and only nuclear weapons mattered: 'what we have forgotten is that the only instrument of peace these last fifty years was the fear of mutual assured destruction' (Delmas, *The Rosy Future of War*, p. 146). In this volume (Chapter 4) van Creveld also strongly defends the point that nuclear weapons, and deterrence generated by them, have been an important factor of peace.

86 Luard, *The Blunted Sword*, pp. 25–56; Mueller, *Retreat from Doomsday*, pp. 110–15, 55–6; and J. Mueller, 'The Essential Irrelevance of Nuclear Weapons', *International Security*, 13, 2 (1988), pp. 55–79. As his contribution to this volume indicates (see Chapter 2), Mueller continues to believe that nuclear weapons and deterrence cannot provide any major explanation of the long peace. Gaddis provides, in turn, evidence that the US and Soviet leaders perceived the military utility of nuclear weapons as very limited; see J. L. Gaddis, *We Now Know: Rethinking Cold War History* (Oxford: Clarendon Press, 1997), pp. 107–8, 230–9.

87 J. A. Vasquez, 'The Deterrence Myth: Nuclear Weapons and the Prevention of Nuclear War', in C. W. Kegley (ed.), *The Long Postwar Peace: Contending Explanations and*

Projections (New York: HarperCollins, 1991), pp. 203–23; T.V. Paul, 'Great Equalizers or the Agents of Chaos? Weapons of Mass Destruction and the Emerging International Order', in T.V. Paul and J. A. Hall (eds), *International Order and the Future of World Politics* (Cambridge: Cambridge University Press, 1999), pp. 373–91; and T.V. Paul, 'Nuclear Taboo and War Initiation in Regional Conflicts', *Journal of Conflict Resolution*, 39, 4 (1995), pp. 696–717. In this volume, Paul refutes the argument that during the Cold War deterrence eliminated the risk of nuclear war and suggests that even today an inadvertent nuclear war is a possibility.

88 Holsti, *Peace and War*. Similarly, Luard notes how the issues behind wars have varied significantly over the last five centuries. Luard, *War in International Society*, pp. 83–131.

89 This perspective is developed further in Adler and Barnett (eds), Security Communities; and H. Haftendorn, R. O. Keohane and C. A. Wallander (eds), *Imperfect Unions: Security Institutions over Time and Space* (Oxford: Oxford University Press, 1999). On the other hand, the critics of the institutional school argue that its conclusions are overblown; see J. J. Mearsheimer, 'The False Promise of International Institutions', *International Security*, 19, 3 (1995), pp. 5–49 and Waltz, 'Structural Realism after the Cold War'.

90 In this volume (Chapter 7), Morgan points to these caveats in the institutional theory of peace, which he otherwise regards as an appropriate approach to the study of major wars.

91 M. Koskenniemi, *The Gentle Civilizer of Nations: The Rise and Fall of International Law 1870–1960* (Cambridge: Cambridge University Press, 2001), pp. 210–22.

92 As van Creveld points out in this volume (Chapter 4), both the terminology and substance of international law has changed to de-legitimize interstate war.

93 M. Ceadel, *Thinking about Peace and War* (Oxford: Oxford University Press, 1987).

94 This argument is placed in a historical perspective by J. A. Hall, *Liberalism: Politics, Ideology, and the Market* (Chapel Hill: University of North Carolina Press, 1987), pp. 125–52; and J. A. Hall, 'Peace, Peace At Last?', in J. A. Hall and I. C. Jarvie (eds), *Transition to Modernity: Essays on Wealth, Power, and Belief* (Cambridge: Cambridge University Press, 1992), pp. 343–67. See also C. Kaysen, 'Is War Obsolete? A Review Essay', *International Security*, 14, 4 (1990), pp. 42–64.

95 P. K. Lawrence, *Modernity and War: The Creed of Absolute Violence* (London: Macmillan, 1997).

96 Thompson, *Toynbee's Philosophy of World History and Politics*, pp. 68–70. This analysis is taken to the ideological level by those who suggest that the Western way of warfare has been, in the past, lethal, exactly because it has been democratic and individualistic. The West has acquired military prowess and global hegemony because its armed forces have bonded together free men who are ready to both kill and die. Now a 'huge federal government and global corporations have reduced the number of Americans who work as autonomous individuals,' which reduces, in turn, their capacity to fight. On the other hand, both Western military and civilian technology are quickly spreading to new countries, enhancing the risk that the Western nations may again fight each other, with devastating consequences; see V. D. Hanson, *Carnage and Culture: Landmark Battles in the Rise of Western Power* (New York: Doubleday, 2001).

97 This line of inquiry was initiated by M. W. Doyle, 'Kant, Liberal Legacies, and Foreign Affairs', *Philosophy and Public Affairs*, 12, 2 and 3 (1983), pp. 205–35 and 323–53. It has been since then empirically tested by dozens of authors; for empirical work, see B. M. Russett, *Grasping the Democratic Peace: Principles for a Post-Cold War World* (Princeton: Princeton University Press, 1993); and B. Russett and J. Oneal, *Triangulating Peace: Democracy, Interdependence, and International Organizations*

(New York: W.W. Norton, 2001). For an overview and further development of the existing scholarship, see also S. R. Weart, *Never at War: Why Democracies Will Not Fight Each Other* (New Haven: Yale University Press, 1998).

98 T. Barkawi and M. Laffey, 'The Imperial Peace: Democracy, Force and Globalization', *European Journal of International Relations*, 5, 4 (1999), pp. 403–34.

99 This is the position adopted in this volume (Chapter 9) by Thompson who also stresses the need to embed the regime change in broader economic and cultural contexts. See also W. R. Thompson and R. Tucker, 'A Tale of Two Democratic Peace Critiques', *Journal of Conflict Resolution*, 41, 3 (1997), pp. 428–54.

100 J. U. Nef, *War and Human Progress: An Essay on the Rise of Industrial Civilization* (New York: W.W. Norton, 1978 [1950]), pp. 359–75 (the quotation is on p. 368).

101 C. Coker, *War and the Illiberal Conscience* (Boulder: Westview, 1998); and H. Joas, 'Die modernität des Krieges: Die Modernisierungstheorie und das Problem der Gewalt', *Leviathan*, 24, 1 (1996), pp. 13–27. See also H. Joas, *War and Modernity* (Cambridge: Polity Press, 2003).

102 The chief advocate of the theory of capitalist peace has been J. A. Schumpeter, 'The Sociology of Imperialisms', reprinted in R. Swedberg (ed.), *The Economics and Sociology of Capitalism* (Princeton: Princeton University Press, 1991 [1919]). Other classics supporting similar conclusions include August Comte, John Stuart Mill, Thorstein Veblen, Werner Sombart, and Karl Polanyi. As I point out in this volume (Chapter 10), the relationship between capitalism and war has been historically variable and appears to be positive mostly in the case of financial capitalism.

103 See Russett and Oneal, *Triangulating Peace*, pp. 125–55; S. M. Macmillan, 'Interdependence and Conflict', *Mershon International Studies Review*, 41, 1 (1997), pp. 33–58; H. Hegre, 'Development and Liberal Peace: What Does It Take To Be a Trading State?', *Journal of Peace Research*, 37, 1 (2000), pp. 5–30; and K. Barbieri, *The Liberal Illusion: Does Trade Promote Peace?* (Ann Arbor: Michigan University Press, 2002).

104 W. H. Mott IV, *The Economic Basis of Peace: Linkages between Economic Growth and International Conflict* (Westport: Greenwood Press, 1997).

105 See, e.g., P. Wallensteen, 'Incompatibility, Confrontation, and War: Four Models and Three Historical Systems, 1816–1976', *Journal of Peace Research*, 18, 1 (1981), pp. 57–90; and J. A. Vasquez, *The War Puzzle* (Cambridge: Cambridge University Press, 1993). In this volume (Chapter 1), Schroeder explores the long peace of 1763–1914 in the triangle composed of the Habsburg Empire, Prussia/Germany, and Russia. This approach suggests that the periods of long peace can also be studied in the subsets of major powers and only in the entire international system.

Part I

DEBATING THE PAST
AND FUTURE
OF MAJOR WAR

1

THE LIFE AND DEATH OF
A LONG PEACE, 1763–1914

Paul W. Schroeder

What is the question, and can history help answer it?

One could approach the task of assessing historical trends to help answer the question of whether major war is currently waning, and if so, whether that trend will endure, in various ways – for instance, by discussing the history of peace movements and their results, or tracing the historical origins and development of the institutions, norms, rules, and practices in international politics that many now see as promoting an end to major war, or analyzing the roots and growth of the broader economic, social, technological and scientific, and cultural developments allegedly contributing to the obsolescence of major war. One could even try the heroic task of surveying the historical causes of major wars to help determine whether these causes persist or have receded.

Yet all such historical approaches fail to address or answer the central question, 'Is major war waning?' directly. They all tacitly consign history (specifically the area I will discuss here, European and world politics from its origins somewhere in the late Middle Ages down to about 1945) to the stage crew rather than the cast of the play, assigning it the task of setting the stage with background information and perspective, but no role in the actual play, saying something specific about present and future trends.

This assignment of a modest, ancillary role to history is understandable and to a certain point justified. History is an uncertain, slippery guide in assessing the present and predicting the future (so, one might add, is social science). But the consignment of history to the stage crew also derives from certain common assumptions as to what this particular segment of history is about and what it has to tell us, assumptions affecting the framing and meaning of the question central to this volume: 'Is major war waning?' The prevailing assumption among both scholars and the general public is that until recently the history of international politics has been dominated by war. More precisely, the history of international politics is a history of competition between autonomous units over opposed, often irreconcilable interests waged within a structure of anarchy, i.e., the absence of any recognized law or effective lawgiver and enforcer. This competition, waged within the anarchic structure of international politics (in contrast to the more hierarchic, law-bound one of domestic politics) has of necessity led to frequent wars of all kinds, many being large-scale struggles between individual great powers (major wars), and some being widespread conflicts involving most or all the great powers (general and systemic wars). The question 'Is major war waning?' would therefore seem to ask merely whether at some time in the recent past, the most plausible and widely cited date being 1945, the start of John Lewis Gaddis's well-known Long Peace, this historic pattern of structural conflict and endemic war has changed to one of overall cooperation and general relative peace. If so, what caused this recent change and how real, durable, and profound can we expect it to be?

This chapter challenges that question as thus posed and the assumptions behind it as misleading, and proposes a different view of the overall course of international history over the centuries, one that enables history to address the question of the waning of major war directly, and that, without pretending to provide the whole answer, offers a useful, necessary part of it. Given limitations of time and space, the argument for this different view will be very compressed, sketchy, and apparently dogmatic. It starts with some fundamental premises about international history, here asserted without evidence or even much illustration.

Why international history is more about explaining peace than war

1   International history as defined earlier, the history of international politics within the evolving European/world international system from about 1500 to 1945, consists at least as much of the history of peace as of war. That is, the quest by various units (mostly states) to attain various ends and acquire various goods in international affairs (peace and tranquility, security, recognition, status, rights and honor, prosperity, etc.) through establishing a viable and durable international order has always been as central and important a driving force in international relations as the quest for these same goods and others (territory, wealth, power, glory and prestige, domination, etc.) through state-organized violence. The two kinds of quests for goods, by peace and by war, are in fact interwoven and inseparable; neither can be understood without the other.

2   Peace (i.e., international order) is not just the absence of war – a condition of being left alone, not overtly threatened or attacked, such as Robinson Crusoe enjoyed on his desert island or as some isolated communities and societies may experience in history. Peace understood as international order is far more complex. It means a condition in which states or other units belong to and participate in an international society in which vast numbers of transactions and interchanges (political, commercial, social, cultural, religious, personal, etc.) go on regularly under orderly, controlled conditions without the constant threat or actuality of organized inter-unit violence. This makes peace therefore not merely more complicated than war, which though complex in practice is simple

in nature and purpose (to impose one's will on the enemy and prevent it from imposing its will on oneself) but also inherently more artificial than war. Wars often simply happen, through loss of control and entropy. Peace is always the product of contrivance and governance, the establishment and maintenance of order and system.

3   Peace is therefore harder to account for and explain than war. Most wars (all the ones in history with which I am familiar) are easy to explain in two broad senses – why wars in general can and do happen, and what events, causes and issues in general were involved in bringing this particular war on. The historical controversies and debates over the origins of wars concern the details of these generally known and accepted elements, the weighting and assessment of different factors involved. In contrast, it is often difficult to detect the origins and growth of peace and even harder to explain them. Why there should be international wars is no puzzle; why there should be peace is a puzzle.

4   The task of accounting for peace becomes still more important given the fact that in concrete empirical reality international history consists more of peace, i.e., of the emergence and development of international order, than of war, i.e., the recurrent incidence of organized inter-unit violence. Whether war has grown or declined in the European/world system over the centuries between 1500 and 1945 is a debatable question whose answer depends on complex calculations and controversial assumptions.[1] But international peace, defined as the joint membership of independent organized communities in a society within which each can seek various goods for itself and carry on practices vital to its existence and well-being on a regular, calculable basis relatively free of force, fraud, and organized violence, has indisputably grown and developed enormously over these centuries. Vast, vital areas of international relations once historically in the zone of war, governed only by force, fraud, and violence, now, for those states operating within the international system, belong predominantly in the zone of peace. These include international trade and finance, travel by land, sea and air, exploration and discovery, communications of all kinds, scientific, technical, and cultural exchange, tourism, ownership and use of property, even to some extent civil and human rights – and this sphere of international peace is being constantly expanded.

Why great wars are not inevitable and instances of long peace not rare

These premises, if accepted, add up to at least a prima facie case for seeing the history of international politics as one of progress toward peace, i.e., greater international order. But many, while not necessarily denying these premises or rejecting the arguments or the empirical evidence for the growth of peace in the sense just indicated, would deny that this is decisive, because none of this 'progress toward peace' obviates or even greatly reduces the permanent possibility of war, and any large-scale war almost automatically destroys this whole nexus of peace, at least for a time and for the belligerent parties. Another great general war could conceivably destroy civilization over the whole planet.

There is certainly something to this view that peace, even if it has grown, is always fragile and vulnerable. But behind this objection that peace is always on notice to quit and that therefore the permanent structural possibility of large-scale war remains the dominant reality in international politics lies an unarticulated assumption of the 'Murphy's Law' variety: so long as wars remain possible, they will eventually happen. New causes and occasions for war have always arisen as the old ones are overcome or die away. Therefore we must regard the new phenomenon of general peace among most major states since 1945 as probably a temporary, ephemeral phenomenon.

The answer, and the main argument of this chapter, is that this view of European/ world international history from 1500 to 1945 is wrong. Wars have not come along like streetcars; the phenomenon of general long peace is not new, restricted to Europe and the world since 1945, but rather something familiar. As a result of historical developments, a sizeable number of recognizable, important instances of long peace have occurred since the mid-eighteenth century, in particular since 1815.

How can one show this and at least make it plausible in a brief overview?

Heinz Duchhardt, the leading authority on international politics in early modern Europe, has suggested that a fundamental shift occurred over the course of the eighteenth century in the development of the European states system, dividing the late medieval/early modern system from the modern one, so that the practice of international politics in the seventeenth century is closer to that of the late fourteenth or early fifteenth than the eighteenth, and that of the eighteenth closer to the nineteenth and twentieth centuries than the seventeenth.[2] Duchhardt's suggestion of an eighteenth century divide seems not only perceptive in general, but also particularly important on a point central to our concerns: the capacity of the units involved in the game of international politics to impose order on their relations and on the system as a whole and thereby to avoid or reduce war and expand the possibility of peace.

A fair generalization about international politics in the fifteenth, sixteenth, or seventeenth centuries is that most wars that were at all likely to start did so; most serious crises in these centuries led within a relatively short time to war. As Duchhardt and many other scholars of early modern Europe have shown, this was not due to the lack of a desire for order and peace, or of ideas and instruments for trying to achieve it. All the institutions and practices that would later be effective for peace and order in the nineteenth century – institutionalized diplomatic machinery, the balance of power, the Concert of Europe, congresses and conferences, special associations and leagues for peace, mediation and arbitration by neutrals, international law – were known and to some extent developed and tried in this era.[3] With some possible exceptions (e.g., Francis I of France or Charles XII of Sweden) the leading princes and statesmen of early modern Europe wanted durable order and peace as well as conquest or glory; some of them pursued it almost desperately, others, including Louis XIV, were driven to seek it. Yet nothing really worked, at least for very long. However one explains the bellicism of early modern Europe, whether one emphasizes the weakness, fragility, and internal incompleteness and instability of most of the unit-actors and the resulting deficits in equality, institutionalization, and autonomy throughout the system,[4] or the destabilizing and conflict-breeding propensities of the prevailing system of territorial possession through dynastic succession,[5] or the underdeveloped state of early modern diplomatic instruments, practices, and rules and the limited choices they offered governments and rulers,[6] or blames it on many other obvious factors – the lack of stable power relationships and of geographic coherence in the system of states, or the fragility of all alliances and interstate ties, or the divisive impact of religious and dynastic rivalries, or the persistence of so-called feudal elements in politics (divided and limited sovereignty, overlapping jurisdictions, the existence of actors like Poland, the German Empire, and many small ecclesiastical, princely, and urban units that could not play the same game as the major states but also could not be ignored) – whatever the sources and causes of war-proneness in early modern Europe, the inescapable conclusion is that the international system could not successfully manage them to the end of significantly preventing war and producing peace and stability.

But increasingly in the eighteenth and nineteenth centuries it could. Starting in the early eighteenth century (a convenient date and turning point being the Peace of Utrecht in 1713–15), continuing through the wars of the mid-century, and climaxed by the revolutionary and imperialist wars at its end and the transformation produced by the Vienna Settlement of 1815, we see emerging a more stable, comprehensive state system endowed not merely with permanent players and better and more widely acknowledged rules, practices, and institutions, but also as a result with greater ability to manage international politics short of overt war. To some extent in the eighteenth century, to an even greater extent in the nineteenth, most wars that could have happened did not happen; most crises were managed more or less successfully.[7]

Cases of general and specific long peace

The most striking proof of this lies in instances of long peace, both general and specific. By a general long peace I mean a significant period in which there was no major war at all within the core international system, though there might be important peripheral conflicts (just as there have been in the post-1945 long peace). The two obvious instances of this in Europe are the Vienna-era peace of 1815–54 and the Bismarckian and post-Bismarckian peace of 1871–1914. In both periods, no wars were fought between major powers in Europe, despite many crises and occasions for it. Both these eras of general peace are well known, have often been analyzed, and need no further discussion here. Less recognized but also striking are instances of specific long peace – i.e., cases in which two or more powers, historic rivals and frequent foes in war, ceased to fight each other even though their rivalry continued, or cases in which historic areas or regions of chronic war remained at peace for long periods even though they continued to be centers of vital strategic, political, and economic conflicts of interest.

Here is a list of six such instances of specific long peace, with just enough description of each to explain its inclusion:

1   The Swiss long peace, 1815 to the present. Switzerland, a vital strategic area, had been fought over for centuries up to and including the wars of the French Revolution and Napoleon. In 1814–15 the great powers reconstituted the Swiss Confederation under a new constitution and guaranteed its neutral confederate status. Save for a brief, small-scale civil war in 1847 it has since experienced no war, despite serious disputes and major wars directly on its frontiers, including two world wars.

2   The long peace in the Low Countries, 1815–1914. The Low Countries constituted for centuries the prime cockpit of Western Europe. The Vienna settlement united these lands into one kingdom and protected them against foreign invasion, and when that union was broken by the Belgian revolt in 1830, the great powers acting in concert replaced it with an even better and more effective international settlement successfully neutralizing and guaranteeing Belgium up to World War I.

3   Peace in the Baltic between Russia, Sweden, and Denmark. This area was almost continually fought over from 1560 to 1721 by these powers and others (Prussia, Poland, other North German principalities, the German Emperor, and the Dutch United Provinces). Yet after 1721, despite important British, Russian, French, and German competition for influence and control in the area, peace in the Baltic between Russia, Sweden, and Denmark was interrupted only briefly and occasionally, almost entirely as a result of wider conflicts spilling over to include them (1788–90, 1808–9, 1813–14, 1863–4, and 1940).

4   Anglo-American peace, 1814 to the present. These states had fought two major wars; each saw the other as the main regional enemy and as a potential threat to its vital interests. Throughout the nineteenth century and well into the twentieth, serious issues divided them and created potential occasions for war. None ever led to war or, with the possible exception of the American Civil War, a major crisis, and from the turn of the century on the two powers, despite growing commercial, naval and imperial competition, experienced a rapprochement that led to their alliance in both world wars.

5   Anglo-French peace, 1815 to the present. These two great powers had been, as everyone knows, quintessential rivals and enemies since the fourteenth century. Their struggles between 1688 and 1815 have been termed a second Hundred Years War. Yet after 1815, despite persistent distrust and dislike on both sides, continued naval, colonial, and commercial rivalry, and some serious

crises and war scares (1839–40, 1860–1, and 1898), they never fought each other again,[8] and they were allies in two world wars.

6   Anglo-Russian peace, 1762–1945. This 'peace', to be sure, differs significantly from others on the list. It did not begin with traditional enmity – for most of the eighteenth century the two powers were important trading partners and politically at least potential allies – and the peace was broken twice, in 1808–12 by a war confined mainly to commerce and in 1854–6 by a genuine war in the Crimea. The significant fact remains, however, that for most of the nineteenth century, beginning as early as 1791 (the Ochakov Crisis) the two powers were competitors for empire in several regions of the world (the Near and Middle East, Central and South Asia, the Far East, and even for a short time the Americas and Africa), and this rivalry gave them many occasions to fight over imperial issues. They never did, and ended up as entente partners before 1914 and allies in two world wars.

A few observations on these examples of long peace are needed before taking up a final instance of long peace, the most important and remarkable one. My claim here is not that these particular instances of long peace before 1945, and/or peace as a collective general phenomenon, are mysteries, difficult or impossible to explain. Some explanations of these individual cases are reasonably clear and fairly obvious, and a satisfactory explanation of the growth of peace as a general phenomenon, though it would be too complicated to present and defend here, is also not new or mysterious. Nor do I claim that these instances of general and specific long peace are unique, the only such in the history of the world. Other eras of 'long peace' could doubtless be mentioned (though I do not know enough about any of them to discuss them seriously) – the Pax Romana, peace between medieval China, Japan, and Korea, and perhaps general peace in Latin America in the nineteenth and twentieth centuries, for example. I contend only that these instances of general and specific long peace in the European/world system before 1945 are real and add up to something important. None of the others really represents the same phenomenon, i.e., peace between numerous states and units that co-exist within a closely knit system, constantly interact, are juridically equal, jealously claim and defend their individual sovereignty, are capable of war and in many cases were specifically created for purposes of war, and have permanent conflicts of interest and compete with each other over scarce resources. Clear instances of long peace achieved under these circumstances, I contend, represent a historically unique and uniquely important phenomenon demanding recognition and explanation – particularly since they were achieved under the kind of system existing today, and the only one we can seriously conceive as prevailing in the future. As historical phenomena these instances of long peace should therefore be taken seriously, not ignored or dismissed with purely individual, ad hoc, contingent explanations as if there were nothing significant to discuss or explain, or as if only war, not peace, required explanation.

A special long peace: Austria, Germany, and Russia
1763–1914

The last instance of specific long peace before 1945, however, was special even when compared to the others. First of all, it was triadic rather than dyadic, prevailing between the Habsburg Monarchy, Prussia–Germany, and Russia from 1763 to 1914. It also differed from these first six in its character and structure, its causes, the reasons for both its remarkable duration and its ultimate demise, and its implications for the debate over the waning of major war today. In other words, there are good reasons for concentrating on it.

Proving that this peace existed is simply a matter of facts and dates. From 1762 to 1914, Prussia, which after 1871 constituted the core of Imperial Germany, never went to war with Russia.[9] Similarly, Austria (after 1867 Austria-Hungary) and Russia never really fought each other from the time Russia first emerged on the European scene early in the eighteenth century as a major power until 1914.[10] The case of Prussia and Austria, to be sure, is more complicated. They had fought each other in two major wars between 1740 and 1763, remained bitter rivals for decades thereafter in Germany and Eastern Europe, particularly Poland, and fought two wars between 1763 and 1914 for mastery in Germany – the first brief and indecisive in 1778–9, the second brief and decisive in 1866. Nonetheless, except for these two overt wars, in a long, close, intimate relationship which made each always an important neighbor to the other, often the most important, so that there were always grounds for tension and rivalry, the record between these two traditional enemies over these 150 years was mainly one of peace and alliance.[11]

This fact about Austro-German relations, that the two powers were always intimately involved with each other, could not ignore each other, and always had occasions for conflict, applies equally to all three powers and again makes their peace special. Statistically, most peace between the many dyads and triads in the world could be characterized as negative peace. The absence of war results simply from the absence of significant relations and occasions for war.[12] These three powers, however, could never dream of this. Peace between them had to be positive and active, the product of conscious policy and efforts to manage their complex, conflict-ridden relations rather than merely to avoid war. This is demonstrated, though not explained, by the fact that most of the time these three powers, though still rivals, were also allies and partners, warily and distrustfully working with one another.

Explanations of this long peace that fail to explain it

The explanation of this long peace must therefore likewise be special. Many factors used to explain peace between other great powers do not help here. Examples of explanations that are obviously irrelevant are: an absence of common frontiers, thus eliminating the possibility of territorial disputes or border clashes; or a decision by one of the rivals to drop out of the competition, yielding the palm to the other;

or the ability of one rival or both to achieve a natural security from attack (e.g., Britain's insular security once it assured itself of world naval supremacy, or the continental security enjoyed by the United States). Plainly none of these apply to this triangular relationship. Equally unhelpful are some of the cultural or institutional explanations of peace currently popular. Since all three powers were and remained military monarchies in which the army was the central pillar of the state, and none achieved real democracy or parliamentary government before 1914 (Germany and the Austrian half of Austria-Hungary coming closer than Russia, which remained the most authoritarian), theories of democratic peace or peace through liberal institutions plainly do not work here.

Other general explanations for international peace seem at first glance to help explain this long peace, but break down under examination. Peace can emerge between rivals if one of them wins so clear-cut and irreversible a victory that the loser gives up the struggle for supremacy or cannot mount a further challenge (e.g., Russia and Sweden after 1721, Britain and France after 1815). But this explanation holds good only for Prussia's victory over Austria in 1866, sealed by Germany's victory over France in 1870, and while this outcome settled the contest for supremacy in Germany and thereby arguably promoted durable peace between these two powers, it certainly did not promote peace in the triangular relationship overall, for several reasons. Far from solving the German question as a whole, Prussia's victories only settled which power would control the main part of Germany (so-called Little Germany). This outcome thereby raised the historic German question in Central and Eastern Europe as a whole to a new and ultimately more dangerous level, leaving the most crucial and difficult issues involved in the German question unanswered and even more pressing than before: the fate of the Habsburg Monarchy with its mixture of Austro-Germans and other peoples, the relations of this united and powerful Little Germany to the non-German peoples of Eastern Europe, the reaction of Russia to this powerful new Germany, and finally – most deadly of all – a possible collision of the two largest ethnic groups of Central and Eastern Europe, Teutons and Slavs, in the next battle for supremacy.

Sometimes ideological solidarity and cultural affinity serve to foster peace (e.g., between Britain and the United States). No doubt the reconciliation between Austria and Prussia after 1866 was helped somewhat by a sense of German ethnic and cultural affinity, which also cemented their alliance after 1879. Similarly, monarchical kinship and conservative solidarity were a major factor in the relations between all three governments, especially from 1815 to the mid-nineteenth century. But these feelings were never the most powerful factors in their relationship, and over time were increasingly outweighed by the ideological, cultural, religious, and ethnic differences between and within these powers, especially later in the era.

Shared goals and programs can help promote peace. The three powers often did have common goals, particularly those of combating revolution and preserving the existing political, territorial, and social status quo, especially in the Vienna era (1815–48). But in other periods before and after this era their respective internal programs and aims diverged sharply and drove them apart rather than together.

41

The chances for peace between quarreling states greatly improve when (if ever) they recognize that the stakes over which they are fighting are not worth a war and can be settled by compromise. While this feeling did help avoid war among these three powers on certain occasions (e.g., between Austria and Prussia in 1779, 1791, 1795, and 1849–50), more frequently the prevailing conviction was that the interests in dispute were vital state interests not capable of mutually satisfactory compromise. Even issues on which the three somehow managed to reach agreements (the joint partitions of Poland in 1772–95 and the further revision of that partition in 1814–15, or the German settlements in 1814–15 and in 1849–50) were bitterly contested, left behind recriminations and bad feelings, and remained potential sources of rivalry. Meanwhile, the perennial bones of contention between Austria and Prussia (Germany) and between Austria and Russia (the Balkans) defied any easy or durable compromise or settlement.

It promotes peace if rivals come to realize that even if they waged war against a particular opponent and won it, the victory would create new enemies and dangers outweighing the possible gains. There were occasions when this recognition helped restrain one or more of these powers from taking the plunge into war, e.g., Austria against Russia in 1772 and against Prussia in 1794–5, all three over the Polish–Saxon question in early 1815, and Austria and Germany against Russia until 1914. But clearly this will not do as a sufficient or central explanation of the long peace, for on numerous occasions between 1763 and 1914 one or more of these three powers discounted this danger, believing that it had the opportunity to start a war against one of the others, localize it, win it, and profit from it without serious adverse consequences. Yet only twice did any of these states actually exploit these supposed opportunities – Frederick II of Prussia unsuccessfully in 1778 and Bismarck successfully in 1866.

Sometimes international agreements promote peace between rivals by fencing off a contested area or issue from great-power conflict. Neutralizing Switzerland and Belgium are obvious examples. This approach played a certain role in this triangular peace. The German Confederation established at the Vienna Congress helped to keep Austro-Prussian rivalry in Germany under control from 1815 to 1866; certain international agreements over the Near East (e.g., the Münchengrätz Agreement in 1833 and the Straits Convention in 1841) helped limit Austro-Russian rivalry in the Balkans. But these arrangements clearly were not sufficient in themselves to account for peace, and broke down over time.

Economic interdependence and trade can under certain circumstances promote peace. Economic ties connecting Prussia/Germany to both Russia and Austria were always important and grew steadily closer right up to 1914. Yet these ties actually promoted more tension and conflict than peace and friendship between the three powers, especially between Germany and Russia after 1890, but also even between Germany and Austria as allies. Germany, for example, became Austria's most dangerous economic competitor in the Balkans.

Finally, one diplomatic device for promoting peace between rivals was particularly vital in this long peace: the restraining alliance. A restraining alliance is a formal or informal alliance that either intentionally or by force of circumstances primarily serves the purposes not of power politics, as a means of capability aggregation and weapon of military security and possible war, but of management, as an instrument for influencing, controlling, and managing the policy of other states, in particular one's ally. Restraining alliances are common in history; in fact, every alliance, however prominent its power-political and security features, also includes this managerial purpose and function to some extent.[13] Some major European alliances have functioned almost entirely as instruments of restraint, serving mainly to keep two rivals tied together as an alternative to war – the Austro-French alliance from 1763 to 1792 and the Austro-Italian alliance from 1882 to 1914, for example. The Austro-German-Russian relationship, however, offers an even better illustration of the importance and potential effectiveness of restraining alliances. Nothing contributed more to peace among these partners than the ways in which they used restraining alliances to manage each others' policies, with one of them usually leading the way and controlling the outcome. I can only list the main examples here: Russia's maintenance and exploitation of parallel alliances with Prussia and Austria from 1764 into the Napoleonic wars; the revival in 1813 of a three-power alliance after the disasters promoted by their disunity in two decades of war against revolutionary and Napoleonic France; their so-called Holy Alliance from 1815 to 1854; the parallel Austro-Prussian partnership in leading the German Confederation from 1815 into the early 1860s; the Three Emperors League formed in 1872–3; the Austro-German Dual Alliance in 1879 (above all a German device to control Austria and manage Austro-Russian and Russo-German relations); the Three Emperors Alliance in 1881, with similar purposes; the Russo-German Reinsurance Treaty of 1887–90, to reassure and restrain Russia; and the Russo-Austrian agreements for cooperation in the Balkans between 1897 and 1908. Every one of these alliances or ententes functioned at least as much for mutual management and restraint as for security and power. Without these agreements this long peace could not have survived, and once the hope of reviving any such restraining alliance disappeared after 1908, the problems of managing this critical and delicate triangular relationship became insuperable.

Yet while understanding the role of restraining alliances helps explain how this long peace survived and worked, it does not really tell us why it did. It indicates the principal instrument and method these states used, but does not disclose their reasons for using it – explain why the three powers so often chose this method of managing their relations to avoid direct confrontation and war, and why they finally abandoned it. To restate the question: why and how were three great military monarchies, always potential rivals and usually active ones, territorially contiguous, having many conflicting and overlapping interests, always facing potential or actual occasions and causes for war, always armed against each other, always believing in war as a legitimate final resort, and never willing to sacrifice their vital interests or great-power status for the sake of peace and tranquility, nonetheless able to spend 150 years not just technically at peace with each other while locked in Cold War, but mainly as each others' partners and allies?

The importance of this long peace

This long peace is as important as it is surprising. It formed the central pillar of the international system. From the time in the mid-eighteenth century (1763, to be precise) when it became clear that these three states, all fairly recent entries into the great power club, would remain permanent members of it, they and their region, Central, Eastern, and Southeastern Europe, constituted the epicenter of European politics. The French Revolution and Napoleon temporarily shifted the fulcrum westward, and had Napoleon been more reasonable and less ruthlessly imperialist his victories could have made this shift more permanent. But as things went, these powers remained at the center of action in the European states system after 1815 even more than before, and the general peace that prevailed between them made possible the long nineteenth century peace in Europe. Granted, the British navy enforced a Pax Britannica overseas that contributed to general European stability (a stability that Britain's loss of undisputed industrial, commercial and imperial hegemony and its shift from informal paramountcy to formal empire overseas in the age of New Imperialism helped undermine). But general peace on the continent was not the result of a Pax Britannica. That is a myth. Except perhaps briefly under Lord Castlereagh's leadership as Foreign Secretary in 1814–20, the British did not organize and lead the European states system and the Concert of Europe, though they repeatedly used it for their purposes, nor did peace prevail on the continent because Britain held the balance of power and acted as arbiter. In most crises throughout the nineteenth century, whether or not they led to war, British policy either played little role or served to heighten tensions. As for France, whatever goal it pursued, whether revision of the treaties after 1815 or overthrow of the system and French hegemony in the 1850s and early 1860s or revision, security, and revanche after 1871, the effect of French policy was more to disturb the peace than to organize and manage it.

Just as the Austro-German-Russian peace accounts for Europe's relative peace and stability, so its breakdown accounts for the systemic collapse into general war. This was partly the case in 1787–92, when war by Russia and Austria against the Ottoman Empire and a crisis over Poland preceded war with France and helped produce it, and it was wholly so in 1914. To say that the breakdown of this triangular peace accounts for the systemic collapse and general war in 1914 is not to state the banal fact that the First World War broke out in southeastern Europe between these powers, but to claim that a general European war could only have broken out here, in this region and between these particular powers, and that the breakdown of the Austro-German-Russian relationship was the central cause of the war. Certainly other grave sources of rivalry and tension existed in Europe and the world, sufficient to assure that an Austro-German-Russian war would become general. But these other rivalries did not bring on World War I, and without an Austro-German-Russian conflict could not have. The Anglo-German rivalry over commerce, colonies, general European and world politics, and above all naval armaments was serious, and their mutual threat perception made it likely by 1914 that Britain would take the French and Russian side in a general conflict. Yet barring two improbable scenarios, namely, a British preventive strike against the German navy or a German preventive attack on France, this rivalry would not by itself have led to war. By 1914 Britain had won the colonial and naval race, and even if Admiral Tirpitz refused to admit it the German government knew it and was concentrating on the continental land arms race it had hitherto neglected and was losing.[14] The Anglo-German colonial issues were being settled, and their commercial and industrial relations, however competitive, were so close that both powers had a strong commercial disincentive to fight and no plausible pretext for doing so.[15] Franco-German rivalry was even more serious and incurable. Superficially and emotionally it stemmed from France's loss of Alsace-Lorraine in 1871; the more profound cause was the mutual insecurity and threat perception created by Germany's victory and growth in power, heightened by 1914 by their rival alliances and the general arms race. But again, unless some extraordinary incident led to an armed clash and war (and a series of such incidents between 1875 to 1913 had been managed well short of war) Franco-German rivalry would not have led to war. The French refused to renounce or forget Alsace-Lorraine, but by 1914 had lost any desire for a war to retake it,[16] while Germany, never eager for another struggle with France, twice in the decade before 1914 passed up good opportunities for a preventive war to remove the French threat. The rivalry between Austria and Italy over the Adriatic, the western Balkans, and Italian irredentism was just as deep-seated and incurable – each side in secret regularly referred to the other as the allied enemy – but once again, barring the preventive attack on Italy which Austria's sometime chief of staff, Conrad von Hoetzendorf, regularly advocated and the Austrian emperor and government regularly rejected, this rivalry was incapable of producing a general war. Both powers were too weak, vulnerable, and fearful to launch a war on their own, and both were allied to Germany, which would not permit it. Tensions and rivalries in the Balkans were of course extremely high, both between the Balkan states themselves and between some of them and great powers, and Mediterranean, Middle Eastern, and North African problems and rivalries also complicated the picture. Yet again, unless Austria, Germany, and Russia went to war over any of these issues, they would not and could not produce a general war. It can hardly be stated too strongly: Europe in 1914 was not a seething cauldron full of bitter rivalries, any of which could have touched off a general war. It was a seething cauldron full of bitter rivalries, only one of which, Austro-German-Russian rivalry, could have touched off a general war. The key to peace or war lay in whether that rivalry came to the boil. This conclusion suggests another: without the breakdown of this particular long peace resulting in this general war, one cannot see how a second, much worse world war could have arisen in the same arena, basically between the same main foes, Germany and Russia.

Explaining the long peace: the right starting point

While the need to analyze this long peace should be obvious, it might be less obvious that the analysis has to ask first, 'Why this long peace?' rather than 'Why the eventual war?' – that it should start with what made this long peace possible and durable rather than with what caused it finally to break down. The reasons are not merely that explaining the origins of World War I has been done over and over, while explaining the long peace remains neglected, or that the final breakdown was no surprise while the long peace is. The main reason is that to try to explain the origins of Austro-German-Russian war without first understanding what made this long peace possible and how it worked is like trying to explain a fatal heart attack without first understanding how a healthy cardiovascular system works. It takes hold of the wrong end of the stick, and almost assures that one will get the explanation of both the peace and the war wrong.

The stages of this peace, and what they show

Plainly a serious historical analysis cannot be attempted here. What I can offer is just enough sketchy history to underpin and illustrate some key points, unavoidably oversimplifying greatly. An indisputable fact about the pattern of this long peace, in any case, is that it did not persist unchanged over time, but underwent striking changes and metamorphoses. The stages in the triangular relationship might be encapsulated thus:

1   1763–92: intense Austro-Prussian rivalry, contained and exploited by Russia within an unstable, aggressive Russian hegemony.
2   1792–1815: repeated crises and breakdowns in the triangular relationship, in part the result of internal conflicts, in part of a French Revolutionary– Napoleonic threat that the rifts between the three powers made more terrible. The resultant disastrous wars finally taught all three powers that they had to unite and cooperate in war and peace if any of them were to survive and prosper.
3   1815–48: Austro-Prussian partnership in Germany, combined with latent rivalry there, and a similar Austro-Russian partnership and latent rivalry in the Near East, under the general aegis of an inactive, relatively tolerable Russian hegemony in the region.
4   1848–71: alienation between Austria and Prussia over the German question in and after the 1848 Revolutions, followed by alienation between Austria and Russia during and after the Crimean War. The result was an end to Russian support for Austria's leading position in Italy, leading to Austria's expulsion, and Russia's hesitant acceptance and support of Prussia's victories over Austria and France and a Prussian-led unification of Germany, excluding Austria there as well.
5   1871–90: a labile German half-hegemony within this triangular relationship and in Europe generally, sufficient to preserve general peace and keep the

growing Austro-Russian rivalry and hostility in the Near East under control, but only at the price of increasingly artificial German expedients and entanglements.

6   1890–1908: a final breakdown of the tenuous connection between Germany and Russia, followed by growing German-Russian tension fed by their opposed alliances, economic quarrels, rival nationalisms, and world policies. This rivalry, however, neither created a serious threat of Russo-German war nor prevented repeated attempts at a rapprochement, especially by Germany. Meanwhile, Austria and Russia engaged in limited and mistrustful cooperation to keep the Balkans from exploding and to facilitate Russian imperialism elsewhere.

7   1908–14: the total alienation of Russia from Austria-Hungary, and a deepened though still not irreversible alienation of Russia from Germany, heightened by an accelerated arms race in which for the first time each is arming mainly against the others, and by a series of crises in which war between them appears likely.

This bare-boned outline of stages in the relationship illustrates again how some apparently plausible explanations for the long life and ultimate demise of the long peace are inadequate – e.g., the operation of the balance of power. Power relationships within the triad, as the outline indicates, were highly labile and normally not balanced in any conventional sense. One power, either Russia or Germany, was almost always the hegemon, the pattern changed repeatedly in different eras, and the period in which power became most evenly balanced among them in a military and strategic sense, from 1890 on, was the one in which the triangular peace progressively broke down. It would be easier to argue for a hegemonic–power shift version of realist theory, that different kinds of hegemony sustained the peace, but that explanation is also too simple. Nor can one contend simply that the three powers stayed together out of solidarity against a common foe or foes, and became enemies when the common threat (France, revolution, liberalism, the West, whatever) disappeared. Overall their relationship was characterized less by such solidarity than by perceptions of betrayal and defection from their alliance. Nor did they stick together because they had no alternatives, could find no other allies. All three repeatedly considered other alliances and alignments, often at the expense of one or both of the others, and they sometimes actively pursued and obtained them.

The elements making this long peace possible and sustainable

Something more deep-rooted therefore had to be sustaining this peace over its surprisingly long life. I detect three elements, so overlapping and interlocking that they virtually constitute a single whole. First, throughout this era the three powers each recognized that while their security concerns were not strictly speaking shared and mutual, they were at least compatible in one major sense: that each power would gain greatly in security through good relations and close ties with the others. Russia always saw a 'friendly' (i.e., non-threatening) Prussia/Germany and Austria as a valuable buffer or glacis against threats from the West, useful both for projecting Russia's influence westward and for protecting Russia's rear while Russia was expanding in the Middle East, Central Asia, and the Far East. For Austria, a friendly Russia secured one of its numerous vulnerable frontiers, and could be a vital ally against other threats. The same held for Prussia/Germany vis-à-vis Russia. As for the two German powers, even when locked in rivalry they were always aware that if they could somehow cooperate, each would be more secure not only against other threats, especially from France, but also against Russian domination and manipulation. The task for each power of balancing these various security concerns and working out the problems of interdependence and leadership within the triadic relationship was never easy and occasionally impossible, but usually the potential gains were worth the effort.

Second, these powers recognized that beyond their strictly defined security needs they also faced general regional problems affecting them all directly or indirectly, problems from which they could not exclude the others without grave danger and the possible use of force, so that these had to be managed jointly. Obvious examples are Poland, the fate of the Ottoman Empire and the Balkan states, the general defense of the monarchical order and their individual political and social systems, and to some extent the management of their internal problems with discontented national, ethnic, and religious minorities (especially when, as with the Poles and Ukrainians, these minorities overlapped their respective frontiers).

These two broad motives for partnership, shared security concerns and shared managerial tasks in the region, merge into a broader third, the real bedrock of their relationship. All three powers learned over time, especially through the great trials by fire in the Napoleonic wars, that willy-nilly, whether they liked it or not, they had to accept, tolerate, endorse, and under certain circumstances even actively support the continued existence of the others as great powers (which included respecting their vital internal concerns and influence in their respective neighbor-hoods) if they were to remain independent great powers themselves. This meant rejecting the option of eliminating or seriously weakening any of them as a great power because each played a role in the region and the states system for which no practical substitute existed or could be devised, so that eliminating any partner, even when it was troublesome and dangerous, would promote problems of an even worse, more unmanageable kind. This understanding meant, at a minimal level, that if war did arise between them, it could not be pursued so far as to eliminate any one as a great power or to reduce it to manageable size (as Russia and Austria had tried to do to Prussia in 1756–63, and that certain leaders in all three countries would propose later at different times).[17] On the more normal, everyday level of inter-national politics it meant solving or managing problems between them politically, without resort to war. At a higher level, but one attained on a number of important occasions, it meant taking concrete action jointly or separately to prevent any of the three from being destroyed or crippled as a great power.[18] To reduce this to a formula: the long peace was made possible and sustained by a mutual recognition among these three great powers of a relation of complex interdependence between them which at a minimum proscribed actions that would destroy or cripple any of the partners as a functioning great power and at a maximum prescribed actions to preserve and promote that status.

Why the underpinnings of this peace were unusual, and yet endured

There is nothing inherently startling about this analysis or this phenomenon, that great powers should recognize their interdependence within the states system and tacitly accept and endorse the existence and vital interests of other great powers as inseparably bound up with their own. Indeed, some such recognition is virtually a presupposition of a working, stable international system. One of the basic functions of the balance of power is supposedly to preserve the existence and functions of all essential actors. But if this phenomenon of mutual recognition of interdependence is not an aberration in international politics, it is hardly a normal or routine phenomenon, and even if balance of power theory and principles call for it and require it in the abstract, actual balance of power practices and politics frequently undermine it. More often than not the power-political mandate to maximize one's own interests and security and pursue one's own relative advantage sweeps aside the theoretical requirement of preserving the balance through maintaining the existence and functions of all essential actors. When therefore three great powers can be seen actually to have observed this rule of respecting each others' existence, status, and vital interests as great powers over a considerable time, this must be the result of something more than normal balance of power politics plus a dash of ideological solidarity and good will. Deliberate policy, hard choices had to be involved, and were. The long peace endured because at a series of critical moments and junctures, one or another of these great powers or all three, faced with a choice between respecting and supporting the existence of the others as great powers or allowing and abetting their destruction, came down concretely on the side of the former alternative.

This claim, to be convincing, would need backing by concrete evidence on how this happened between 1763 and 1914 – a demonstration possible, but far too complicated to be undertaken here, so that the claim must be left as another fairly naked assertion. One can show, however, that this principle was not only embodied in individual decisions and policies, but also institutionalized and carried out through more or less formal institutions and practices – partly those of the European Concert, but above all through the instrument mentioned earlier, restraining alliances. To a considerable degree one could write the whole history of this long peace in terms of the restraining alliances reached between these three powers and what happened to them – the parallel Russo-Prussian and Russo-Austrian alliances after 1764, the failed alliances of 1792–1807, the successful one forged in 1813–14, the so-called Holy Alliance after 1815, the Austro-Prussian restraining alliance in

Germany and the Austro-Russian one in the Balkans, the Prusso-German-Austrian alliance that restrained both Austria and Russia in the Crimean War, the Three Emperors League, the Three Emperors Alliance, the Reinsurance Pact, the Mürzsteg Punctation (1903–7), and the disastrous failure of the last serious attempt to revive the Austro-Russian Balkan entente and the Three Emperors League in 1908.

Explaining the breakdown: not German challenge, but Russian defection

An obvious rejoinder might be: If this peace was so valuable, why did it die so horrible a death, with such disastrous consequences? What destroyed it? Every student of the question knows the standard answer, and most accept it. Germany and Austria-Hungary wrecked this triangular peace and the general European peace with it – Germany by its growing power and restless world policy, Austria-Hungary by aggressive foreign policy moves intended to meet its internal crises and prove it was still a great power. These together directly challenged Russia's prestige and vital interests in the Balkans, the Straits, and Asiatic Turkey. The Central Powers particularly confronted and humiliated Russia in the Bosnian Crisis of 1908–9, obstructed Russian interests and threatened Russia's allies in the Balkan wars, and finally threw down a deliberate, unacceptable challenge to Russia in the July Crisis.

This is not the place to discuss the origins of World War I, but it is the place to discuss the breakdown of this particular peace, and to show that the difference in approach and perspective makes a difference. If one's goal is to explain the origins of the war and one's method is that of analyzing events and developments before 1914 from the standpoint of how they led to the outbreak of war – the standard aim and method – then a case making Germany's power, ambitions, and aggressive behavior the root causes of the war and Austria-Hungary's weakness and desperation the triggering factor can be constructed. (It does not convince me, but no matter.) If, however, as claimed here, explaining peace is logically prior to explaining war and more important; if the objective should be first to analyze the roots and sources of this long peace and on that basis explain its breakdown, and thereby better understand the origins of the war; and if that analysis (as outlined here) concludes that the long Austro-German-Russian peace depended fundamentally on having all the partners continue to recognize, respect, and at least passively support the continued existence of the others as independent great powers, then any scenario making the German powers primarily responsible for the breakdown becomes untenable. Germany and Austria-Hungary, especially the former, can plausibly be accused of doing things that increased tensions and raised the general danger of war in Europe, but not of a failure to observe this rule in respect to Russia. The opposite is true. In the decades before World War I both Germany and Austria-Hungary constantly courted and appeased the Tsarist government, hoping to win it back from the arms of France and Britain. In the Far East Germany from the early 1890s on supported and cooperated with Russia in its imperialist expansion, and got no thanks for it.[19] In Turkey and the Middle East the Germans sought and eventually secured a deal protecting Russia's interests in the Baghdad Railway project, after Russia had deliberately excluded Germany from Persia by its convention dividing Persia with Great Britain.[20] Both Germany and Austria-Hungary rejected repeated Turkish requests for a defensive alliance against Russia.[21] Unlike Britain and France, they regularly supported Russia's goal of achieving a favored position at the Straits. Though Russia and Germany quarreled over tariffs, Russia was more protectionist than Germany and Germany remained its most valuable economic partner. The land arms race between them after 1910 was launched by Russia's military programs, not Germany's, and the Austrians, who were most threatened by that arms race, essentially gave up trying to keep pace. Austria-Hungary's policies in the Balkans, though they were undoubtedly anti-Serbian and anti-Italian in reaction to these countries' clearly anti-Austrian ones, were never anti-Russian in purpose or even in effect.[22] Austria proposed and loyally carried out the Austro-Russian agreements between 1897 and 1907 that put the Balkans on ice, at a time when Russia urgently needed to keep that theater quiet in order to concentrate on its imperialist expansion in the Far East, and subsequently to survive the disastrous war against Japan and the revolution its imperialist policy had provoked.[23] Austria-Hungary's last two foreign ministers in 1906–14, Baron Aehrenthal and Count Berchtold, were the most pro-Russian ones it had had since Count Rechberg in the early 1860s. Both wanted to revive the Three Emperors League, as did the heir-apparent, Archduke Francis Ferdinand.

Even if some of these claims are challenged (as some scholars doubtless would do), there is one particularly striking proof of the German powers' continued recognition and support for Russia's existence as a great power. Their policy in 1904–6 saved the Tsarist regime from overthrow by revolution. Had either of these powers in 1905 done anything at all to threaten Russia when it was paralyzed by defeat and revolution – mobilized, ordered troop movements, even merely renounced their public stance of benevolent neutrality – the regime would have gone down. This is not speculation. The only way the Russian premier Count Witte was able to persuade Russia's generals, strongly opposed on general principles to using the army for internal policing, to let their forces be dispersed over the Russian country-side to stamp out the revolution was to assure them that there was absolutely no possibility of a military threat on Russia's western front.[24] This assurance both German governments had already given Russia, Austria by a formal neutrality agreement, Germany informally, and they stuck by it. The Russian response to this, once order was restored, was first to back France and Britain in imposing a humiliating defeat on Germany over Morocco at the Conference of Algeciras; then to make a separate deal with Britain over Persia and Central Asia deliberately designed to exclude Germany; and next to break Russia's longstanding cooperation with Austria-Hungary in the Macedonian question in favor of working with Britain.

This is not to say that the Central Powers acted in a generous or altruistic fashion and Russia with ingratitude and treachery. The prevailing ethos of imperialism and *sacro egoismo* in that era rendered such terms irrelevant and almost meaningless, and Russia's conduct more or less normal. What this does prove is that Germany and Austria-Hungary still conceived their own interests and acted upon them in ways required for the long peace to survive. Russia did not. The Russian government, backed by Russia's political elites and Russian society (which basically consisted of some 300,000 gentry and aristocratic families), still wanted general peace in Europe, desperately needed for economic, military, and political recovery, but had already in spirit repudiated this Austro-German-Russian peace. Its minimal requirements were now seen in Russia as intolerably onerous and humiliating, because the reigning Russian attitude toward its partners, in particular one of them, had decisively changed. Though Russia had allied itself with France against Germany and Austria-Hungary already in 1891–4, making Germany its main military rival and opponent, the Russian government and public continued to recognize Germany as a great power and take it seriously – in fact, to try in many respects to emulate it. Even if the Russian government increasingly gravitated toward France and Britain from 1906 on, it wanted to keep a line open to Berlin. The lively Russian debate within the government, the Duma, and the press between pro-Westerners and pro-Germans persisted until 1914, though the pro-Western side slowly gained ground. In short, Russo-German relations deteriorated overall, but this did not lead to Russia's ceasing to recognize and treat Germany as an independent great power. Even during the world war, it continued to expect Germany to survive defeat and emerge as a major power, just as Britain and France did.

Toward Austria-Hungary the Russian attitude was completely different. Ever since the Crimean War, Russia had at best tolerated Austria-Hungary's continued existence as a great power, rather than endorsing or supporting it, as it had done before. Well before 1900, from the 1870s on, most influential Russians ceased to consider Austria-Hungary a great power or an equal, fit partner for Russia in any sense. Russia's generals, despite French arguments for concentrating on the German threat, always insisted on making Austria Russia's primary military target in any war arising from the Russo-French alliance. Before 1908, however, Russian hostility and contempt for Austria-Hungary had not yet become active enmity. On particular questions of Russia's national interests, the Russian government was still willing to deal with the Habsburg Monarchy and tolerate its existence, though not at the price of any effort or sacrifice to sustain its great-power status and integrity.

The Bosnian Crisis of 1908–9 that supposedly ended in Russia's humiliation at the hands of Germany and Austria-Hungary changed Russian hostility and aversion into active enmity. Thereafter Russia in cooperation with Italy and France set out to block every Austrian action or initiative, supported the anti-Austrian territorial ambitions of small powers (Romania and Montenegro as well as Serbia), worked to bring Serbia, Montenegro, Bulgaria, Greece, and even Austria's ally Romania and its potential ally the Ottoman Empire into a Russian-led Balkan League directed against Austria, and while still reluctant to risk war, looked forward to the Habsburg Monarchy's expected demise with anticipation rather than fear or regret. As everyone knows, Austria-Hungary touched off World War I in July 1914 by its ultimatum to Serbia, intended to provoke a local war to eliminate Serbia as a political factor in the Balkans. Virtually every historian sees this as an unacceptable challenge to Russia as a great power. Few have recognized that Russia's policy for the previous five years was directed toward gradually eliminating Austria-Hungary as a political factor in the Balkans, or have seen this as an unacceptable challenge to Vienna.[25]

Two illustrations of Russia's defection, and a bit of explanation

While I again believe that ample evidence supports this controversial view, it cannot be presented here.[26] To keep the argument from resting simply on assertion, however, let me quickly cite two incidents to show how Russia had already abandoned the central requirement of this long peace vis-à-vis Austria-Hungary, respect for the other's existence as a great power, well before their supposedly decisive confrontation and breach in 1908–9. These incidents also illustrate how much difference it makes if one examines events with an eye to explaining peace rather than war.

The first incident, well known but too little noticed, occurred in 1899, when the French Foreign Minister Théophile Delcassé worked out with Russia a reinterpretation of their alliance changing it from the original simple defensive alliance of 1894 directed solely against the Dual Alliance into a general instrument for upholding the European balance of power. While Delcassé had general strategic and power-political aims in mind, he was prompted to seek the change in the alliance at this time because Austria-Hungary, in the throes of a severe domestic crisis, seemed likely to suffer an internal collapse and breakup. Delcassé wished to ensure that France and Russia, together with Italy, Austria's hostile ally, would control the resulting territorial partition of Austria-Hungary, preventing Germany from taking Austrian territories dangerous to them, especially Trieste with its outlet to the Adriatic and Mediterranean, and possibly enabling France to recover Alsace-Lorraine as the payoff for Germany's expected aggrandizement with German portions of Austria-Hungary.[27] That Delcassé, a pure French nationalist and *Realpolitiker*, should adopt this policy of exploiting Austria-Hungary's anticipated collapse and partition is no surprise. Throughout the nineteenth century *sacro egoismo* was always as much France's principle as Italy's. That Russia, however, should also treat Austria-Hungary's demise and breakup purely from the standpoint of competitive power politics, and that Russia's foreign minister and its chief of staff should discuss with the French then and later how to exploit it for purposes of military security and relative advantage, says a great deal – not, true, directly about how war started in 1914, but about how and why the long Austro-German-Russian peace declined and died.

The second incident has gone virtually unnoticed. In early 1905, with Russia already in deep trouble in its war with Japan and feeling the rumblings of revolutionary discontent at home, but with Austria-Hungary also undergoing another grave internal crisis, the German Foreign Office proposed to Russia that the two powers, in order to encourage elements loyal to the throne in Austria, join in a simple declaration of their disinterest in any territorial aggrandizement at Austria-Hungary's expense. The Russian Foreign Minister Count Lamsdorff, after first expressing some interest, then proceeded to evade the proposal, despite Germany's renewing it and offering to agree to any wording of the declaration Lamsdorff would propose. As a result the proposal died.[28] The *éminence grise* at the German Foreign Office, Friedrich von Holstein, interpreted the incident, reasonably enough, not as a sign that Russia had actual territorial ambitions at Austria's expense (though in fact Tsar Nicholas II did entertain some in regard to eastern Galicia), but that the government was completely unwilling to do anything that might be criticized by the Panslavs in Russia.[29]

Once again, the incident says nothing directly about the origins of World War I. From that standpoint the German proposal can be ignored as unimportant or dismissed as one of many German efforts to lure Russia into its camp.[30] But it says something important about the life and death of the long Austro-German-Russian peace. This suggestion was to my knowledge the only one ever made before 1914 for any collective international action to help stave off an eventuality, Austria-Hungary's collapse, that everyone recognized as a grave threat to international stability and peace. The action Germany proposed, minimal and innocuous though it was, stood squarely in the tradition and spirit of this long peace – resembling, for example, the Münchengrätz and Berlin conventions in 1833 pledging Russia, Austria, and Prussia to try to maintain the territorial integrity of the Ottoman Empire as a way to help keep the Ottoman Sultan on his throne. Yet the Russian government, which itself at this time desperately needed diplomatic support from Germany and Austria to survive, and was receiving that support from both powers, refused to make even this Platonic gesture in favor of Austria-Hungary's continued existence.

A full explanation of this Russian animus toward Austria and the remarkable failure to see any connection between the anticipated downfall of the Habsburgs and the fate of the Romanovs would break the already overstretched bounds of this chapter. Suffice it to say that one can easily explain this on normal historical grounds – the traditional Russian contempt for Austria as a weak, treacherous neighbor; the extraordinary stupidity and stubbornness of Tsar Nicholas II, who finally decided Russian foreign policy; the image of Austria as enemy that had been forged already by the Crimean War and was deepened by the Eastern crises of the 1870s and 80s; the influence of domestic politics and of ethnic, nationalist, and religious antipathies, etc. These elements and others supply ample grounds for a normal 'rational' explanation. Yet I cannot escape the feeling that these factors, while relevant, stop short of a satisfying explanation. In his influential book *Retreat from Doomsday*, John Mueller argues that modern war has become obsolescent in advanced societies because it has become subrationally unthinkable, like dueling or slavery.[31] Whatever one thinks of the thesis in regard to war, the concept is useful here. The very idea of doing anything to support Austria-Hungary's existence as a great power had by 1914 become subrationally unthinkable in Russia – and not only there.

What does it all mean?

This chapter would seem to have strayed far from its original theme and purpose. What is all this in aid of? What can it tell us about the waning of major war today?

Perhaps nothing. There may be no real connection. One could easily argue that the global situation today is so different from the one prevailing in the eras discussed here, and that the particular circumstances and forces either favoring or threatening the current long peace in the world are so remote from the ones operative in Europe then, that this discussion is as important for this theme as the manual typewriter is for current business.

Nonetheless, the argument here may have some relevance. To be precise, it offers a clear answer to one part of our question, and two hints or suggestions on other aspects of it. First, to the basic question 'Is major war on the wane?', it offers a direct answer: 'Yes, of course. It started waning long before the current Long Peace began.' The undeniably horrible wars and atrocities of the first half of the twentieth century and the unique dangers posed by new weapons of mass destruction make no difference on this score. There is a common belief that two world wars and the nuclear age destroyed the reigning nineteenth-century illusion of a steady progress toward peace. It is wrong on at least two counts. That illusion did not reign in the nineteenth century, especially toward its end. The great majority of leaders and opinion-makers everywhere believed the opposite: that war was natural and more or less inevitable. More important, the mere fact that two great world wars and a host of smaller ones have occurred, and that World War II especially was accompanied by horrors and crimes unprecedented in scale and in certain respects unique in kind, cannot disprove the reality of progress toward international peace any more than the occurrence of new epidemics and catastrophic illnesses, like the flu epidemic in 1918 that killed more people than died in World War I or the AIDS epidemic now, refutes the reality of medical progress. It should not have been a surprise, at least to historians and other scholars, that human beings organized in large rival communities can and do commit unspeakable crimes against each other in wartime, using all the means their wealth and ingenuity can devise in the process. Scholars ought to take that for granted. The surprise lies in any progress made in reducing and preventing this. In any case, none of this disproves the claim that there is now more peace in the world (defined as stated at the outset) than there was in the nineteenth century, just as there was more in the nineteenth than in the eighteenth.

The salient question, of course, is whether that growth in peace will endure or end in a cataclysm much worse and more final than 1914–18. No one (certainly no historian) can answer that question confidently, but the argument here about the life and death of this remarkable long peace in modern history gives at least two hints or indications on what the greatest dangers leading to that latter outcome might be.

One common argument about the current long peace is that though it may seem satisfactory and reasonably secure to us now (satisfactory, that is, to the billion people or so in the developed world as opposed to the five billion outside it), one can detect already present or looming on the horizon dangers and problems for which both the current international system and its component governments are unprepared and unsuited to cope, especially in an era marked by the supposed decline and weakening of even advanced national states and the undeniably fragile and impotent state of most governments in the world. In other words, things are very likely to go out of control in the face of new forces and problems. Anyone can list some of these – globalization, the growing gap between rich and poor both between and within regions and countries, the clash of civilizations, ethnic and religious rivalry, terrorism, population growth, uncontrolled migration, pressure on resources and the environment, etc. These problems, that are not now being solved and are likely to get worse, will sooner or later lead some governments or movements or groups to do things to try to solve them, or pretend to solve them, or distract attention from them, or defend themselves against them, that will snowball into another great war.

This view of the future closely resembles one of the broad standard explanations of the causes of the First World War, according to which the war happened basically because escalating problems caused things to go out of control. Governments swept along in a maelstrom of escalating international challenges and responses lost control not simply of their own foreign policies, but even more important, well before this began losing effective governance of their own states and societies in the face of challenges and problems that these governments, especially the authoritarian and semi-authoritarian ones, could not manage, much less solve. These included nationalism, especially the romantic ethnic integral nationalism pervasive in Central and Eastern Europe, Social Darwinism, racism, the stresses of industrialization and urban growth, economic competition, imperialism, militarism, radical ideologies and revolutionary movements, the rise of mass politics and of incomplete and immature democracy, the pressures of uneven development, conflicting demands from old threatened elites and new rising parties, interests, and classes – challenges that overwhelmed governments with their often old-fashioned decision-making processes. Partly in an effort to deflect these pressures, to paper over internal divisions, and to stay in power, partly in direct response to demands and pressures generated from below, various governments, again especially the more authoritarian ones, took refuge in an aggressive foreign policy, hoping by success there to meet these challenges or distract attention from them. Ultimately this made them even more the prisoners of their own policies and unsolved problems and produced the slide into war.

I will comment only on what this historical explanation might suggest about present prospects. The view that governments before 1914 became overwhelmed by problems of rapid change they could not solve and responded with policies of social imperialism and secondary integration that escalated into war deserves respect and contains considerable truth. Among the governments involved, it applies to some degree to Britain and France, considerably more to Germany and Austria-Hungary, and most of all to Russia, Serbia, and Italy.[32] But as an overall explanation for the war, and as the main explanation of the foreign policies of these individual states, it is unconvincing. There is simply too much evidence that in 1914 all the governments, including the authoritarian ones, were still acting on the basis of rational calculation and choice, however narrow they felt their alternatives might be.[33] Moreover, their motives and reasons for action, even where extremely misguided, reflected normal foreign policy decision-making, based primarily on conventional statecraft.[34] Though the various leaders were certainly under pressures, both internal and external, they did not feel driven by forces beyond their ability to manage until very late, perhaps July 30, when the general feeling arose that the game they were playing had escaped their control. I have the sense, for whatever it is worth, that the same general situation still prevails. Massive problems and pressures face the world and could threaten international peace; some already do. But this does not mean that governments, or those that count for purposes of major war, cannot manage these so as to avoid major war over them, and still less that their response must be to do reckless things that will cause one. That did not happen in 1914 or 1939, and it need not now.

So much for a hopeful hint from history. The more grave and decisive question, before 1914 and now, is however not whether governments can do the things necessary to sustain peace, but whether they will, and the crucial lesson taught by the long peace of 1763–1914 is that while they may repeatedly decide prudently and act rationally for a surprisingly long time, nothing guarantees that this sane decision-making and prudent collective action will continue indefinitely. Powerful structural reasons may indeed work against this, and the very success experienced in keeping a long peace going may help hasten its demise.

Why? Because that very success in managing crises and avoiding war promotes, not so much overconfidence and recklessness as a reliance on simple formulas for preserving peace. If one has the right balance of power ('right' meaning usually a preponderance of power in the hands of the right, peace-loving states), or the right alliances and military means, or the right diplomatic and international organizations to promote it, or the right kinds of governments (namely, democratic ones) in power, or the right willingness to make compromises and adjustments, or some combination of these, peace will follow.

A certain version of such thinking clearly prevailed in Europe before 1914. None of the great powers or even the smaller ones desired a great war. But they all believed in and followed simple formulas for making peace endure, basic policies that can be stated in brief sentences without serious distortion. For the British, the formula was to maintain the balance of power, defined as a stable deterrent balance between the two continental alliance systems, with Britain as arbiter of the peace through its naval and financial supremacy. For France the formula was simply to maintain the existing alliances rigid and intact. For Germany it was to make sure that Germany remained strong enough to fight a two-front war, thus deterring any attack or unacceptable threat, meanwhile trying to improve its position by wooing Russia away from France and keeping Britain neutral. For Russia the formula was to become so strong by 1917 that Germany would not dare attack, meanwhile keeping Austria-Hungary quiet in the Balkans. For Italy, concerned less to prevent a great war than to stay out of it unless and until it could gain from entering, it was to continue playing both sides against the other. Only Austria-Hungary had no simple formula for maintaining peace, because all the expedients it tried, mainly ones of marshalling German and European Concert support for its legal position, kept failing, until it finally resorted to the simplest and most drastic measure of all – a preventive local war to rid itself of its most immediate foe.

All these simple formulas were defective. Not merely were they inadequate as individual prescriptions for continued peace and in glaring contradiction to each other, each one requiring that the other side or some other power accept something it considered flatly unacceptable. Above all, they shared the same Utopian illusion that certain basic conditions – correct balance of power, firm alliances, clear commitments, superior strength, whatever – would make the system work so that the concrete details of peace – the negotiations, the compromises, the necessary adjustments on the ground – would follow. That idea, though seductive, is illusory. Not only does it overemphasize peace through positive measures of deterrence and compellence, neglecting the still more important aspect of limits, what one cannot and must not do if one wishes to preserve peace. It also consigns politics, the process of reaching consensus and compromise, to the tactical periphery of international politics and peace, making it merely the practical means of executing policy, realizing certain predefined goals and ends, when in genuinely critical situations politics is the essence of policy, and peace depends on changing goals, redefining vital interests, and stretching the limits of the acceptable and desirable.

1914 illustrates this. The reliance then on simple formulas for peace rested on something deeper than mere habit, superficial thinking, or inadequate leadership. Holger Herwig has suggested that behind the universal failure of all the powers' carefully worked-out war plans in 1914 lay something which he calls a pathology of strategic planning, a deep, pervasive disconnect between means and ends – an intriguing concept that can be adapted here. Behind the reliance on illusory formulas for peace in 1914 lay a general pathology of European politics, of political thinking and decision-making. The essence of pathological political thinking is to will an end without willing the necessary means, or to pursue an end by clearly counter-productive means. A fanatic is someone who, facing evidence that he is headed in the wrong direction, redoubles his efforts. This kind of fanaticism is found in the policies of all the major powers and some smaller ones, but I will confine myself to one already designated here as the worst and most central offender, Tsarist Russia. The Russian government, it is clear, wanted and needed peace, not war. To secure it, it hoped to restrain Germany from attack and to keep Austria-Hungary quiet in the Balkans. Both aims were in principle reasonable. But to restrain Germany from attacking Russia now, while Russia was still relatively unprepared, it openly adopted a massive arms program avowedly designed to achieve an insuperable military superiority over both Germany and Austria-Hungary by 1917, and to keep

Austria-Hungary inactive in the Balkans Russia actively and successfully pursued an anti-Austrian alliance under Russian leadership intended to unite all the Balkan states, including Austria's worst enemy Serbia, its nominal ally Romania, and its potential ally the Ottoman Empire, thus isolating Austria. It also pledged itself to defend Serbia, whose avowed purpose was the eventual acquisition of large tracts of Austro-Hungarian territory, and its ambassador to Serbia encouraged the revolutionary campaign of subversion, propaganda, and terrorism Serbia was waging against Austria-Hungary. In other words, it did almost everything possible to prompt Germany and Austria-Hungary to act against Russia now before it was too late. Pursuing peace by such directly counterproductive means is irrational. This was not the first time. A decade earlier Russia had blundered into an unwanted, disastrous war with Japan through a very similar pattern of thinking and decision-making.

Something more than the usual suspects – divided counsels, bad leadership, bureaucratic infighting, lack of intra-governmental coordination, and the like – lies behind this. Here again John Mueller's concept of subrational unthinkability can be applied to general European thinking and decision-making in high politics. War, including a great general war, remained rationally thinkable, while some of the most important policies and actions that had created and sustained the long peace became subrationally unthinkable. Again the easiest and most obvious examples are found in Russia. It is not hard to say what Russia should and could have done after 1905 to ensure for itself the peace and quiet it needed, especially in the Balkans. It needed simply to recognize, as it had done through most of the previous 160 years, that though Russia and Austria had overlapping and competing interests in the Balkans and Eastern Europe that could not be disentangled or easily settled by compromise, and that both states found the other one dangerous and difficult to get along with, they could still coexist in peace, so long as each recognized the other as a great power with legitimate interests in the region and worked with the other in managing their shared concerns. In other words, Russia needed to get along with Austria-Hungary simply because it was there, like it or not, and because without some kind of working relationship there could be no stable, durable peace. Austria-Hungary wanted this relationship and constantly pursued it. No concrete Russian interests (as opposed to ones of pure prestige) would have been hurt by this, and Russian ambitions in the Straits would have been advanced. Russia could have retained its alliances with France and even with Serbia and other Balkan states provided they were not pointed (as they were) squarely against Austria-Hungary. Why then was it impossible for anyone in Russia (even Count Witte, perhaps the most sensible of Russian statesmen and the one most open to the idea) even to suggest reviving this traditional stance toward Austria-Hungary, returning to something like the Three Emperors League? Because, as noted earlier, the idea had become subrationally or irrationally unthinkable. It would be an insult to Russia's honor, a blow to Russia's greatness, a betrayal of its historic mission and of its co-religionists and Slav brethren whom the Austrians were oppressing, another humiliation like the Crimean War or like 1877–8, when Austria had robbed Russia and its fellow Slavs and Orthodox believers of the fruits of their blood and sacrifice. None of this was really true, all of it even if true was irrelevant to Russia's present concrete needs and aims, and that fact made no difference.

This kind of political thinking and decision-making is as commonplace and dangerous today as ever, and no international system and principles or weapons systems or diplomatic procedures are sure prophylactics against it or its effects. Against a sufficient level of collective stupidity and national hubris produced by a pathological institutionalized pattern of political thinking and decision-making, nothing avails. This, I believe, constitutes the greatest threat to the current and future long peace.

Notes

1 Some of the factors involved would be the definition of war as opposed to informal but widespread violence, the distinction between international and civil war, the calculation of the losses and damage due to war as opposed to other concurrent causes, the number and size of the units in the international system at different times, the size and extent of the wars, their numbers and extent in relation to the numbers and size of units involved within size of system as a whole, etc. It is not that these problems are necessarily insoluble or that little work has been done on them – quite the contrary. The statistical and quantitative study of war is an impressive industry, beginning with the pioneer work of Quincy Wright and Lewis Richardson and stretching down to the many works of J. David Singer and his collaborators and the Coordinates of War project today. For a very useful survey and analysis, see J. S. Levy, *War in the Modern Great Power System, 1495–1975* (Lexington: University Press of Kentucky, 1983). However, as a historian I remain unconvinced that statistical and quantitative research alone, however valuable and sophisticated it is, can finally answer the central question: has war grown or declined over the centuries?

2 See his magisterial survey of eighteenth-century international politics, H. Duchhardt, *Balance of Power und Pentarchie 1700–1785* (Paderborn: Schöningh, 1997).

3 H. Duchhardt, *Gleichgewicht der Kräfte, Convenance, Europäisches Konzert* (Darmstadt: Wissenschaftliche Buchgesellschaft, 1976); H. Duchhardt, *Studien zur Friedensvermittlung in der frühen Neuzeit* (Wiesbaden: Steiner, 1979); H. Duchhardt (ed.), *Zwischenstaatliche Friedenswahrung im Mittelalter und früher Neuzeit* (Cologne: Böhlau, 1991).

4 J. Burkhardt, 'Die Friedlosigkeit der Frühen Neuzeit: Grundlegung einer Theorie der Bellizität Europas', *Zeitschrift für Historische Forschung* 24, 4 (1997), pp. 510–74.

5 J. Kunisch, *Staatsverfassung und Mächtepolitik: Zur Genese von Staatenkonflikten im Zeitalter des Absolutismus* (Berlin: Duncker & Humbolt, 1979).

6 H. Duchhardt (ed.), *Rahmenbedingungen und Handlunsspielräume europäischer Aussenpolitik im Zeitalter Ludwigs XIV* (Berlin: Duncker & Humbolt, 1991).

7 Two illustrations of this point: A recent book by Jost Dülffer and others entitled *Vermiedene Kriege* examines an impressive list of instances of wars avoided by de-escalation in the last half of the century. Such a book could not be written on the seventeenth century or before. Neither could a book on successful cases of crisis management such as J. L. Richardson's *Crisis Diplomacy*. J. Dülffer (ed.), *Vermiedene Kriege Deeskalation von Konflikten der Grossmächte zwischen Krimkrieg und Erstem Weltkrieg (1865–1914)* (Munich: R. Oldenbourg, 1997); J. L. Richardson, *Crisis Diplomacy: The Great Powers since the Mid-Nineteenth Century* (Cambridge: Cambridge University Press, 1994).

8   Never, that is, unless one counts the conflict between Britain and the Vichy government after mid-1940, which the British insisted was not waged against the French state or people, but solely against Nazi Germany.

9   An apparent exception proves the rule: in 1812 Napoleon forced Prussia against its will to be France's auxiliary in his invasion of Russia. After Napoleon's defeat in Russia the Prussian government defected and joined Russia in the War of Liberation.

10 Again the apparent exceptions really prove the rule. In 1809 Russia under strong French pressure half-heartedly fulfilled its alliance commitment by declaring war on Austria after it had opened war on France. In 1812, Napoleon coerced Austria into taking a role in the Russian campaign. Without Napoleon's coercion, neither would have fought each other, and in neither case did they fight very hard against each other. Once Napoleon's grip on Central Europe was loosened, Austria eventually joined Prussia, Russia, and Britain in war against France.

11 To guard against a possible objection, it could plausibly be argued that while the dates of 1763 to 1914 for this long peace are formally correct, the character of the triangular relationship for the first fifty years was so different from that of later eras that including these decades in the long peace is misleading. From 1763 to 1792, though the only war that occurred between them was the brief and almost bloodless Austro-Prussian one of 1778–9, their relations were so tense and managing their crises involved so much violence and instability (two major eastern wars, the first Partition of Poland, frequent war scares) that peace between them was almost accidental. Had the Revolutionary–Napoleonic challenge not forced them to fight France, they would surely have fought each other. Thus this long peace really dates only from 1813 to 1914. As noted, the argument contains some truth, and in any case the point about its dates is not central here. Nonetheless, the fact remains that these three powers stayed at peace with each other through this period of constant crises and wars, by using some of the same means employed later, so that the broader dates can be defended.

12 However, one cannot assume that the dying out or obsolescence of old causes for rivalry will lead to a long peace. A major counter-example is the relationship between France and the Habsburg Monarchy from 1715 to 1918. With the Peace of Utrecht, all the main traditional reasons accounting for Habsburg–Valois and Habsburg–Bourbon rivalry since 1494 disappeared or became obsolescent. The two powers instead came to have important shared interests and common rivals and enemies. Yet they remained rivals most of the time, fought six wars between 1715 and 1918, some of them major and prolonged ones, and never succeeded in becoming effective allies or partners. See P. W. Schroeder, 'A Pointless Enduring Rivalry: France and the Habsburg Monarchy, 1715–1918', in W. R. Thompson (ed.), *Great Power Rivalries* (Columbia: University of South Carolina Press, 1999), pp. 60–85.

13 P. W. Schroeder, 'Alliances, 1815–1945: Weapons of War and Tools of Management', in K. Knorr (ed.), *Historical Dimensions of National Security Problems* (Lawrence: University Press of Kansas, 1976), pp. 227–62.

14 S. Förster, *Der doppelte Militarismus: Die Deutsche Heeresrüstungspolitik zwischen Status-Quo-Sicherung und Aggression 1890–1913* (Stuttgart: F. Steiner, 1985); D. Stevenson, *Armaments and the Coming of War. Europe, 1904–1914* (Oxford: Oxford University Press, 1996); I. N. Lambi, *The Navy and German Power Politics, 1862–1914* (Boston: Unwin Hyman, 1984); H. Schottelius and W. Deist (eds), *Marine und Marinepolitik im kaiserlichen Deutschland, 1871–1914* (Düsseldorf: Droste, 1972).

15 G. Schöllgen, *Imperialismus und Gleichgewicht: Deutschland, England und die orientalische Frage 1871–1914* (Munich: R. Oldenbourg, 1984).

16 J. F. V. Keiger, *France and the Origins of the First World War* (London: Palgrave Macmillan, 1983). Allan Mitchell's work on the German influence on France after 1871, especially A. Mitchell, *Victors and Vanquished: The German Influence on Army and*

Church in France after 1870 (Chapel Hill: University of North Carolina Press, 1984) shows that from 1871 on French policy was always more centered on security against Germany than on revanche.

17 Examples: The proposal of German General Count Waldersee, Chief of the Prussian General Staff, for a preventive war in 1888 to destroy Russia's offensive potential against Germany and Austria-Hungary, or various Pan-Slav proposals before 1914 to destroy the Habsburg Monarchy.

18 Examples: Nicholas I's intervention in Hungary in 1849 to help save the Habsburg Monarchy, or Frederick William IV's determination not to take advantage of Austria's troubles in that same year, or the Austrian decision in 1850 not to push the German crisis to the point of war against Prussia, or Bismarck's decision in 1866 to preserve the Austrian empire, or the German and Austrian decisions in 1904–5 not to take advantage of the crisis of Russia's defeat by Japan and the Russian revolution to weaken or destroy Russia.

19 R.-H. Wippich, *Japan und die deutsche Fernostpolitik 1894–1898* (Stuttgart: F. Steiner, 1987).

20 F. Kazemzadeh, *Russia and Britain in Persia, 1864–1914: A Study in Imperialism* (New Haven: Yale University Press, 1968); B. Martin, *German–Persian Diplomatic Relations, 1873–1912* (The Hague: Mouton & Co.:'s-Gravenhage, 1959); D. McLean, *Britain and Her Buffer State: The Collapse of the Persian Empire, 1890–1914* (London: Royal Historical Society, 1979).

21 B. F. Schulte, *Vor dem Kriegsbruch 1914: Deutschland, die Türkei und der Balkan* (Düsseldorf: Droste, 1980); U. Trumpener, *Germany and the Ottoman Empire, 1914–1918* (Princeton: Princeton University Press, 1968); F. G. Weber, *Eagles on the Crescent: Germany, Austria, and the Diplomacy of the Turkish Alliance, 1914–1918* (Ithaca: Cornell University Press, 1970).

22 M. Behnen, *Rüstung, Bündnis, Sicherheit: Dreibund und informeller Imperialismus, 1900–1908* (Tübingen: M. Niemeyer, 1985).

23 S. W. Sowards, *Austria's Policy of Macedonian Reform* (Boulder: East European Monographs, 1989). On the Russo-Japanese war, see A. M. Malozemoff, *Russian Far Eastern Policy, 1881–1904* (Berkeley: University of California Press, 1958); J. A. White, *The Diplomacy of the Russo-Japanese War* (Princeton: Princeton University Press, 1964); S. Okamoto, *The Japanese Oligarchy and the Russo-Japanese War* (New York: Columbia University Press, 1970); R. Esthus, *Double Eagle and Rising Sun: The Russians and Japanese at Portsmouth in 1905* (Durham: Duke University Press, 1988). Russian policy toward China was just as aggressive and reckless; see S. C. M. Paine, *Imperial Rivals: China, Russia, and Their Disputed Frontier* (London: S. E. Sharpe, 1996). Particularly revealing on the formation of Russian policy is D. M. McDonald, *United Government and Foreign Policy in Russia, 1900–1914* (Cambridge: Harvard University Press, 1992). An even more devastating picture of the general policies of the Russian government in this era can be found in O. Figes, *A People's Tragedy: the Russian Revolution, 1891–1924* (New York: Jonathan Cape, 1997); and T. E. Weeks, *Nation and State in Late Imperial Russia: Nationalism and Russification on the Western Frontier, 1863–1914* (DeKalb: Northern Illinois University Press, 1996).

24 W. C. Fuller, *Civil–Military Conflict in Imperial Russia, 1881–1914* (Princeton: Princeton University Press, 1985).

25 This is the more surprising in that some contemporaries saw this quite well. The French President Raymond Poincaré, for example, learning very late about Russia's promotion of a Balkan League under its auspices, told the Russians bluntly that this would encourage the Balkan states to go to war against Turkey and that Austria would justifiably consider it a provocation, raising the danger of general war. But having denounced Russia's action, Poincaré, true to his principle of alliance loyalty at all cost, promised to support

Russia whatever the consequences. Keiger, *France and the Origins of the First World War*, fn. 14.

26 One clear sign can be mentioned, however. Two excellent books describe and analyze Russian governmental and public opinion and decision-making in this era: D. McDonald, *United Government and Foreign Policy in Russia, 1900–1914*; and C. Ferenczi, *Aussenpolitik und Öffentlichkeit in Russland, 1906–1912* (Husum: Matthiesen Verlag, 1982). Both make clear, without intending to do so or discussing the subject explicitly, that while there were always pro-Western and pro-German parties and factions, there was never a voice, much less a party, favoring a pro-Austrian policy or connection. This notion was simply out of bounds. Indeed, one of the arguments used in favor of rapprochement with Germany was that then Germany would clamp down on Austria-Hungary and force it to stop obstructing Russian interests.

27 C. Andrew, *Théophile Delcassé and the Making of the Entente Cordiale: A Reappraisal of French Foreign Policy, 1898–1905* (New York: St Martin's Press, 1968), pp. 127–35.

28 The documents from February to April 1905 are in J. Lepsius (ed.), *Die Grosse Politik der Europäischen Kabinette, 1871–1914* (Berlin: Deutsche Verlag Gesellschaft für Politik und Gesichte, 1927), 40 vols in 54 parts, XXII, pp. 9–19.

29 N. Rich and M. H. Fisher (eds), *The Holstein Papers IV* (Cambridge: Cambridge University Press, 1955–63), pp. 444–5, 461–3.

30 Norman Rich, editor of the Holstein papers, does not mention it in his biography of Holstein, N. Rich, *Friedrich von Holstein: Politics and Diplomacy in the Era of Bismarck and Wilhelm II*, 2 vols (Cambridge: Cambridge University Press, 1965).

31 J. Mueller, *Retreat from Doomsday: The Obsolescence of Major War* (New York: Basic Books, 1989).

32 Incidentally, Italy affords another illustration of the difference it makes whether one seeks primarily to explain the origins of the war or the breakdown of the peace. R. J. B. Bosworth in two excellent books criticizes Italy's constant efforts to make itself into the great power it never had the capacity to become, and demonstrates how these gravely threatened and destabilized the international system. R. J. B. Bosworth, *Italy the Least of the Great Powers* (London: Cambridge University Press, 1979) and R. J. B. Bosworth, *Italy and the Approach of the First World War* (London: Macmillan, 1983). Yet he exonerates Italy of any responsibility for the war, on the factually correct ground that Italy was only a bystander in the July Crisis. Thus we have the odd conclusion that Italy was to a serious degree responsible for undermining the peace, but entirely innocent of causing the war.

33 See David Stevenson's argument on this point in his book and his article, Stevenson, *Armaments and the Coming of War*; D. Stevenson, 'Militarization and Diplomacy in Europe before 1914', *International Security*, 22, 1 (1997), pp. 125–61.

34 This is true even of Russia. See, in addition to McDonald, *United Government and Foreign Policy in Russia, 1900–1914*, D. Geyer, *Der russische Imperialismus: Studien über den Zusammenhang von innerer und auswärtiger Politik, 1860–1914* (Göttingen: Vandenhoeck and Ruprecht, 1977). For a general critique of the concept of diversionary war by a political scientist, see J. S. Levy, 'The Diversionary Theory of War: A Critique', in M. Midlarsky (ed.), *Handbook of War Studies* (Boston: Unwin Hyman, 1989), pp. 259–88.

2

ACCOUNTING FOR THE WANING OF MAJOR WAR

John Mueller

In early 1989 I published *Retreat from Doomsday: The Obsolescence of Major War*, a book that dealt with war among developed countries. Military and diplomatic historian Michael Howard reviewed the book at the time with considerable skepticism about its central thesis, helpfully suggesting the 'prudent reader will check that his air raid shelter is in good repair'. But then, in 1991, he mused that it had become 'quite possible that war in the sense of major, organised armed conflict between highly developed societies may not recur, and that a stable framework for international order will become firmly established'.[1]

Two years later, the military historian and analyst, John Keegan, concluded in his *A History of Warfare* that the kind of war he was principally considering could well be in terminal demise:

> War, it seems to me, after a lifetime of reading about the subject, mingling with men of war, visiting the sites of war and observing its effects, may well be ceasing to commend itself to human beings as a desirable or productive, let alone rational, means of reconciling their discontents.[2]

By the end of the century, Mary Kaldor was suggesting that 'The barbarity of war between states may have become a thing of the past', and by the beginning of the new one, Robert Jervis had concluded that wars among the leading states 'will not occur in the future' or, in the words of Jeffrey Record, may have 'disappeared altogether'.[3]

The world seems, then, to have continued, even accelerated, its retreat from doomsday – a word that has, in fact, picked up a slight aura of quaintness over the last decade and half. And, however imprudently, many air raid shelters do seem to have been allowed to lapse into disrepair.

Not only did developed countries manage to stay out of war with each other during the Cold War, but there have been remarkably few international wars of any sort since World War II. The only truly notable exception since 1975 (and it is an important one) was the bloody war between Iran and Iraq that lasted from 1980 to 1988. Moreover, it is probably significant that, although armed contests between the Israeli government and Palestinian rebels remained plentiful, no Arab or Muslim country was willing after 1973 to escalate the contest to international war by sending its troops to participate directly. Also in decline, it appears, are conventional civil war, colonial war, and ideological civil war.

Changing attitudes toward war

This remarkable phenomenon chiefly stems, it seems to me, from the way attitudes toward the value and efficacy of war have changed, particularly over the last century, and the key to the development lies in the machinations of idea entrepreneurs. A profound disillusionment with war took place in Europe at the time of World War I. This came about not because that war was peculiarly destructive and costly, but because of the success of the idea entrepreneurs of the prewar antiwar movement in presenting their once-novel argument that war – by which they primarily meant war among developed states – ought to be abolished.[4] World War II in Europe was almost single handedly created by one man, Adolf Hitler: historical conditions in no important way required another continental war in Europe, and the major nations there were not on a collision course. The Cold War, in my view, was primarily caused by Communist devotion to an ideology about violent revolution and international class warfare that seemed threateningly expansionary to the democratic, capitalist West. However, despite the severe ideological dispute between the Communist and the non-Communist world and despite a surrogate war in Korea that permanently seems to have discredited limited military probes as a revolution-enhancing technique, major war was never really on the cards.[5]

For almost all of history war has been accepted as a natural, inevitable, and, often, desirable element in human affairs. However, over the course of the last century, it appears that the institution has been losing that casual acceptance and is moving toward obsolescence rather in the manner of slavery and dueling before it. In particular, while still entirely possible in a physical sense, it seems that major war – war among developed countries – is becoming increasingly unlikely as developed countries seize control of their destinies and decide that war with each other should not be part of them. By now, war between many former enemies in the developed world, such as France and Germany, has become subrationally unthinkable – it doesn't even come up as a coherent option and, if it ever did, would be rejected not so much because it is unwise, but because it is absurd.[6]

The apparent decline in war, or at least in the most discussed types of war, may be part of a broader trend, at least within the developed world, away from the acceptance of a number of forms of deliberate, intentional killing. Infanticide, for example, has declined over the centuries as has human sacrifice – something that, Barbara Ehrenreich reminds us, was once a 'widespread practice among diverse cultures, from small scale tribes to mighty urban civilizations'.[7] A more recent development is summed up by David Garfield:

At present there is a measure of agreement – though not unanimity – among historians that the period between 1700 and the present has seen a change in sentiments with respect to violence, a growing antipathy toward cruelty of all kinds, and the emergence of a new structure of feeling which has changed the nature of human relationships and behaviour.[8]

To begin with, there has clearly been a decline of unofficial justice as carried out by vigilantes, lynch mobs, or posses, and forms of private justice that previously had been tolerated – vendetta and blood feuds – seem generally to be in decline in many cultures. Donald Horowitz also notes the remarkable, and presumably related, decline of deadly rioting in the West.[9] Formal dueling, too, once a very common practice among certain social sets, has become obsolete. Official murder, generally known as capital punishment, has also been eradicated in most of the developed world, and corporal punishment, once standard practice and very common, has ceased to be either. Finally, a number of studies have suggested that homicide – and, indeed, civil violence more generally – was far more common centuries ago, particularly in rural areas.[10]

Alternative explanations for the decline of war

In focusing on changing attitudes toward war to explain the institution's decline, I find myself in agreement with Robert Dahl's observation that:

> because of their concern with rigor and their dissatisfaction with the 'softness' of historical description, generalization, and explanation, most social scientists have turned away from the historical movement of ideas. As a result, their own theories, however 'rigorous' they may be, leave out an important explanatory variable and often lead to naive reductionism.[11]

Since beliefs and ideas are often, as Dahl notes, 'a major independent variable', to ignore changes in ideas, ideologies, and attitude is to leave something important out of consideration. That is, ideas have consequences.[12]

However, a number of other explanations have been advanced to explain the decline of war. Some of these stress the impact of technology, particularly nuclear weapons, others economic development, increasing costs of war, the rise of democracy, increased international trade, or the role of international institutions.

Nuclear weapons

In seeking to explain history's greatest non-event – the utterly unprecedented absence of major war over the last half century – many analysts point to the fortuitous invention in 1945 of nuclear weapons and emphasize the peculiar terror they induce.[13] These analyses accept what can be called the 'Churchill counterfactual', a proposition that notes the emergence after World War II of a 'curious paradox' and a 'sublime irony' whereby nuclear weapons vastly spread 'the area of mortal danger' with the potential result that 'safety will become the sturdy child of terror, and survival the twin brother of annihilation'.[14] Rendered in more pointed, if less eloquent, phraseology, the Churchill counterfactual holds that if, counter to fact, nuclear weapons had not been invented, disaster was pretty much inevitable. That is, the people running world affairs after 1945 were at base so incautious, so casual about the loss of human life, so conflagration-prone, so masochistic, so doom-eager, so incompetent, and/or simply so stupid that in all probability they could not have helped plunging or being swept into a major war if the worst they could have anticipated from the exercise was merely the kind of catastrophic destruction they had so recently experienced in World War II. Accordingly, those who abhor war should presumably take the advice of Kenneth Waltz and 'thank our nuclear blessings' or, as Elspeth Rostow proposes, bestow upon it the Nobel Peace Prize.[15]

To me, the opposite counterfactual seems more plausible. It suggests that if, counter to fact, nuclear weapons had not been invented, the history of world affairs would have turned out much the same as it did.[16] Specifically, nuclear weapons and the image of destruction they inspire were not necessary to induce the people who have been running world affairs since 1945 to be extremely wary of repeating the experience of World War II (or for that matter, of World War I). After all, most of these figures were either the same people or the direct intellectual heirs of the people who tried desperately, frantically, pathetically, and ultimately unsuccessfully to prevent World War II. They did so in part because they feared – correctly, it gave them no comfort to discover – that another major war would be even worse than World War I.[17] I find it difficult to understand how people with those sorts of perceptions and with that vivid and horrifying experience behind them would eventually become at best incautious about, or at worst eager for, a repeat performance. But that, essentially, is what the Churchill counterfactual asks us to believe.

And there were several additional important war-discouraging factors. The world since 1945 has been ruled by the victors of World War II, and they have generally been content with the territorial status quo. Furthermore, although Communist ideology – the chief upsetting element during the Cold War – did embrace violence, it emphasized subversion and internal revolution, not over-the-border aggression, and it came accompanied with a cautious emphasis on tactics from Lenin.

None of this, of course, is to deny that nuclear war is appalling to contemplate and mind-concentratingly dramatic, particularly in the speed with which it could bring about massive destruction. Nor is it to deny that decision-makers, both at times of crisis and at times of non-crisis, have been well aware of how cataclysmic a nuclear war could be. It is simply to stress that the horror of repeating World War II is not all that much *less* impressive or dramatic, and that leaders essentially content with the status quo would strive to avoid anything that they feel could lead to *either* calamity. A jump from a fiftieth-floor window is probably quite a bit more horrible to think about than a jump from a fifth-floor one, but anyone who finds life even minimally satisfying is extremely unlikely to do either.[18]

However, while visions of mushroom clouds haven't been necessary to keep the leaders who have actually run world affairs since 1945 cautious about major war, there are imaginable circumstances under which it might be useful to have the weapons around – such as the rise of another lucky, clever, risk-acceptant, aggressive fanatic like Hitler. Moreover, there are circumstances in which nuclear weapons could have made a difference. For example, Iraq might not have attacked Iran in 1980 or Kuwait in 1990 if those countries had had nuclear weapons with which to retaliate. The argument is not that nuclear weapons *cannot* make a difference, but rather that their existence has not been necessary to create the long peace the developed world has enjoyed now for more than a half century.

Economic development and the industrial revolution

In attempting to assess the rise of war aversion in the developed world, Michael Howard proposes economic development as a causative factor. At one time, he notes, the developed world was organized into 'warrior societies' in which warfare was seen to be 'the noblest destiny of mankind'. This was changed, he suggests, by industrialization which 'ultimately produces very unwarlike societies dedicated to material welfare rather than heroic achievement'.[19]

The main problem for this generalization, as Howard is quite aware, is that industrialization spoke with a forked tongue. Between 1750 and 1900 the developed world experienced the industrial revolution, enormous economic growth, the rise of a middle class, a vast improvement in transportation and communication, surging literacy rates, and massive increases in international trade. But if this phenomenon encouraged some people to abandon the war spirit, it apparently propelled others to fall, if anything, more fully in love with the institution. Howard himself traces the persistence, even the rise, of a militaristic spirit that became wedded to a fierce and expansionist nationalist impetus as industrialization came to Europe in the nineteenth century. Thus industrialization can inspire bellicism as much as pacifism. Howard never really provides much of an explanation for how or why industrialization must inevitably lead to an anti-military spirit, and he rather vaguely attributes the horrors and holocausts that accompanied industrialization to 'the growing pains of industrial societies'.[20]

The rising costs of war

Carl Kaysen has concluded that major war is becoming obsolete, and he has advanced an argument similar to Howard's, but with far more detail about the process, particularly its economic aspects. He argues that 'for most of human history, societies were so organized that war could be profitable for the victors, in both economic and political terms'. However, 'profound changes . . . following the Industrial Revolution, have changed the terms of the calculation' causing the potential gains of war to diminish and the potential costs to rise.[21]

Kaysen tends to minimize the economic costs of war before the modern era, but many studies suggest they could be extremely high for winners and losers alike. The expression 'Pyrrhic victory', after all, stems from a battle fought in 279 BC.

According to Frederick the Great, Prussia lost one-ninth of its population in the Seven Years War, a proportion higher than almost any suffered by any combatant in the wars of the twentieth century. Germany's population dropped by about 15 or 20 per cent in the Thirty Years War, and Kalevi Holsti calculates that, 'if measured in terms of direct and indirect casualties as a proportion of population', it was Europe's most destructive armed conflict.[22] And, as Lawrence Keeley documents, far higher death rates have routinely been suffered in primitive warfare than those inflicted in either World War.[23] Many early European wars were fought to the point of total economic exhaustion. Richard Kaeuper's analysis of the economic effects of decades of war in the late middle ages catalogues the destruction of property, the collapse of banks, the severing of trade and normal commerce, the depopulation of entire areas, the loss of cultivated land, the decline of production, the reduction of incomes, the disruption of coinage and credit, the hoarding of gold, and the assessment (with attendant corruption) of confiscatory war taxes. The Thirty Years War set back the German economy by decades and the Seven Years War brought Austria to virtual bankruptcy, while many primitive wars have essentially destroyed whole societies. Moreover, civil wars have often been cosmic exercises in masochism, destroying both sides, and many primitive wars have essentially eradicated whole societies – in fact, notes Keeley, since the costs of warfare are relatively higher for primitive societies, war should be less common among them than it is among states and empires, but the opposite seems to be the case.[24]

By contrast, within a few years after World War I, most of the combating nations had substantially recovered economically: by 1929 the German economy was fully back to prewar levels, while the French economy had surpassed prewar levels by 38 percent, and Germany recovered economically from the destruction of World War II in five years, while Japan, poorer to begin with, and even more devastated in World War II, recovered in less than ten. Among the winners, World War II was probably economically profitable for the United States (and the casualties it suffered were, as a percentage of its population, tiny compared to those suffered in a huge number of earlier wars). Not only have there long been many hideously destructive, even annihilative, wars, but many wars have been believed to be even more horrible than they actually were. Often – in fact, *typically* – war stories would substantially exaggerate the extent of the destruction and bloodshed. For example, a legend prevailed for centuries after the Thirty Years War holding that it had caused Germany to suffer a 75 percent decline in population.[25] Yet beliefs and experiences like this had never brought about a widespread revulsion with war as an institution nor did they inspire effective, organized demands that it be banished. Instead war continued to be accepted as a normal way of doing things.

The 'most meaningful question', observes Alan Milward, 'is whether the cost of war has absorbed an increasing proportion of the increasing Gross National Product of the combatants. As an economic choice war, measured this way, has not shown any discernable long-term trend towards greater costliness.'[26] Moreover, as with Howard's argument, the problem is that the great expansion of economic growth in Europe in the nineteenth century was accompanied not only by a rising peace movement (eventually), but also by a renewed romantic yearning for the cleansing process of war.

The expansion of democracy

When ideas have filtered throughout the world in recent centuries, they have tended to do so in one direction. Without passing on the quality or value of the ideas so transmitted, it does seem that there has been, for better or worse, a long and fairly steady process of what is often called 'Westernization': Taiwan has become more like Canada than Canada has become like Taiwan; Gabon has become more like Belgium than Belgium has become like Gabon.[27] In the last few centuries, major ideas that have gone from the developed world to the less developed world include Christianity, the abolition of slavery, the acceptance of democratic institutions and Western economic and social forms, and the determined application of, and faith in, the scientific method. Not all of these have been fully or readily accepted, but the point is that the process has largely been unidirectional and that there has so far been little in the way of a reverse flow of ideas – the few that suggest themselves include cuisine, of course, karaoke, acupuncture, and some elements in the arts. Sometimes ideas which have had a vogue and become passé in the West can still be seen to be playing themselves out in the less 'advanced' world: the romance about violent class revolution, largely a nineteenth-century Western construct, has been mostly discredited in the West, but it continues to inspire a (declining) number of revolutionaries in other lands.

The growth in acceptance of the idea of democracy seems best explained by this sort of analysis.[28] Like soccer and Shakespeare and fast food and the cotton gin and the airplane and the machine gun and the computer and the Beatles, democracy caught on first in one corner of the world and is in the process, except where halted by dedicated forces, of spreading worldwide. Eventually, I suppose, it could fall from fashion, but for now things look pretty good.

In the last decade or so there has been a burgeoning and intriguing discussion about the connection between democracy and war aversion.[29] Most notable has been the empirical observation that democracies have never, or almost never, gotten into wars with each other. This relationship seems substantially spurious to me. Like most important ideas over the last few centuries, the notion that war is undesirable and inefficacious and the idea that democracy is a good form of government have largely followed the same trajectory: they were accepted first in northern Europe and North America and then gradually, with a number of traumatic setbacks, became more accepted elsewhere. In this view, the rise of democracy not only is associated with the rise of war aversion, but also with the decline of slavery, religion, capital punishment, and cigarette smoking, and with the growing acceptance of capitalism, scientific methodology, women's rights, environmentalism, abortion, and rock music.

While democracy and war aversion have taken much the same trajectory, however, they have been substantially out of synchronization with each other: the movement toward democracy began about 200 years ago, but the movement against war really began only about 100 years ago. Critics of the democracy/peace connection often cite examples of wars or near-wars between democracies. Most of these took place before the experience of World War I – that is, before war aversion had caught on.[30]

Democracy, as H.L. Mencken put it, is 'the theory that the common people know what they want, and deserve to get it good and hard'. At base, democracy is merely a gimmick – a good one in my view – for aggregating preferences, and democratic publics at various times have wanted all sorts of things only to change their minds about it later (see Box 2.1).[31] Thus, if the people happen to want war, they will tend to get it. And before 1914, democracies were often poised for war, even with other democracies: France and England certainly neared war in the Fashoda crisis, and both the war of 1812 and World War I could be considered to have democrats on both sides. Moreover, if Cuba had been as brutally run by democratic Belgium in 1898 as it was by at best semi-democratic Spain, the resentment triggered in the United States is unlikely to have been much less. Belgium and Holland, democracies by some standards, got into a war in 1830, and Switzerland in 1847 and the United States in 1861 cascaded into civil wars in which the two sides remained essentially democratic. Since World War I, the democracies have been in the lead in rejecting war as a methodology – even though this has not necessarily caused them to adopt a pacifist approach.

Thus, while democracy and war aversion have often been promoted by the same advocates, the relationship does not seem to be a causal one. And when the two trends are substantially out of step today, democracies will fight one another. It is not at all clear that telling the elected hawks in the Jordanian parliament that Israel is a democracy will dampen their hostility in the slightest. The same phenomenon, it seems, could be found in the various elected parliaments in the former Yugoslavia. A necessary, logical connection between democracy and war aversion, accordingly, is far from clear.[32]

And, of course, the long post-World War II peace between developed countries includes not only the one that has prevailed between democracies, but also the one between the authoritarian east and the democratic west.

Increased trade, interdependence

Peace may be associated with increased trade and other international interconnections. But to the degree this is true, it seems to me that peace is more nearly the essential cause of the connection than the reverse. Although expanding trade and interactions may enhance or reinforce the process, attitude toward war is likely to be the key explanatory variable in the relationship.

It has frequently been observed that militarized disputes between countries reduce trade between them. By contrast, if a couple of countries that have previously enjoyed a conflictual relationship lapse into a comfortable peace and become extremely unlikely to get into war, businesses in both places are likely to explore

Box 2.1 Democracy's record

Democracies variously have:

gone to war with enthusiasm and self-righteousness	*and*	sought to outlaw the institution
banned liquor	*and*	allowed it to flow freely
welcomed or committed naked aggression	*and*	fought to reverse it
raised taxes to confiscatory levels	*and*	lowered them to next to nothing
refused women the right to vote	*and*	granted it to them
despoiled the environment	*and*	sought to protect it
subsidized certain economic groups	*and*	withdrawn subsidies
stifled labor unions	*and*	facilitated their creation
banned abortion	*and*	permitted and subsidized the operation
tolerated drug use	*and*	launched massive 'wars' upon the practice
devolved into vicious civil war	*and*	avoided it by artful compromise
embraced slavery	*and*	determinedly sought to eradicate it
tolerated and sometimes caused humanitarian disaster in other parts of the world	*and*	sought to alleviate it
persecuted homosexuals	*and*	repealed the laws that did so
seized private property	*and*	turned over state assets to the private sector
discriminated against racial groups	*and*	given them preferential treatment
embraced colonialism	*and*	rejected the practice entirely
banned pornography	*and*	allowed it to be distributed freely
adopted protectionist economic policies	*and*	been free traders
tolerated the organization of peaceful political opposition	*and*	voted themselves out of existence by withdrawing the right to do so

the possibilities for mutually beneficial exchange. For example, the Cold War, as Edward Yardeni has pointed out, was among other things a huge trade barrier and, once it ended, trade and other connections grew greatly.[33] And one reason for the remarkably enhanced international trade that occurred in Europe in the nineteenth century was surely the unprecedented absence of continental war, interconnections that obviously did not prevent Europe from stumbling into such a war in 1914.[34] It is peace that causes, or facilitates, the trade and other interconnections, not the other way around.[35]

There are also problems when one seeks to apply the interdependence argument to wars other than interstate ones. Civil wars, which are far more common than international ones – and very often far more destructive to the participants – are usually fought between groups whose interdependence, economic and otherwise, is close to total. And in his study of primitive warfare, Keeley concludes that 'economic exchanges and intermarriages have been especially rich sources of violent conflict . . . exchange between societies is a context favorable to conflict and is closely associated with it'.[36]

The development of international institutions and norms

International institutions and norms often stress peace, but to the degree that is true, they, like expanded trade flows, are not so much the cause of peace as its result. Many of the institutions that have been fabricated in Europe – particularly ones like the coal and steel community that were so carefully forged between France and Germany in the years following World War II – have been specifically designed to reduce the danger of war between erstwhile enemies. However, since it appears that no German or Frenchman in any walk of life at any time since 1945 has ever advocated a war between the two countries, it is difficult to see why the institutions should get the credit for the peace that has flourished between those two countries for the last half century and more.[37] They are among the consequences of the peace that has enveloped Western Europe since 1945, not its cause. As Richard Betts puts it for institutions of collective security, 'peace is the premise of the system, not the product'.[38]

A similar argument holds for the impact of the rise of international norms like the one about territorial integrity. Since World War II, there have been exceedingly few instances anywhere in the world in which an international border has changed through warfare.[39] But this norm was specifically fabricated and developed because war-averse countries, noting that disputes over territory had been a major cause of international war in the past, were seeking to enforce and enshrine the norm. Its existence did not cause them to be war averse, but rather the reverse.

The remnants of war

With only a few exceptions, two kinds of war remain.[40] By far the most common are unconventional civil wars, most of them taking place in the poorest countries of the world. Many of these have been labeled 'new war', 'ethnic conflict', or, most grandly, 'clashes of civilizations'. But, in fact, most, though not all, are more nearly opportunistic predation waged by packs – often remarkably small ones – of criminals, bandits, and thugs who engage in armed conflict either as mercenaries under hire to desperate governments or as independent or semi-independent warlord or brigand bands. The damage perpetrated by these entrepreneurs of violence – who commonly apply ethnic, nationalist, civilizational, or religious rhetoric – can be extensive, particularly to the civilians who are their chief prey, but it is often scarcely differentiable from crime.

The other remaining type of war, far less frequent, includes what might be called 'policing wars'. These comprise militarized efforts, mostly successful, by developed countries to bring order to the civil conflicts or to topple the thuggish regimes that are, after the apparent demise of international war, the chief remaining sources of unnatural human destruction in the world. However, although the developed countries have brought the civil warfare that once plagued them under control, have generally abandoned warfare among themselves, and have arrived, after the Cold War, at a substantial consensus about the desirable shape the world should take, they are unlikely systematically to carry out such actions for several reasons. These include a severe aversion to casualties, a fundamental lack of interest, an aversion to long-term policing (something likely to be increased by America's experience in Iraq), the lack of political gain from success, a deeply held bias against war and aggression, and the misguided, but convenient, assumption that civil conflicts stem from immutable and inexplicable ethnic hatreds that cannot be remedied by well-intentioned outsiders.

The best solution to the problems presented by civil warfare lies in the development of effective domestic governments – that is, not in international policing, but rather in the establishment of competent domestic military and policing forces tracing a process Europe went through in the middle of the last millennium. After all, it was not efforts by the international community that brought warfare, particularly civil warfare, under control in Europe, but rather the development of what Charles Tilly calls 'high capacity' governments.[41]

In fact, in an important sense many civil wars have effectively been *caused* by inept governments that through impatient overreaction adopt policies that are ineffective or counterproductive. If policing forces are sufficiently brutal and systematic, the methods can sometimes be successful (particularly in the short run).[42] But inept ones applying the same methods court disaster, turning friendly or indifferent people into hostile ones and vastly increasing the size of the problems they are trying to deal with. However, when poor countries adopt sound and accommodating political policies, they can often do quite well. Thus, ethnic violence has been avoided in Bulgaria and Romania even though those countries are hardly more developed than Serbia or Bosnia and even though they have variously experienced considerably greater ethnic tension.[43]

Thus the fabrication of capable government is ultimately the most promising method for the long-term control, and even potentially for the eradication, of civil war. And there is some suggestive, but by no means conclusive, evidence that governments are becoming generally more effective even in the poorest areas of the world.

Over the course of the last few decades there has been something of a decline in the number of regimes that are vicious and/or criminal, and an increase in the number of countries that are led by effective people who, instead of looting their country's resources, seem to be dedicated to adopting policies that will further its orderly development – something Robert Rotberg labels 'positive leadership'.[44] This has happened in almost all of Latin America as well as in many places in Asia, such as South Korea, the Philippines, Malaysia, and Thailand – areas that, not coincidentally, have also experienced a considerable decline of warfare. Whether Africa – the area that continues most to be plagued by civil warfare – will follow that pattern is yet to be determined, but there are at least some hopeful signs. At one time, the model, as found in Nigeria for example, was one in which military leaders waited in line to take over the country to loot it even more effectively than they were doing as senior officers. But such venal and kleptocratic leaders may now be in the process of being replaced by ones whose style is not egomania and whose primary goal is not self-enrichment. Rather, they seek to make their mark in history by guiding their countries to coherence and prosperity.

As attitudes toward war have changed, the institution has waned, and it is violence and predation by bands of thugs that today most disrupts the peace. What is needed to keep them in check – to establish peace and order – is good government, following the path the developed world fell upon in the middle of the last millennium. Sometimes international authorities, working out of or under the direction of, the developed countries, have been able to aid or speed the process. And they can certainly be of assistance when a country sincerely desires to develop the kinds of competent military and police forces that have helped bring peace and prosperity to the developed world. Moreover, the example of the developed societies – civil, prosperous, flexible, productive, and free from organized violent conflict – can be most attractive, as indicated by the masses of people from the developing world who are trying to emigrate there, abandoning in fear and disgust the turmoil and violence of their home countries. However, unless the developed world wants once again to engage in a form of colonialism (and despite all the punditry surrounding the American invasion of Iraq in 2003, it doesn't), it is likely that exercises in nation building that are productive of peace and order will have to be accomplished – and, ultimately, with results that are most likely to be lasting – by forces that are domestic.

There are signs, particularly in the last decade, that this process is underway – that in an increasing number of places fanatics, criminals, and thugs, the chief authors and organizers of what remains of war in the world, are being brought under control or sometimes aptly coopted by effective governments. Criminality and criminal predation will still exist and so will terrorism which, like crime, can be carried out by individuals or very small groups. And there will certainly be plenty of other problems to worry about – famine, disease, malnutrition, pollution, corruption, poverty, politics, and economic travail.

JOHN MUELLER

However, a further (or continuing) decline in what remains of war, while far from certain, does seem to be an entirely reasonable prospect. If the process continues, war – *all* war, not just major war – will recede from the human experience.

Notes

1 M. Howard, 'A Death Knell for War?', *New York Times Book Review*, 30 April 1989, p. 14; M. Howard, *The Lessons of History* (New Haven: Yale University Press, 1991), p. 176.
2 J. Keegan, *A History of Warfare* (New York: Knopf, 1993), p. 59.
3 M. Kaldor, *New and Old Wars: Organized Violence in a Global Era* (Cambridge: Polity Press, 1999), p. 5; R. Jervis, 'Theories of War in an Era of Leading-Power Peace', *American Political Science Review*, 96 (2002), p. 1; J. Record, 'Collapsed Countries, Casualty Dread, and the New American Way of War', *Parameters*, Summer (2002), p. 6. See also M. Mandelbaum, 'Is Major War Obsolete?', *Survival*, 40, 4 (1998–9), pp. 20–38; M. Mandelbaum, *The Ideas That Conquered the World: Peace, Democracy, and Free Markets in the Twenty-first Century* (New York: Public Affairs, 2002); P. Johnson, 'Another 50 Years of Peace?', *Wall Street Journal*, 9 May 1955; A. Mack, 'Civil War: Academic Research and the Policy Community', *Journal of Peace Research*, 39, 5 (2002), p. 523.
4 See J. Mueller, *Quiet Cataclysm: Reflections on the Recent Transformation of World Politics* (New York: HarperCollins, 1995), ch. 9.
5 See J. Mueller, *Retreat from Doomsday: The Obsolescence of Major War* (New York: Basic Books, 1989), chs 3–9. On Hitler, see also J. Mueller, *The Remnants of War* (Ithaca: Cornell University Press, 2004), pp. 54–65.
6 See Mueller, *Retreat from Doomsday*, pp. 240–4.
7 B. Ehrenreich, *Blood Rites: Origins and History of the Passions of War* (New York: Metropolitan, 1997), p. 61. See also R. C. Forsberg, 'Socially-Sanctioned and Non-Sanctioned Violence: On the Role of Moral Beliefs in Causing and Preventing War and Other Forms of Large-Group Violence', in R. Stanley (ed.), *Gewalt und Konflikt in Einer Globalizierten Welt: Festschrift für Ulrich Albrecht* (Wiesbaden: Westdeutscher Verlag, 2001).
8 D. Garfield, *Punishment and Modern Society: A Study in Social Theory* (Chicago: University of Chicago Press, 1990), p. 232.
9 D. L. Horowitz, *The Deadly Ethnic Riot* (Berkeley: University of California Press, 2001), pp. 560–5.
10 On capital punishment, see Garfield, *Punishment and Modern Society*, pp. 225–9. On homicide trends, see J. B. Given, *Society and Homicide in Thirteenth Century England* (Stanford: Stanford University Press, 1977); T. R. Gurr, 'Historical Trends in Violent Crime: A Critical Review of the Evidence', *Crime and Justice*, 3 (1981), pp. 295–353; Garfield, *Punishment and Modern Society*, pp. 230–1; L. H. Keeley, *War Before Civilization: The Myth of the Peaceful Savage* (New York: Oxford University Press, 1996), p. 118; C. Tilly, *The Politics of Collective Violence* (New York: Cambridge University Press, 2003), pp. 60–1. Dueling faded mainly because it came to be taken as a ridiculous mode of behavior, not because it was superseded by some other method to resolve disputes. See Mueller, *Retreat from Doomsday*, p.10.
11 R. A. Dahl, *Polyarchy* (New Haven: Yale University Press, 1971), pp. 182–3, 188.
12 Ibid. See also A. Wendt, *Social Theory of International Relations* (New York: Cambridge University Press, 1999), ch. 3.
13 For example R. Jervis, 'The Political Effects of Nuclear Weapons', *International Security*, 13, 2 (1988), pp. 28–38; J. L. Gaddis, *The United States and the Cold War:*

Implications, Reconsiderations, Provocations (New York: Oxford University Press, 1992), ch. 6; Johnson, 'Another 50 Years of Peace?'; J. L. Gaddis, 'Conclusion', in J. L. Gaddis, P. H. Gordon, E. R. May and J. Rosenberg (eds), *Cold War Statesmen Confront the Bomb: Nuclear Diplomacy since 1945* (Oxford: Oxford University Press, 1999), pp. 260–71; M. van Creveld, 'The Future of War', in R. G. Patman (ed.), *Security in a Post-Cold War World* (New York: St Martin's, 1999), pp. 30–3; M. van Creveld, *The Rise and Decline of the State* (Cambridge: Cambridge University Press, 1999), pp. 337–44.

14 E. R. May, 'Introduction', in J. L. Gaddis, P. H. Gordon, E. R. May and J. Rosenberg (eds), *Cold War Statesmen Confront the Bomb: Nuclear Diplomacy since 1945* (Oxford: Oxford University Press, 1999), pp. 1–2. Elsewhere, and more specifically, Churchill advanced the 'melancholy thought' that 'nothing preserves Europe from an overwhelming military attack except the devastating resources of the United States in this awful weapon'. W. Churchill, *In the Balance: Speeches 1949 and 1950* (Boston: Houghton Mifflin, 1951), p. 356.

15 K. N. Waltz, Presidential Address, in Annual Meeting of American Political Science Association, Washington, DC, September 1998; Rostow quoted in May, 'Introduction', p. 3.

16 For a much more extended development of this argument, see Mueller, *Quiet Cataclysm*, ch. 5. See also J. Mueller, 'The Essential Irrelevance of Nuclear Weapons: Stability in the Postwar World', *International Security*, 13, 2 (1988), pp. 55–79; J. Mueller, 'Epilogue: Duelling Counterfactuals', in J. L. Gaddis, P. H. Gordon, E. R. May and J. Rosenberg (eds), *Cold War Statesmen Confront the Bomb: Nuclear Diplomacy since 1945* (Oxford: Oxford University Press, 1999), pp. 272–83.

17 In 1953, Averell Harriman, a former ambassador to the Soviet Union, observed that Stalin 'was determined, if he could avoid it, never again to go through the horrors of another protracted world war'. Quoted, *Newsweek*, 16 March 1953, 31.

18 See also E. Luard, *War in International Society* (New Haven: Yale University Press, 1986), p. 396; E. Luard, *The Blunted Sword: The Erosion of Military Power in Modern World Politics* (London: I.B. Tauris, 1988), pp. 25–31; J. L. Ray, 'The Abolition of Slavery and the End of International War', *International Organization*, 43, 3 (1989), pp. 428–31; R. L. Holmes, *On War and Morality* (Princeton: Princeton University Press, 1989), pp. 238–48; J. A. Vasquez, 'The Deterrence Myth: Nuclear Weapons and the Prevention of Nuclear War', in C. W. Kegley, Jr (ed.), *The Long Postwar Peace: Contending Explanations and Projections* (New York: HarperCollins, 1991), pp. 205–23. On military initiatives non-nuclear countries have taken against nuclear ones, see T. V. Paul, *Asymmetric Conflicts: War Initiation By Weaker Powers* (New York: Cambridge University Press, 1994).

19 Howard, *The Lessons of History*, p. 176.

20 Howard, *The Lessons of History*, p. 1. Actually, industrialization may have enhanced war's appeal by making possible the 'splendid little war': as Luard observes, 'very short wars (two months or less) have been virtually confined to the last century or so, since it is only in this period that mobility has been sufficient to allow the type of lightning military campaign required' (Luard, *War in International Society*, p. 79).

21 C. Kaysen, 'Is War Obsolete?' *International Security*, 14, 4 (1990), p. 49.

22 K. J. Holsti, *Peace and War: Armed Conflicts and International Order 1648–1989* (Cambridge: Cambridge University Press, 1991), p. 313.

23 Keeley, *War Before Civilization*, pp. 89–94, 160.

24 R. Kaeuper, *War, Justice and Public Order* (New York: Oxford University Press, 1988) pp. 77–117. On Frederick, see Luard, *War in International Society*, p. 51. On twentieth century wars, see M. Small and J. D. Singer, *Resort to Arms: International Civil Wars, 1816–1980* (Beverly Hills: Sage, 1982), pp. 82–99. On the Thirty Years War, see

G. Parker (ed.), *The Thirty Years' War*, 2nd edn (New York: Routledge, 1997), p.188. During the Thirty Years War almost two-thirds of the expenditures of the city of Nordlingen were devoted to direct military demands and the average wealth declined precipitously; although the city gradually recovered during the next twenty years, then another cycle of wars left it 'helpless to solve its own financial problems', and it took fifty more years to recover (and then only with outside intervention) at which point it was plunged once again into deep debt by the wars of the French Revolution. C. R. Friedrichs, *Urban Society in an Age of War* (Princeton: Princeton University Press, 1979), pp. 154, 169.

25 On 1929, see R. J. Overy, *The Nazi Economic Recovery 1932–1938* (London: Macmillan, 1982), p. 16. On the Thirty Years War legend, see C. V. Wedgwood, *The Thirty Years War* (London: Jonathan Cape, 1938), p. 516.

26 A. S. Milward, *War, Economy and Society, 1939–1945* (Berkeley: University of California Press, 1977), p. 3.

27 On this issue, see also E. A. Nadelmann, 'Global Prohibition Regimes: The Evolution of Norms in International Society', *International Organization*, 44, 4 (1990), p. 484.

28 J. Mueller, *Capitalism, Democracy, and Ralph's Pretty Good Grocery* (Princeton: Princeton University Press, 1999), ch. 8.

29 See, for example, M. W. Doyle, 'Liberalism and World Politics', *American Political Science Review*, 80, 4 (1986), pp. 1151–69; B. Russett, *Controlling the Sword: The Democratic Governance of National Security* (Cambridge, Mass.: Harvard University Press, 1990); M. Singer and A. Wildavsky, *The Real World Order: Zones of Peace, Zones of Conflict* (Chatham: Chatham House, 1993); B. Russett and J. R. Oneal, *Triangulating Peace: Democracy, Interdependence, and International Organizations* (New York: Norton, 2001).

30 For example, C. Layne, 'Kant or Cant? The Myth of the Democratic Peace', *International Security*, 19, 2 (1994), pp. 5–49.

31 H. L. Mencken, *Prejudices: Second Series* (New York: Knopf, 1920), p. 203. See also Mueller, *Capitalism, Democracy, and Ralph's Pretty Good Grocery*, chs 6–8; R. L. Schweller, 'Correspondence', *International Security*, 27, 1 (2002), p. 184.

32 It is often asserted that democracies are peaceful because they apply their domestic penchant for peaceful compromise (something, obviously, that savagely broke down in the United States in 1861) to the international arena or because the structure of democracy requires decision-makers to obtain domestic approval (for a discussion, see Russett and Oneal, *Triangulating Peace*, pp. 53–8). But authoritarian regimes must also necessarily develop skills at compromise in order to survive, and they all have domestic constituencies that must be serviced such as the church, the landed gentry, potential urban rioters, the nomenklatura, the aristocracy, party members, the military, prominent business interests, the police or secret police, lenders of money to the exchequer, potential rivals for the throne, the sullen peasantry. See also S. Rosato, 'The Flawed Logic of Democratic Peace Theory', *American Political Science Review*, 97, 4 (2003), pp. 585–602; M. F. Elman (ed.), *Paths to Peace* (Cambridge, Mass.: MIT Press, 1997).

33 E. Yardeni, 'The Economic Consequences of the Peace', in J. Mueller (ed.), *Peace, Prosperity, and Politics* (New York: Westview, 2000), p. 94.

34 In fact some people at the time argued that economic interdependence made war more tolerable. For example, war glorifier Heinrich von Treitschke concluded that economics would keep war in Europe from becoming too unpleasantly costly. He explained his reasoning this way: 'Civilized nations suffer far more than savages from the economic ravages of war, especially through the disturbance of the artificially existing credit system, which may have frightful consequences in a modern war. . . . Therefore wars must become rarer and shorter, owing to man's natural horror of bloodshed as well as to the size and quality of modern armies, for it is impossible to see how the burden of a

great war could long be borne under the present conditions' (H. von Treitschke, *Politics* (New York: Macmillan, 1916), p. 70). John Maynard Keynes was prominent among those who expected the war to be brief for such reasons even after it started (see Mueller, *Quiet Cataclysm*, p. 190).

35 Disputes reduce trade: B. Pollins, 'Conflict, Cooperation, and Commerce: The Effect of International Political Interactions on Bilateral Trade Flows', *American Journal of Political Science*, 33, 3 (1989), pp. 737–61; B. Pollins, 'Does Trade Still Follow the Flag?', *American Political Science Review*, 83, 2 (1989); Q. Li and D. Sacko, 'The (Ir)Relevance of Militarized Interstate Disputes for International Trade', *International Studies Quarterly*, 46, 1 (2002), pp. 11–34. Russett and Oneal conduct a limited effort to test the proposition that militarized disputes disrupt trade (Russett and Oneal, *Triangulating Peace*, pp. 224–6). There is an effect even though the analysis deals with militarized disputes (not war alone) and even though it only looks at the effect from one year to the next rather than over a longer term.

36 Keeley, *War Before Civilization*, pp. 123, 126.

37 But they do: 'The creation of a security community has made armed conflict between France and Germany ... unthinkable' (Russett and Oneal, *Triangulating Peace*, p.158). See also G. J. Ikenberry, *After Victory: Institutions, Strategic Restraint, and the Rebuilding of Order after Major Wars* (Princeton: Princeton University Press, 2001), ch. 6.

38 R. K. Betts, 'Systems for Peace or Causes of War? Collective Security, Arms Control, and the New Europe', *International Security* 17, 1 (1992), pp. 23–4, emphasis removed. See also R. L. Schweller, 'The Problem of International Order Revisited: A Review Essay', *International Security*, 26, 1 (2001), p. 183.

39 M. Zacher, 'The Territorial Integrity Norm: International Boundaries and the Use of Force', *International Organization*, 55, 2 (2001), pp. 215–50; van Creveld, 'The Future of War', pp. 28–9.

40 For a development of this argument, see Mueller, *The Remnants of War*.

41 Tilly, *The Politics of Collective Violence*.

42 See B. Valentino, *Final Solutions* (Ithaca: Cornell University Press, 2004), ch. 6.

43 On Bulgaria, see V. I. Ganev, 'Bulgaria's Symphony of Hope', *Journal of Democracy*, 8, 4 (1997), pp. 125–39; Z. Barany, 'Bulgaria's Royal Elections', *Journal of Democracy*, 13, 2 (2002), pp. 141–55. On Bulgaria and also Lithuania, see E. J. Gordon and L. Troxel, 'Minority Mobilization Without War', Paper presented at the conference on Post-Communism and Ethnic Mobilization at Cornell University, 21–2 April 1995. On Romania, see R. Brubaker, 'Ethnicity without Groups', *Archives Européennes de Sociologie*, 43, 2 (2002), pp. 163–89. On Romania and also Slovakia, see R. H. Linden, 'Putting on Their Sunday Best: Romania, Hungary, and the Puzzle of Peace', *International Studies Quarterly*, 44, 1 (2000), pp. 121–45.

44 R. Rotberg, 'New Breed of African Leader', *Christian Science Monitor*, 9 January 2002, p. 9. On this trend, see also M. G. Marshall and T. R. Gurr, *Peace and Conflict, 2003: A Global Survey of Armed Conflicts, Self-Determination Movements, and Democracy* (College Park: Center for International Development and Conflict Management, University of Maryland, 2003), pp. 17–25.

3

TRENDS IN MAJOR WAR

Too early for waning?

Peter Wallensteen

Is major war waning?

The thesis that major wars are waning is attractive. It means that the world gradually comes closer to the first lines of the goal in the UN Charter: we are beginning 'to save succeeding generations from the scourge of war'. Is it also possible to establish such a trend over the past decades and to make a prognosis that such a trend is likely to continue? This is what will be discussed in this chapter, in two ways. First, is there an absolute change in numbers of different types of war, and secondly, is there a trend of declining probability of war in categories of war? This would help to confirm the general thesis or specify its range. Either way it means that the thesis is challenging, even provocative, and thus requires a closer scrutiny.

There is no doubt that the thesis fits well with a change in the intellectual and cultural trends in global political thought. War has never been acceptable and it has always been constrained by moral rules in all cultures. There is also good documentation of such a tendency in the understanding of the utility of wars.[1] Since the end of World War II major war has only been justified as a matter of self-defense or based on a decision by the UN Security Council. The two world wars were strong antidotes to war enthusiasm. The danger of nuclear war reaffirmed this basic attitude.

To this we could add that the twentieth century has demonstrated a change in the priorities of the path-setting states: building welfare, developing economic growth and reducing social inequality have been more important than sovereignty, national defense and the pursuit of major war. Social movements have transformed societies. Democracy has changed the domestic agenda, and, to a larger extent, made international affairs subservient to domestic concerns. This development can also be documented by opinion data in leading Western states showing an increasing reluctance to send soldiers to distant wars, be it for intervention or peacekeeping. Thus, the first sentences in the UN Charter seem to be confirmed: basic sentiments have shifted.[2]

It means that global culture may have changed, but the interest in actually pursuing war may not, even in so-called developed, industrial or democratic societies. *War is feared, but not excluded* as a possible necessity and last resort. Even Mueller finds that deterrence might have been a necessary strategy against Hitler or that strong police forces could do the job to take on organized criminal activity.[3] This means that war may still be justified, even though we can use different labels for the actions. If a particular operation is termed deterrence (requiring military force to be credible) or police action (requiring considerable police forces to back it up) this does not change the fact. Self-defense may be legitimate, but the actions may still be war. Major war is something more than a change in tactics, labels or justifications.

Although this attitudinal trend is discernible, the actions by states and peoples around the world do not necessarily speak the same language. The number of armed conflicts since 1946 is 226 (by 2002), and 111 of these reached the level of war.[4] This can be translated into an average initiation of four new armed conflicts per year and two becoming wars. It is a considerable war experience. It can be compared to the first part of the twentieth century, for which the Correlates of War reports wars, i.e. armed conflicts with more than 1,000 deaths, at 84 for the period 1900–1945, that is two per year.[5] These figures almost suggest the opposite of the thesis: armed conflicts are actually increasing, not decreasing, but the war frequency is not affected. Clearly, we can state that, in spite of the increasingly negative cultural and intellectual attitude to war, armed violence remains a political option used by decision-makers.

These data cover the entire world and all types of armed conflict that fit the definition. It includes international and internal wars, colonial and civil wars, separatism and major terrorism. In the absolute sense war is not disappearing. It could possibly be argued that this trend is parallel to global population growth, perhaps also to the increase in the number of states, and thus to be expected, if we believe that the probability of war is related to such basic changes. The thesis should, however, look for a decline in either absolute numbers or in probabilities of war.

Let us pursue this by noting that the thesis of waning war may depend on what we include as 'wars'. No doubt, there are geographical areas with less experience of war than others. There might be some societies and relations that do not have war at all and there might be changes over time. Thus, applying different definitions may result in different profiles of the war experience, and, relating to this, the expectation and probability of war. This is what will be attempted in this chapter. It serves as a basis for a discussion on the conditions under which major war may actually become a declining phenomenon. Five different definitions will be discussed in the next section and we return to the implications of this in the final section.

Are *some* major wars waning?

Warfare changes. What remains are some basic elements, such as deliberate destruction to gain advantage; the killing of soldiers, bystanders, civilians; the search for a moral justification. In most other respects wars are likely to change. If we are to make statements about general trends there is a need for a reasonable definition which can work across time and space. In this way, the war phenomenon can be compared and it becomes possible to determine whether a particular form of major war is disappearing or increasing. In the following, five different definitions (with some subversions) will be used to give an answer to the question if some major wars are on the wane.

Definition 1: major war as Prussian warfare

In a long historical perspective, the two world wars were atypical. Still, they inevitably color our thinking as we as researchers and citizens continue to live in the shadow of these two mega-wars. It means we may be inclined to think that this is the type of war which we will confront in the future. However, history tells us that history does not repeat itself in such a uniform manner. Thus, it is interesting to search for particular traits of the world wars.

Let us first note that a shared feature is that both world wars were highly industrial wars, clearly belonging to an era of manufacture and commercial development. This can be seen in the use of mechanized vehicles, the development of rapid transportation and, later on, the emergence of an air force. The integrated armies consisted of trained soldiers and large numbers of conscripts, with clear chains of command, food and medical services. Remarkable was the ability of the state to extract resources from the society and make decisions on behalf of all citizens.

Much of this industrial feature applies also to a nuclear war. The way such a war was conceived during the Cold War period included the use of long-range missiles, submarines, bombers, satellite navigation techniques and electronics, that is, technology that meant a further elaboration of previous techniques. Also in this case, the strength of the decision-maker center was taken for granted. The result would – in all likelihood – have been a human-created disaster more than a traditional military-directed strategy. Although using the same logic, the 'war' would have been one of all-out destruction, rather than military strategy.

The cultural reactions against war have been particularly strong against such industrial wars. It is possible that the origin of this warfare dates to Prussian military organization. It included highly disciplined centralized armies, with specially trained officers, authoritarian political leadership, full support from all governmental structures, and with little transparency in decision-making. The political ambitions were directed towards territorial conquest and expansion (*Lebensraum*). Several such wars took place during the nineteenth century as well. The most obvious precursor was the Franco-Prussian War of 1870–1.[6] This means that the major wars in Central Europe during the late 1800s and much of the 1900s exhibit traits that are not typical of all wars. These wars may, in fact, have been closely tied to a specific German experience. This war technique was, after all, developed in a country in the middle of a continent, surrounded by open space, with few natural boundaries for its protection, thus searching for strategic depth for defense. State survival was seen to require bold, determined and highly competent military action. Thus, the warfare techniques were tied to a particular military strategy. There are societies in similarly exposed strategic positions including the potential of sudden attack from an overwhelming force but they are few; for instance, Israel, South Korea and Taiwan. Some of their military strategies are closer to a Prussian model than many other military forces. Thus, there is a phenomenon of organized warfare that can be found in many countries: Prussian warfare.

Prussian warfare might have had its origin in Europe, but it is now seen in other parts of the world. In the European context, we can safely suggest that Germany is no longer likely to be an independent war-making actor. It finds its security by being increasingly embedded in regional cooperation and economic inter-dependence. Thus, we can conclude that it is likely that the Prussian type of warfare and military strategy is on the wane. Even for the originator, Prussian survival is replaced by human interconnection. It is relevant for some specific parts of the world, but not for the world in general. Here is an element of limited support for the waning war thesis.

If one form of warfare declines, however, it does not exclude the possibility that it is replaced by others. Our search has to continue.

Definition 2: major war as war between major powers

A second way of defining a major war focuses on the actors of war, rather than warfare strategies. It seems rather obvious that if there are major powers involved these are likely to be major wars. This definition brings our analysis a step forward. It requires us to define 'major power' in a historically consistent way. There are three valid definitions of major war that can be pursued here:

1   Major wars as wars between states which at least have a regional military reach, sometimes also of global significance.
2   Major wars as wars between the most important, permanent members of the UN Security Council.
3   Major wars as wars where major powers (according to point 2) support local wars against the forces of another major power.

Let us deal with these definitions, one by one. First, the major states that fought World War I were at least regionally strong powers. Few of them compare to the global superpowers that we later have become accustomed to regard as 'major powers'. The state that initiated World War I, Austria-Hungary, was a regional power with limited military interest outside its neighborhood and immediate area of political control. It was nevertheless regarded at the time as a major power.

Applying such a definition to the present, major power status could fit a large set of states. It would include all the permanent members of the Security Council. In addition, we would have to add states of regional significance, such as Israel, Iraq, Iran, Pakistan, India, Vietnam, Indonesia, Egypt, South Africa, Nigeria, Brazil and Argentina. If these countries are at war with one another, that would correspond to the states that were major powers in World War I, at least at the beginning of that war. It would make, for instance, the repeated wars between India and Pakistan major wars. The same would be true for the war between India and China, and the one between Iran and Iraq. Other candidates would be the Falklands/ Malvinas War between Britain and Argentina, and wars between Israel and some Arab states.

With this as the definition, it is interesting to see that such interstate wars among major powers are not many in the post-World War II period. Looking at the Uppsala data, there is no discernible trend. Such wars have come at a pace of one or two per decade, as these examples make clear. They are rare, but not unheard of, and they are as frequent (or infrequent) in absolute numbers as they have been before. As the list makes clear, however, there are more states that fit this category than ever before. Although they do get into wars with one another at the irregular frequency, it might be argued that the likelihood of a particular pair of such major powers entering war with one another is increasingly low. This is particularly so if we look at some that share borders with one another. Cold war or cold peace has replaced hot wars in a number of relations (e.g. Iraq–Iran, Israel–Egypt, Argentina–Brazil, Argentina–UK, Vietnam–China, China–India). A closer study will also show that this relates to the way the most recent (last?) war or confrontation ended and the efforts at containment, even settlement of issues, that have occurred since then. With this definition, we see no waning of major war, nor is there an increase in frequency. In terms of probability of war, however, it may have declined. As many of the same states, however, are belligerent vis-à-vis other actors it may be more easy to attribute this to changed international alliances, preventive efforts and other international factors, rather than a change in the culture of peace.

Pursuing this discussion one step further, we can reduce major power status to those states that more customarily are included in this category. That could be equated to states that are permanent members of the UN Security Council. For instance, the Correlates of War project has a definition which includes as major powers countries with wide networks of diplomatic relations and with considerable military force. This would give us only five major powers for the post-World War II period. With this definition, the war patterns become considerably closer to the suggested thesis. There has been no war directly between major powers since the Korean War of 1950–3, when the USA (under the UN banner) was fighting against the People's Republic of China (although the Communist regime was not seated in the UN, China as such was). Half a century without such a major war is clearly a contrast to the first part of the same century. This would give some support for the thesis.

There might be at least one alternative explanation, however: the major powers have become fewer. In the customary way of thinking, the major powers of 1914 were eight: Britain, France, Russia, Germany, Austria-Hungary, Italy, Japan and the United States. They all, with the exception of Austria-Hungary, had significant colonial possessions and held considerable military force to maintain their control. By 1945, the number had declined to five, all members of the Security Council (USA, Britain, France, the Soviet Union and China). The realities of the Cold War and the rapid process of decolonization made clear that there were only three that were independent enough. These were also the ones that most vigorously developed their nuclear capacity (USA, USSR/Russia, China). With fewer major powers we would also expect fewer major wars. The low number of major states might reduce the likelihood of the countries misunderstanding each another. Here there could be a danger of circularity in the waning war thesis: it may pick up that the number of major powers has become fewer, which makes the number of possible war relations fewer as well. There is, in other words, a plausible almost mathematical alternative to the waning war thesis.

To this could be added that historically global wars or their equivalents are rare. In fact, there is only a history of two such events. Both came in the first part of the twentieth century, suggesting that there was something very special with that period, and that we might now have a more 'classical' relationship, where the strongest actors continuously monitor each other, are rivals, exhibit occasional confrontations, but mostly abstain from attacking each other directly.

Still, this is not the full picture. There is an additional complication alluded to in the third sub-definition above: military interventions by major powers. Undoubtedly, the Cold War experience was one of continuous interference in internal wars by the major actors. The Cold War culture was very brutal. The public pictures of 'Communists', 'anti-Communists', 'Democrats', 'Socialists', 'Capitalists' and 'Imperialists', etc. were highly simplified, very hostile and close to mirror images. From this followed that much violence could be accepted, as the other side was demonized. Thus, the wars in Korea, Vietnam and Afghanistan were highly vicious, although the number of killed in the intervening forces (China, USA and Soviet Union) may have been a lesser share of all the casualties. The importance of the global confrontation made the three major powers interested in other, more local conflicts. Such conflicts only rarely were on their own borders or of a high strategic significance.

Being involved in a local situation was to some a strategic way to affect the strength of the opponent in the global confrontation. In the Reagan Administration, for instance, one group was called the 'bleeders', as they expected that an intensive and protracted war in Afghanistan would serve to bleed the Soviet society of its resources. Thus, the US government became interested in arming guerrillas, be they democrats, Islamists or something else. Similar arguments were used for the Soviet and Chinese support for the North side in the Vietnam War. It was expected that it would weaken the international standing of the USA and change 'the correlation of forces'. The fate of the local victims was of little regard. Major powers may, in other words, be quite heavily involved in wars against each other, only keeping their own troops at a minimum, and protecting themselves from risk of direct attack. It means letting other people die for your causes.

In moral terms, these strategies are hardly a civilizational improvement. Looking more closely, we can see that such interventions were particularly pronounced in conflicts where the danger of escalation to nuclear war was the least apparent. The low risk may have made commitments to parties in these wars more acceptable to domestic audiences, particularly in the open democratic societies. With these arguments local wars (be they in the Middle East, Indochina, Afghanistan, Central America, Southern Africa) might also be seen as major wars: they would not have been pursued without the support of major powers. That support may have made many wars more protracted, destructive and unsolvable than otherwise would have been the case. Such proxy wars constituted an important element in the armed conflicts throughout the Cold War.

After the Cold War, such involvement has been more rare. Instead, peacekeeping operations have been frequent, but their motive and support is different. Most of them enter *after* wars, rather than as parties *to* wars. The reduction in one-sided interventions could plausibly be an effect of the end of the Cold War and the major power confrontation rather than stemming from a long-term general reluctance to war. The reactions of the American public to the September 11, 2001 events show that interventions again can become a leading theme for at least one major power.

Thus, it is hard to document a trend that major wars defined as sizeable wars between major powers or their proxies actually have been on the wane. However, our comments suggest an interesting change in the international system. There are today more countries with a regional reach and they are on the whole more peaceful than has historically been the case. At the same time there is a reduction in the number of very strong actors. That has, historically, been a level with few direct wars. World wars remain rare. The phenomenon of interventions, however, may remain, taking new forms after the end of the Cold War (peacekeeping operations and, more recently, counter-terrorism interventions).

Definition 3: major war as wars by developed countries

If we restrict the definition in another way and ask for the wars that involve developed countries a different set of observations emerges. These are countries which have achieved at least the industrial level that is comparable to the leading countries at the time of World War I. This means that we search for conflicts between countries of a certain industrialization, military capacity and urbanization. A crude measure is membership of the OECD, as suggested by Holsti.[7] Another is to say that the leading European countries that fought World War I were developed. Thus, criteria that fit them at that time could also be used for other countries at a later time to define their level of development.

When we bring this definition to the different data sources we have to conclude that there is no particular trend. In fact, the war involvement of OECD countries and industrial countries has been almost constant. It is a small fraction of all wars, no doubt, but there is no trend in a particular direction. Possibly, however, open, democratic, industrial and wealthy societies have fewer conflicts between themselves. The industrialized world shows a more peaceful way of relating to each other than to other parts of the world. We have already alluded to the significance of the integration of Germany into the European regional framework.

At the same time, these countries are willing to use military forces against non-industrialized countries. Throughout the period we find British, French and American forces in conflicts in Africa, Indochina, Central America, and now also in Central Asia and the Middle East. The waning war thesis in this case has to be rephrased to concern peace among industrial countries, where at the same time, the same peaceful countries demonstrate interventionist tendencies vis-à-vis other, poorer societies.

Even so, this revised thesis has some challenges. The internal peace of developed states is not without disturbing internal (or domestic) wars, something which also has to be considered. This can be seen even in the case of democratic industrial societies. France in the 1950s found itself in a civil war (by the official French definition Algeria was a legal entity of the motherland of France) which led to considerable upheaval, a military coup and the demise of an entire constitutional order (the Fourth Republic). The United Kingdom is only of late able to extract itself from a protracted conflict in Northern Ireland (after more than thirty years of 'troubles'). The United States has been exposed to occasional riots (1960s, 1990s) and armed violence (1993, 1995) emanating from the internal situation of the country. Similarly Germany (1970s), Japan (1970s, 1990s), Spain (the protracted Basque insurgency) and Italy (1970s) have found themselves having to deal with armed action by domestically recruited and organized groups. Albeit on a smaller scale than major wars, it suggests that war and violence still have not been eradicated from the political arena of internal affairs even in highly industrialized countries.

Again, this information does not yield a trend. There is, however, an element of inter-industrial peace. Countries with a higher level of industrialization act today more peacefully to each other than they did at the beginning of the twentieth century. With increasing economic wealth among more countries, the likelihood of war between them could be expected to decrease. It does not mean that they exhibit the same pacific attitude to other, non-industrial countries, however.

Definition 4: major war as regional war

A different way to understand a major war is to go by its consequences for a larger region. Does the war lead to new relationships in a region, bringing people and states closer or further away from each other? World War I and World War II certainly had such consequences which turned them into historical watersheds. Primarily, those effects could be seen in a regional context (Europe), but also in global relationships. With this in mind, we can go back to the conflict data in search for other patterns.

First, such a search shows that there are wars between major powers which were not major wars. They did not result in realignments among major states. Power relations were not changed. To these belong, for instance, the Crimean War in the nineteenth century or the Russo-Japanese War in 1905. Perhaps even the Korean War of 1950–3 would be such a war of lower regional significance, as it did not result in marked realignments, although it strongly cemented the relations that were emerging.

Second, there have been such regional wars throughout the last part of the twentieth century. Several of them are located in the Middle East. The creation of Israel in 1948, the Suez Crisis of 1956, the wars of 1967 and 1973 all impacted on the regional dynamics. This has not ended. For instance, the Gulf War of 1991 showed that the Cold War was over, and that cooperative relations were now preferred among the major states. At the same time this crisis became central in regional diplomacy for the following decade. Certain wars have had regional effects by the fact that they have been highly protracted (the Kashmir conflict for South Asia as a whole, the Iran–Iraq War for the Middle East) or have been highly intensive (the Vietnam War for Indochina and Southeast Asia). The effects can linger for a long time. 'Normalization' did not follow in Indochina until the beginning of the 1990s, although the USA militarily left the region twenty years earlier. These were wars with linkage to major powers, however defined. There is no discernible trend of such regional wars becoming fewer.

Third, a major regional war, such as the Central African War that began in the middle of the 1990s, could be defined as a major war, although it did not involve any major power. In an unprecedented way, this war engaged neighboring countries and groups in a complicated web of dependencies and rivalries. The major powers shied away from this conflagration, at the same time as being reluctant to let the UN take up the challenge. As a consequence, it turned into a tragic major war for Africa. Some regionally significant countries were directly involved, but rather on a peacemaking mission (South Africa, Nigeria).

Surveying the list of regional wars since 1945 it is hard to find a clear precedent of the Central African War. This would say that with this definition, we are able to point to a new war phenomenon. The post-Cold War conditions may have created a milieu where local actors are able to pursue protracted wars using local resources. Early observations on such changes were made by Mary Kaldor.[8] The important aspect is that the new international conditions initially made it possible for rogue actors to pursue local ambitions without international checks. The wars around Liberia and in the southern Caucasus qualify as well. How novel this is can be debated, but it has not been part of the Cold War experience.[9] The use of weak states as the staging ground for new types of threats, be they terrorism or drug trade, highlights the significance of state failure in warmaking. The probability of future regional wars is difficult to estimate, but the increasing number of failed states may be an indicator of rising threats.

Definition 5: major war as war with global impact

Some wars are more important than others, but the outcome is of course not known at the time the war is initiated. World War I was, at its inception, expected to be a short local war in the Balkans. It was seen to be no different from many of the other wars that had been fought in the region during the preceding decades. This was a misjudgment of monumental proportions. It dawned on the decision-makers a few days later, when Russia mobilized and Germany attacked, in accordance with its

Prussian understanding of its own vulnerability. By then it was clear that the local crisis had become a Great War, and when it finally ended, more than four years later, the world was different. World War II, similarly, started with high expectations of victory by the Nazi German leadership. It seemed to work according to plan. It took horrendous sacrifice to thwart these ambitions. In the end, the Nazi regime was eliminated. Again a world order had to be created. This means that the term major war can be associated with important rearrangements among major powers and their relations. What would the conflict data say about trends, using such a definition?

Some wars are more important for global development than others. It could be because they engage more actors than other wars. Since 1945, some wars have been special by invoking alliances and the UN in support of one or the other actor. Thus, the wars in Korea, Vietnam, Afghanistan, the Gulf and the Balkan regions were all major wars with this definition. They involved a host of other countries, drawn from outside the region of conflict. Major powers as well as smaller actors were parties to the conflict. Such major wars do not form a declining trend. Each one seems to be initiated approximately ten years after the previous one ended, or even sooner.

The following examples illustrate this. The Korean War cemented an alliance between China and the USSR against the USA, thus making the Cold War a profoundly global line of division. The Vietnam War led to a military defeat for the USA and considerable changes in its military strategy. The same is true for the Soviet war in Afghanistan, possibly contributing to the downfall of the entire Soviet system. The Gulf War built on unprecedented cooperation between major powers, a pattern which was to be repeated the following decade. The Kosovo War, however, was close to derailing this newly developed partnership.

The effects of the attack on the United States mainland on September 11, 2001 do not easily fit with established definitions. The global impact of this event went beyond the death of close to 3,000 civilian, unprotected inhabitants. It provided global insecurity. The following escalation of the war in Afghanistan made the fate of that country central in international affairs. The events received full global attention. The engagement of the United States made them strategic. The Afghanistan War of 2001 had the support of a large coalition, making this a war of not only regional, but also global significance. It was followed by the Anglo-American intervention in Iraq in 2003, which did not have similarly wide international support. This may constitute a break, as the public, particularly in Western Europe, was unwilling to give the war its blessing. The extent of anti-war demonstrations was something not seen for a whole generation.

Also with a definition of major war as wars with global impact, we still have difficulties in documenting a trend of waning wars. The debate over the 2003 Iraqi War may, however, contain some of the elements that the thesis builds on. There was a widespread reluctance among the public to engage in this situation.[10]

Summary

After applying five different definitions of major war we have not been able to ascertain the existence of a uniform, declining trend of such war. Some types of war may have disappeared or become more rare due to changes in security alternatives (Prussian warfare) and causes for conflict (relations between industrial states, between regional powers). Some new types may have emerged (the regional war without major powers, as seen in Central Africa, and the war on global terrorism). The September 11 attack shows that popular opinion can shift quickly. The US public was willing to accept a major war to eliminate terrorism and restore the self-image of the strength of the United States. Months earlier, this sentiment would have been marginal.

This has consequences for the thesis of the waning of major war. Clearly, the thesis has to be narrowed in range. It fits only a limited category of wars: wars done in a particular way, conducted between particular parties. This should not be dismissed as insignificant, however. It is important that there have been no wars in Western Europe, notably between France and Germany, for more than 50 years. It is a shift in European history. Prior to this, this particular pair of states recorded three major wars in less than 75 years. Another 25 years without war, which seems likely, will make the non-war relationship of states a 'normal' one. For several generations, peace has been the experience, not war. The probability of war has declined dramatically.

Nevertheless, in what historically is a very recent period, we have to note that there were several serious nuclear confrontations. War planning was advanced and at times peace seemed entirely dependent on the unwillingness of the other actor to start a war, rather than actors having a will to avoid war altogether. Neither side wanted to begin and none gave the other side an opportunity to start. It means deterrence may have worked. But this, then, seems to be the result of gamesmanship rather than cultural development.

This data shows that it is too early to claim a universal ending to major war. In fact, there have been long periods without major war. It has been noted that the triangle of Austria–Germany–Russia saw 150 consecutive years without war (1763–1914). Still this very relationship is where the series of world wars of the twentieth century started.[11] A large number of years passed without war does not help to reduce the danger of war. Indeed, Sweden has had no war with Russia since 1809, but for close to two hundred years all Swedish defense planning assumed Russia to be the primary opponent. The image and fear of a particular conflict reemerging did not give way. The attitudes, instead, lingered on and had to be dealt with in their own regard.

Implications: when can we expect the waning of major war?

Changes of attitudes and in culture are important, but not necessarily sufficient factors to bring a contentious relationship from repeating historical paths of war. More needs to be added. In this overview we find that there are now more peaceful relations between industrial countries than there used to be. At the beginning of the twentieth century it was a common expectation that industrial countries had to be rivals and that war between them was likely. This is no longer so. The expectations have changed. It suggests a route away from war. What is today the European Union acquires significance. Cooperation has resulted in a security community which helps to reduce the danger of war. The likelihood of war has receded in Western Europe. It is a good sign that former warrior states today are at peace.

Following this observation, we could canvass the world for situations where there have been wars in the previous half-century to see if there are similar peacebuilding processes in place. Among the major powers we find few such examples. The relations between the USA and the West on the one side and Russia on the other have not come that far. NATO is still feared in Russia. Russia is regarded as a potential trouble spot in the West. In the aftermath of September 11, 2001 political relations have become closer, even personally cordial on the Presidential level. The fear of terrorism seems to be stronger to both leaderships than the fear of the other. Whether this is an alliance of convenience or a lasting re-arrangement will depend on the ability to use this opportunity to improve connections throughout society.

American (including other Western countries and Japan) relations with China remain contentious. The marks left from the confrontations during the Cold War, the battle over Korea, the crises on Taiwan, the disagreements on human rights, may still be too fresh to exclude an escalation of this conflict. The disagreement on desirable types of governance remains fundamental (Communism–Democracy). The peacebuilding initiatives for this region are few, and have so far had little impact. This provides a reason for more creative thinking.

Let us, then, pursue this discussion on when major wars actually can be expected to decline. The reduced propensity of war between industrial states is interesting and might provide some clues to the conditions under which major wars might be waning. It squares well with findings relating to the democratic peace.[12] It suggests that what is needed is not industrialization per se (that is, development), but rather the rise of democratic institutions. The correlation between democratic states and the absence of war is stronger than the one between developed countries and the lack of war. For instance, the two world wars took place between developed countries, but not between democratic ones. Certainly there is a large debate on this, and there are also empirical objections (notably the fact that there are internal wars in democratic states, such as the conflicts over Northern Ireland or northern Sri Lanka). There are also studies pointing to the dangers of the democratization process.[13] Thus, democracy is not a full solution, and, indeed, its establishment globally is a long-term proposition.

A contrasting hypothesis, also with support in the data, is that the danger of major war depends heavily on major power relationships. If they are cooperative and *universalistic* this will reduce the likelihood of major war (at least understood as major war among the major powers themselves).[14] The increased cooperation between the major powers after the Cold War has served to reduce the danger of major war between this set of actors. The de facto alliances formed after September 11 make this even more important. As the post-Cold War experience also makes clear, this is not correlated with a reduction in armed conflicts in other countries. Something important might be gained, but at the same time new entanglements may occur. For instance, internal dynamics of smaller and bigger countries may be less connected to types of major power relationships.

Shifts in relations between major powers often have to do with changes in their internal affairs. Such transitions might be particularly important and may go in different directions. In cases where it reduces the political distance to other major powers it could improve relations between them (e.g. Russia since 1986 and 1991 in relations with the West). If it increases distance, tension is likely to follow (e.g. Russia after November 1917 in its relations with the West). Wars might stem from such transitions.[15] Understanding the shifts and finding ways in which political change can be peaceful is, in other words, of central importance. Particularly this is a concern that relates to major powers. Today, this puts the onus on China. Will it be able to transform into an Asian form of democracy without violence and without the dissolution of the Chinese Empire, as we know it today?

Clearly it can. It is a matter of foresight and incremental change. This furthermore provides some clues as to where to look in society for such shifts. The role of violence, new forms of heroism, the role of new groups in power, are all likely to impact on the way members of society see themselves and their role, and the way the society will manage its own conflicts. If this is developed properly it has to start with the recognition that grievances seldom are remedied through major wars. For instance, some of today's independent countries gained this status with violence, but the path-setting country (India) used non-violence and most countries used neither one nor the other. If the use of violence is an important element in the normative messages to a population, it is likely to cement the early resort to coercive measures in that society.

A peacebuilding approach to achieve a reduction in (the likelihood of) major war requires both an ambition to solve ongoing conflicts (where cooperation among major powers may be a necessary condition) and a long-term approach to peaceful transition, in addition to questioning the role of violence. This effort at peace-building would have to involve the restoration of failed states in ways which do not create new authoritarian structures. It is also a challenge to the international community to allow poor states in the South to develop their economies, have equal access to the leading markets in the North, and decent support to their civilian development. The cultural changes suggested by Mueller[16] are part and parcel of this, but alone they cannot accomplish a world without major war.

Acknowledgment

I am grateful for the valuable comments given by Raimo Väyrynen on an earlier version of this intervention at the conference held at the University of Notre Dame, 6–8 April 2001.

Notes

1 J. Mueller, *Retreat from Doomsday: The Obsolescence of Major War* (New York: Basic Books, 1989).
2 D. Reiter and A. C. Stam, *Democracies at War* (Princeton: Princeton University Press, 2002).
3 See J. Mueller's chapter in this volume, Chapter 2.
4 M. Eriksson, P. Wallensteen and M. Sollenberg, 'Armed Conflict, 1989–2002', *Journal of Peace Research*, 40 (2003), pp. 593–607.
5 See *Correlates of War* project website, www.umich.edu/~cowproj/, 12 April 2002.
6 Some would argue that the Crimean War of 1854–5 had these marks as well, but it appears in other respects as a colonial and pre-industrial war using less mechanized instruments of war.
7 See K. Holsti's chapter in this volume, Chapter 6.
8 M. Kaldor, *New and Old Wars: Organized Violence in a Global Era* (Stanford: Stanford University Press, 1999).
9 S. N. Kalyvas, ' "New" and "Old" Civil Wars: A valid distinction?', *World Politics*, 54 (2001), pp. 99–118.
10 Technically it might not qualify as a major war as the battlefield casualties were limited. As an intervention it should then be more acceptable to the public, according to the thesis.
11 See P. W. Schroeder's chapter in this volume, Chapter 1.
12 B. Russett and J. Oneal, *Triangulating Peace* (New York: Norton, 2001).
13 H. Hegre, T. Ellingsen, S. Gates and N. P. Gleditsch, 'Towards a Democratic Civil Peace?', *American Political Science Review*, 95, 1 (2001), pp. 33–48.
14 See M. T. Henehan's and J. Vasquez's chapter in this volume, Chapter 11.
15 See Holsti's chapter in this volume, Chapter 6.
16 Mueller, *Retreat from Doomsday*.

Part II

SYSTEMIC CAUSES OF MAJOR WARS AND THEIR DECLINE

4

THE WANING OF MAJOR WAR

Martin van Creveld

In my view, major war has been on the wane not since 1980 but since 1945. Of course one might argue that, from a historical point of view, even half a century is not a very long period and that it does not represent an adequate basis for judgment; indeed one might argue – applying the reasoning of David Hume – that *no* period however long which has passed since an event took place can guarantee that it will not recur. Granting this, however, it seems to me that five decades are a much better basis than two on which to form our judgment. My starting point, accordingly, will be 1945.

By far the most important factor behind the waning of major interstate war has been the introduction of nuclear weapons. From the beginning of history, political organizations going to war against each other could hope to preserve themselves by defeating the enemy and gaining a victory; but now, assuming only that the vanquished side will retain a handful of weapons ready for use, the link between victory and self-preservation has been cut.[1] On the contrary, at least the possibility has to be taken into account that, the greater the triumph gained over an opponent who was in possession of nuclear weapons, the greater also the danger to the survival of the victor. A belligerent faced with the imminent prospect of suffering total defeat – as, for example, happened first to France and Russia and then to Germany and Japan during World War II – was all the more likely to react by pressing the nuclear button. Or, indeed, by falling on it as his chain of command collapsed and he lost control.[2]

Appearing as they did at the end, and as a result, of the largest armed conflict ever waged, nuclear weapons took a long time before their stultifying effects on future war were realized. During the immediate post-1945 years, only one important author seems to have understood that 'the absolute weapons' could never be used;[3] whether in or out of uniform, the great majority preferred to look for ways in which the weapon could and, if necessary, *would* be used.[4] As always happens when people try to forecast the form of future conflict, inertia and the 'lessons' of World War II played a part. So long as the number of available nuclear weapons remained limited, their power small compared to what was to come later, and their effects ill-understood it was possible to believe that they would make little difference and that war would go on more or less as before. To those who lived during or shortly after the War the outstanding characteristic of twentieth century 'total' warfare had been the state's ability to use the administrative organs at its disposal for mobilizing massive resources and creating equally massive armed forces.[5] Hence it was not unnatural to assume that such resources, minus of course those destroyed by the occasional atomic bomb dropped on them, would continue to be mobilized and thrown into combat against each other.[6]

At first possession of nuclear weapons was confined to one country only, the US, which used them in order to end the war against Japan. However, the 'atomic' secret could not be kept for very long and in September 1949 the USSR carried out its first test.[7] As more and more weapons were produced and stored, there were now *two* states capable of inflicting 'unacceptable damage' on each other, as the phrase went. The introduction of hydrogen bombs in 1952–3 opened up the vision of unlimited destructive power (in practice, the most powerful one built was three thousand times as large as the one that had demolished Hiroshima) and made the prospect of nuclear war even more awful. At the end of World War II there had been just two bombs in existence; but now the age of nuclear plenty arrived with more than enough devices available to 'service' any conceivable target.[8] For the first time, humanity found itself in a situation where it could destroy itself if it wanted to. The decade and a half after 1945 saw the publication of widely read novels such as Aldous Huxley's *Ape and Essence* (1948), Leon Uris's *On the Beach* (1957) and Walter Miller's *A Canticle to Leibowitz* (1959). All three described the collapse of civilization following a nuclear exchange. All three had as their central message the need to prevent such an exchange at all cost.

Even as the possible effects of nuclear weapons were becoming clear, the two leading powers were busily developing better ones. The original device had been too large and cumbersome to be carried in any but specially modified versions of the heaviest bombers of the time; however, during the fifties smaller and lighter versions were built that could be delivered by light bomber, fighter bomber, artillery shell, and even a light recoilless weapon operated by three men from a jeep. The acme of progress, if that is indeed the word, was represented in the form of ballistic missiles. Based on the ones developed by the Germans during World War II, by 1960 their range had been increased to the point where they were capable of delivering a hydrogen bomb from practically any point on earth to any other. The sixties and seventies saw missiles becoming much more accurate so that not only 'area targets' – meaning entire cities – but pin-point targets such as military bases could be aimed at and, with some luck, hit. Miracles of computerization led to the advent of Multiple Reentry Vehicles (MRV) and Multiple Independent Reentry Vehicles (MIRV); this made it possible to put as many as ten warheads on top of a single missile. Also, both ballistic missiles and the smaller cruise missiles could now be based on the ground – either in fixed silos or on top of mobile railway cars – in the air, and at sea where hundreds upon hundreds of them were either put into submarines or mounted on the decks of World War II vintage battleships which were specially refurbished for the purpose.

To focus on the US alone, the number of available weapons rose from perhaps less than a hundred in 1950 to some 3,000 in 1960, 10,000 in 1970, and 30,000 in the early 1980s when, for lack of targets, growth came to a halt. The size of the weapons probably ranged from under 1 kiloton (that is, 1,000 tons of TNT, the most powerful conventional explosive) to as much as 15 megatons (15 *million* tons of TNT); although, as time went on and the introduction of new computers and other navigation aids permitted more accurate delivery vehicles to be built, there was a tendency for the yields of 'strategic' warheads to decline to as little as 50–150 kilotons. With some variations, notably a preference for larger warheads and a greater reliance on land-based missiles as opposed to air- and sea-based ones, these arrangements were duplicated on the other side of the Iron Curtain. At its peak between 1980 and 1985 the Soviet arsenal probably counted some 20,000 warheads and their delivery vehicles. As in the American case, they were linked together by vast and intricate command and control networks consisting of bomb-proof command posts (some of them airborne), radars, satellites, communications, and the inevitable computers.[9] Their purpose was to serve warning against attack and make sure that the retaliatory forces would still be capable of doing their job even after 'riding out' a nuclear attack.

By basing them on the ground, at sea, and in the air, as well as greatly increasing numbers, the nuclear forces themselves could be protected against attack, at any rate to the extent that enough of them would survive to deliver the so-called 'second strike'. However, the same was not true of industrial, urban, and demographic targets. During World War II a defense that relied on radar and combined fighter with anti-aircraft artillery had sometimes brought down as many as a quarter of the bombers attacking a target; so, for example, in the case of the American raid against the German city of Schweinfurt in the autumn of 1943. Should the attack be made with nuclear weapons, though, even a defense capable of intercepting 90 percent of the attacking aircraft would be of no avail, since a single bomber getting through was capable of destroying the target just as surely as Hiroshima and Nagasaki were.

With the advent of ballistic missiles flying at hypersonic speeds, as well as cruise missiles flying so low that they could not be traced by ground-based radar, the problem of defending against attack became even more intractable. From the anti-ballistic missile area of the late sixties all the way to the 'Star Wars' program announced by President Reagan in 1983, tens of billions of dollars were spent and many solutions proposed; in the end, however, none of them appeared sufficiently promising to be developed and deployed on any scale. From a technical point of view, a missile that could be launched at another with a reasonable chance of hitting it in mid-flight (though the meaning of 'reasonable' remained in doubt) appeared feasible. However, how to deal with a missile carrying as many as ten warheads, let alone an attack consisting of numerous missiles and aimed at swamping the defense, was a different question altogether.

In the absence of a defense capable of effectively protecting demographic, economic, and industrial targets, nuclear weapons presented policy-makers with a dilemma. Obviously one of their most important functions – some would say, their only rightful function – was to deter war from breaking out. Previous military theorists, with Clausewitz at their head, had seldom even bothered to mention deterrence;

now, however, it became a central part of strategy as formulated in defense departments and studied in think-tanks and universities. On the other hand, if the weapons were to be capable of exercising a deterrent effect the weapons had to be capable of being used. What is more, they had to be used in a 'credible' manner that would not automatically lead to all out war and thus to the user's own annihilation.

In the West, which owing to the numerical inferiority of its conventional forces believed it might be constrained to make 'first use' of its nuclear arsenal, the search for an answer to this problem started during the mid-fifties and went on for the next thirty years. Numerous theories were developed; though none of them was ever put to the test. In retrospect they may be divided into three types. The first, proposed by Henry Kissinger among others,[10] suggested that an explicit agreement might be concluded concerning the kinds of targets that might be subjected to nuclear bombardment as well as the maximum size of the weapons that might be used to destroy them. The second, variously known as 'flexible response' and 'selective options', also depended on agreement, albeit a tacit one. It rested on the hope that, in exchange for NATO not using every nuclear weapon in its arsenal against every kind of target, the USSR would exercise similar restraint and permit the war to remain limited in terms of geography, targets, or both; this, in spite of repeated Soviet statements to the contrary.[11]

The third, and most hair-raising, 'solution' to the problem was proposed during the mid-eighties and was known as decapitation. Its adherents recognized that the chances of reaching an agreement, tacit or explicit, on the limitation of nuclear use in a war between the superpowers were anything but good; they therefore suggested that the new missiles and cruise missiles then coming into service should be used to 'decapitate' the Soviet Union. By this term they meant a series of super-accurate strikes that would eliminate the leadership and destroy its system of command control and communication, thus hopefully preventing it from launching an effective response.[12]

As the two last-mentioned strategies, dating to the 1970s and 1980s, suggest, by this time the apocalyptic fears so characteristic of the fifties had to some extent evaporated. Such novels as John Hackett's *The Third World War* (1979) and Tom Clancy's *Red Storm Rising* (1984) enjoyed immense popularity; to say nothing of the latter's *A Debt of Honor* (1994), in which a team of American commandos is sent to demolish Japan's nuclear establishment *in order* that a war may be fought against that country. In the years before 1914, the popularity of military fiction was one indication of the approaching slaughter.[13] In Reagan's America, presumably many people would have welcomed an opportunity to test the wonderful weapons put at their disposal by advancing technology. They might, indeed, have brought about a clash if it had not been for the restraining effect of nuclear weapons which, unfortunately, threatened to bring the fun to an end before it had even properly started; not by accident, both *The Third World War* and *Red Storm Rising* come to an end the moment such weapons are introduced. Whatever the precise relationship between fact and fiction, in practice the planners' attempts to devise 'warfighting' strategies for using the smaller bombs and super-accurate delivery vehicles came to naught. Deterrence, 'the sturdy child of terror' as Winston Churchill had once called it, prevailed.

After the Cuban Missile Crisis, which for a few days in October 1962 seemed to have brought the world to the verge of nuclear doom, the superpowers became notably more cautious. There followed such agreements as the Test Ban Treaty (1963), the Nonproliferation Treaty (1969), the two Strategic Arms Limitation Treaties of 1972 and 1977, and the cuts in the number of medium-range missiles and warheads that were achieved in the late eighties by President Reagan and Chairman Gorbachev. Each was brought about under different circumstances, but all reflected the two sides' willingness to put a cap on the arms race; as well as the growing conviction that, should a nuclear war break out, there would be neither winners nor losers. To date, the capstone of these agreements is formed by the one which was signed by Presidents George Bush and Boris Yeltsin and which provided for doing away with the more accurate delivery vehicles (MIRV). This was tantamount to an admission that 'warfighting' was dead, and that the only function of nuclear weapons was to deter.

By the time the Cold War ended the number of nuclear states, which originally had stood at just one, had reached at least eight. From Argentina and Brazil through Canada, West and East Europe, all the way to Taiwan, Korea (both North and South), Japan, Australia, and probably New Zealand, several dozen others were prepared to construct bombs quickly; or at any rate capable of doing so if they wanted to.[14] One, South Africa, preened itself on having built nuclear weapons and then dismantled them; although, understandably, both the meaning of 'dismantling' and the fate of the dismantled parts remained somewhat obscure. Meanwhile, technological progress has brought nuclear weapons within the reach of anybody capable of producing modern conventional arms; as is proved by the fact that states like China, Israel, India, and Pakistan all developed the former years, even decades, before they began building the latter.

The entry of new members into the nuclear club was not, of course, favorably received by those who were already there. Seeking to preserve their monopoly, repeatedly they expressed their fears of the dire consequences that would follow. Their objective was to prove that they themselves were stable and responsible and wanted nothing but peace; however, for ideological or political or cultural or technical reasons this was not the case elsewhere.[15] Some international safeguards, such as the Nonproliferation Treaty of 1969 and the London Regime of 1977, were set up, the intention being to prevent sensitive technology from falling into undesirable hands – which in practice meant those of Third World countries. However, the spread of nuclear technology proved difficult to stop. If, at present, the number of states with nuclear weapons in their arsenals remains limited to eight, on the whole this is due less to a lack of means than to a lack of will on the part of would-be proliferators.

Looking back, the fears of nuclear proliferation proved to be greatly exaggerated. Worldwide, the number of devices produced reaches into the high tens of thousands; fifty years after they were first introduced, however, the only ones actually used in anger remain those which were dropped on Hiroshima and Nagasaki. First the superpowers, which were sufficiently terrified by the Cuban Missile Crisis to set up so-called hot lines; then their close allies in NATO and the Warsaw Pact, which signed various agreements designed to prevent the outbreak of accidental nuclear war; then the USSR and China, which settled their border dispute in 1991; then China and India, which have not seen a shot fired across their borders since the 1961 war between them; then India and Pakistan; and finally Israel and its neighbors – each in turn found that ownership of such weapons did not translate into as much military power as they had thought.

Instead, the nuclear arsenal tended to act as an inhibiting factor on military operations. As time went on, fear of escalation no longer allowed these countries to fight each other directly, seriously, or on any scale. As time was to show, the process took hold even where one or more of the nuclear states in question was headed by absolute dictators, as both the USSR and China were at various times; even when the balance of nuclear forces was completely lopsided, as when the US possessed a ten to one advantage in delivery vehicles over the USSR during the Cuban Missile Crisis; even when the two sides hated each other 'for longer than any other two peoples on earth' (Pakistani Prime Minister Zulfikar Ali Bhutto), as in the case of India and Pakistan; and even when officials denied the existence of the bomb, as in both South Asia and the Middle East.

In fact, a strong case could be made that, wherever nuclear weapons have appeared or where their presence is even strongly suspected, major interstate warfare on any scale is in the process of slowly abolishing itself. What is more, any state of any importance is now by definition capable of producing nuclear weapons; as the examples of China, Israel, India, Pakistan, and South Africa show, often they can do so even before they are in a position to build advanced conventional ones. To the extent that major war still exists, it can only be waged either between or against third and fourth rate states. To the extent that it is waged between or against first and second class states, it is no longer major.

Since, in the years since 1945, first and second rate military powers have found it increasingly difficult to fight each other, it is no wonder that, taking a global view, both the size of the armed forces and the quantity of weapons at their disposal have declined quite sharply. In 1939 France, Germany, Italy, the USSR, and Japan each possessed ready-to-mobilize forces numbering several million men. The all-time peak came in 1944–5, when the six main belligerents (Italy having dropped out in 1943) between them probably maintained some 40 million men under arms. Since then the world's population has tripled, and international relations have been anything but peaceful; nevertheless, the size of regular forces has declined to a mere fraction of this and is still declining.[16]

To adduce a more specific example, in 1941 the German invasion of the USSR, as the largest single military operation of all time, made use of 144 divisions out of approximately 209 that the Wehrmacht possessed; later during the Russo-German war the forces deployed on both sides, but particularly by the Soviets, were even larger. By contrast, since 1945 there has probably not been even one case when any state used over twenty full-size divisions on any single campaign, and the numbers are still going nowhere but down. In 1991 a coalition that included three out of five members in the Security Council brought some 500,000 troops to bear against Iraq; which was only about one third as many as Germany, counting field forces only, used to invade France as long ago as 1914. As of the late nineties, the only states that still maintained forces exceeding a million and a half (for the US alone, the 1945 figure stood at 12,000,000) were India and China – and, of them, the last-named had just announced that half a million men would be sent home. In any case most of those forces consisted of low quality infantry, some of which, armed with World War I rifles, were suitable – if at all – more for maintaining internal security than for waging serious external war.

As major war against major enemies became less and less likely, the system which had been used to provide it with cannon fodder – general conscription – also came under critical scrutiny. As is well known, in 1792 Revolutionary France became the first modern country to introduce conscription.[17] The period of reaction after 1815 witnessed a move back towards small professional armies; however, after Prussia with Moltke at its head showed how the combination of conscription and railways could lead to armies much larger and more efficient than any others in history until then most other countries were also compelled to adopt the system. By 1914 the only important exceptions were Britain and the US. Both of them introduced conscription in World War I, and both of them did so for the second time during World War II.

In 1963, Britain became the first major country to abolish the system and return to professional forces made up entirely of volunteers. In 1973, this move was followed by the US as the largest military power of all. Since then their example has been followed by almost every other developed country, and with good reason: as was demonstrated with particular force when the French tried to go to war in the Gulf in 1991 and found it almost impossible to do so. By the 1990s conscription itself had become almost synonymous with military backwardness. Even Israel, which owing to the lopsided demographic balance between it and its Arab enemies has been more dependent on the system than perhaps any other state since 1945, was having second thoughts. If, at the present time, the Israel Defense Force (IDF) has not yet gone so far to abolish it, already now the proportion of Israeli youths who are inducted each year has fallen very sharply.[18]

While the decline in the number of troops – both regulars and, even more so, reservists – has been sharp indeed, the fall in the number of major weapons and weapon systems has been even more precipitous. In 1939, the air forces of each one of the leading powers counted their planes in the thousands; during each of the years 1942–1945, the US alone produced 75,000 military aircraft on the average. Fifty years later, the air forces of virtually all the most important countries were shrinking fast. The largest one, i.e. the United States air force, bought exactly 127 aircraft in 1995, including helicopters and transports;[19] elsewhere the numbers (if any) were down to the low dozens. At sea, the story has been broadly similar. Of the former Soviet navy, on which fortunes were spent and which as late as the

1980s appeared to pose a global threat, little remains but rusting surface vessels and old, under-maintained, submarines that allegedly risk leaking nuclear material into the sea. The US navy is in much better shape, but has seen the number of aircraft carriers – the most important weapon system around which everything else revolves – go down from almost one hundred in 1945 to as few as twelve in 1995. The US apart, the one country which still maintains even one carrier capable of launching conventional aircraft is France; the carriers (all of them decidedly second rate) owned by all other states combined can be counted on the fingers of one hand. Indeed it is true to say that, with a single major exception, most states no longer maintain ocean-going navies at all.

In part, this decline in the size of armed forces reflects the escalating cost of modern weapons and weapon systems.[20] A World War II fighter bomber could be had for approximately $50,000. Some of its modern successors, such as the F-15I, come at $100,000,000 a piece when their maintenance packages (without which they would not be operational) are included; which, when inflation is taken into account, represents a one-hundred-and-fifty-fold increase. Even this does not mark the limit on what some airborne weapon systems, such as the 'stealth' bomber, AWACS and J-STAR – all of them produced, owned, and operated exclusively by the world's sole remaining superpower – can cost. And it has been claimed that the reluctance of the US air force to use its most recent acquisition, the B-2 bomber which carries a $2 billion price tag, against Iraq stems in part from the fact that there are simply no targets worthy of the risk.[21]

Even so, one should not make too much of the price factor. Modern economies are extraordinarily productive, and could certainly devote much greater resources to the acquisition of military hardware than they do at present. Thus, the cost of modern weapon systems may appear exorbitant only because the state's basic security, safeguarded as it is by nuclear weapons and their ever-ready delivery vehicles, no longer appears sufficiently at risk to justify them. In fact, this is probably the correct interpretation; as is suggested by the tendency, which has now been evident for decades, to cut the size of any production program and stretch the length of any acquisition process *ad calendas grecas*. For example, to develop the Manhattan Project – including the construction of some of the largest industrial plant ever – and build the first atomic bombs took less than three years; but the designers of present-day conventional weapon systems want us to believe that a new fighter bomber cannot be deployed in fewer than fifteen. The development histories of countless modern weapon systems prove that, in most cases, only a fraction of the numbers initially required are produced, and then only after delays lasting for years and years. The reason is that, in most cases, the threat – which would have made rapid mass production necessary and incidentally led to a dramatic drop in per unit costs – is no longer there.

At the same time, yet another explanation for the decline in the quantity of weapons produced and deployed is the very great improvement in quality; this, it is argued, makes yesterday's large numbers superfluous.[22] There is, in fact, some truth in this argument. Particularly since guided missiles have replaced ballistic weapons in the form of the older artillery and rockets, the number of rounds necessary to destroy any particular target has dropped very sharply; as the 1991 Gulf War showed, in many cases a one-shot, one-kill capability has been achieved. On the other hand, it should be remembered that for every modern weapon – nuclear ones only excepted – a counter may be, and in most cases has been, designed. However simple or sophisticated two opposing military systems, provided that they are technologically approximately equal the struggle between them is likely to be prolonged and to result in heavy attrition.[23] Expecting more accurate weapons to increase attrition – as, in fact, was the case both in the 1973 Arab–Israeli War and the 1982 Falklands War, each in turn the most modern conflict in history until then – logically late twentieth century states ought to have produced and fielded more weapons, not less. The fact that this has not happened almost certainly shows that they are no longer either willing or able to prepare for wars on a scale larger than, say, Vietnam and Afghanistan; and even those two came close to bankrupting the two largest powers, i.e. the US and the USSR respectively.

To look at it in another way still, during World War II four out of seven (five out of eight, if China is included) major belligerents had their capitals occupied. Two more (London and Moscow) were heavily bombed, and only one (Washington DC) escaped either misfortune. Since then, however, *no* first or second rate power has seen large scale military operations waged on its territory; the reasons for this being too obvious to require an explanation. In fact, the majority of countries which did go to war – or against which others went to war – were quite small and relatively unimportant. For example, Israel against the Arab states; India against Pakistan; Iran against Iraq; the United States first against Vietnam and then against Iraq; and, for a few days in 1995, Peru against Ecuador. When the countries in question were not unimportant, as in the case of India and China during their pre-nuclear days, military operations were almost always confined to the margins and never came near the capitals in question.

The significance of this change was that that strategy, which from Napoleon to World War II often used to measure its advances and retreats in hundreds of miles, now operates on a much smaller scale. For example, no post-1945 army has so much as tried to repeat the 600-mile German advance from the River Bug to Moscow, let alone the 1,300-mile Soviet march from Stalingrad to Berlin. Since then, the distances covered by armies have been much shorter. In no case did they exceed 300 miles (Korea in 1950); usually, though, they did not penetrate deeper than 150 or so. In 1973 Syria and Egypt faced an unacknowledged nuclear threat on the part of Israel. Hence, as some of their leaders subsequently admitted, they limited themselves to advancing ten and five miles respectively into occupied territory – to such lows had the formerly mighty art of 'strategy' sunk.[24] In other places where nuclear powers confront each other, as between India and Pakistan, what hostilities still take place (across the remote, and practically worthless, glacier of Siachen) do not involve any territorial advances at all.[25]

As nuclear weapons restricted the scope of war, it is perhaps no wonder that conventional military theory stagnated. The thinkers who, during the interwar years, taught the world's armed forces how to wage wars with weapons and weapon systems based on the internal combustion engine – Giulio Douhet, John Frederick Fuller, Basil Liddell Hart, Heinz Guderian – did not really have successors worthy of them. It is often believed that, throughout the Cold War, the one thought that occupied the brains of the General Staff in Moscow was how to conduct a 1940-style Blitzkrieg, only much bigger, faster, and more powerful; conversely, 90 percent of all NATO planning concerned the question of how to stop such a Blitzkrieg in its tracks and then, perhaps, go over to the counteroffensive as the British had done at Alamein in 1942.[26] Through all this, the basic analytical terms used to understand large scale military operations – such as advance, retreat, breakthrough, penetration, encirclement, front, line of communications, internal and external lines, direct and indirect approach – remained very much as they had been; with the result that Liddell Hart's *Strategy*, published for the first time in 1929, tended to be reprinted each time a conventional war broke out.[27] Arguably, the only new concept that has appeared on the scene since 1935 or so has been that of vertical envelopment.[28] Involving the use of aircraft and, later, helicopters in order to land troops in the enemy's rear, seize key points, and cut his communications, vertical envelopment was used on a number of occasions during World War II. However, not since the Suez Campaign of 1956 has any army tried to implement it on any scale; its use in counterinsurgency apart, the most innovative idea of all (which itself is over half a century old) has remained purely on paper.

Initiated by the development of nuclear weapons, and accompanied by a drastic decline in the size of military establishments as well as the equipment at their disposal, the decline of major interstate war was also reflected in international law and *mores*. For centuries if not millennia, the most important reason why politically organized societies, including (after 1648) states, went to war against each other had been to carry out conquests and acquire territory. It was by sword and fire that Louis XIV conquered Alsace, Frederick II Silesia, and Napoleon (however temporarily) most of Europe. This was also the case in 1815 when Prussia emerged from the Napoleonic Wars in possession of the Rhineland, a territory that had never previously belonged to it; and when the US occupied huge tracts of Mexican territory in 1846–8. As late as 1866 it was by means of war, and the peace agreements concluded in its wake, that Prussia annexed some of the North German states and Italy obtained Venice from Austria. Over the next half-century the acquisition of territory in Asia and Africa, where society had not yet been organized in states, continued and even accelerated. Not so in Europe itself. There, the spread of nationalism – meaning the growing identification of people with the state whose citizens they were – was probably already beginning to make conquest more difficult both to bring about and to legitimize.

In retrospect, the turning point in the process that eventually made the annexation by one state of territory belonging to others into a legal and practical impossibility probably came in 1870–1. Having won their war against France, the Germans like countless conquerors before them demanded payment in the form of real estate.

That real estate was duly signed away by the newly established, but legitimate, republican government of Adolphe Thiers; however, it very soon became clear that, in sharp contrast to similar events in the past, the French people simply refused to let go. On the contrary, the very fact that they had been conquered by force caused Alsace and Lorraine to be designated 'sacred'; during the second half of the twentieth century, that was to become the fate of *every* bit of occupied territory, no matter how insignificant. The land being sacred, they waited for *la revanche* which it was now the patriotic duty of every Frenchman and Frenchwoman to prepare as best they could. As Bismarck himself had expressly foreseen,[29] the change in attitudes turned the annexation of the two provinces – carried out at the insistence of Moltke and the General Staff – into the worst political error he ever made. From now on, every other state that nursed a grudge against Germany could invariably count on French support.

The idea that complete sovereignty, including the unrestricted right to wage war, was too dangerous to entertain in the age of modern technology suffered another blow as a result of World War I and the 10 million casualties (in dead alone) that it wrought.[30] Ever since the first half of the seventeenth century, numerous suggestions had been made to limit the right of states to make war against their neighbors. The idea was to establish some kind of international organization that would stand above individual states; arbitrate in disputes that broke out among them; and bring force to bear against disturbers of the peace. Those who floated schemes of this kind included the Abbé Cruce, William Penn, Jean-Jacques Rousseau, Emmanuel Kant, John Stuart Mill, and the Swiss jurist Johann Bluntschli; in short, many of the leading intellectuals of the period between about 1650 and 1900.[31] Finally, in 1919, the vision was partly realized and the League of Nations established. Its Covenant, and especially Article 10, represented a new departure in international law. For the first time ever, the territorial integrity and political independence – in other words, the right to be free of conquest – of states were recognized as a fundamental international norm.

The next step was taken in 1928 and took the form of the Kellogg–Briand Pact. In this Pact, originally designed by the foreign ministers of the US and France, the signatories formally undertook 'to renounce war as an instrument of national policy'. During the years that followed this obligation was joined by sixty-one additional states; since there was no time limit, technically speaking the Pact remains in force to the present day.[32]

In the event, these and other 'international kisses', as they have been called by their self-styled 'realist' critics, failed to prevent the unleashing of World War II as the greatest war of conquest of all time. This, however, does not mean that, as indicators of the public mood, they were completely without significance. Once World War II was over, those persons considered most responsible for launching it were brought to justice in Nuremberg and Tokyo. The courts which were set up by the Allies used the Kellogg–Briand Pact as the legal basis for charging them with a new crime, such as had not been heard of since Hugo Grotius;[33] namely, planning and waging 'aggressive' war.[34] The arguments of the defendants' lawyers, namely that this was a *post facto* indictment for a crime which had not been recognized as such at the time when it was allegedly committed, remained unheeded. The most important Nazi and Japanese war criminals were convicted – for this as well as other crimes – and, the majority of them, duly executed. Moreover, thirteen months had not yet passed since the end of hostilities when the prohibition on aggressive war and the use of force in order to annex territory belonging to other sovereign entities were written into Article 2(4) of the United Nations Charter. As additional states joined the UN, in time the latter was to develop into the most subscribed-to document in human history.

Article 39 of the Charter left the decision as to what constituted aggression in the hands of the Security Council which, especially in view of the disagreements between its members, found the task remarkably difficult.[35] Nevertheless, it could be argued that the attempt to prevent states from enjoying the fruits of aggression in the form of territorial aggrandizement has been remarkably successful. The last time international war led to the annexation of territory on any scale was in 1945 when the USSR took over lands belonging to Poland (which itself annexed German lands), Germany, Czechoslovakia, and Japan; since then, though, international borders have become all but frozen. Remarkable as it seems, not the Korean War, nor the three Indo-Pakistani Wars, nor the Indo-Chinese War, nor any of the Arab–Israeli Wars, ended with important pieces of territory being ceded by one side to another; indeed the great majority did not lead to any territorial changes at all. At most, a country was partitioned and a new international border created. This, for example, was what took place in Yugoslavia between 1991 and 1995. This, too, was what happened in Palestine in 1948–9 when Israel, having been established by means of a United Nations Resolution, occupied somewhat more territory than had been allocated to it by the Partition Plan. At that time King Abdullah of Jordan, who may have been acting in concert with Israel, used the opportunity to take over some 2,000 square miles known as the West Bank. However, in the whole world the only two countries to recognize the annexation were Britain and Pakistan; and in any case it has since been formally annulled.

Elsewhere the idea that force should not be used for altering frontiers, which was reaffirmed once again by UN Resolution 2734 of 1970, prevailed.[36] Before 1945, the attainment of military victory usually led to the surrender of the vanquished, a peace treaty, and the cession of territory; now, however, almost without exception the most that an occupant could obtain was an armistice. Particularly in the Middle East, the state of no war, no peace that ensued proved itself capable of lasting for decades on end; as a result, many of the maps in current use have two lines marked on them, namely a green one showing the international border (which was only in effect during the first nineteen years after 1948) and a purple one indicating the ceasefire line that was established in 1967. Indeed, so strong has the prevalent bias towards the *status quo ante* become that it prevailed even in those cases when the defeated plainly did not have the ability to eject the victor. This is what happened when India occupied several thousand square miles of Pakistani territory in 1971; and also after China invaded Vietnam in 1979.

Moreover, the decline of major war has led to a change in the terminology by which it was surrounded. All but gone are a whole series of terms, such as 'subjugation' and 'the right of conquest', which even as late as 1950 or so formed a normal part of legal discourse in a work on international law written by such a highly civilized authority as His Britannic Majesty's Government's official adviser.[37] Of the two, the former has acquired an archaic, not to say outlandish, ring. The latter is regarded almost as a contradiction in terms; given that might, as exercised by one sovereign state against another, by definition can no longer create right. Gone, too, are the 'war ministries' of the various states, every last one of which has had its name changed into ministry of defense, ministry of security, or something of that kind. Needless to say, the change in nomenclature did not always mean a different kind of activity. As they had done for centuries past, 'defense' officials of many countries continued to plan and prepare for wars at least some of which were aggressive. What it did do was to emphasize the growing force of international law to delegitimize war; or, at any rate, war as waged by one state against others.

The Iraqi invasion of Kuwait, which took place in 1990–1, marked yet another step towards the delegitimization of interstate war. Against the background of changing international norms, perhaps not since the time of Korea had there been a similar clear-cut attempt to occupy a sovereign state and wipe it off the map. The question of oil apart, no wonder Saddam Hussein faced the opprobrium of the whole world; as it turned out, he was unable to get his annexation recognized even by the handful of countries that supported him, such as Cuba, Jordan, Yemen, and the Sudan.

On the other side of the dispute, the states that formed the coalition against Iraq did not respond by declaring war on their own accord. Following a precedent set in the matter of Korea in 1950, they asked the Security Council (in which, of course, their own influence was paramount) for a mandate to end the aggression or, in plain words, throw the Iraqis out. As was noted at the time,[38] the procedure selected by President Bush raised the question whether states still had the right to use force in order to pursue their interests; or whether they had to ask for permission in the manner of medieval princes appealing to the Pope. Nor, as events were to show, was the precedent thus set without significance. Much of 1995 was spent wrangling over the question whether NATO, as a mere alliance of sovereign states, was entitled to send troops to Bosnia without requiring a mandate from the United Nations. Early in 1998, as it was trying to punish Saddam Hussein for allegedly 'stonewalling' the arms inspections to which Iraq had been subject for the last seven years, the United States found that going to war without permission from the Security Council would incur a heavy political price.

In law as well as in fact, as the twentieth century was approaching its end major war – at any rate as it applies between states – appeared to be on the retreat. The right to wage it, far from being part and parcel of sovereignty, had been taken away except in cases involving strict self-defense; even when states *did* wage war in strict self-defense (and for precisely that reason) they were no longer allowed to benefit by bringing about territorial change. Thus has such war lost its chief attraction. At the same time, as far as important states were concerned, the stakes were raised many times over by the introduction of nuclear weapons. No wonder that its incidence, among those states at least, was diminishing.

As to the interstate wars that still took place, with hardly any exception they were waged between, or against, third and fourth rate states – the 2003 campaign against Iraq being, of course, a perfect case in point. This means they could not be major by definition; even though, from the point of view of the unfortunate people who were caught up in them, this fact was by no means as apparent as to those sitting in the world's main capitals and watching the wars in question unfold on TV. From the Middle East to the Straits of Taiwan, the world remains a dangerous place and new forms of armed conflict appear to be taking the place of the old.[39] Nevertheless, compared to the situation as it existed even as late as 1939 the change appears momentous.

Notes

1 See above all T. S. Schelling, *Arms and Influence* (New Haven: Yale University Press, 1966), ch. 1.
2 The best work about the breaking of the link between victory and survival and indeed nuclear strategy in general, remains Schelling, *Arms and Influence*.
3 B. Brodie (ed.), *The Absolute Weapons* (New York: Columbia University Press, 1946), ch. 1; also B. Brodie, 'The Atom Bomb as Policy Maker', *Foreign Affairs*, 27, 1 (1948), pp. 1–16.
4 The best history of nuclear 'strategy' remains L. Freedman, *The Evolution of Nuclear Strategy* (New York: St Martin's Press, 1981).
5 See e.g. J. F. C. Fuller, *The Conduct of War* (London: Eyre & Spottiswode, 1961), p. 321ff.
6 P. M. S. Blackett, *The Military and Political Consequences of Atomic Energy* (London: Turnstile Press, 1948), ch. 10.
7 For the Soviet road to the bomb see most recently D. Holloway, *Stalin and the Bomb* (New Haven: Yale University Press, 1994).
8 See A. Enthoven, *How Much is Enough? Shaping the Defense Budget, 1961–69* (New York: Harper & Row, 1971) for the kind of calculation involved.
9 For the arrangements in question see P. Bracken, *The Command and Control of Nuclear Forces* (New Haven: Yale University Press, 1983).
10 H. A. Kissinger, *Nuclear Weapons and Foreign Policy: The Need for Choice* (New York: Harper & Row, 1957), pp. 174–83.
11 On these doctrines, which for the sake of brevity have been bundled together, see e.g. R. van Cleave and R. W. Barnett, 'Strategic Adaptability', *Orbis*, 18, 3 (1974), pp. 655–76; and L. E. Davis, *Limited Nuclear Options: Deterrence and the new American Doctrine*, Adelphi paper No. 121 (London: International Institute for Strategic Studies, 1976).
12 C. S. Gray, 'War Fighting for Deterrence', *Journal of Strategic Studies*, 7, 1 (1984), pp. 5–28.
13 See I. V. Clark, *Voices Prophesizing War* (Middlesex: Penguin, 1963), ch. 5.
14 See on this T. Rauf, 'Disarmament and Non-Proliferation Treaties', in G. A. Wood and L. S. Leland, Jr (eds), *State and Sovereignty: Is the State in Retreat?* (Dunedin: University of Otago Press, 1997), pp. 142–88.
15 On the Soviet bomb, see e.g. M. Strunk, 'The Quarter's Polls', *Public Opinion Quarterly*, 14, 1 (1950), p. 182. On the Chinese bomb, see R. Ducci, 'The World Order in the

Sixties', *Foreign Affairs*, 43, 3 (1964), pp. 379–90. On the Indian bomb, see A. Myrdal, 'The High Price of Nuclear Arms Monopoly', *Foreign Policy*, 18, spring (1975), pp. 30–43.

16 The International Institute of Military Studies, *The Military Balance, 1999–2000* (London: IISS, 2000) gives a country by country overview of the armed forces currently in existence.

17 See G. Best, *War and Society in Revolutionary Europe* (London: Fontana, 1982), pp. 82–98.

18 See on this most recently Y. Lifschitz, 'Managing Defense After 2000', in H. Golan (ed.), *Israel's Security Web: Core Issues of Israel's National Security in Its Sixth Decade* [Hebrew], (Tel Aviv: Maarachot, 2001), pp. 57–63; and Y. Levy, *The Other Army of Israel* [Hebrew], (Tel Aviv: Yediot Acharonot, 2003), p. 462.

19 World War II figures from R. Overy, *The Air War 1939–1945* (London: Europa, 1980), pp. 308–9; 1995 ones from D. M. Snider, 'The Coming Defense Train Wreck', *Washington Quarterly*, 19, 1 (1996), p. 92.

20 The best analysis of cost trends remains F. Spinney, *Defense Facts of Life* (Boulder: Westview, 1986).

21 BBC, 25 February 1998.

22 For some calculations pertaining to his subject see N. Brown, *The Future of Air Power* (New York: Holmes & Meier, 1986), p. 88; J. A. Warden, III, 'Air Theory for the Twenty-First Century', in K. P. Magyar (ed.), *Challenge and Response: Anticipating US Military Security Concerns* (Maxwell: Air Force University Press, 1994), pp. 313 and 328; also D. T. Kuehl, 'Airpower vs. Electricity: Electric Power as a Target for Strategic Air Operations', *Journal of Strategic Studies*, 18, 1 (1995), pp. 250–60.

23 Cf. M. van Creveld, *Technology and War, from 2000 B.C. to the Present* (New York: Free Press, 1988), chs 9 and 11.

24 For the effect of nuclear weapons on the Arab–Israeli conflict see S. Aronson, *The Politics and Strategy of Nuclear Weapons in the Middle East* (Albany: State University of New York Press, 1992).

25 For the ongoing Siachen conflict see A. S. Wirsing, 'The Siachen Glacier Dispute, part 1', *Strategic Studies*, x, 1 (1987), pp. 49–66; A. S. Wirsing, 'The Siachen Glacier Dispute, part 2', *Strategic Studies*, xi, 3 (1988), pp. 75–94; A. S. Wirsing, 'The Siachen Glacier Dispute, part 3', *Strategic Studies*, xii, 1 (1988), pp. 38–54.

26 See for example A. A. Sidorenko, *The Offensive* (Washington DC: Government Printing Office, 1970).

27 B. H. L. Hart, *The Decisive Wars of History* (London: Faber & Faber, 1929), reprinted as *Strategy: The Indirect Approach* in 1946 and 1954 and as *Strategy* in 1967 and 1991.

28 See above all N. Browne, *Strategic Mobility* (London: Praeger, 1963); and R. Simpkin, *Race to the Swift* (London: Pergamon Press, 1985).

29 O. von Bismarck, *Reflections and Reminiscences*, Vol. 2. (London: Smith, 1898), pp. 252ff.

30 For what follows see F. Przetacznik, 'The Illegality of the Concept of Just War under Contemporary International Law', *Revue de Droit International, des Sciences Diplomatiques et Politiques*, 70, 4 (1993), pp. 245–94.

31 For these and other attempts at international organization see A. Saita, 'Un Riformatore pacifista Contemporaneo de Richelieu: E. Cruce', *Rivista Storica Italiana*, 64 (1951), pp. 183–92; W. Penn, *An Essay Towards the Present and Future Peace of Europe* (Hildesheim: Olms, 1983 [1699]); Abbé de Saint Pierre, *A Scheme for Lasting Peace in Europe* (London: Peace Book, 1939 [1739]); O. Schreker, 'Leibnitz, ses Idées sur l'Organisation des Relations Internationales', *Proceedings of the British Academy*, 23 (1937), pp. 218–19; E. Kant, *Plan for a Universal and Everlasting Peace* (New York: Garland, 1973 [1796]); J. Lorimer, *The Institutes of the Law of Nations* (Edinburgh:

Blackwood, 1883–4), ch. 14; J. G. Bluntschli, *Gesammelte kleine Schriften*, Vol. 2. (Nordlingen: Beck'sche Buchhandlung, 1879–81), pp. 293–5.

32 For these developments see F. Przetacznik, 'The Illegality of the Concept of Just War under Contemporary International Law', *Revue de Droit International*, 70, 4 (1993), pp. 245–94.

33 H. Grotius, *De Jure Belli ac Pacis* (Amsterdam: Jansunium, 1632), bk 2, ch. 23, s. 13; bk 1, ch. 3, s. 1.

34 See G. Best, *War and Law since 1945* (Oxford: Clarendon Press, 1991), pp. 181–2.

35 For two attempts to grapple with this question see Y. Melzer, *Just War* (Leiden: Sijthoff, 1975), pp. 83 ff.; I. D. de Lupis, *The Law of War* (Cambridge: Cambridge University Press, 1987), pp. 58 ff.

36 The relevant paragraphs are printed in S. D. Bailey, *Prohibitions and Restraints on War* (London: Oxford University Press, 1972), appendix I, p. 162.

37 H. Lauterpacht, *International Law: A Treatise* (London: Longman, 1947).

38 See G. Picco, 'The UN and the Use of Force', *Foreign Affairs*, 73, 5 (1994), pp. 14–18; also, in general, A. Roberts, 'The United Nations: A System for Collective of International Security?' in G. A. S. C. Wilson (ed.), *British Security 2010* (Camberley: Camberley Staff College, Strategic and Combat Studies Institute, 1996), pp. 65–8.

39 See M. Kaldor, *New Wars for Old* (London: Pergamon, 1998).

5

THE RISK OF NUCLEAR
WAR DOES NOT BELONG
TO HISTORY

T. V. Paul

The end of the Cold War has heralded an era of unprecedented peace among the major powers. Nuclear weapons that supposedly prevented major power war still exist in large numbers in the post-Cold War world, but with political relations among the leading actors having altered for the better, their prominence has been waning both in official pronouncements and public discourse. This limited, yet meaningful politico-military depreciation of nuclear weaponry in the major power system has occurred despite the fact that the long peace of the Cold War years was presumably the result of the nuclear standoff, which nonetheless involved the high risk of a nuclear war breaking out between the superpowers and their allies. The fear of an all-out nuclear war seemed to have exerted enormous caution in the behavior of the nuclear powers even when dealing with the central security issues vital to them in the conflict-ridden environment of the Cold War years. Although we cannot say with absolute certainty that nuclear deterrence was the key source of systemic stability, the empirical reality is that, during the fifty years of the nuclear age, fortuitously a catastrophic major power war was averted.

In this chapter I argue that, in the post-Cold War world, the probability of the outbreak of an advertent or premeditated nuclear war among the major powers has declined while the danger of an inadvertent nuclear war still exists. Although the occurrence of major wars involving nuclear weapons is of low probability, war-generating situations are likely to emerge both at the regional and global levels as the international system evolves from a near-unipolar to a multipolar system. Systemic and structural changes, caused by political, technological and economic factors that affect the balance of power and that have a bearing on the probability of nuclear conflict are possible over the long-term time horizon. These changes are likely to manifest themselves in the politico-military doctrines and actual behavior of the hegemonic power, the United States, the declining power, Russia, and the rising power, China, in terms of the offensive, defensive and deterrent value they attach to nuclear weaponry. The technological advances, such as near-perfect missile defense systems and other revolution in military affairs (RMA) capabilities that allow the possessor of such systems high levels of precision in offensive operations, might alter the relative utility of nuclear weapons for the affected states.

The prospects of a nuclear war involving the US and a regional state have increased since the 1990s. The new US nuclear strategy under the Bush Administration allows the use of nuclear weapons preemptively or preventively against 'rogue states' or terrorist groups that hold weapons of mass destruction (WMD) as well as to keep open the option of retaliating with nuclear arms if such actors actually use WMD. Further, the US is in the lead for developing mini-nuclear weapons meant to penetrate deeply buried bunkers or other underground facilities of regional foes.

In addition, the risks of nuclear war, advertent and inadvertent, among the new nuclear states – India, Pakistan, Israel and North Korea – do exist, although the first category will decline as time passes by and as these states establish reliable command, communications and control (C3) systems. In the near term, however, risks of nuclear war exist because of the vulnerabilities in their deterrent relationships in terms of crisis, arms control and strategic instability and also their dearth of highly effective technical and political controls necessary to prevent a possible accidental nuclear war. Moreover, the 'stability–instability paradox' seems to be rampant among the new nuclear states, signifying that, although at the strategic level new nuclear states do not experience major wars, at the sub-strategic level the incidence of low intensity conflicts has increased. Further the possibility of inadvertent accidental or unauthorized nuclear use exists among the new nuclear states.

A final category of potential nuclear use involves sub-state actors, especially terrorist groups, the states that sponsor them and the states that are targets of the activities of such groups. If a terrorist group acquires nuclear weapons and succeeds in using them against a nuclear state, the pressure on the latter to retaliate in kind could be high. This contingency, although far-fetched until September 2001, seems not inconceivable in the future. For instance, the Al-Qaeda network could obtain nuclear weapons through disgruntled Pakistani military and scientific personnel, especially if Pakistan collapses as a state with the military losing control of the country and its nuclear arsenal. Once in possession of nuclear weapons, this group may resort to nuclear use against a country or society that it detests, as the deterrence logic may not apply in such conflict situations. Moreover, there may be circumstances under which the US could be under intense pressure to use small tactical weapons to eject terrorists holed up in specific unreachable locations.

Risk of nuclear war during the Cold War era

At this point, a discussion of the probability of nuclear war to have occurred during the Cold War would help illuminate the chances of such wars in the post-Cold War world. Throughout the Cold War era, the risk of nuclear war existed for the following reasons:

1   Nuclear war was a possibility during a substantial decline in political and diplomatic relations, i.e., crisis, between the superpowers. A general nuclear

war would have been the result of the escalation of crises involving the major powers in the two core regions of the world, Europe and Asia. This would have been the result of the failure of mutual deterrence, of both the general and the immediate categories.[1] The periods of the Berlin Blockade, Korean War, Cuban Missile Crisis and the Afghan conflict serve as examples of this type of situation when the political relations between the superpowers deteriorated sharply and the outbreak of a nuclear war was a possibility.[2]

2   A related contingency of nuclear use would have been a preemptive strike by either superpower as nuclear-armed adversaries attempted to limit the damage of a feared or actual impending attack on their forces.[3] Thus, one of the nuclear rivals could have gone to war, believing that the opponent was about to strike and that, by attacking first, it would limit the damage to its homeland and gain significant advantages in the post-war settlement.[4] A possible example of nuclear war of this nature would have been a preemptive strike by either superpower during the Cuban Missile Crisis, fearing that the other was about to launch a nuclear attack. The 'reciprocal fear of surprise attack', despite the perverse logic inherent in it, continued to plague policy-makers' thinking throughout the Cold War era.[5]

3   A 'bolt from the blue', premeditated attack by either superpower in order to achieve coercive bargaining advantage forms another danger that existed during the Cold War era.[6] Such an attack could have been a single launch or multiple launches by one superpower aimed at compelling the other to make concessions. However, as the nuclear era advanced and the mutual assured destruction (MAD) relationship was well in place the probability of this category of nuclear war breaking out declined substantially for reasons of credibility. Despite the low likelihood of this type of war occurring, the nuclear doctrines of both superpowers contained the fear of 'bolts from the blue' attacks as evident in their force postures, weapons deployment and general weapons acquisition patterns.[7]

4   A limited nuclear war, preceded by crises and limited wars in regional theaters where both superpowers had perceived high stakes in the protection of their regional allies, was a fourth category of prospective nuclear war that existed during the Cold War era. The protection of allies through extended deterrence or nuclear umbrellas constituted a declared core function of the superpower nuclear weapons, especially that of the United States. Regional conflicts in Europe, East Asia and the Middle East could have escalated to a nuclear exchange involving the superpowers, especially in the event of the US or the USSR actively intervening in the defense of their allies. The Middle East conflict of 1973, when the US alerted its nuclear forces, provides the closest example of this contingency.[8]

5   A preventive strike, purportedly to forestall the nascent nuclear programs of a country, was another contingency that could have led to a nuclear war during the Cold War years. The preventive strike situation could also have included a nuclear adversary expecting dramatic decline in its power position or dramatic

rise in the capabilities of another, especially through the introduction of a new offensive weapon system or defensive weapon system that would make its deterrent capabilities redundant. However, preventive strikes were mostly possible in the context of a new state acquiring nuclear weapons while an established nuclear power attempted to forestall such acquisitions. The US striking the nascent nuclear weapons programs of Russia and China or Russia striking China's nuclear facilities constituted possible cases that never materialized. However, newly declassified official documents suggest that the United States under the Kennedy Administration seriously contemplated preventive attack against China to stop it from acquiring nuclear arms.[9] Similarly, the possibility existed for China attacking the Indian nuclear facilities and India striking Pakistani facilities, but these also never materialized. A preventive conventional attack prior to these states building nuclear weapons was more plausible as opposed to a nuclear attack after they had acquired such weapons.[10] However, it is possible that even a conventional preventive attack on some of these emerging nuclear nations could have escalated into a major counterattack in Europe (in Russia's case) forcing NATO/US to use nuclear weapons consistent with their extended deterrent obligations.

6   Inadvertent or accidental nuclear wars due to misperceptions, miscalculations, wrong signals, faulty organizational procedures and failures caused by technical factors beyond human control were possibilities that existed throughout the Cold War era. The dangers were accentuated by the short decision time of minutes at the disposal of decision-makers in a nuclear crisis.[11] Loss of control resulting from 'fragmented political authority, domestic pressures that leaders are powerless to resist, or an institutional malfunction or breakdown', and miscalculation 'when one of the adversaries crosses the other's threshold to war in the false expectation that his action will be tolerated'.[12]

The superpowers created extensive technical and diplomatic measures to avert nuclear wars under all these contingencies, especially the last category. The technical hurdles included: installation of permissive action links (PALs), radar facilities and ballistic missile early warning systems (BMEWS) in several parts of the world, extensive command and control requirements, and a hotline connecting Moscow and Washington DC allowing the top political leaders to communicate promptly in times of crisis. Political–diplomatic hurdles were established mostly through the arms control process and confidence building measures that were introduced following the Cuban Missile Crisis. The PAL systems that would allow intercontinental ballistic missile (ICBM) launches only after the insertion of specially controlled codes were introduced in the 1960s. Other systems, such as the positive control launch (PCL), were installed on bombers and a complex system of procedural checks and balances was established over sea-based nuclear weapons.[13] These technical systems were buttressed by 'negative control' over nuclear weapons and delivery systems, and institutional checks such as the 'two-man rule', i.e., nuclear weapons from missile silos or submarines could be launched only with the coordinated actions of two separate individual commanders.[14] Over time, both superpowers had introduced different systems intended to avoid inadvertent nuclear attacks, and these measures provided reasonable assurances that an accidental war involving the superpowers would be averted.[15]

In retrospect, the political–technical–diplomatic preventive measures did work and mutual deterrence prevailed. A nuclear war between the superpowers and other nuclear powers was prevented despite some close calls.[16] Some say it was sheer luck, while others contend that it was the result of a prudent mixture of states-manship and actual politics that averted a global war.[17] Still others maintain that nuclear weapons just did not matter, as a third world war involving the major powers would not have occurred in any event.[18]

Post-Cold War relations among nuclear powers

Relations among the major powers have been substantially altered as a result of the end of the Cold War. The zero-sum competition that was characteristic of the Cold War era has become a muted political rivalry. The vital interests on which past great power conflicts occurred have become less salient in the day-to-day affairs of the major powers. During the early post-Cold War years, the major powers in some cases depreciated or devalued nuclear weapons as the key instrument for managing mutual relations and have opted for other means or assets to achieve their security objectives.[19] The latter include increased use of the United Nations and of multilateral sanctions including economic instruments of statecraft and coercion. Indiscriminate economic sanctions, as in the case of Iraq, have inflicted 'more damage than weapons of mass destruction', and they constitute 'an extreme case of mass destruction through economic warfare'.[20] In the short and medium terms, a nuclear war under the first five categories identified above has become less probable. Major nuclear arms reductions by the US and Russia and the removal of tactical nuclear weapons from most theaters of the world have also helped to improve stability in the international system. However, the sixth possible cause of nuclear war identified in this chapter, inadvertence and accidents, exists among all nuclear weapons states, old and new.

Let us discuss the probability of war under each of these categories in the post-Cold War era. Premeditated, preemptive and preventive attacks are most likely to occur during intense crises involving adversarial states that believe in the possibility of easy victory. During the past major power conflicts and in many minor power wars, such calculations were clearly present. If statesmen believe that they can gain quick victories at a low cost to themselves, war probability increases.[21] The near-unipolar power structure that emerged in the 1990s assured that no single power could unilaterally attempt to alter the international order through war or coercive means in the short and medium terms. Because of their possession of nuclear weapons, second-ranking nuclear powers know that the hegemonic power is unlikely to coerce them or challenge them beyond a point. Further, the dissatis-faction level required for a violent system change does not exist in the present-day world. None of the great powers, including China, professes revisionist ideologies of the Nazi, Fascist or even Stalinist varieties. The major powers most dissatisfied with the current international order are Russia and China, but they do not have the ideological fervor to initiate a catastrophic war. Russia did not fight a war to keep itself together, a war it could have waged as evident in its own history and the history of many declining empires. Although not completely integrated into the international order, China has gradually accepted many of the institutions, regimes and norms of the current world order.[22] It is also a beneficiary of increased economic interaction and is unlikely to go on the warpath, except for limited conflicts in the Taiwan Straits. Taiwan thus is the most likely source of conflict that would raise the risks of a US–China confrontation and even of a nuclear war, as the declaration of full independence by Taipei could provoke China to intervene militarily. However, China's attempt to forcibly occupy Taiwan could compel the US to act, lest the credibility of its power in East Asia and the protection it guarantees to allies would weaken substantially. War under these circumstances is a possibility but, even in this case, limited indirect engagements and brinkmanship crisis behavior are more in the realm of possibility. The common enemy of terrorism has, since the attacks on the US in September 2001, unified the three powers, at least in the short run. Russia has mellowed its opposition to the expansion of NATO eastward, while allowing the US to use Russian airspace for the airlift of American military and relief cargoes to Central Asian republics.[23]

The normative foundations against nuclear war have also been strengthened during the last five decades. The tradition of non-use or 'nuclear taboo' has probably been strengthened as a result of the end of the Cold War. The nuclear taboo is an unwritten prescriptive norm that prohibits a nuclear attack, i.e., that nuclear states shall not use their nuclear weapons, especially against non-nuclear states, even when it could be militarily beneficial to them to use these weapons.[24] However, the normative restraints have weakened somewhat as the nuclear weapons states follow through with their plans to target non-nuclear states in order to deter chemical or biological attacks by these states as well as by terrorist groups.

Although political relations among the major powers are at a fairly stable plateau, nuclear war cannot be completely ruled out as the politico-military doctrines of the nuclear powers still call for resort to nuclear attack under some contingencies. The US war-fighting doctrines underwent only very limited change under the Clinton Administration.[25] The US military strategy is still driven by fears of surprise attack, and allows the use of nuclear weapons as a hedge against surprise attacks and as a last resort weapon in case of a crisis involving Russia. Although the arms control agreements such as the Strategic Arms Reduction Treaties (START I and II) and the Strategic Offensive Reductions Treaty (SORT) of May 2002 would reduce the 5,000–6,000 odd US and Russian strategic warheads each down to 1,700–2,200 in a decade, there are questions regarding the value of these agreements. For instance, the SORT does not make it mandatory to destroy the removed warheads; instead they could be placed in storage and could be resurrected at some future point if political conditions warrant so.[26] In addition, 'both sides would still retain the capability in a crisis to deploy thousands of additional warheads by increasing warhead loadings on existing missiles and bombers'.[27] The US, in fact, sees value in maintaining nuclear weapons as part of the overall grand strategy to perpetuate its primacy in the international system. The US also wants to possess a high number of nuclear weapons in order to continue to offer extended deterrence to civilian powers like Germany and Japan so as to dissuade them from exercising the nuclear option.[28] Further, the US has also extended the use of nuclear weapons to deter chemical and biological attacks by selected developing countries labeled as 'rogue states' as well as by terrorist groups. According to one analysis, over a thousand targets of states with chemical, biological and nuclear programs are now selected for nuclear attack by the US for the purposes of deterrence.[29] Thus the US counter-proliferation strategy has inherent dangers of nuclear escalation, even if the US follows a conventional counterforce strategy.[30]

The end of the Cold War has not substantially reduced the 'usability paradox', i.e., 'the two central objectives of US policy – to deter aggression against the United States and its allies and to prevent accidental war require that the U.S. nuclear force be usable, but not too usable'.[31] Further, both Russia and the US are still driven by fears of surprise preventive and preemptive attacks, as evident in their continued maintenance of contingency planning, pre-delegation of authority to launch nuclear weapons in case the President is incapacitated, and the provisions for the movement of the political and bureaucratic elite into bunkers, which are supposedly able to withstand nuclear attack, enabling the top surviving decision-makers to carry on their retaliatory function.

The fear of preemptive attack bedevils the arms control postures of both the US and Russia. During the entire Cold War era, both these powers were deeply worried about 'windows of vulnerability', as evident in the positions they took during SALT and START negotiations. While negotiating SALT II, the US negotiators were worried about the Soviets surreptitiously slipping additional warheads on to their very large ICBMs 'in order to overwhelm' the US preemptively. During the START II negotiations, one of the US objectives was to 'eliminate all Russian ICBMs capable of carrying more than one warhead to prevent them being able to load up extra warheads for pre-emptive purposes'.[32] Russia and China's opposition to the US National Missile Defense (NMD) program, and their plans for mobile missiles all arise from the fear of preemptive and preventive attacks. These fears point to the worst case assumptions that characterize US–Russia security relations even after the end of the Cold War and the considerable improvement in political relations between the two states. Further, the extreme contingency thinking of their militaries inhibits these countries from developing military doctrines and strategies based on most-probable threat assessments.

All nuclear powers, except China and India, also officially adhere to a first use policy, i.e., they would launch a nuclear attack in case their opponent initiates a conventional war. Most prominent are the nuclear postures of the US, NATO alliance and Russia, which all adhere to a 'first use policy'. Russia, after maintaining a no-first use policy, reverted to it in 1993 under Boris Yeltsin in the face of a declining conventional military capability. In early 2000, in response to NATO's Kosovo war, Russia approved a new military doctrine and national security concept which reemphasized nuclear first use in response to large-scale conventional attack or to the use of nuclear or other types of weapons of mass destruction against it or its allies.[33]

The United States and NATO continue to maintain the first use policy because of the perceived 'benefits from a posture of calculated ambiguity. The implied threat of nuclear attack might be just what it takes to deter some would be aggressor.'[34] This policy is also touted as necessary to give teeth to extended deterrence as well as to deter chemical and biological attacks by 'rogue states' and terrorist groups. In fact, this adherence to first use posture is more for reasons of dogma than for much of a practical utility.[35]

Accidental wars

The probability of accidental or unauthorized use of nuclear weapons by the established nuclear powers still exists. There are several contingencies of this nature that were identified by a study on the future of US nuclear weapons policy by the National Academy of Sciences. Some of these contingencies arise from the 'alert' policies of the nuclear powers and the possible erroneous use of nuclear weapons, caused by hasty decision-making or false alarms and wrong signals. Although the Clinton–Yeltsin agreement of 1994 on de-targeting took away the day-to-day targeting of missiles, the danger still exists.[36] Possible examples of inadvertent nuclear war

> include a decision to launch nuclear weapons in response to false or ambiguous warning of actual or impending attack, or misinterpreting a demonstration shot, unauthorized attack, or an attack on another country as a massive attack on one's own country. The reported deterioration of Russia's missile attack warning system is particularly troubling in this regard.[37]

The alert policies of the US and Russia are of particular concern in this respect. 'Launch on warning' became the accepted policy of the superpowers, and these countries have pursued this policy beyond the Cold War.[38] The National Academy of Sciences study warns:

> Despite the end of the Cold War, both the United States and Russia maintain the technical capability, even during peacetime, to launch thousands of nuclear warheads on short notice. This is particularly true of the United States, which maintains two thirds of its submarines and virtually all of its land-based missiles in a high state of alert. Alert practices make deterrent forces immediately responsive, but they also increase the chances of an unauthorized or even accidental detonation of a nuclear

120

weapon and contribute to the possibility of triggering a war that neither side intends.[39]

Rapid reactions to nuclear threats could provoke a response even if it is based on erroneous warnings. The Russian forces are especially vulnerable to an attack by the more accurate US Trident, Minuteman and MX missiles. Such attacks could wipe out Russian command and control facilities in less than 20 minutes. In order to protect its largely land-based forces against a feared sudden attack, Russia relies heavily on a launch on warning strategy. The degradation of Russia's attack warning systems has compounded the problems that Moscow faces in this regard. Argues one analyst: 'By deploying relatively large, lethal, and alert forces to deter the increasingly improbable circumstances of a deliberate surprise Russian attack, the United States may prompt Russia to adopt a posture that greatly increases the risk of erroneous or unauthorized launch.'[40]

The end of the Cold War thus has not dramatically modified the complex organizational and procedural structures of American and Russian nuclear command and control systems. In fact, in Russia's case, this organizational structure has weakened in terms of the ability of the political leadership to exert effective control in peacetime and in crisis time. Given the exceedingly short reaction time that is available to decision-makers, there is all the more reason to worry about a 1914 scenario of misjudgments, miscalculations and strategic fatalism occurring in the future, especially in times of crisis involving third parties, this time of a larger magnitude.

Systemic changes and the prospects of major power nuclear war

Although a calculated or premeditated nuclear war involving the present-day major powers is unlikely to occur, systemic changes that can increase the prominence of nuclear weapons in the relations among the major powers do exist. These changes involve the status quo power, United States, rising powers, China and India, and the declining power Russia. The sources of these changes are largely political, military–technological and economic, the factors that power transition theorists have identified (see for instance Chapter 9 in this volume). In the near-term, the most prominent challenge to major power-based system stability will come from technological developments, especially those that favor the United States. While there can be an argument that structural factors are driving the technological competition, the causal arrow may sometimes be reversed, i.e., the structural competition pushes dominant actors to acquire capabilities in order to maintain or increase their preponderance and to prevent weaker actors from militarily challenging them while the introduction of new military capabilities results in more structural competition.

Missile defense systems and strategic stability

The technological changes that may favor the US are in the missile defense area and space-based weapons, as well as precision-guided munitions. Successful testing and deployment of national missile defense systems and theater missile defense systems could leapfrog the capabilities of the US while decreasing the power of the nuclear deterrent of other states that do not have matching systems. The RMA process is occurring in several areas and most of it favors the United States, at least in the short run. These areas include technological changes that allow for greater ability for surveillance, information processing and precision-guided targeting. The changes could affect the realm of social and organizational status of military forces and, more importantly, strategies and doctrines of the affected states.[41] Some critics argue that the US missile plans also derive from a desire to colonize space, the last frontier open to humankind.[42] Under these circumstances, China and Russia could devise countermeasures, such as increasing offensive weapons in their armory, and mining space with anti-communication satellite devices. These arms developments, involving China, would propel India to improve its nuclear capabilities as well, which in turn would put pressure on Pakistan to acquire more and more arms. In this climate of general arms race involving the nuclear-armed major powers and new nuclear powers, the probability of war occurrence, both advertent and inadvertent, could increase. An arms race in outer space would not only violate existing arms control agreements, but would also vitiate the general political and military climate of planet earth.

The probable consequences of a successful deployment of missile defenses by the US would be a stepping up of nuclear modernization by China which has already warned of a ten-fold increase in its twenty or so ICBM force in response to US deployment. Further, the deployment of theater missile defense (TMD) in Taiwan and Japan could provoke a crisis involving China and the US.[43] The Russian response to missile defenses was initially oppositional, but has mellowed over time. With Russia as a financially broken former superpower attempting to readjust to the changing realities and the common cause of terrorism binding the agendas of Washington and Moscow closer, Russia has agreed to the scrapping of the Anti-Ballistic Missile (ABM) Treaty. However, it is unlikely that barring major political accommodation, the Russian suspicions over NMD would fully disappear. Russian concerns arise from the fact that, despite US official assurances that the missile defense system is not aimed at Russia, once deployed, the system will weaken the potency of the Russian deterrent. Because of its deteriorating economic conditions, Russia will not be able to fully modernize its ICBMs in the near term. The United States, along with its defensive systems, will also retain several hundred accurate ICBMs and submarine-launched ballistic missiles (SLBMs) that would allow it first strike advantages. The Russians are especially concerned about Trident II SLBMs 'which could potentially exploit gaps in the crumbling Russian early warning system to attack and destroy each hardened target with little or no warning'. 'The planned C3 phase of the NMD, with its 200 to 250 interceptors, could appear as a direct threat to Russia's retaliatory capability.'[44]

Although not articulated in so many words, the NMD debate underlines an increasing lack of faith among some of the US military and political top brass in deterrence, based on mutual assured destruction (MAD). The doubts about deterrence have been aired in the context of the likely behavior of a regional rogue challenger state with nuclear-armed ICBMs and intermediate range ballistic missiles (IRBMs). Although the NMD plans come out of a stated desire to eliminate America's vulnerability to nuclear attacks by these states, they have effects that go beyond such regional powers. They create conditions for the US to assume strategic and offensive dominance, which would undermine the logic of deterrence. The nuclear states that perceive themselves to be the most vulnerable would opt for countermeasures, which in turn could create more strategic vulnerabilities. The spiral effect of acquisition of new systems could generate arms races and intensify the classic security dilemma problem, even though the affected great powers may be in a waiting mode for now.

Missile defenses and instability

The deployment of effective national and theater missile defense systems could have major consequences for strategic, crisis and arms race stability, the three pillars of the nuclear order in the Cold War era. This, in turn, could increase the probability of a nuclear war. Strategic stability meant the ability of both superpowers to mount a second strike even after absorbing a first strike. Crisis stability meant that neither side would be vulnerable to a preemptive strike during a crisis. Finally, arms race stability 'prevails when neither side fears that its opponent is developing weapons that could endanger strategic stability or crisis stability'.[45] Assuming that the end of the Cold War has diminished the prospects of instability in all these three areas, it is still possible that a new round of intense arms race can feed into rivalry and lead to further instability in the international system.

Long-term structural and systemic changes are most difficult to predict and have the most telling effect on weapons, strategy and the probability of war. There is somewhat of an agreement among systems theorists that the American dominance of the international system is a passing phase, and that some form of multipolarity is likely to occur, although they differ on the precise time-frame when this will happen. To some neo-realists, nuclear multipolarity brings in additional problems.[46]

The Russian strategy is still based on MAD and is likely to continue so for the foreseeable future even if the US abandons the concept. Russia's renewed enthusiasm for nuclear weaponry results from the realization of its political leadership that, in terms of conventional weaponry and capability, Russia is in a position of profound inferiority to the Western countries, especially the US. This does not necessarily mean that nuclear war is likely to happen. But the over-reliance on nuclear weapons by a weakened great power and a rising power shows that nuclear weapons are valued by these states for the role of 'great equalizers'. The disintegration of Russia's nuclear infrastructure is a particular source of concern. Over six thousand warheads are on hair-trigger alert in Russia, which are controlled by an early warning network of radars, satellites and computers that often functions partially or erratically. The country's command and control personnel are also affected by the socio-economic hardships and maladies of the society and are called upon to make decisions within a short period of warning time.[47] An incident in January 1995 forcefully reminded the world of the dangers of hair-trigger alerts by the nuclear powers, especially Russia. The Russian early warning system detected an unidentified ballistic missile over Norway, possibly heading for Russia, and the Russian commanders initiated the early phases of launch on warning procedures. For the first time, the Russian nuclear briefcase carried by the President was activated, an emergency telecommunications conference of the President and his national security advisers was held and the missile launch posts were given an alert broadcast. Nuclear attack was averted by only a few minutes when the missile was recognized as a Norwegian scientific research rocket.[48]

We have no assurance that geopolitical competition will end forever or that we have reached the historical endpoint in terms of ideological rivalries. One thing is certain, however, that the historical process of the rise and fall of great powers is likely to continue although we do not know the manner in which future transitions will occur. One does not have to be a structural realist to contend that the American primacy that is perhaps maintaining international order at the beginning of the twenty-first century is unlikely to last forever.

The new US national security strategy and nuclear use

Another major source of concern is the new US nuclear strategy vis-à-vis regional challengers. The US military planners seem to be prepared to consider using nuclear weapons against states possessing chemical, biological and nuclear weapons as these weapons are believed to have spread or are spreading to several states and possibly to terrorist groups. The 'calculated ambiguity' policy under the Bush (Sr) and Clinton Administrations was meant to deter the use of chemical or biological weapons by a regional adversary. The first Gulf War and the disclosures about Iraq's clandestine nuclear weapons program accelerated the adoption of the new policy. During the war, the US leaders made several references to the possibility of nuclear use in the event of Iraq using weapons of mass destruction against US troops or American allies. The top secret Nuclear Weapons Employment Policy (NUWEP) issued in January 1991 by the then Defense Secretary authorized the use of nuclear weapons under some circumstances.[49] The Presidential Decision Directive (PDD) 60 signed by Bill Clinton in November 1997 permits US nuclear strikes in retaliation against chemical or biological weapons use by enemy states.[50]

The Bush (Jr) Administration has enlarged the potential role for nuclear weapons by assigning three purposes to them: to deter, to preempt the use of WMDs – including chemical and biological weapons – and to prevent their buildup by new states. Thus the US could use nuclear weapons preemptively if it believes that a regional adversary is planning to use WMDs in the battlefield or against US troops stationed abroad. The preventive aspect implies that the US could prevent the contingency of a regional adversary developing WMD by attacking the WMD facilities early on before they become a security threat. Both the prevention and pre-emption urges are driven by the notion that deterrence is not workable against 'rogue states' and terrorist organizations.[51] If the adversary is hiding WMDs in deep bunkers or facilities that are not destroyable through conventional strikes, the US should keep the option of using all capabilities, including the bunker-buster mini-nukes, now under development. The terrorist attacks of September 2001 accelerated these changes. The new nuclear policy is embodied in the following documents: *The National Security Strategy of the United States of America* of September 2002, the *National Strategy to Combat Weapons of Mass Destruction* (NSCWMD) of December 2002 and *Presidential Directive 17*, signed 14 September 2002.[52] These new policies came to be tested prior to and during the 2003 Iraq War when military planners were understood to have studied a list of potential targets for the use of tactical nuclear weapons in response to or in order to preempt an Iraqi use of chemical or biological weapons or to destroy deeply buried command and control facilities.[53] The US officials also warned the Iraqi regime against the use of WMD by threatening to use any means necessary without ruling out nuclear retaliation.[54]

The US has accelerated the development of deep bunker-busting mini-nukes and earth-penetrating nuclear devices. The Robust Nuclear Earth Penetrator (RNEP) that the Pentagon proposed to the House and Senate Armed Services Committee in March 2003 is meant to destroy command and control facilities buried deep underground. Despite a Congressional ban on the development of low-yield weapons, the US weapons labs have continued their active research of such devices although their deployment is still restricted by Congressional opposition. Once proved to be feasible, deployment is likely to occur, especially if US domestic politics turns rightward further, which may be accelerated by possibilities of terrorist attacks and nuclear weapons development by North Korea and Iran.[55]

While the prospects of nuclear use by the US in regional theaters have increased, the new nuclear states, both declared and undeclared, generate another serious source of concern.

Prospects of nuclear war among the new nuclear states

The probability of a nuclear war involving the new nuclear states is perhaps higher than that among the old nuclear powers, although the apocalyptic and politically motivated predictions coming from military and intelligence establishments of the nuclear weapons states seem far-fetched. The prospects for nuclear stability among nuclear states are presented to be grim because of the higher likelihood of 'bolts from the blue', preventive and preemptive strikes in their intense conflict environments, characterized by intermittent crises. Moreover, the potentially dangerous stability–instability paradox exists in these regional theaters, somewhat higher than that which existed between the superpowers during the Cold War period. Glenn Snyder, who presented this paradox in the 1960s, argued that MAD at the strategic level allowed nuclear states to fight conventional wars at the sub-strategic level safely as they were assured that war would not escalate to the nuclear level.[56] A new nuclear state, anticipating no escalation to the nuclear level, as happened in South Asia in 1999, could push hard at the conventional level to achieve its tactical or political aims.[57]

Nuclear conflicts are also possible given the short flight time that characterizes the decision-making of the new nuclear states. If the US and Russia have twenty to thirty minutes to assess and make decisions on whether to retaliate or not to retaliate, India and Pakistan may have only five to ten minutes to do so. The problems are further complicated by the fact that one of these states, Pakistan, does not subscribe to a no-first use policy. Thus, in the South Asian asymmetric dyad, Pakistan poses a major risk of nuclear use. Its lack of civilian control, its military's obsession with Kashmir, its intense desire to balance India even when it has a numerical inferiority of five to one in most measures of capability, its willingness to engage in continuous crisis behavior even when such behavior is hurting its economy and societal fabric, all could be argued in support of the proposition that nuclear capability is not a guarantor of peace, but a source of instability in South Asia. Pakistan values nuclear weapons as a 'great equalizer' in its asymmetrical power relationship with India and relies on the threatened nuclear retaliation to prevent an Indian conventional attack deep into Pakistani territory.[58] The Pakistani military is known for its high risk-taking behavior and brinkmanship strategies, as evident in its limited war/guerrilla operations in Kargil in 1999.

Unlike Pakistan, whose military controls its nuclear arsenal, the Indian weapons are under civilian control. India has also made a no-first use pledge.[59] Despite this pledge, India may be forced to initiate a nuclear response first if a localized conflict cannot be contained in Kashmir and its conventional military operations need to be expanded and there is an impending danger of Pakistan using nuclear weapons. Under such circumstances, preemption could become a necessary alternative, even in the face of partial information that Pakistan is about to launch a nuclear attack. India's evolving conventional military doctrine is also problematic as, in the face of a Kargil type situation, it has contemplated engaging in 'hot pursuits' and 'limited conventional wars'.[60] Conventional escalation by India could pressure Pakistan to up the nuclear ante, for its first use strategy calls for such escalation. The virtual absence of arms control and confidence building measures between these two countries also causes concern. The strategic situation in South Asia urgently calls for effective technical and political measures to prevent an accidental or inadvertent nuclear war.

Israel is the third new nuclear state that holds a large number of nuclear weapons, perhaps more than that of India and Pakistan combined. It has maintained this arsenal since 1967 and has strengthened it over time. During two wars in which it was involved since then – 1973 and 1991 – it seems to have contemplated the use of nuclear weapons. However, during both crises, Israel did not cross the Rubicon, although some amount of temptation existed at different levels of the military and political elite. Analysts like Avner Cohen put the Israeli reluctance to use nuclear weapons down to the 'nuclear taboo'. Part of this may be explained by the fact that no existential threat to Israel existed during these crises, a condition which would have provoked an Israeli nuclear response.[61]

Despite the near-optimism of Israeli nuclear restraint, Israel remains a strong candidate to use nuclear weapons in an intense crisis involving Arab states such as Iraq or Syria. The fact that nuclear-armed Jericho missiles were mobilized for possible retaliation against Iraqi Scud missile attacks in 1991 suggests that, if Iraq had succeeded in inflicting heavy casualties or used chemical weapons as Scud warheads, Israel would have been under tremendous pressure to respond disproportionately, i.e., with nuclear weapons.[62] Although the Iraqi chemical attack would not have constituted an existential threat, enshrined in the Israeli military doctrine as the necessary condition for nuclear use, Israel would have been tempted to respond with nuclear weapons. In the volatile context of the Middle East, where Iraq, Iran and Syria all possess chemical weapons, nuclear retaliation by Israel in response to chemical or biological attack is not a total improbability. Further, Israel does not have to worry about an assured nuclear retaliation in the short or medium terms, as none of the Arab states possesses operational nuclear weapons.

The latest addition to the nuclear club, North Korea, also presents a major case of future nuclear war, given its intense militarized conflict with South Korea, and rivalry with the US and Japan. The reclusive North Korean regime could also engineer a nuclear crisis for diplomatic or economic bargaining with the US. In addition to North Korea, since September 2001, transnational terrorists have brought forth a new dimension to the nuclear war in the current international arena.

Terrorism and nuclear war

The September 2001 terrorist strikes in the United States brought into sharper focus the possibility of nuclear use by a terrorist group, by a state that sponsors such a group or by a nuclear state that wants to destroy such groups. The Al-Qaeda network under Osama Bin Laden has been attempting to buy nuclear weapons and materials from various sources, while some reports suggest that the network has already acquired crude bombs or bomb materials. In addition, Bin Laden has laid claims on Pakistan's nuclear weapons on the basis that he supported the Pakistani tests in 1998.[63] There is also the possibility of a nuclear-armed Pakistan disintegrating, with its nuclear weapons spreading to terrorist groups such as the Taliban, which have strong support within the Pakistani army and the intelligence service. If Islamic militants could gain access to these weapons, their possible use in conflict with India and the US cannot be ruled out. A related contingency is a possible preventive strike by the US or India on Pakistan's nuclear capability if these countries see an imminent possibility of nuclear weapons falling into terrorist hands. If such a group as Bin Laden's acquires nuclear weapons and succeeds in using them against a nuclear state, the pressure on the nuclear state to retaliate in kind could arise. This contingency, although far-fetched until September 2001, seems not inconceivable in the future. The impact of nuclear use by a group for cataclysmic terrorist strikes could be much higher than the September 11 airplane strikes in the US.

Part of the reason for grave concern in this matter is that, unlike state actors, terrorist groups that hold millenarian views may not be deterred from using nuclear weapons or nuclear materials in the furtherance of the particular creed or ideology they propagate. The deterrence logic, predicated on rationality, may not apply to these groups. Compellence and deterrence are most relevant in the context of state to state interactions where rationality often prevails among decision-makers. The deterrence logic is premised on the implicit assumption that 'avoiding societal destruction represented an instrumental limit on rational action. The universal view of deterrence can be challenged therefore by recognizing the possibility that there may be societal conceptions of rational behavior that instrumentally include the potential for societal destruction' in the pursuit of millenarian goals.[64] Studies on terrorism suggest that, while formerly terrorist groups were often small collections of individuals engaged in selective and discriminate acts of violence in order to further a political or ideological cause, in recent years the motivations and capabilities of terrorist groups have become more transcendental with global reach. It seems the new terrorists do not mind using cataclysmic events to propagate their goals. This change from instrumental terrorism to transcendental terrorism means nuclear weapons are valuable assets for a group fighting for millenarian causes.[65]

Conclusions

Whether a nuclear war among the great powers or between the new nuclear states will occur or not is a highly conjectural question. This chapter has identified the plausible scenarios under which war would have happened during the Cold War period and the possibility of nuclear war occurring under such conditions in the post-Cold War era. In the post-Cold War environment, nuclear war among states was fairly ruled out under the premeditated, preventive and preemptive strike categories, but the possibility of accidental or inadvertent wars does exist. Nuclear war involving non-state actors and their state sponsors is a possibility in the emerging scenarios of global conflict dynamics. Finally, the long-term prospects of nuclear war as a result of systemic and structural changes have been discussed as these changes could arise from power transitions, military–technological changes, and economic forces.

Acknowledgment

I thank Alan Dowty, Baldev Nayar, Raimo Väyrynen and David Welch for their comments on an earlier version of this chapter.

Notes

1 On the distinction between general and immediate deterrence, see P. M. Morgan, *Deterrence: A Conceptual Analysis* (Beverly Hills: Sage Publications, 1977), pp. 30–1. See also, P. Morgan, *Deterrence Now* (Cambridge: Cambridge University Press, 2003).

2   On these crises, see B. McGeorge, *Danger and Survival* (New York: Random House, 1988).

3   D. Frei and C. Catrina, *Risks of Unintentional Nuclear War* (Totowa: Allanheld Osmun, 1983); C. L. Glaser, *Analyzing Strategic Nuclear Policy* (Princeton: Princeton University Press, 1990), p. 112; B. G. Blair, *Strategic Command and Control: Redefining the Nuclear Threat* (Washington DC: The Brookings Institution, 1985), p. 17.

4   R. N. Lebow, *Nuclear Crisis Management: A Dangerous Illusion* (Ithaca: Cornell University Press, 1987), pp. 25, 32.

5   On this, see T. C. Schelling, *The Strategy of Conflict* (Cambridge: Harvard University Press, 1960), pp. 207–29.

6   Glaser, *Analyzing Strategic Nuclear Policy*, p. 112.

7   On how this concern enters the deployment patterns of the US in the context of the MX ICBM missiles, see S. Turner, *Caging the Nuclear Genie: An American Challenge for Global Security* (Boulder: Westview Press, 1997), pp. 42–3.

8   On this, see R. N. Lebow and J. G. Stein, 'Nuclear Lessons of the Cold War', in K. Booth (ed.), *Statecraft and Security: The Cold War and Beyond* (Cambridge: Cambridge University Press, 1998), pp. 71–86.

9   W. Burr and J. T. Richelson, 'Whether to "Strangle the Baby in the Cradle": The United States and the Chinese Nuclear Program, 1960–64', *International Security*, 25, 1 (2000), pp. 54–99.

10 The Israeli attack on the Osiraq facility of Iraq in 1981 and the US-led coalition's attack on Iraq in 1991 constitute examples of military strikes driven by the preventive logic. Iraq could not retaliate with nuclear weapons presumably because it had not fabricated an effective bomb yet.

11 On this, see S. D. Sagan, *The Limits of Safety: Organizations, Accidents and Nuclear Weapons* (Princeton: Princeton University Press, 1993); B. G. Blair, *The Logic of Accidental Nuclear War* (Washington DC: The Brookings Institution, 1993).

12 Lebow, *Nuclear Crisis Management*, p. 26.

13 S. D. Sagan, *Moving Targets* (Princeton: Princeton University Press, 1989), pp. 138–9. See also, A. B. Carter, J. D. Steinbruner and C. A. Zraket (eds), *Managing Nuclear Operations* (Washington DC: The Brookings Institution, 1987).

14 Lebow, *Nuclear Crisis Management*, p. 40. See also P. Bracken, *The Command and Control of Nuclear Forces* (New Haven: Yale University Press, 1983).

15 Accidental war was still possible as evident from the several incidents involving nuclear weapons that occurred during the Cold War era. The crashing of a B-52 bomber carrying two hydrogen bombs near Golsboro, North Carolina in January 1961 and the June 1980 wrong warning of the launching of Soviet SLBMs by a faulty North American Aerospace Defense Command (NORAD) warning system are some examples. The latter incident resulted in the US initiating preliminary preparations for a nuclear response, which was removed after realizing the technical failure. For these incidents, see Sagan, *Moving Targets*, p. 145.

16 Blair, *The Logic of Accidental Nuclear War*, p. 9.

17 The nuclear revolution has been unparalleled as it drastically altered the meaning of 'victory'. R. Jervis, *The Meaning of the Nuclear Revolution: Statecraft and the Prospect of Armageddon* (Ithaca: Cornell University Press, 1989), pp. 5–8.

18 J. Mueller, 'The Escalating Irrelevance of Nuclear Weapons', in T. V. Paul, R. Harknett and J. Wirtz (eds), *The Absolute Weapon Revisited: Nuclear Arms and the Emerging International Order* (Ann Arbor: University of Michigan Press, 1998), pp. 73–98.

19 P. J. Garrity, 'The Depreciation of Nuclear Weapons in International Politics: Possibilities, Limits, Uncertainties', *Journal of Strategic Studies*, 14, 4 (1991), p. 465. Further, several technologically capable states have chosen to forswear nuclear weapons. On this, see T. V. Paul, *Power versus Prudence: Why Nations Forgo Nuclear Weapons* (Montreal and Kingston: McGill-Queen's University Press, 2000).

20 J. Mueller and K. Mueller, 'The Methodology of Mass Destruction: Assessing Threats in the New World Order', *Journal of Strategic Studies*, 23, 1 (2000), p. 180.

21 S. V. Evera, *Causes of War: Power and the Roots of Conflict* (Ithaca: Cornell University Press, 1999), pp. 14–34. Even weaker opponents went to war, expecting war would be limited and that massive reprisals would not take place, T. V. Paul, *Asymmetric Conflicts: War Initiation by Weaker Powers* (Cambridge: Cambridge University Press, 1994), pp. 24–9.

22 S. Chan, 'Chinese Perspectives on World Order', in T. V. Paul and J. A. Hall (eds), *International Order and the Future of World Politics* (Cambridge: Cambridge University Press, 1999), pp. 197–212.

23 P. E. Tyler, 'Russia and U.S. Optimistic on Defense Issues', www.nytimes.com, 19 October 2001.

24 On the taboo, see T. V. Paul, 'Nuclear Taboo and War Initiation in Regional Conflicts', *Journal of Conflict Resolution*, 39 (1995), pp. 696–717; N. Tannenwald, 'The Nuclear Taboo', *International Organization*, 53 (1999), pp. 433–68.

25 An overemphasis on counterforce still dominates US policy. See E. Mlyn, 'U.S. Nuclear Policy and the End of the Cold War', in Paul, Harknett and Wirtz (eds), *The Absolute Weapon Revisited*, pp. 137–66.

26 For these treaties, see www.armscontrol.org/act/2002_06/factfilejune02.asp.

27 National Academy of Sciences, Committee on International Security and Arms Control, *The Future of U.S. Nuclear Weapons Policy* (Washington DC: National Academy Press, 1997), p. 28.

28 M. Mastanduno, 'Nuclear Weapons and US Grand Strategy Today', in D. G. Haglund (ed.), *Pondering NATO's Nuclear Options* (Kingston: Queens Quarterly, 1999), pp. 59–79.

29 B. G. Blair, *Global Zero Alert for Nuclear Forces* (Washington DC: The Brookings Institution, 1995), p. 7. Despite high hopes of change in nuclear policy, the 1994 Nuclear Posture Review (NPR) left intact most of the previous Bush Administration's nuclear policy. Mlyn, 'U.S. Nuclear Policy and the End of the Cold War', p. 204; J. E. Nolan, *An Elusive Consensus: Nuclear Weapons and American Security after the Cold War* (Washington DC: Brookings Institution Press, 1999), pp. 58–9.

30 J. J. Wirtz, 'Counterproliferation, Conventional Counterforce and Nuclear War', *Journal of Strategic Studies*, 23, 1 (2000), pp. 5–23.

31 Sagan, *Moving Targets*, p. 4.

32 Turner, *Caging the Nuclear Genie*, p. 91.

33 For these documents, see A. G. Arbatov, 'The Transformation of Russian Military Doctrine: Lessons Learned from Kosovo and Chechnya', *The Marshall Center Papers*, 2 (2000), p. 36.

34 Turner, *Caging the Nuclear Genie*, p. 77.

35 On how the first use dogma got well entrenched in NATO, see J. D. Steinbruner and L. V. Segal (eds), *Alliance Security: NATO and the No-First Use Question* (Washington DC: The Brookings Institution, 1983); J. Mendelsohn, 'NATO's Nuclear Weapons: The Rationale for No-first Use', *Arms Control Today*, July/August (1999), pp. 3–8.

36 How fragile these promises are, and how susceptible they are to changing political relations, was brought home in April 1999 when President Yeltsin ordered re-targeting of strategic missiles against states engaged in the bombing of Yugoslavia. Arbatov, 'The Transformation of Russian Military Doctrine', p. 29.

37 *The Future of U.S. Nuclear Weapons Policy*, p. 17. The possibilities of theft as well as unauthorized use of nuclear weapons also exist, due largely to the decline in the morale of Russian military forces. Ibid.

38 Blair, *The Logic of Accidental Nuclear War*, p. 173.

39 *The Future of U.S. Nuclear Weapons Policy*, p. 41.

40 Ibid.; Blair, *Global Zero Alert*, p. 4.

41 P. M. Morgan, 'The Impact of the Revolution in Military Affairs', *Journal of Strategic Studies*, 23, 1 (2000), pp. 132–61; B. Owens, *Lifting the Fog of War* (New York: Farrar, Strauss, Giroux, 2000), pp. 15–16.

42 J. Valleau, 'The Final Frontier', *Globe and Mail* (Toronto), 15 January 2001, p. A9. The twenty-first century is likely to see the gradual militarization of space, with the US taking the lead and other states like Russia, China, India and Japan following suit. The possible weapons systems for deployment may include anti-satellite weapons and space-based lasers intended to destroy missiles and targets on earth. 'Escalating Space Race', www.stratfor.com, 5 January 2001.

43 D. Shambaugh, 'Facing Reality in China Policy', *Foreign Affairs*, 80, January/February (2001), p. 52.

44 G. Lewis, L. Gronlund and D. Wright, 'National Missile Defense: An Indefensible System', *Foreign Policy*, 117, winter (1999/2000), p. 131.

45 L. V. Sigal, 'No First Use and NATO's Nuclear Posture', in J. D. Steinbruner and L. V. Sigal (eds), *Alliance Security: NATO and the No-First Use Question* (Washington DC: The Brookings Institution, 1983), p. 107. On the NMD controversy, see K. S. McMahon, *Pursuit of the Shield: The U.S. Quest for Limited Ballistic Missile Defense* (Lanham: University Press of America, 1997), p. 48. See also M. O'Hanlon, 'Star Wars Strike Back', *Foreign Affairs*, 78, November/December (1999), pp. 68–82.

46 See K. Waltz, 'The Emerging Structure of International Politics', *International Security*, 18, 2 (1993), pp. 44–79; C. Layne, 'The Unipolar Illusion: Why New Great Powers Will Rise?', *International Security*, 17, 4 (1993), p. 7.

47 Moreover, Russian politicians and commanders have on several occasions raised the specter of nuclear attack to quell the uprising in Chechnya. S. F. Cohen, *Failed Crusade: America and the Tragedy of Post-Communist Russia* (New York: W.W. Norton, 2000), pp. 200–2. Russia's poor training of personnel and low maintenance of equipment was clearly evident in the sinking of the nuclear powered cruise missile submarine, the *Kursk*, in the Barents Sea in August 2000. On Russia, see also, A. M. Khazanov, 'A State without a Nation? Russia after Empire', in T. V. Paul, G. J. Ikenberry and J. A. Hall (eds), *The Nation-State in Question* (Princeton: Princeton University Press, 2003), pp. 79–105.

48 H. A. Feiveson (ed.), *The Nuclear Turning Point* (Washington DC: The Brookings Institution Press, 1999), p. 4; R. Green, *The Naked Nuclear Emperor* (Christchurch: The Disarmament and Security Center, 2000), p. 7.

49 Cited in H. M. Kristensen, 'Nuclear Futures: Proliferation of Weapons of Mass Destruction and U.S. Nuclear Strategy', *BASIC Research Report*, March (1998), p. 10.

50 R. J. Smith, 'Clinton Directive Changes Strategy on Nuclear Arms', *The Washington Post*, 7 December 1997, p. A01.

51 J. J. Wirtz and J. A. Russell, 'U.S. Policy on Preventive War and Preemption', *The Nonproliferation Review*, spring (2003), pp. 113–23.

52 US President, 'The National Security Strategy of the United States of America', www.whitehouse.gov/nsc/nss.pdf, September 2002, p. 15; US White House, 'National Strategy to Combat Weapons of Mass Destruction', www.whitehouse.gov/news/releases/2002/12/WMDStrategy.pdf, December 2002, p. 3.

53 N. Kralev, 'Bush Approves Nuclear Response', *The Washington Times*, 31 January 2003.

54 P. Ritcher, 'U.S. Weighs Tactical Nuclear Strike on Iraq', www.latimes.com, 26 January 2003; 'U.S. Warns Iraq over Using Mass Destruction Arms', www.reuters.com, 26 January 2003.

55 *The Washington Post*, 7 March 2003, p. A25.

56 G. Snyder, 'The Balance of Power and the Balance of Terror', in P. Seabury (ed.), *The Balance of Power* (San Francisco: Chandler, 1965), pp. 184–205.

57 On the debate between proliferation optimists and pessimists see J. W. Knopf, 'Recasting the Proliferation Optimism–Pessimism Debate', *Security Studies*, 12, autumn (2002), pp. 41–96; D. J. Karl, 'Proliferation Pessimism and Emerging Nuclear Powers', *International Security*, 21, 3 (1996/97), pp. 87–119.

58 For the Pakistani nuclear calculations, see Z. I. Cheema, 'Pakistan's Nuclear Use Doctrine and Command and Control', in P. R. Lavoy, S. D. Sagan and J. J. Wirtz (eds), *Planning the Unthinkable: How New Powers will Use Nuclear, Biological and Chemical Weapons* (Ithaca: Cornell University Press, 2000), pp. 158–81.

59 For an analysis of India's no-first use policy, see K. Bajpai, 'India's Nuclear Posture after Pokhran II', *International Studies*, 37, October–December (2000), pp. 267–301.

60 Defense Minister G. Fernandes, 'Presentation', *on the National Seminar on Challenges of Limited War*, New Delhi, Institute for Defense Studies and Analysis, 5–6, January 2000.

61 On this, see A. Cohen, 'Nuclear Arms in Crisis under Secrecy: Israel and the Lessons of the 1967 and 1973 Wars', in P. R. Lavoy, S. D. Sagan and J. J. Wirtz (eds), *Planning the Unthinkable: How New Powers will Use Nuclear, Biological and Chemical Weapons* (Ithaca: Cornell University Press, 2000), pp. 104–24.

62 For this analysis, see D. A. Welch, 'The Politics and Psychology of Restraint: Israeli Decision-making in the Gulf War', in J. G. Stein and L. W. Pauly (eds), *Choosing to Cooperate: How States Avoid Loss* (Baltimore: Johns Hopkins University Press, 1993), pp. 128–69.

63 P. Webster and R. Watson, 'Bin Laden's Nuclear Threat', *The Times* (London), 26 October 2001. Bin Laden's terrorist network has been known to make several attempts to acquire nuclear materials from Russia, South Africa and Europe; *The Gazette* (Montreal), 15 October 2001, p. B8; cgi.refiff.com/cgi-program/print/printpage.cgi, 10/16/ 2001.

64 W. C. Martel, 'Deterrence and Alternative Images of Nuclear Possession', in T. V. Paul, R. Harknett and J. Wirtz (eds), *The Absolute Weapon Revisited: Nuclear Arms and the Emerging International Order* (Ann Arbor: University of Michigan Press, 1998), pp. 213–34.

65 B. Hoffman, 'Terrorism Trends and Prospects', in I. O. Lesser (ed.), *Countering the New Terrorism* (Santa Monica: Rand Corporation, 1999), pp. 7–38.

Part III

THE INTERNATIONAL
SYSTEM AND INSTITUTIONS

6

THE DECLINE OF INTERSTATE WAR

Pondering systemic explanations

Kalevi J. Holsti

If major war is becoming obsolete, what properties in the international system can help explain the trend? We must raise several questions about the obsolescence of war before we enter the realm of explanation. In his justly famous book, John Mueller is not entirely clear on what constitutes a 'major' war.[1] In places he implies that it would be a war between the Soviet Union and the United States. In others he suggests that any war in the 'developed world' would qualify as major. Important questions on methodology and criteria for inclusion and exclusion remain, as Chapter 3 suggests.[2] However, if we delete the 'major' criterion and use the more traditional definition of war as organized and publicly authorized violence between established states (interstate war) involving a minimum of 1,000 casualties, then we can see significant trends.

The figures in Table 6.1 are reasonably stark. On one hand, interstate wars break out more frequently today (every 1.5 years since 1991) compared to the nineteenth century (every 3.4 years), but raw incidence is misleading because there are many more states in the central system today than in nineteenth century Europe. The probabilities or risks of war for any state in an average year have declined significantly since the era of early modern Europe, from one chance in 59 in the period after the Westphalia treaties (1648–1714) to only one chance in 250 today. In so far as classical interstate war (including armed interventions) is concerned, the world is significantly safer today than in any previous period since 1495. Obsolescence does not mean obsolete, however; interstate wars still occur with regularity, but they have not kept up with the growth in the number of states.

If we disaggregate the global numbers by region, we can locate those areas of the world where obsolescence is tending toward the obsolete, and those where major war remains a distinct possibility. Although there have been numerous militarized crises and a few brief border skirmishes with casualties in the hundreds, there has been no sustained war in South America since 1942. There has been no armed conflict in North America since 1916 when the United States invaded Mexico. The Caribbean and Central America, in contrast, have been areas of repeated American armed interventions, though not formal wars. If we exclude the Balkans, there has

Table 6.1 Incidence of interstate wars (central system), 1495–2003*

Period	Average no. of states in central system	No. central system interstate wars	Onset of interstate war, every	Interstate wars per state per year	Risk of war involvement by state per year
1495–1600	18	40	2.6 years	0.021	1 in 48
1648–1714	20	22	3.0 years	0.017	1 in 59
1715–1814	19	36	2.8 years	0.019	1 in 53
1815–1914	21	29	3.4 years	0.015	1 in 67
1918–1941	30	25	0.9 years	0.036	1 in 28
1945–1990	145	38	1.2 years	0.006	1 in 167
1991–2003	181	8**	1.5 years	0.004	1 in 250

Source: Adapted and amended from Q. Wright, *A Study of War* (Chicago: University of Chicago Press, 1965), pp. 641–2; K. J. Holsti, *The State, War, and the State of War* (Cambridge: Cambridge University Press, 1996), p. 24; and K. J. Holsti, *Taming the Sovereigns: Institutional Change in International Politics* (Cambridge: Cambridge University Press, 2004), Table 10.2.

Notes:
* Excludes European imperial expansion wars, wars among or against non-members of the central state system (e.g., Boxer rebellion, nineteenth century wars in Latin America), post-1945 wars of 'national liberation', or internal wars. The list includes armed interventions resulting in significant loss of life.
** The 1991 Gulf War, Yugoslavia–Croatia, Yugoslavia–Bosnia, Kosovo, Eritrea–Ethiopia, Nagorno–Karabakh, Afghanistan, and US coalition–Iraq.

been no war in continental Europe since 1945, and the probabilities of such are difficult to imagine. Russia and its peripheries have seen a good deal of military activity since the end of the Cold War, but nothing that could be classified as a major war. Central Asia and the Middle East are the regions with the highest incidence of armed conflict since 1945 and continue to be the scenes of armed interventions, wars, and high tensions.

Africa has remained remarkably free of interstate wars since the colonies became independent. The recent border war between Eritrea and Ethiopia and the numerous armed interventions into the Congo quagmire have marred that record. The first was relatively brief and contained to a specific and limited region. The latter is likely to continue indefinitely because of state and leadership weakness in the Congo.

South Asia contains the perennial India–Pakistan problem that has broken out in war three times already and is the most likely scene of a limited nuclear war in future. Southeast Asia since the Vietnam War has become pacified in terms of interstate relations, although serious territorial disputes with China over the Paracel and Spratly islands remain unresolved. East Asia, including China, Japan, Taiwan, and the Koreas, remains an area of unsolved issues, increased military spending, high tensions, occasional saber rattling, and probabilities of war that are significantly higher than those in Europe or Russia and its peripheries. Any war there, moreover, would have a high probability of escalation.

When we survey the world in these regional terms, the probabilities of major war seem to be low and receding in the Western Hemisphere, Southeast Asia,

Africa, and Europe. East Asia, South Asia, and the Middle East constitute the major danger zones of interstate wars, whereas domestic wars, civil wars, and secessionist wars remain significant problems in Africa, the Middle East, and Central Asia.

Of the lengthy list of changes in the international system that could be linked to the decline or obsolescence of interstate war,[3] this chapter will concentrate on four types: ideas, norms, power distributions, and social learning. I approach each as a systemic rather than actor characteristic.

Changes in the international system: the role of ideas

European history since at least the fifteenth century has been characterized as a struggle between two visions of a political order: a hierarchical, organic unity under central direction – as it was at least symbolically during much of the mediaeval period – and an anarchical realm comprised of sovereign states. The mediaeval papacy and Holy Roman Empire gave expression to the first design; the Treaty of Westphalia laid some of the foundations for the second. The idea of a Europe united under some form of hegemony has never died, and indeed has been a major source of all of Europe's major wars since the early sixteenth century. There were first the aspirations of Charles V, the Holy Roman Emperor who sought to reinvigorate the Empire's juridical and political predominance in large parts of Europe. This meant re-establishing a hegemony it had shared with the papacy until approximately the thirteenth century. A second challenge came in the early seventeenth century. One of the major issues of the Thirty Years War (1618–1648) was the widespread fear of the Habsburg search for 'universal monarchy' and the imposition of Catholic supremacy in Protestant domains. We must remember that the Peace of Westphalia was as much a religious document as one enshrining the historic rights of the estates of the Empire. It in effect guaranteed certain rights for Christian religious minorities (tolerance), and reduced the power of the Empire so that it could never again challenge the emerging European sovereign states.

Louis XIV offered the next threat to the Westphalian system of political decentralization. His attempt to join the French and Spanish Bourbon crowns led to Europe's next major conflagration, the War of the Spanish Succession (1702–1713). Whether Louis sought to reunite Europe under a single crown remains a matter of debate, but clearly his enemies feared him as a potential European hegemon and branded his diplomacy and expansionist dynastic and territorial claims as inconsistent with the provisions of the Westphalia settlement.

Napoleon represented the next assault on the Westphalian system. He carved up, annexed, reconfigured, partitioned, and sold territory as if it were a personal possession. His proclivity for placing his commoner relatives on various thrones throughout the continent (including Spain) represented an assault and insult to European monarchical sensibilities and their support in the doctrine of divine right. Napoleon's plan for Europe looked distinctly like a family and Paris-based empire, where the norms associated with sovereignty would become hollow and symbolic at best. He treated his conquests and erstwhile allies (usually allied through compulsion rather than free consent) as parts of an empire rather than as equal sovereign states.[4] The Napoleonic wars involved not only new military strategies and tactics, but also systematic looting and draconian occupation policies that violated the notions of tolerance and political pluralism incorporated in the Westphalia treaties. Here was another instance of one man's dreams for unifying Europe clashing with the principles and practices of political fragmentation and tolerance.

We move forward yet another century until the next attempt at establishing hegemony over Europe. Debate about Germany's war aims in 1914 continues, but the peace imposed on Bolshevik Russia at Brest-Litovsk in 1918 indicates that Germany's purposes were not consistent with the Westphalian settlement. It sought not just to rectify a few borders or to gain access to strategic points, but to provide a basis for a clear hegemony over the continent. At the same time, the Bolshevik leaders were dreaming of world revolution and the total destruction of the Westphalian system, a system that had spawned the great European, American, Japanese, and Russian imperial expansion of the late nineteenth century. The Bolsheviks renounced the Tsar's debts, violated numerous norms dealing with diplomatic immunities and privileges, and openly promoted and sustained revolutionary activities in other countries. By the early 1920s, however, the Bolshevik commitment to an anti-Westphalian world revolution petered out, as economic weakness forced Lenin and his successors to emphasize 'socialism in one country' and to seek entry into the club of states.

Adolph Hitler represented the next, and probably the last, attempt to unify Europe by force of arms. He denounced Westphalian principles such as sovereignty, non-intervention, political tolerance, and numerous doctrines of international law.[5] He sought to build a hierarchical order centered on the dominion of the Aryan/ Teutonic races, with the Slavs at the bottom of the pyramid. Jews, homosexuals, gypsies, and other undesirables were to be exterminated. This dream (and its imperial Roman or Confucian prototypes in Italy and Japan) and the military assault it inspired, ended up costing 50 million lives, the political collapse of Europe and Japan, and the emergence of the Soviet Union and the United States as the two new world powers. What is particularly notable in the Hitler saga is the consistency between his main ideas of world order and his actions. Between the publication of *Mein Kämpf* (1922) and his attack on Poland in 1939, he altered strategic and tactical plans, but he never lost sight of his long-range dreams. We cannot appreciate the historical significance of Hitler and World War II without understanding Hitler's main political ideas. Ideas were the sources of his behavior; power relations were just the means.

Ideas also played a role in the major Western imperial expansion of the late nineteenth and early twentieth centuries. Though these did not lead to major wars defined in Eurocentric terms, the numbers of native civilians killed in 'pacifying' operations numbered in the millions. Zero-sum strategic expansionism was the predominant structural characteristic of modern imperialism.[6] It is unlikely, however, that the British, French, American, and Germans would have become involved throughout the peripheries of the world, as well as some centers such as China, had their policy-makers not been imbued with paternalistic ideas about Europe's civilizing mission, the duty to uplift the less fortunate, and a missionary zeal to eradicate primitive and repugnant practices by savages, barbarians, and pagans. Not the least of the ideas promoting imperialism was the crusade to end slavery. Finally, a number of Darwinian and racist ideas helped sustain the great costs of imperial expansion.[7]

If great men and their ideas account in part for the incidence and location of Europe's great wars, then recent changes in the contemporary discourses of international politics provide substantial support for Mueller's thesis. There are no prominent leaders today who espouse ideas and purposes that seek to transcend or replace the essential characteristics of the Westphalian system. We have no contemporary counterparts to Charles V, Louis XIV, Napoleon, or Hitler. The dream of world revolution pretty much ended in the early 1920s, although it was official Soviet doctrine until the Gorbachev era. Soviet leaders, however, frequently pushed further into the future the time when we could have expected the demise of imperialism, capitalism, and the states system it sustained. With the fall of the Berlin Wall and Gorbachev's announcement of the 'Sinatra Doctrine' – an eminently Westphalian concept that allows countries to 'do it their way' – the Bolshevik dream of transcending the states system came officially to an end.

Those states that might be problematic in the future, including Russia and China, evidence no characteristics reminiscent of Louis XIV, Napoleon, Hitler, or Stalin. They seek to operate *within* the system, not to destroy it. China's entry to the WTO, Russia's inclusion in the G-8, and many other acts reveal calculations that the best way to promote their domestic and international interests is through present international institutions and organizations, rather than through revolutionary activities. Would-be regional potentates such as Saddam Hussein or Muammar Qaddafi have been removed from office by armed intervention, or have been diplomatically isolated. The heroes of our era – if we have any – include Nelson Mandela, Julius Nyerere, Jean Monnet, and Itzak Rabin. They bear no relationship to the role models of Hitler or Stalin. Their dreams have been of peace, reconciliation, and development, not conquest, racial superiority, or violent revolution. Other candidates such as Ayatollah Khomeini have had little influence outside of their homeland. Muslim extremists have gained transnational notoriety and popularity in the past few years, but their agenda has been more to harm and destroy than to build the intellectual edifice of an alternative world vision.

To this point I have emphasized the ideas and dreams of leaders and statesmen. But ideas about war are also cultural; they float around and dominate the popular imagination. In the past two centuries, we have witnessed dramatic changes in popular thinking about war. The arts and literature of the seventeenth and eighteenth centuries portrayed war as a heroic, virtuous activity that brought fame, *majesté*, and *gloire* to kings and potentates. Dissent followed in the form of the early peace societies, but in this era they were popularly regarded as groups of cranks and misfits. By the late nineteenth century, a variety of social Darwinists, racists, and cultural imperialists were convinced that war was a mighty regenerative tonic for societies reeling under the impact of industrialization, democracy, secularism, and social degeneracy.[8] Hitler, Mussolini, and the Japanese military resurrected a variety of militaristic slogans and attempted to inculcate a spirit of *amour de guerre* throughout their societies. But the disasters of the Great War effectively de-bellicized most of the rest of Europe. Peace societies flourished, universities developed courses and degree programs around the great issues of peace and war, and in popular discourse and the arts, war was increasingly portrayed as a tragedy, horrible mistake, curse, disease, or evil. World War II and the obliteration of Hiroshima and Nagasaki effectively undermined most cults of warrior virtue.

These changing ideas about war were not shared universally, as the great task of decolonization required popular mobilization and in at least nineteen cases, prolonged wars of national liberation. Major theorists of 'people's' war such as Mao Tse-tung, Regis Debray, and Nguyen Vo Giap, apologists for anti-colonial violence such as Franz Fanon, and some Muslim extremists praised war for its revolutionary or religious inspiration, but did not glorify it as an enduring and redeeming activity, as eighteenth century analysts and Hitler had done. Nor did they lionize national aggrandizement – interstate war – as a means of empire building.

Mueller is thus largely correct to emphasize the ideational and cultural context of war. War is an international institution in the sense that it is surrounded and supported by ideas and norms. And these have changed significantly in the past century. They are a necessary part of any explanation of the decline in major war incidence.

But Mueller does not believe that the developing world has yet embraced the anti-war ethic. War within the Third World remains a serious problem. He has been joined by a number of analysts who predicted that the post-Cold War international system would be characterized by 'the coming anarchy', a 'new world disorder', and 'zones of peace and zones of turmoil'.[9] Major war would be more not less likely in such an environment. But these authors implicitly expressed old Western imperial thinking habits. They constructed the Third World as a zone of ceaseless conflict, calamity, and disaster, continuing a long tradition of portraying non-European peoples as exotic at best, and more typically savage, unstable, bloodthirsty, and violent. They supported such visions by suddenly discovering 'ethnic wars', wars that supposedly broke out because the overlay of the Cold War was now gone. The superpowers had imposed a bit of order in the world, and with their strategic withdrawal from many areas of the Third World, primordial hatreds were ready to take over.

The problem with this type of analysis is that these 'ethnic' wars – often a serious mislabeling – began long before the end of the Cold War. They were largely invisible in the West because strategic analysts here had been so mesmerized with the Cold War and its strategic problems that they ignored or were blind to domestic wars in Burma (starting in 1962), Sri Lanka (1983), Nigeria (1967), and many other places. These wars had a great deal to do with the legacies of colonialism and the weakness of states, but the important point is that they were predominantly civil wars and/or wars of secession, and not interstate wars. In fact, if the Third World is indeed a zone of turmoil or anarchy, why have there been so few interstate wars in this vast region? The record of interstate warfare in the Third World is more favorable than the record of interstate war throughout European history until 1945. In fact, genuine interstate wars within the Third World have been relatively scarce events. If we eliminate major armed interventions by the great powers (e.g., Vietnam, Afghanistan, Panama, Grenada, and the like), decolonization wars, and the three wars involving Israel, there have been only twenty-three classical interstate wars in the whole of the Third World since 1945. Some of these barely passed the 1,000 casualty threshold, so there have been probably not more than a dozen wars that could be classified as serious. Given the large number of Third World countries and the many dangerous neighborhoods they populate, the low incidence of interstate war hardly supports the image of 'anarchy' or 'new [third] world disorder'.

In fact, the Third World states have been among the most vocal supporters of the Westphalian principles enshrined in the United Nations Charter. They were the ones who sanctified state sovereignty by declaring (Resolution No. 1514) in 1960 that any challenges to the independence and territorial integrity of the new states would constitute a violation of the Charter. Most significantly, these referred to challenges emanating within states, and not just to those from the external realm. This was a clear statement to undermine the legitimacy of secessionist movements. The same states have seriously questioned all attempts to compromise sovereignty principles, including the establishment of no-fly zones in Iraq and Bosnia, and the NATO bombing of Kosovo, an act which was not consistent with the United Nations Charter. Moreover, many of these states denounced Saddam Hussein's conquest of Kuwait in July 1990 and joined in the armed coalition directed to restore Kuwait's sovereignty and independence. In terms of their international behavior, then, most states in the Third World have been the main defenders of the Westphalian order and of the ideas and norms that help sustain it. Many are embroiled with their neighbors in various kinds of quarrels but for the most part they have desisted from acts of aggression and military conquests reminiscent of those notorious Europeans, Bismarck, Hitler, Stalin, Mussolini, or even Lenin. Thus, since the end of World War II, and even with more emphasis since the demise of communism, the strong commitment to Westphalian principles by most states most of the time vastly reduces the probabilities of major war.

The declining incidence of interstate war: norm-based explanations

Ideas relevant to international relations do not include only long-range visions, dreams, and values. We should include norms as well. Although the theoretical literature on international norms is immense and contested, we can apply the common sense notion of rules that indicate socially constructed appropriate and inappropriate

141

behavior. Two types of norms have been particularly important and can be linked to the declining incidence of interstate wars. The first we might call the anti-conquest norm. It condemns as illegitimate all forms of aggression and militarized threats against the independence and territorial integrity of states. Reversing a traditional European concept of conquest as an integral prerogative of sovereign authority, the Congress of Vienna in 1815 began to circumscribe that right. The authors of the Vienna Treaty stipulated that any subsequent conquests in Europe and the Balkans had to be legitimized by the great power concert. A century later, the League of Nations Covenant articulated in Article X the members' commitment to 'respect and preserve against external aggression the territorial integrity and political independence of all Members of the League'. This statement in effect abrogated the old, sovereignty-based right of conquest. The anti-conquest norm is repeated in Article 2(4) of the United Nations Charter and in many regional organizations and treaties, including the Helsinki Final Act, the Charter of Paris, and the founding documents of ASEAN, OAS, and OAU. To these we can add numerous General Assembly resolutions condemning colonialism and de-legitimizing enduring forms of national domination over dependent territories. Although these resolutions and charters were never applied to the Soviet Union's relations with its 'fraternal' allies, their spirit has become universal since the end of the Cold War. More general international legal instruments such as the United Nations Covenant on Civil and Political Rights (1966) and the UN Declaration on Principles of International Law concerning Friendly Relations and Cooperation among . . . States (1970) clearly state that the subjection of peoples to alien rule is a violation of the principles of self-determination and thus a denial of fundamental human rights. Since World War II, we have seen the *principle* of self-determination transformed into a *right*. Conquest, in short, has been thoroughly de-legitimized. Its incidence since World War II is probably the lowest in history. No state has recognized Israeli conquests resulting from the 1967 war and the regime in place in those territories is considered to be a temporary occupation. Only Australia recognized Indonesia's conquest of East Timor in 1975. India's invasion of Goa in 1961 represents one of the few acts of military conquest that has been recognized generally by the international community.[10]

We can look at this problem from yet another perspective. What has been the fate of weak and collapsed states? In the realist scheme of things we would predict that the great powers, faced with power vacuums and easy opportunities for expansion, would move into the areas of state failure to establish supremacy. But this has not been the fate of Somalia, Sierra Leone, Lebanon, Kampuchea, and many others. Instead, the international community through the United Nations has attempted to resuscitate failed states, to restore some correspondence between their *de jure* sovereignty and their ability to act as sovereigns. Where they have failed, as in Somalia, they have simply walked away. There has been no great power scramble to carve out spoils, to establish spheres of influence, or in any other way to copy European, Russian, and American imperial practices of the late nineteenth and early twentieth centuries. As Jackson and Rosberg point out, none of the Black African states have been destroyed or even significantly changed. No country has . . . been absorbed into a larger one against the wishes of its legitimate government and as a result of violence or the threat of violence. No territories or people – or even a segment of them – have been taken over by another country.[11]

This pattern stands in stark contrast to the entire recorded history of European diplomatic relations when conquest was a regular practice at least until the mid-twentieth century. Robert Jackson has summarized succinctly the strength of the anti-conquest norm in the contemporary society of states:

Nowadays all states possess a virtual guarantee of non-aggression and non-intervention – including states which are internally chaotic and even those . . . which scarcely exist as organized political systems. The possibility of international legal existence as a sovereign entity (juridical statehood) in the absence of internal socio-political existence as an effective state (empirical statehood) became a noteworthy feature of international society in the second half of the twentieth century. . . . That unusual condition is a direct consequence of changes in norms of state recognition connected with the right of self-determination and the abolition of colonialism. It is unprecedented and has no clear parallel with any previous period of modern international history.[12]

Norms against forceful territorial revision are no less important than norms relating to conquest or the extinguishing of sovereignty in states. In the settlements following World War I, territorial claims had to be legitimized either by means of public expression such as plebiscites or by information on population distributions. The Covenant of the League of Nations prohibited states from threatening or using force to change international boundaries. The main function of the organization was to protect the independence and territorial integrity of its members, and forceful attempts to alter territorial boundaries constituted a violation of the norm of national self-determination. The Kellogg–Briand Pact of 1928 committed the signatories to respect international boundaries and outlawed all acts of war to alter them. In 1931, the American Secretary of State, Henry Stimson, announced that the United States would not recognize as legal any alterations of territorial boundaries resulting from Japan's invasion of Manchuria. The League of Nations subsequently adopted his position as an international norm. 'The intended effects of these pronounce-ments', claim Jackson and Zacher was 'to freeze the political map of the world in its existing pattern of state jurisdiction'.[13] Alteration of territorial boundaries in the future had to be accomplished through consent.

These norms did not of course accord with subsequent practices in the 1930s and during World War II. The military conquests of this era were obviously incom-patible with them, but in the sense that World War II was a contest to preserve the

Westphalian states system against those who wanted to build regional or universal empires based on racial or Confucian principles, the norms prevailed. But not entirely, even in the immediate postwar settlements. Most of the states of Europe retained their prewar frontiers. The Soviet Union was the major exception. Through peace treaties and other arrangements, it retained its territorial conquests from Finland, Poland, Germany, Romania, and Japan. However, the major Western powers did not recognize as legal the Soviet annexation of the Baltic states. The 1930s and 1940s thus present many instances of throwbacks to earlier European territorial practices.

But perhaps it is best to see the interwar period as one of transition, where norms and rules expressed hopes rather than realities. The territorial institution was still weak because its main ideas and norms were not consistent with state behavior. In contrast, since 1945 practices have become increasingly consistent with the territorial norm.

Numerous multilateral agreements and resolutions have clearly specified that territorial revision without consent has no international legitimacy. The United Nations Charter explicitly links territory to people and declares that non-consensual territorial revision violates the principle of self-determination. It also declares that the threat or use of force to change the territorial status quo is a 'threat to international peace and security', thus justifying international sanctions, including armed force. Regional collective defense arrangements allowed under Article 51 are also premised on the idea that parties can legitimately use armed force against any attack on their territorial integrity.

Since 1960, the legal principle of *uti posseditis*, which originally arose in the context of the independence of the former Spanish colonies in South America, has become universal. It was enshrined in the Charter of the Organization of African Unity in 1963 and has served as the basis for all attempts to mediate or resolve African territorial disputes. The 1961 Vienna Convention on Treaties specified that the principle of *rebus sic stantibus* no longer applies to internationally recognized borders. That is, states can no longer claim that changing circumstances or conditions justify claims to change borders. The Helsinki Final Act (1975) of the Conference on Security and Cooperation in Europe reiterated the older norms associated with notions of self-determination and declared that 'frontiers can [only] be changed . . . by peaceful means and by agreement', that is, by consent. The Charter of Paris (1990), a document that established the principles upon which the post-Cold War territorial order in Europe would be based, reiterated the principle of consent and negotiation and ruled out the threat or use of force as a means of promoting or accomplishing territorial change.

Overall, we see an increasing consistency between territorial norms and practices.[14] We are therefore justified in claiming that conquest and territorial revision through armed force have become de-legitimized. The territorial map of the world has the quality of being 'frozen', norms have effective application and have become internalized, and boundaries have taken on social values that far exceed those found in traditional polities or among earlier European states. On matters of territoriality, states for the most part pursue policies and practices of 'appropriateness'; they follow the norms and rules of territoriality rather than of opportunity.[15] Thus, although disputes over the location of boundaries or claims to territorial revision continue, the incidence of armed conflicts fought primarily to alter territorial possession has declined significantly.[16] And where armed violence has been used, internationally sanctioned territorial changes have been few. Zacher provides support for the generalization: controlling for the much larger number of states in the international system, he found that the number of war-resulting territorial redistributions per country year declined from 0.0032 for the 1816–1850 period, 0.0035 for 1851–1900, and 0.0073 for the first half of the twentieth century, to 0.0015 for the 1951–1998 period.[17] The last figure is less than one-third the incidence per state year of territorial war-resulting redistributions found in the period between the Napoleonic wars and the end of World War II. If the incidence of interstate war has declined significantly, if not steadily, over the last four centuries, so has territorial change through the threat or use of force. The anti-conquest and territorial revision norms, buttressed by the principle of self-determination, may not account fully for this significant change in international practices, but they must be part of the explanation. The use of force for conquest and/or territorial revision has become a relatively rare event. Prior to the twentieth century (and during the 1930s) it was a common occurrence.

The normative foundations of the contemporary international system have come under scholarly scrutiny only in the last several decades.[18] Under realist doctrine, the prevailing analytical framework for studying international politics during most of the twentieth century, the texture of international politics is similar wherever they are structured by formal anarchy. I believe this characterization of the essence of international politics is incorrect. The vast variation in the incidence of interstate war and territorial revision cannot be explained adequately by structural analysis. If great power war was one of the defining features of the European states system and its Cold War legacy, as Levy suggests,[19] and if anarchy continues as the main structural principle of international politics, how can we explain the decline not only of great power war, but also the diminution of all interstate wars? I believe the institutionalization of norms helps to explain what is probably more than a passing anomaly. The norms of sovereignty, independence, self-determination, and territoriality, all enshrined in the United Nations Charter and numerous other diplomatic instruments, must be part of the explanation. But it may not be a sufficient explanation. Most realists, for example, argue that when norms and interests collide, the latter prevail.[20] The element of power must be built into any analysis of significant change in international relations. The problem is that analyses based on changing power configurations lead to contradictory explanations and outcomes.

Changing power distributions in the international system and the decline of war

Scholars of international relations have seldom emphasized the ideational and normative foundations of major wars specifically, or of other significant characteristics of the international system in general. Rather, they have theorized a great deal about changes in power relations: realist lore has long held that major war is the result of imbalances of power, or of the drive by potential great powers to replace existing hegemons.

Robert Gilpin has offered one of the most compelling power-based explanations for the repetition of major power wars throughout the history of the Westphalian system.[21] He characterizes the international system as a modified anarchy. States are sovereign, but within the collectivity of states there is always one predominant power. It establishes the main rules of the system, including territorial distribution. The 'top dog' is in fact a hegemon. But thanks to the universal laws of uneven economic development and diminishing returns, the hegemon's position is always insecure. Its relative power position tends to wane over time. Challengers arise and in the extreme stage of competition, major war breaks out. Either the hegemon wins (Great Britain in 1815 and 1918), or is replaced by a new hegemon (Great Britain replaces the Dutch Republic after three brief naval wars in the late seventeenth century). International politics has historically been a 'game' of national rise and decline, of challenge and response, and systemic war. This is the theory of power transition. Today's great power is likely to be tomorrow's minor power. The development of nuclear weapons only makes this historical pattern more dangerous. Another major war might well end the whole process. Gilpin offers no respite from the historical pattern. His answer to Mueller's war obsolescence thesis would probably be that we must wait for longer historic periods in which the competition and contradictions among the great powers lead to war. British hegemony lasted for more than a century, and although Russia no longer fits the role of a challenger, China and possibly Europe might well challenge American predominance within the next fifty years. If so, the probabilities of a great power war will rise. The Soviet challenge has receded, but the law of uneven economic development does not cease with the collapse of communism. We live today in an era of respite, not structural change or the reversal of historical patterns. We cannot predict when the next major war will occur, but we remain in an anarchical system and the configuration of power and its dynamics of change will continue. For Gilpin, the decline of major power war is not yet an established trend. It is only the manifestation of *temporary* American hegemony, a hegemony that is likely to be challenged in due time. Mueller, Gilpin might argue, confuses a temporary postwar period with a fundamentally new state of affairs.

William Pfaff, in a severe critique of American hegemonic behavior, lends support to a Gilpin-style analysis.[22] In his view, the current 'unipolar' moment is likely to be transitory. 'Eventually a pluralism of power will re-establish itself, whether the United States resists it or not.' The critical question is whether the

United States will adjust to a balancing by recognizing and accepting the different interests of the other major powers, or whether it will 'come in conflict and bitterness, with unpredictable consequences'.[23]

But many other power analysts challenge Gilpin's determinism and Pfaff's prognostication. They point out that the development of nuclear weapons effectively rules out another hegemonic war as a means of resolving contradictions in the system or maintaining American hegemony. Although Mueller rejects the 'peace through nuclear terror' argument, it still has a number of adherents.[24] The development of nuclear weapons, according to many, was perhaps the major change in the international system at the end of World War II.[25]

The Soviet Union and the United States comprised a new category of lethal capacity: the superpowers. Had the United States and the Soviet Union been armed only with conventional weapons, speculation goes, the likelihood of war between them would have been very high. Nuclear weapons changed all this. With each side having a secure second strike retaliatory force, the whole logic of using military force to promote national goals was undermined. No nuclear great power could behave as Frederick the Great, Louis XIV, or Napoleon had. If it tried to do so, it would immediately destroy itself. The shift in the major function of weaponry from war fighting to deterrence constituted, then, a major systemic change of historic proportions. The whole historical pattern of territorial expansion, conquest, balancing, and hostile challenges to hegemony had to end. If it did not, states and the states system would end. The decline or obsolescence of major interstate war is thus best explained by a revolutionary technological development: nuclear weapons and the rocketry available to hit any target in the world with a high degree of accuracy. These developments render Gilpin's *post hoc* explanation for major wars problematic.

The difficulty with the obsolescence through nuclear power thesis is that it can help explain only the decline of war incidence between those powers that possess atomic weapons; it cannot account for the decline of *all* interstate wars, the pattern that is the focus of this exploration. What of broader balance of power theories?

Traditional balance of power theory, because of its ambiguities and contradictory empirical findings, neither explains Mueller's prognostication, nor challenges it. Balance of power theory fails for at least two reasons: (1) empirically, numerous studies find little or no relationship between power configurations and the incidence or absence of war in the international system[26] and (2) theoretically, balance of power theories do not predict consistent outcomes from balances and imbalances. The literature, for example, predicts peace (the absence of major power war) both from a state of approximate equilibrium *and* from the predominance of a single power.[27]

According to the most common version of the theory, when one power reaches a position of predominance or potential hegemony, the others coalesce into a counter-coalition. This was a pattern in the late seventeenth century and again during the Napoleonic period. World Wars I and II also seemed to confirm the theory. But the end of the Cold War presents difficulties. Most observers argue that we now live in a unipolar world. The contemporary United States is the sole state with pre-eminence in every dimension of power – economic, military, technological, and cultural – with the capacity to pursue and defend its interests in every part of the world. It has unrivaled coercive capacity. With a defense budget of more than $420 billion and rising under the Bush administration, the United States spends more than the next twenty-four largest military spenders *combined*.[28]

In such a power distribution, according to traditional balance of power theory, counterbalances will arise to challenge the hegemon, and as Pfaff predicts, the danger of war will increase consequently. Christopher Layne similarly maintains that 'states do indeed balance against the hegemon's unchecked power'.[29] Military or security competition among *all* the great powers should therefore remain the distinguishing feature of international politics. We are, in short, returning to the traditional patterns of diplomacy; the Cold War was the aberration. But since Layne wrote these words, the world has not moved in the direction of a counter-coalition. Despite America's actions and statements that clearly establish a hegemonic pattern of diplomacy and coercion (see below), no counter-coalition is forming. Why not?

Hegemonic stability theory, as articulated by liberal institutionalists and others, might offer an explanation to the non-event. A *benign* hegemon provides a number of public goods – primarily security – that act as the foundation for a tolerable international order. Under this theory, enough states benefit from the hegemon that they are willing to compromise their autonomy and put off consideration of establishing counter-alliances. This is a major alteration of classical balance of power theory and implicitly validates American international predominance. The United States does not act as traditional hegemons typically did; it is a 'lite' hegemon. Michael Mastanduno argues, for example, that:

> If balancing is a response solely to capabilities, then by now we should have witnessed other states attempting to counter US preponderance. But if balancing behavior is also triggered by threat, then whether or not states balance against the dominant state will depend on the international environment and on the foreign policy behavior of the dominant state. . . . A dominant state that is aggressive or provocative is more likely to inspire balancing behavior than one that is reassuring or accommodating.[30]

John Ikenberry more recently has argued that paramountcy in an international order can be sustained if the hegemon practices self-restraint.[31] It must institutionalize its power, that is, exercise leadership by co-opting others to join multilateral institutions such as the United Nations and NATO. The Russians have apparently learned to live with NATO expansion because they do not fear (so much) a military alliance that is composed of democracies that pool their resources and act only after wide public debate. The purpose of the United States today is not to create 'universal monarchy', as was the great European fear in the seventeenth and eighteenth centuries, but to maintain a benevolent predominance that brings benefits to all. Hegemonic stability theory is an amended realist portrait that lends weight to American exceptionalism. The failure to create a counter-American coalition stems not only from the relative weakness of the other great powers, but also from a lack of fear and motivation. The United States is not a real threat except to those, like al-Qaeda, who seek to harm it through heinous means.[32]

But many would challenge this portrait of 'lite' American hegemony. The hegemon, they suggest, seeks a more brutal form of world domination, one that directly threatens the Westphalian principles of sovereignty, independence, tolerance, and legal equality. America's purpose is not to provide public goods for all, but to create a system in which its values and interests predominate at the expense of local and national cultures, the sovereign independence of states, and the right of people to conduct their internal affairs according to their own choices. The evidence of American unilateralism, blithe disregard for others' sensibilities and interests (e.g., in the Middle East), arrogance, and domination, they suggest, is more than anecdotal. There is a long list of signs of malevolent intent, of challenges to Westphalian principles, and of the use of force to compel states to meet standards set unilaterally by the United States. The United States, they suggest, enjoys a hegemonic position that it intends to maintain at any cost. The benign portrait of the United States presented in the works of Mastanduno, Ikenberry, and others is not consistent with a litany of actions that suggests a more dangerous picture. Here is a partial list:

- A major drive to undermine various collaborative and peace-enhancing projects of the international community. The United States has sought to subvert the new International Criminal Court, to avoid the commitments of the Land Mines Treaty, to evade the commitments of the Comprehensive Test-ban Treaty, and it has walked out of the protocols of the Biological Weapons Convention.
- Application of extraterritorial rules contrary to international law. This includes the Helms-Burton law and various incidents of American violations of sovereignty in Mexico and Colombia.
- The unilateral use of force to oust governments that do not meet underspecified and unilaterally declared American standards. Victims include Guatemala, Panama, Grenada, Cuba, and Iraq.
- American complicity or planning in the assassination and subversion of rulers it does not like. Victims or near-victims include Patrice Lumumba, Fidel Castro, Ngo Dinh Diem, Salvador Allende, Muhammad Mossadegh, Jacobo Arbenz, Manuel Noriega, Muammar Qaddafi, Saddam Hussein, and probably a few others who have not yet come to light. No other modern great power, including Hitler's Germany, has indulged in more subversion and assassination of its adversaries than has the United States.
- A continued defiance of the Non-Proliferation Treaty (NPT) *quid pro quo*, where the nuclear states would disarm their weapons in exchange for pledges by others not to acquire them. The United States clearly seeks to maintain its nuclear predominance and to threaten those that might challenge it. The United States is committed to eliminating all 'weapons of mass destruction'

(not clearly defined) in the world, except its own and those of its closest allies, including Great Britain, France, and Israel. Indeed, as the United States seeks to prevent proliferation of WMDs, it is proliferating its own arsenals and has consistently refused to adopt a 'no first use' nuclear weapons posture.

- Abrogating the Anti-Ballistic Missile (ABM) treaty by developing a national missile defense system that will undermine China's minimal deterrent capability and assure American nuclear predominance throughout the world. The national defense system is also probably a precursor to an American attempt to station weapons in space.
- Predatory trade policies that severely punish states that do not adhere to an American-defined model of 'free markets', and that vastly subsidize American agricultural products that drive competitors, primarily from the developing countries, out of international markets.
- Enunciating a national strategic doctrine that justifies pre-emptive strikes against adversaries for underspecified threats and that proclaims the intention to maintain American military paramountcy throughout the world into the distant future.

No single incident provides greater grist for the malevolent hegemon theory than American actions in Iraq. In this case, the United States planned and organized for an attack on a sovereign country. The decision to attack Iraq was made long before (e.g., spring 2002) the issue went to the United Nations in September 2002. It was placed on the agenda there only because the American Secretary of State persuaded George W. Bush – contrary to the wish of other administration officials – that the United States should obtain a legitimizing resolution from the Security Council. It obtained a resolution (unanimously) to impose a strict regime of arms inspection on Iraq, but failure to uncover evidence of weapons of mass destruction, and a finding by the International Atomic Energy Agency that Iraq did not have an ongoing nuclear weapons program, led to a major confrontation in the Security Council between those who wanted to continue inspections and those who wanted to 'disarm' Iraq by force. The United States and its 'coalition of the willing' (most of whose members joined for domestic political reasons rather than the merits of the case) attacked Iraq in March 2003 without an authorizing resolution from the Security Council. Despite the odious nature of the Hussein regime in Iraq, the attack was a direct violation of the United Nations Charter and more evidence of a government bent on pursuing its interests without respect for, or interest in, the views of other members of the organization, including its closest allies. In justifying the attack, President George W. Bush invoked the old eighteenth century corollary of the doctrine of sovereignty: the United States had the *right* to attack any country which it deemed to be a threat to its national security, even in the absence of demonstrable imminent danger.

For our analysis, it is only important to point out that whether 'lite' or malevolent, American hegemonic behavior has not led to the construction of a counter-coalition. Current realities are not consistent with balance of power theories.

Because power theories come to such diametrically opposed predictions, I argue that explanations of the decline of interstate war that emphasize ideas and norms have greater purchase.[33] Except for the interwar period (1918–1941), the decline in the incidence of interstate war, when adjusted for the number of states, has been fairly steady across all sorts of power distributions, multipolar, tripolar, bipolar, and unipolar, and different degrees of polarity. The 500-year pattern of war decline transcends any particular pattern of power.

Social learning and the decline of interstate war: special kinds of ideas

Ideas help to explain the decline of interstate war and the robustness of norms such as those prohibiting conquests and armed territorial revision. But where do these ideas come from?

Mueller's thesis about the obsolescence of major war rests upon a social theory of learning. Contrary to those who proclaim that structural features of international relations constrain and predispose policy-makers to behave in certain ways, Mueller and many liberal internationalists – whom we might characterize as proponents of the UNESCO view that 'war begins in the minds of men' – argue that human-kind (generically speaking) creates social institutions to serve its needs, interests, and values. But when those needs, interests, and values change, humankind changes institutions accordingly. Nothing motivates it to do so more than the failures and high costs of established practices. In the realm of international politics, Kant first proposed that humankind would learn to abolish the institution of war only after a series of increasingly devastating conflicts. The Great War effectively pacified large parts of Europe, but Hitler and his mimics and acolytes reverted to more primitive ideas to justify a new round of conquests and aggressions. If World War II did not de-bellicize the whole world, at least nuclear weapons fundamentally changed the calculus underlying classical interstate wars. They could only serve the interests of deterrence and prestige; they could not be used as instruments of conquest and expansion. The great wars of the twentieth century and the subsequent era of mutual assured destruction were profound learning experiences and they led to worldwide movements in support of disarmament, arms control, and the pacific resolution of international conflicts. Kant's prediction seemed to be coming to pass.[34]

Mueller accepts this view. For a variety of reasons (and not just cost–benefit calculations), humankind is changing the institution of war. It is making it obsolete, just as it did with organized slavery and the slave trade, and more recently with colonialism. Mueller rejects both biological and neo-realist theories that war is a constant in human affairs and that except for balances of power there are no palliatives to this condition. War is a social institution, because as Rousseau argued, 'One kills in order to win; no man is so ferocious that he tries to win in order to kill.'[35] War has known purposes that are always a matter of choice rather than necessity. If the purposes of states change, let us say, from the conquest of territory to the invention of technology and the maximization of welfare and employment, then the use of force in international relations may become not only irrelevant, but counterproductive. The Japanese gained little from their conquests of the 1930s compared to what they have achieved through peaceful trade, de-militarization, and investment in education and productive capacity. Armed force against others no longer serves national needs, interests, or values, and thus will be used only *in extremis*, as during the Kosovo episode, to promote the international community's interests. While Louis XIV fought two major wars primarily for his personal glory and reputation,[36] contemporary wars have little to do with such values. As for the spate of secessionist, ethnic, and civil wars, they must continue because they reflect the inherent weakness of many contemporary states. But few of them threaten *international* peace and security, and hence they are not likely to escalate or attract competitive outside intervention. We must remember that Mueller is not proclaiming the disappearance of violence in human affairs, but only the obsolescence of major interstate war.

Many of the arguments employed by Kant and Mueller make sense and may help account for the decline in the incidence of interstate war. It is not difficult to reject the determinism of biological and neo-realist theories of war. Humankind *can* change social institutions, and does learn though often only after catastrophic experiences.

Kant and Mueller share optimism in people's ability to learn, adjust, and change. For Kant, the source of change is pain; the horrible lessons learned from increasingly destructive wars. For Mueller (p. 217), change comes from cost–benefit analyses and changing norms. The world, or at least the OECD world, has learned that war is 'abhorrent – repulsive, immoral, and uncivilized – and methodologically ineffective – futile'. The obsolescence of interstate war is consistent with a progressivist view of history. International institutions such as the slave trade have become obsolete, and there is a good deal of evidence that the institution of war, particularly in its conquest format, is dramatically receding in incidence. The ancient *right* of conquest, a doctrine that developed to justify European expansion starting in the fifteenth century, has no legal standing today. The United Nations Charter and dozens of counterparts for regional organizations seriously proscribe the use of force to achieve or defend foreign policy objectives. The overwhelming international reaction to Saddam Hussein's attempted conquest of Kuwait in July 1990 suggests that those who choose to behave this way will pay a heavy price. Increasingly, the use of force requires international validation.

Even if we concede that learning may alter structural patterns – Kant trumps Waltz – we must still ask the question whether learning must always be progressive. Is there some inevitable course of history in which human behavior and social institutions 'improve'? If we look at the historical development of war as an international institution – that is, as a set of ideas, norms, rules, and practices – then by almost any measure humankind regressed between Kant's time and World War II. European wars of the eighteenth century were models of decorum, restraint, rule-guided behavior, and concern over the welfare of non-combatants when compared to the carnage, planned butcheries of civilians, and massive atrocities committed during World War II. War in the eighteenth century was an activity of gentlemen with unfortunate but low military casualties, more attributed to disease and illness than to fighting. By the twentieth century, armies had become vast killing machines directed as much against civilians as combatants. All sides between 1939 and 1945 systematically violated most of the laws of war developed so painstakingly in the eighteenth and nineteenth centuries. War, in fact, became de-institutionalized in the sense that rules and norms failed to restrain violence. In the case of Hitler, Rousseau's assertion no longer held. Hitler *did* seek to win in order to kill. He overturned the classical Clausewitzian concept of war as a rational activity to promote the interests of the state. Clausewitz could not have imagined that a state could seek conquest in order to turn its subjugated population into slaves, or to eliminate an entire people. The course of war as a practice has hardly been progressive.

It is the case, then, that what humankind learns can also be regressive or forgotten. New technologies and ideological purposes can transform the character of war from an instrument of state policy to a medium of genocide and extermination. There is also the problem of context. Did learning lead to the hypothesized abandonment of war, or was war just 'put on the shelf' during a historical era of unprecedented economic and social development? The period since 1945 has been relatively benign compared to the interwar period. De-colonization – a major institutional change – proceeded for the most part through peaceful means, although the wars in Algeria and Vietnam were major wars when viewed from the perspective of their Algerian and Vietnamese victims. The global economy, with some exceptions such as the decade of inflation in the 1970s, grew strongly and benefited most societies, although not equally. The end of the Cold War terminated the most virulent forms of arms racing, reduced the fear of accidental war, and prompted most states to reduce their defense expenditures. The global trading system expanded at unprecedented rates. Once poor, many of the newly industrialized countries (NICs) joined the ranks of the rich. Today, Hong Kong, Kuwait, and Singapore rank fourth, fifth and sixth in GDP per capita in purchasing power parity (PPP). Brazil has the world's eighth largest economy. While many poor countries have regressed economically over the last half century, far more have moved significantly higher and today enjoy economic levels close to the OECD average of only two decades ago. Do any of these elements help explain the absence of major war? In other words, have we *learned* not to use force in interstate relations, or has there been an *absence of necessity*?

Many analysts today write about 'new' security agendas. Pollution, ecological degradation, the drug trade, increasing resource scarcity – the sale of African resources to Western economies largely finances Africa's contemporary wars – the depletion of fisheries, and illegal migration (from areas of poverty to areas of wealth) are now commonly characterized as new types of threats or the constituent units of the 'new security agenda'. To them we would add terrorism in its various manifestations. These have replaced interstate war as the major problems of our era. But if we examine them closely, we see that they are mostly problems generated by economic abundance. The demand for drugs, for example, comes mostly from wealthy societies. They provide the market for an illicit drug trade that approaches one trillion dollars annually. It is the wealthy societies that create most of the environmental 'threats'. They are manifestations and costs of a world of plenty, of dramatic economic growth, and of good times. There is little necessity in this kind of environment.

What if we speculate about economic breakdown? Would Mueller's prognostications regarding war hold in an environment of economic and financial collapse? In such an environment, necessity might replace choice. The world economy today is far more complex and interconnected than at any other time in history. The cascading effects of severe difficulties in one country or region are immediate and often amplified by the 'electronic herd',[37] the hundreds of millions of investors and speculators who move billions of dollars in minutes. The links between economic depression and war were strong in the 1930s. At a time of extreme hardship, heroes and strongmen returned to fashion. Hitler and Stalin had their emulators all over the world. Domino effects, spillover, and cascading processes guaranteed that the worst effects of depression in one major industrial center would spread throughout most regions of the world. Today they would be quicker, more robust, and more devastating.

We have not recently speculated on or studied these problems because of the optimism generated by a long period of relative peace and prosperity. Today, it is more fashionable to focus on new types of threats, threats that are mostly peculiar to systems characterized by prosperity. But a system heading to breakdown, high unemployment, a major contraction of trade and investment, or the depletion of a major resource could herald a new era of more traditional security threats, wars of conquest, and copy-cat aggressions.

I do not predict any of this, but mention them as an antidote to optimistic learning theories, assumptions regarding historical progress, and notions of institutional change that have only happy outcomes. Pessimistic economic scenarios are of course not the only possibilities. Revolutions have also been a major source of war (and vice versa) throughout history, and we are not yet in a position to predict that we have seen the last of them.[38] What would be the probabilities of major war in the event of revolution or the collapse of governance in China or Russia? Could such major events be quarantined? Whether we emphasize ideas, norms, learning abilities, or certain power distributions, we should recall that the Mueller-type thesis is not new. Books announcing the end of interstate war were also popular in the late nineteenth and early twentieth centuries. Norman Angell became a major figure with his arguments that war does not pay, is not rational, and can be overcome through cost–benefit analysis and learning. William Pfaff reminds us that the twentieth century began

in circumstances of apparent security more reassuring than those of today. No one in 1900 could have imagined the events that only 14 years later would destroy the existing international system and unleash the wars of totalitarianism that would dominate world affairs for most of the rest of the century.[39]

There have been numerous, significant changes in the international system over the past half century. I have emphasized those in the realm of ideas and norms that give further credence to Mueller's thesis. Yet, there are also reasons for skepticism. Any notion of a progressivist, inevitable trend requires hesitation. The realists who emphasize structure and capabilities provide some of the ammunition for counter-arguments, but the confusion surrounding balance of power theory and analysts' consistent portrayal of the United States as a benevolent hegemon render their counter-arguments problematic.

Conclusion

This chapter has explored four avenues for explaining the historical decline in the incidence of interstate war. Ideas, norms, and social learning are closely related, although in some ways distinct. Power distributions and balances/imbalances are also systemic characteristics, but for many reasons they suffer from severe explanatory limitations such as inconsistent and contradictory findings and the fact that the secular decline of interstate war incidence has occurred in the context of many different power configurations. Much of the power-based analysis today consists of attempted refinements and location of exceptions to classical balance of power theory. Thus, there are debates whether at time x power was in approximate balance or not, whether there were two or many poles of power, and whether a hegemon was or is benign or aggressive. In the narrow context of a particular time frame – say five years – this kind of debate has meaning, but over the long haul of several centuries it makes little sense. To repeat the earlier point: war incidence has been declining except during the 1918–1941 period at a steady rate in *all* power contexts.

Scholars have only in recent years come to recognize the power of ideas as shaping the texture of international politics in any given era. In fact, military power in the European pre-modern and in the global modern era has almost always been in the service of sets of ideas[40] and sometimes to enforce norms. Certainly ideas may contain rationalizing rhetoric that masks more mundane or greedy foreign policy purposes – was the American attack on Iraq in 2003 designed to rid the world of a military menace, or was it an attempt to gain control of Iraqi oil, to obtain a new locale for American military bases, and a means of escaping the clutches of OPEC? – but often the ideas and power considerations become hopelessly mixed. Yet it is difficult to think of any major foreign policy initiative during the last century or so that was not an attempt to buttress and promote ideas and some image of a better world or region within it. Thus, in approaching the question of explaining the decline of interstate war, we must pay attention to the ideas and attitudes of both policy-making elites and broad publics. The significant change in the practice of using force in international politics over the past two centuries or so has to be seen as a critical reflection of underlying changes in public attitudes toward war and the anti-conquest norm that has become inscribed in dozens of major charters, treaties, and declarations. Often in the late seventeenth century, the first option considered when diplomatic purposes were incompatible was to declare war. Today, in contrast, war is commonly portrayed as the last option, to be used only when all other courses of action have failed. Thus, bringing back ideas, norms, and learning experiences into the study of international politics is essential if we wish to understand the texture of the times.

Finally, these systemic characteristics have to be married to explanatory protocols that emphasize the characteristics of key actors – actor-level variables, as it were. This is where the democratic peace literature fits in, because of the strong correlation between the declining incidence of war and the spread of democratic institutions. Political arrangements within states are actor characteristics, but if aggregated across many actors, they become system properties. They then bear a close relationship to my notion of transnational ideas. Francis Fukuyama has expressed this succinctly: '[t]he argument [about democracy and peace] . . . is not so much that liberal democracy constrains man's natural instincts for aggression and violence, but that it has fundamentally transformed the instincts themselves and eliminated the motive for imperialism.'[41] Fukuyama here is speaking of a broad cultural revolution that transcends any particular state. If his assertion is correct, then we are back in the realm of ideas as systemic properties. In international politics, purpose comes before power. To explain a phenomenon or trend such as Mueller's, we need to look at purpose first.

Notes

1 J. Mueller, *Retreat from Doomsday: The Obsolescence of Major War* (New York: Basic Books, 1989). For more recent studies that highlight the secular decline of interstate war, see for example N. P. Gleditsch, *The Future of Armed Conflict* (Ramat Gan: The Begin–Sadat Center for Strategic Studies, 2003) and M. Sarkees, F. Wayman and J. D. Singer, 'Inter-State, Intra-State, and Extra-State Wars: A Comprehensive Look at their Distribution over Time', *International Studies Quarterly*, 47, 1 (2003), pp. 49–70.

2 Peter Wallensteen, 'Trends in major war: too early for waning', this volume, pp. 80–93.

3 Mueller is not the only analyst to predict and account for the obsolescence of major war. 'Globalists' have explained the phenomenon or trend in terms of (1) interdependence and the transnationalization of production, (a type of 'war does not pay' argument); (2) because states are losing authority – upwards, sideways, and downwards – and thus unable to mobilize for mass warfare; and (3) because of democratization and the fact that democracies rarely fight each other. These and other similar explanations for the obsolescence of interstate war can be found in P. Drucker, 'The Global Economy and the Nation-State', *Foreign Affairs*, 76, 5 (1997), pp. 170–2; J. Rosenau, 'New Dimensions of Security: The Interaction of Globalizing and Localizing Dynamics', *Security Dialogue*, 25, 3 (1994), pp. 255–81; and R. D. Lipschutz, *After Authority: War, Peace, and Global Politics in the 21st Century* (Albany: State University of New York Press, 2000). For a summary of and rejoinder to these arguments, see T. V. Paul, 'States, Security Function and the New Global Forces' (Montreal: Group d'Étude et de

Recherche sur la Securité Internationale/Research Group in International Security, Université de Montréal/McGill University, 2001, Note de Recherche/Working Paper 10).

4 S. Woolf, *Napoleon's Integration of Europe* (New York: Routledge, 1991).

5 Hitler claimed that '[t]he "nation" is a political expediency of democracy and liberalism. We have to get rid of this false conception and set in its place the conception of race. . . . The new order cannot be conceived in terms of the national boundaries of the peoples with an historic past, but in terms of race that transcend those boundaries.' H. Rauschning, *Hitler Speaks: A Series of Conversations with Adolf Hitler on his Real Aims* (London: Thornton Butterworth, 1939), p. 229. Hitler's ultimate goal was, as he claimed to his dinner guests in 1942, to destroy not just the Treaty of Versailles, but ultimately the Treaty of Westphalia. See A. Hitler [N. Cameron (Translator), R. H. Stevens (Translator) and H. Redwald Trevor-Roper], *Hitler's Table Talk 1941–1944* (Oxford: Oxford University Press, 1953), p. 66.

6 Cf. R. Robinson and J. Gallagher, *Africa and the Victorian Mind: The Official Mind of Imperialism* (London: Macmillan, 1965).

7 For an extended analysis of the ideational justifications for imperialism, see W. Bain, *Between Anarchy and Society: Trusteeship and the Obligations of Power* (Oxford: Oxford University Press, 2003), esp. ch. 1.

8 Cf. J. Mueller, *Retreat from Doomsday*, pp. 38–52; K. J. Holsti, *Peace and War: Armed Conflict and International Order, 1648–1989* (Cambridge: Cambridge University Press, 1991), esp. ch. 9.

9 See R. Kaplan, 'The Coming Anarchy', *The Atlantic Monthly*, 273 (1994), pp. 44–76; S. Hoffmann, 'Watch out for a New World Disorder', *International Herald Tribune*, 26 February 1991, p. 6; and M. Singer and A. Wildawsky, *The Real World Order: Zones of Peace/Zones of Turmoil* (Chatham: Chatham House Publishers, 1993).

10 China's conquest of Tibet and North Vietnam's conquest of the south might be included, although there are arguments that neither case fits the criterion of the military and permanent conquest of a sovereign state.

11 R. H. Jackson and C. G. Rosberg, 'Why Africa's Weak States Persist: The Empirical and the Juridical in Statehood', *World Politics*, 35 (1982), pp. 1–24.

12 R. H. Jackson, *The Global Covenant: Human Conduct in a World of States* (Oxford: Oxford University Press, 2000), p. 207.

13 R. H. Jackson and M. W. Zacher, 'The Territorial Covenant: International Society and the Stabilization of Territories' (Vancouver: Institute of International Relations, University of British Columbia), Working paper No.15, 1997, p. 5.

14 For a case by case analysis of these practices, see ibid. and M. W. Zacher, 'The Territorial Integrity Norm: International Boundaries and the Use of Force', *International Organization*, 55, 2 (2001), pp. 215–50.

15 For a general discussion of the processes of norm diffusion, see K. Alderson, 'Making Sense of State Socialization', *Review of International Studies*, 27, 3 (2001), pp. 415–34; and for the instrumental and ideational sources of the territorial norms in particular, see Zacher, 'The Territorial Integrity Norm'.

16 Cf. K. J. Holsti, *Peace and War*, esp. ch. 12; J. Vasquez, *The War Puzzle* (Cambridge: Cambridge University Press, 1993).

17 Zacher, 'The Territorial Integrity Norm', p. 224.

18 H. Bull, *The Anarchical Society* (London: Macmillan, 1977) stands as the first comprehensive examination of the role of norms and 'rules of the game' in international politics.

19 J. Levy, *War in the Modern Great Power System, 1495–1975* (Lexington: University of Kentucky Press, 1983).

20 Cf. S. Krasner, *Sovereignty: Organized Hypocrisy* (Princeton: Princeton University Press, 1999).

21 R. Gilpin, *War and Change in World Politics* (Cambridge: Cambridge University Press, 1981).
22 W. Pfaff, 'The Question of Hegemony', *Foreign Affairs*, 80 (2001), pp. 221–32.
23 Ibid., p. 231.
24 Mueller, *Retreat from Doomsday*, p. 6.
25 Cf. M. Mandelbaum, *The Nuclear Revolution: Politics Before and After Hiroshima* (Cambridge: Cambridge University Press, 1981).
26 J. A. Vasquez, *The Power of Power Politics: A Critique* (New Brunswick: Rutgers University Press, 1983); A. N. Sabrosky (ed.), *Polarity and War: The Changing Structure of International Conflict* (Boulder: Westview, 1985); C. S. Gochman, 'Capability-Driven Disputes', in C. S. Gochman and A. N. Sabrosky (eds), *Prisoners of War? Nation-States in the Modern Era* (Lexington: Lexington Books, 1990); F. W. Wayman and T. C. Morgan, 'Measuring Polarity in the International System', in J. D. Singer and P. F. Diehl (eds), *Measuring the Correlates of War* (Ann Arbor: University of Michigan Press, 1990); and E. Mansfield, 'The Concentration of Capabilities and the Onset of War', *Journal of Conflict Resolution*, 36 (1992), pp. 3–24.
27 Cf. A. F. K. Organski, *World Politics*, 2nd edn (New York: Alfred A. Knopf, 1968). Classical balance of power theory did not predict variation in the incidence of war as a result of balance or imbalance. Analysts generally agreed that war could be used to redress the balance. The purpose of balancing was to prevent 'universal empire', not war.
28 T. V. Paul, 'States, Security Function and the New Global Forces', p. 19.
29 C. Layne, 'The Unipolar Illusion: Why New Great Powers Will Rise', *International Security*, 17, 4 (1993), p. 13.
30 M. Mastanduno, 'A Realist View: Three Images of the Coming International Order', in T. V. Paul and J. Hall (eds), *International Order and the Future of World Politics* (Cambridge: Cambridge University Press, 1999), p. 31.
31 J. G. Ikenberry, *After Victory: Institutions, Strategic Restraint, and the Rebuilding of Order after Major War* (Princeton: Princeton University Press, 2001).
32 The contemporary cheerleaders of American supremacy naturally see it as benign. William Kristol and Robert Kagan, for example, have argued that '[T]he United States does not pursue a narrow, selfish definition of its national interests, but generally finds its interests in a benevolent international order. In other words, it is precisely because the United States infuses its foreign policy with an unusually high degree of morality that other nations feel they have less to fear from its otherwise daunting power.' Quoted in Pfaff, 'The Question of Hegemony', p. 224. Comments such as these bring to mind E. H. Carr's view that 'Utopians argue that what is best for the world is best for their country, and then reverse the argument to read that what is best for their country is best for the world. . . . British [and today, American] writers . . . have been particularly eloquent supporters of the theory that the maintenance of British [American] supremacy is the performance of a duty to mankind.' See E. H. Carr, *The Twenty Years Crisis, 1919–1939* (New York: Harper Torchbooks 1964 [1946]), pp. 79, 72.
33 A more sophisticated treatment of the problem of hegemony, one that balances power considerations with ideas, norms, and culture is T. Knutsen, *The Rise and Fall of World Orders* (Manchester and New York: Manchester University Press, 1999).
34 For corroboration, see L.-E. Cederman, 'Back to Kant: Reinterpreting the Democratic Peace as a Macrohistorical Learning Process', *American Political Science Review*, 95, 1 (2001), pp. 15–32.
35 C. E. Vaughan, *The Political Writings of J. J. Rousseau* (Cambridge: Cambridge University Press, 1915), I, p. 313.
36 Cf. I. Dunlop, *Louis XIV* (New York: St Martin's Press, 1999), esp. chs 16, 21.
37 T. L. Friedman, *The Lexus and the Olive Tree* (New York: Random House, 2000), ch. 7.

38 F. Halliday, *Revolution and World Politics: The Rise and Fall of the Sixth Great Power* (Durham: Duke University Press, 1999).

39 Pfaff, 'The Question of Hegemony', p. 230.

40 A recent and persuasive analysis of the power of ideas in helping to bring about the dissolution of the colonial system is N. Crawford, *Argument and Change in World Politics: Ethics, Decolonization, and Humanitarian Intervention* (Cambridge: Cambridge University Press, 2002).

41 F. Fukuyama, *The End of History and the Last Man* (New York: Avon Books, 1993), p. 263.

7

MULTILATERAL INSTITUTIONS AS RESTRAINTS ON MAJOR WAR

Patrick M. Morgan

It is possible that this topic is too simple. With regard to the 'Long Peace', the absence of systemwide military struggles or large wars involving great powers, multilateral institutions cannot be said to be *responsible*. The reasons are straight-forward. Multilateral institutions (MIs) have not been responsible for physically, politically, or morally preventing great powers from fighting each other, because they are not capable of this. They cannot overpower great powers verging on a major war, nor overpower states that have entered into such a war and refuse to stop, at least not as MIs work now – at best they might legitimize an effort by other great powers to do this and those actors are unlikely to try. They cannot politically compel great powers to avoid such wars either; no MIs command such authority and legitimacy. Finally, they have never been so morally esteemed – and values they embody have never been so fully accepted – that they can disperse a looming major war by condemning the very idea of it. All this seems not only true but obvious. (It was, roughly speaking, Inis Claude's critique years ago.[1]) Maybe there is no need to carry on further and the chapter is done.[2]

On second thought (no academic lacks second thoughts), they can have an impact without being responsible; the title, after all, refers to 'restraints' on major wars. Perhaps MIs do things that restrain the incidence of such wars, modestly or other-wise. If so, why not a few words about that impact (no academic is at a loss for words). Of course, they have to be put in proper context: suitable definitions of terms, refinements in relevant concepts, references to applicable theories (what academic can resist this?). Sounds like a chapter after all.

On the relevant wars

What is 'major interstate war?' In arguing that major wars are obsolete, Mandelbaum referred to systemwide wars – the great powers fighting at length with enormous consequences for governments and the global system.[3] That is too narrow; this is what 'major war' means to me. First, a major interstate war involves major states

160

– it involves the great powers in the *relevant international system*. The world has a global system and a number of regional systems. The global system great powers are identifiable: the US, Britain, France, Germany, Japan, China, and Russia (though the last three are borderline).[4] In a regional system the great powers are its most significant states, in military and/or other capabilities, regularly operating in the system centered identifiably on that particular region. Thus the US is part of the East Asian regional international system, as it is of the Middle Eastern regional international system (as was the Soviet Union in the past). Physical location in the relevant region is not required to be a major player in the associated international system. This means that regional powers in regional systems can also generate major wars.

With this in mind, the wars between Egypt and Israel, Iran and Iraq, and the US and Iraq were major wars. On the other hand, the Israeli invasion of Lebanon was not a major war; fighting between Egypt and the Sudan would not be a major war, nor fighting between the US and Libya. A major war is initially, or eventually, intended to have a large political effect on, and in, the system where it occurs. Since most states, even very powerful ones, mainly focus on their relations within a regional system, a war that seriously disturbs (or could disturb) that system is 'major'. While a war among smaller states sometimes comes close, wars among major states always have this potential; any war among them is highly disturbing for almost anyone in the associated system. This is better than having 'major' wars only on a global scale since that system is a bit remote for most states until a global war occurs. It is better than thinking about 'major' in terms of other consequences (like casualties and destruction), since they are difficult to evaluate relatively and can be ephemeral in impact.[5] A minor war (in participants and political consequences) might involve many casualties – and a major war can involve few.

Next, there must be significant military activity intended. Casualties are a normal way of measuring military activity but this is insufficient. The major states must mobilize significant portions (or all) of their military might for the war and fully intend to conduct it at high intensity in combat, lethality, and destructiveness, whether that is how the war actually goes or not. In this sense, the Gulf War was major as were the Arab–Israeli wars of 1956 and 1967, even though they were over quickly and with few casualties. Many border skirmishes, regardless of how passionately they are pursued, are not major in terms of forces readied for combat. The Falkland Islands was not a major war, nor was the Sino-Soviet border fighting in the late 1960s, nor is the ongoing India–Pakistan border conflict.[6]

Thus a decline in major war is not just the absence of world wars but a paucity of regional systemwide and regional great-power wars. The latter have become scarce too – there have been none in Latin America for decades, or in the Far East or Europe since 1945. They were once common in the Middle East and South Asia but not lately.

On multilateral institutions

For discussing multilateral institutions we can focus on either international organizations or organized international behavior. The latter is the more inclusive; it encompasses the former plus less formal and institutionalized, yet organized, ways of acting. The case for treating any organized behavior as an institution is not as strong as many claim, but has become widely accepted as the best way to proceed. Hence: in a general way, an 'institution' can be viewed as a relatively stable collection of practices and rules defining appropriate behavior for specific groups of actors in specific situations.

Practices and rules are 'embedded in structures of meaning and schemes of interpretation' as well as in 'resources and the principles of their allocation'.[7] Extending this leads to international institutions: as a set of rules that stipulate the ways in which states should cooperate and compete with each other. They prescribe acceptable forms of state behavior, and proscribe unacceptable kinds of behavior.[8]

John Mearsheimer adds that these rules are negotiated by states, usually taken to rest on the acceptance of higher norms, formalized in international agreements, and often embodied in international organizations.[9] There is debate over whether states obey more or less on their own volition – not by command. However, if the higher norms constitute a 'normative order', these orders clearly vary in the degree to which states feel free to do what they please.[10]

As for 'multilateral', there are two relevant versions. In the first a multilateral institution is one with more than two states involved. Various analysts add that states are not the only participants in developing rules and not necessarily the only actors to whom the rules apply; however, 'multilateral' is seldom applied to institutions where states are not the members. The second version of multilateralism is more complex, more stringent, and is discussed later.

Do states obey only if they want to? Not necessarily. States can collectively establish institutions and grant them, whether they have organizations or not, the power to command – upheld by force if necessary either by the members as a whole or selected members acting on everyone's behalf. We learned in the 1990s that the Korean War was no fluke, that serious enforcement can be undertaken by MIs. In such institutions only very powerful states can readily feel they are governed only if they choose to obey. All others face the possibility of being forced to obey. This applies to states that agreed to establish the institutions and ceded their right to suspend obedience whenever they wish. But it might also apply to states that did not participate in establishing them – the members may insist on applying the institution universally, or in areas near the members, or in especially egregious instances of unacceptable behavior by nonmembers.

On MIs as restraints on major war Raimo Väyrynen has offered a review of alternative explanations on the waning of major war and a broad conclusion:

> Multilateral regimes have not influenced national policies primarily by means of deterrence and prevention, but more so by establishing new

normative standards, communication channels, and institutional practices. Thus, new norms, patterns of consultation, and learning opportunities embedded in multilateral institutions, rather than specific constraints, have modified the behavior of states, restricted the resort to arms, and thus contributed to the decline of major war.[11]

His conclusion is that 'institutions, instead of shaping behavior independently or reflecting deeper material changes, are actually expressions of more fundamental changes in ideas, values, and norms concerning the use of military force'.

This seems likely to be true, leaving no need to carry on further. Ah, but what about second thoughts? And what would be the basis for them?

Thinking about MIs and major wars

A realist perspective tends to dismiss multilateral institutions because of the decentralized nature of international systems – the actors have a great deal of power plus the right and/or ability to make major decisions on their own. Institutions cannot *command* and expect to be obeyed when it comes to preventing war, thus institutions are not effective. However, even though institutions aren't always effective this view is not correct. We must avoid the mistake of insisting on total success and cite the continued existence of wars as evidence that institutions cannot rule. For one thing, norms are involved and 'norms are counterfactually valid. No single counterfactual occurrence refutes a norm. Not even many such occurrences necessarily do.' As a result the violation of norms 'is not the beginning, middle, and end of the compliance story'.[12] In particular, we must distinguish between *disobedience* and outright *rejection*. With the former, system governance suffers a failure but its existence and purpose are not threatened, but the latter calls its existence into question. Though no domestic system eliminates violations of established laws and norms this does not make its control of violence meaningless. And while governments have enforcement capabilities, the domestic control of violence readily collapses if people massively withdraw willingness to behave – if even a modest number do so, crime and violence can run rampant. As in international politics, institutions work only if enough members behave.[13]

So the main difference seems to be that, for domestic politics, only when a state and society have dangerously unraveled is violence a real threat to overwhelm the state. Domestic warfare is abnormal, an extraordinary situation. In international politics, on the other hand, war has classically not been abnormal, both in its presence and as a standard, even logical, part of life. The reason is the lack of authoritative and forceful constraints, so actors can readily choose not to behave.

However, the notion of interstate war as normal deserves less respect than it gets. Interstate war is not common (much less so today than intrastate war). Most states, most of the time, are not at war, do not expect to be any time soon, and are not seriously planning for one. War has been declining. During 180 years of the modern state system there were no interstate wars in 81 of them; 150 states did not experience a war at all and 49 had only one or two; only eight had ten or more.[14] The number of wars being conducted since 1945 has risen steadily but two-thirds are internal, a much higher percentage than in earlier eras, and only 17 percent seem like classic interstate wars.[15] Thus wars are not 'normal' in international politics. Ah, but is this due to a successful MI-based way of preventing war? That seems hardly the case.

It is possible to construct very potent institutions for preventing wars, ones that go well beyond peacemaking or peacekeeping and are readily capable of providing *deterrence* of war and *enforcement* of norms and rules against war, the two ultimate functions involved. For instance, the highly developed East–West deterrence system during the Cold War can be described as a regime with well-established norms and rules, some institutionalized, that sharply constrained major wars.[16] (There might be a question as to how multilateral it was.) The same is true of the multilateral hegemonic arrangement found in Europe today; it is quite capable of preventing war via both deterrence and enforcement. Other multilateral arrangements capable of both deterrence and enforcement against war are a great-power concert and Wilsonian collective security.

In short, we need not rely on actors behaving themselves to have international politics without war – in principle. Multilateral institutions can go beyond indirect assistance to directly prevent or constrain war. This does not mean they are powerful constraints on warfare, just that in principle they can be. For an international institution to perform that function it must ultimately have an action capability, a suitable concentration of power. Just as in domestic affairs, there must be a deterrence/enforcement capability – not everyone will behave all the time. This in turn requires:

1   That those with the necessary power be *willing* to provide the required deterrence/enforcement.
2   That the opposition be weak enough to coerce.

Both requirements are problematic, but they are problematic in domestic systems too. The chief complaints about MIs' effectiveness in producing peace often boil down to a failure to meet these two conditions (apart from the usual charges of ineptitude, slow reaction time, etc.).

The first condition is a special problem in international politics. In most political systems, enforcing peace and order is a highly coveted role; candidates readily appear and the state itself is eager to achieve what Weber's definition assigns it – a monopoly on the legitimate use of force and the physical superiority to suppress illegitimate uses. Why isn't this true in international politics? Sometimes it is. It is commonly claimed that major states have often wanted empires, even universal in scope, to bring order out of anarchy. On the other hand, there is widespread concern instead about free riding and buck passing[17] – that states will likely look the other way, eschewing the role of maintaining order and providing security against war.

The task is daunting, the price too high, the burdens too great. Those who now fear the US as an imperial wolf vie with those who fear the US will eventually abandon security management like a neoisolationist sheep.

While a state might feel this way, why wouldn't things be different for members of a strong collective – a hegemonic alliance or the UN? Why wouldn't the very powerful ambition to enforce peace and order and therefore rule in important ways, with all its psychological, political, and other benefits, apply to these institutions? The typical explanation cites, to start with, the concern states have about interventions that weaken sovereignty, even if the cause looks good – the payoff from interrupting sovereignty often seems too low. States will also disagree about what the collective power created is to be used for (in preventing war or other matters) and who is to dominate future decisions on its use; since each fears it may not win those arguments they will be leery of creating the power to intervene in the first place. Also regularly cited is the tendency to ride free or pass bucks, with the result that security and order can be underproduced. Given all this, states will lack confidence that the collective actor can actually provide peace and order, or can do it indefinitely, and will therefore rely more on self-help.

This makes it easy to understand the lack of effective deterrence/enforcement – too often there will be little willingness to provide it. The problem would disappear if each member moved to define its national interest as rooted in an effective system management of war. Then they would drop narrow, short-term conceptions of their interests; they would also need strong confidence that management by collective institutions will not be fleeting, a failure, or injurious to the members. They are most likely to adopt these positions when:

1   States come to see multilateral arrangements as very beneficial, particularly as shown in practice, and conclude that lack of management is unattractive – the payoffs from MIs are high.
2   States enjoy acceptable participation in the multilateral arrangements – a voice and a role. This contributes to feeling that the arrangements are beneficial, allow pursuit of their particular goals, and are *intrinsically valuable* (i.e., a seat at the table).
3   States conclude that system management is good *in principle* even if inadequate or unduly burdensome and harmful at present.

These are stringent but not impossible requirements. States can take important steps to enhance the chance for and durability of cooperation by maneuvering to bring about these conditions.[18] We know the conditions are not impossible since periodically they have been met, particularly on handling wars of modest size. Granted, the record of MIs in preventing or halting wars, even well below major wars, is quite uneven. Nevertheless, collective responses to war have sometimes been impressive – MIs can do effective conflict resolution, peacekeeping, and peace enforcement; sometimes they pull off a major peace imposition.

Hence when we look back at the two conditions listed earlier the ultimate difficulty is not the first condition – willingness to provide, multilaterally, the necessary deterrence and enforcement – but the second. Multilateral deterrence and enforcement for preventing war appears *implausible and unfeasible for major war* because that requires a level of force that is normally beyond system management itself. There are participants in the system too strong to be readily coerced. To attempt to coerce them takes a major war and thus major war ceases to 'wane'.

If power is distributed quite unequally, it is easy to imagine a collective security arrangement working, as long as members are not divided roughly evenly on some fighting issue. All other members can gang up on those who go to war or threaten to, providing the basis for effective deterrence or imposing peace. Since members have markedly unequal capabilities, however, only the most powerful states can readily provide the power suitable for deterrence and enforcement. (Inside collective management lurks a hegemon or concert around which collective effort coalesces politically and operationally.) Those states are beyond deterrence and coercion. One or more might be defeated by the others in combination but this would take a major war and look less like multilateral management than a systemwide war.

The only MI ever devised to *really* prevent *major* wars by concentrating power was Cold War deterrence. It helped do this at the global level, though analysts disagree as to whether it was responsible, very important, or just helpful (some analysts say it did nothing) and thus also disagree about whether it prevents major wars today.[19] However, it was inconsistent in preventing major wars in regional systems. It was also of dubious value for enforcement if a major global war had ever broken out – maybe it would have blocked escalation, maybe not. It's good we never had to find out. It was also not always clearly multilateral.

We are left with a structural problem. Unless major wars cannot occur and will not be planned, deterrence or enforcement will probably be needed sometimes. But MIs cannot do this except in and through their most powerful members who are then beyond MI deterrence and enforcement.[20] This is a familiar problem in government: the central power necessary for governance is simultaneously beyond easy coercion and thus actually or potentially above the law. It may come to be beyond institutional control over the abusive use of force. States possessing this capability cannot readily be deterred from violating the domestic peace or reliably punished for doing so other than by a large civil war. In international politics the necessary coercive power has always been lodged in great powers; as such it resembles a feudal system. Those especially capable of conducting major wars also have much of the power to run the system, and thus power to defy it. There is no consistent check on their going to war unless they balance each other. Others must fear that those states will use multilateral arrangements to serve only their own interests and escape limitations on their freedom of action.[21]

This is how to arrive at the notion – fairly widespread – that MIs do not prevent major wars directly. Global level MIs can prevent or halt smaller wars, as can regional MIs. Global level MIs can prevent or halt war involving a great power of a regional system (as Iraq discovered). However, they cannot coercively prevent major wars directly among global-level great powers and now there is widespread concern that the spread of weapons of mass destruction will enlarge this defect – that many regional great powers will eventually be beyond the coercive power of multilateral institutions.[22]

Can this limitation be avoided? There are three possibilities. The first is that nothing can be done. Multilateral restraints on war are simply not universally applicable and this applies to many, even most, major wars. MIs offer partial constraints, at best, on the worst kind of war. The second possibility is that MIs make a significant contribution but it is not crucial – they cannot prevent major wars. The final possibility is that MIs do not prevent major wars by deterrence/enforcement but can offer a functional equivalent.[23]

Specifically preventing major wars

To assess the contributions of MIs, let's start with the circumstances under which they can be made. We can conjure up at least four kinds of scenario. First, MIs might be important in preventing circumstances from arising that could draw great powers into war, such as by helping to resolve important and sensitive political disagreements among weaker states. This means providing decent system governance. Or MIs could be effective in dealing with a nasty international or domestic political conflict (one with some fighting), thus forestalling a great-power involvement that would make matters worse and possibly thrust great powers into a confrontation. Such tasks arose frequently during the Cold War and can involve MIs acting so that the great powers do not, or arranging that a great-power intervention is cooperative rather than competitive. Next, MIs might take steps to prevent escalation when two or more great powers are embroiled in a very serious but not yet war-threatening conflict (say, the US and China over Taiwan). Finally, if great powers are nearing war in a growing crisis where they are committed to incompatible goals and willing to fight for them (another Cuban Missile Crisis), perhaps MIs can help. Let's refer to these as First-, Second-, Third-, and Fourth-Level War Avoidance.

In addition, to properly assess the role of MIs we must recall that major-power warfare is often linked to international system governance, not simply a recurring headache governance must overcome. Sometimes governance concerns and ambitions provide the impetus for major wars, as suggested by well-known analyses of systemwide wars that determine who runs the system. Sometimes this is not the initial goal but emerges as an important objective and outcome – as for the US in World War II. Great-power wars are so important they inevitably alter system governance, even if this was unintended. When they shift the distribution of power and status they shift the concentration of power available for managing system peace and security.

Often this is taken for granted. Before 1914 a great war was widely anticipated because conflicts over running the European system could only be settled that way. The Axis powers were explicit about constructing a new world order by war. Gilpin and Modelski argue that a systemwide war always decides such matters.[24] In Kennedy's analysis, the 'rise' and 'fall' of great powers is defined by the ability to compete militarily, as ascertained by major wars.[25]

Hence we should explore the contributions of MIs in barring major wars via system governance. First-Level Major War Avoidance is governance good enough to prevent serious great-power conflicts from arising. Second-Level Avoidance is containing, repressing, or eliminating conflicts or crises that could provoke great-power confrontations – dealing with them another way or shaping congenial great-power interventions. Third-Level Avoidance copes with or contains great-power conflicts so they don't escalate, such as governance-related grievances, territorial or other specific disputes, or misperceptions that can lead to a major war. For instance, for a possible US–China war we would want MIs to contain or eliminate the Taiwan issue, or prevent a specific US–China conflict (over missile firings or naval maneuvers around Taiwan) from escalating, or help prevent US or Chinese misperceptions over whether China will violently object to US military sales to Taiwan or the US will really risk Los Angeles over Taiwan.

Fourth-Level Major War Avoidance means halting the movement of hostile great powers toward war. The MI contribution might come in terms of broad governance or in helping defuse the immediate issues. The former is apt to be the most important. Normally, driving the specific events, perceptions, and issues pushing great powers toward a major war is a larger context of rivalry that is the real cause.

Thus four sorts of circumstances offer a danger of major war to which MIs may helpfully respond. Our concern is this: is their response to these circumstances so helpful that they are a major reason for the drop in major wars, that they somehow 'cause' that drop? There are good reasons to think not, especially given their limitations for generating the military power to deter major wars or enforce peace.

Claimed contributions

There are numerous claims about what MIs do for peace and security. Some pertain directly to conflict management and war, others to promoting cooperation in general. It appears that they actually make these contributions at times. The oldest claims reflect what MIs have been designed to do and have demonstrated they can do. MIs facilitate negotiations on conflicts and thereby help contain them or bring them to a peaceful resolution. They provide an arena for diplomatic combat, a substitute for fighting. They provide good offices for negotiations, and apply pressure on the parties to talk and not fight. They are a venue for talks and help bring the parties together. They facilitate through fact-finding and carrying messages. They mediate: generating communication and discussion, offering proposals, sometimes manipulating or pressuring the parties into a deal. So MIs help resolve minor conflicts before they escalate and prevent serious conflicts from generating higher tensions and more grievances.

MIs can also deal with sensitive situations so rival great powers don't have to, avoiding dangerous confrontations, or become vehicles for great-power cooperative management of such situations. If those situations deteriorate, MIs can threaten or initiate intervention via peacekeeping. If that doesn't work they can threaten to suppress fighting and punish those who don't stop. Finally, they can take steps to resolve a conflict after fighting has ended – trying to rebuild political systems, economies, and societies, get combatants disarmed, etc. This range of activity gives us the contemporary terminology for peace efforts of MIs: peacemaking, peacekeeping, peace enforcement, peace imposition, and peace building. These can also be undertaken by, or under the rubric of, noninstitutionalized MIs, such as a nuclear deterrence-based management or an informal concert.

Next comes the neorealist or 'liberal institutionalist' analysis of how MIs contribute.[26] These analysts emphasize that the institutions flourish because they enhance the efficient conduct of international affairs, promote transparency, and ease concerns about cheating or defection that can either prevent agreements or cause them to break down. Thus organizations monitor agreements, investigate complaints, verify compliance, and generate information. MIs, particularly organizations, facilitate agreements through issue linkage, a major lubricant of politics at any level, and help construct focal points around which equilibria coalesce. They reduce transaction costs for negotiations and agreements. They bring more predictability to international life which, with greater transparency, makes future considerations more salient in foreign policies; a lengthened shadow of the future brings greater cooperation and a less self-centered, short-term, focus. They allow governments to shift the onus for unpopular decisions to a higher level or cite international imperatives to justify painful national adjustments.

Finally, there are constructivist conclusions about multilateral institutions.[27] MIs help construct state identities and the elements of community in international politics. They regularize and institutionalize the existence of norms and constitute the essence of rules of behavior. In effect they embody efforts to build commitment to important values and give concrete form to them. Many norms and values would not be taken seriously without an institutional expression.[28] MIs provide a basis and systematic way to invoke norms and challenge instances of noncompliance, helping turn noncompliance into norm reinforcement. In this fashion they shape and build habits, and a history, of cooperation. In particular, they can facilitate the development of reciprocity, especially diffuse reciprocity, as a motivational element in state interactions.

If these are MI contributions, the problem is that they often seem irrelevant to the prevention of *major* wars. In First- and Second-Level Major War Avoidance, their contributions might easily supply better management of international politics. MIs often seem to have their greatest impact here, promoting peace and order below the threshold of great-power competitive intervention. Unfortunately, MI conflict management often rests primarily on the great powers even at these levels. They supply the high profile political influence, the diplomatic leverage, the implied threats of conflict management at work. Some MIs (concerts) are essentially great powers in action; others that can be more than this (collective security) are apt to need the great powers to really make things happen. The more demanding the conflict management task, the more the great powers seem crucial for success. This is particularly so when the task shifts from peacemaking or peacekeeping (First and Second Level) to peace enforcement or imposition, but it is true even at the peacemaking stage. In the Middle East peace process UN involvement was long ago superseded by the role of the US. Sometimes an MI successfully substitutes for the great powers, but often not much will happen without their active participation, particularly if some great powers are the targets.

In dampening or ending outbreaks of fighting (forestalling potential great-power clashes) the MI record is mixed. It is not clear why actors comply (or not) with international agreements[29] including obligations under MI-brokered deals to settle conflicts, but for years analysts like Butterworth, Haas, and Diehl have charted the limited success of the UN in conflict abatement and conflict resolution. For instance the UN is not very effective, once it intervenes, in preventing future conflict between the parties.[30] The surge of UN interventions in the 1990s culminated in widespread complaints that it was overloaded, the achievements were limited, peacekeeping was in 'crisis'[31] and the requisite great-power congeniality was slipping away.[32] Even a generally favorable study on international organizations and peace finds them less influential than the impact of democracy and rising trade.[33]

Regional organizations fare no better or not as well. They are often bereft of resources, making regional great powers even more central to any decision and action they may take.[34] They are frequently disparaged for lacking not just resources but imagination and will, particularly for directly intervening in member states.[35]

At the Third and Fourth Levels, the role of multilateral institutions appears more limited still. For instance, the peacemaking functions of MIs are hard to bring to bear in great-power conflicts, in part because MI efforts often depend on the great powers. Second, great powers often use intermediaries only in simple ways. They resist oversight intrusions into their conflict behavior and regularly get away with it. They often ignore MIs on functions like detection of cheating or verification of compliance, preferring to carry on those tasks themselves. (For instance, the US, Russia, and the EU are not subject in the normal way to International Atomic Energy Agency (IAEA) monitoring.) They often avoid fully implementing transparency measures adopted by MIs for other states, preferring national means of detection in dealing with peers. They rarely turn to mediation of their quarrels by third parties, and seek direct negotiations instead or use an MI simply as a convenient venue; they themselves mediate, but they rarely accept mediation among themselves except as global great power mediating for regional great powers (as in the Israeli–Egypt negotiations).

They clearly prefer dealing with their conflicts by themselves, such as doing their own versions of issue-linkage. There is no recourse to peacekeeping and peace enforcement for them, and rarely any peace imposition in dealing with even regional great powers. It is hard to imagine peacekeeping units being inserted between American and Chinese forces off Taiwan, and the UN was not much of a mediator between Moscow and Washington in the Cold War. India rejects any outside mediation on Kashmir, and the Sino-Soviet dispute was never referred to a third party.

We return to the most serious limitation of MIs, namely that the power needed to deter/enforce for preventing major wars is beyond their control. What can be done about this? Domestic ways of dealing with the problem are instructive. States and societies face the same problem and handle it unevenly. War within societies and within states is common enough so insufficient governance to prevent it is a serious problem. Also serious is that power concentrated to keep the peace often results in governments or rulers that terribly abuse the citizens. It is hard to say which is more common: overweening leaders and states that make war too readily on their populations, or overly weak states forced into war by powerful domestic opponents.

What do domestic systems do? One answer is power balancing but it produces quite uneven results, just as in international politics. There is balancing by the dispersion and sharing of powers. There is the maintenance of multiple and competing specialists in force and violence. Some states keep military capabilities dispersed as militias or powerful provinces, which also provides military resources for use by locals against centrally mounted threats.

Another possibility is the leviathan – powerful central rule that crushes threats of internal resistance or war. Absolutist systems certainly can, at least for a time, keep peace domestically but the price is loss of protection against the state's predations. The third solution is community building so effective that the society and the state are suffused with values and behavior that avoid internal warfare. Within such a community power can be concentrated sufficiently to provide domestic peace while the strength of community ties minimizes the threat that might be posed by illegitimate uses of force and power. These systems can professionalize military forces without detaching them from society's dominant values. Concentration yet containment of military power is achieved via a strong sense of community resting on shared norms, rule of law, and the cherishing of rights.

How relevant are these solutions for MIs? The first is highly suspect, given its past record. With offsetting power balancing in international politics the role of MIs is typically very limited. And while MIs have often been championed as alternatives to power balancing, they need not be. For instance, power balancing might operate within a concert.[36] Concert members might have spheres of influence within which they try to keep peace, with members having agreed to avoid each others' turf. Of course, concert members could collectively exploit less powerful states. Or they might keep out of each other's spheres precisely so each had a free hand in exploiting its own. This was the sort of concert in which Hitler offered membership to Stalin.

The objection to power balancing in international politics, *for preventing major wars*, has always been that it doesn't work consistently and that effective balancing even requires major warfare – sometimes to maintain the system against challengers. That it doesn't work well enough suggests that power is insufficiently concentrated to deter and enforce while the need for war to maintain the system suggests that even when it works well, it works badly.

Some analysts think nuclear deterrence makes power balancing more effective. Advocates of nuclear proliferation suggest that it resolves the problem of major war by dispersing the capabilities needed to deter it, and we can add that it simultaneously protects against overly concentrated power. Power is balanced yet war is not needed to keep it so. However, this approach enjoys much less support than power balancing in general, for which there are many advocates. It is particularly unappealing for those interested in other sorts of multilateral institutions. Few supporters of institutions think of power balancing, or of nuclear deterrence, as the ultimate in major-war avoidance.

As for the leviathan, the parallel in international politics is hegemony. Available analysis concerns the single dominant state. With a hegemon, how are international institutions involved? It depends. International institutions may flourish but as effect rather than cause. The theory of hegemonic stability traces solidly cooperative international relations, and effective international institutions, to the order provided by the hegemon.[37] The theory was used to point out how international institutions, the cooperation, and the related peace and security, would decline when the hegemon did. Keohane argued that this is not necessarily the case, that institutions can survive and flourish after the hegemon fades, but since the hegemon of interest now has not faded it is difficult to be certain.

Not well analyzed is the collective hegemon. NATO is now a collective hegemon, the purveyor of security for Europe. It is a dominant concentration of power, clearly superior even after cutting its overall military capabilities sharply since 1989. At first reluctant to take on hegemonic responsibilities it then resorted to this with vigor. Particularly interesting is that it has been turning itself from an alliance, albeit an unusually institutionalized one, into a genuine multinational organization for security management through the Partnership for Peace Program and the Euro-Atlantic Partnership Council. As its Secretary General likes to say:

> Today the Alliance is the dynamo at the hub of a profound new set of defence relationships. . . . Forty six countries – NATO members, former Warsaw Pact countries and even neutrals, including Switzerland which is not even in the United Nations – now train together, talk about security issues together and even carry out peacekeeping operations together. The value of this inclusive framework is very clear. Every country in Europe has a structure through which they can enhance their security interests.[38]

This makes for stability and predictability so Europeans avoid 'fragile and dangerous security pacts' which might create 'a volatile and weakly anchored security system'.[39]

The regional system in which NATO is immersed is shot through with institutional elements, so much so that states newly associating themselves with it insist on seeking membership in all those institutions. This is a liberalist MI hegemony but it is shifting toward something more like collective security. In this connection it is appropriate that President Putin (like Yeltsin before him) has suggested that Russia some day join NATO and that the US (among others) has never ruled this out. It is a powerful MI arrangement for imposing peace and security when necessary. But there is no sign it could prevent a *major* war in Europe, no sign it has escaped that limitation of other MIs. NATO does not expect to have to force its great-power members to avoid war among themselves on a large scale, and future collective security protection will not be provided with them as the possible threats.

The third recourse in domestic systems is community building. One way to display the existence of a suitable community is to leave the relevant power with the participants – as with a militia. This remains the most plausible way international institutions can be directly responsible for 'restraining' major wars by deterrence and enforcement; states keep the relevant power but an alliance promises to mobilize against the illegitimate use of war, which is collective security. This sounds fine but when tried in the past it failed at both required functions. It did not minimize (to the vanishing point) major wars and deterrence/enforcement were therefore needed (community building was inadequate), and then it did not successfully deter and enforce. The problem of dealing with very powerful war-prone states did not disappear. One critique suggests that its multiple failings mean that 'collective security is fundamentally flawed in its theoretical logic'.[40]

The most disturbing feature of collective security is the great disparity in military might among members of any system because this means that in some instances to enforce rejection of war would take a major war, a violation of the objective (unless required only at the start to lay the basis for the system and its credibility).[41] Proponents of collective security count on nonmilitary enforcement to evade this problem but it has not worked consistently with major states as targets. What is often needed to make collective security work is a hegemon or an effective concert. But what keeps those powerful states from warring on each other or collectively against others?

The end point of community building (short of integration) is a pluralistic security community where the members see no likelihood of wars among themselves and behave accordingly. This is the ultimate liberalist solution,[42] and fits some construc-tivist perspectives too. It eliminates the security dilemma. As for institutions, they can be highly supportive. In the abstract they are unnecessary for a pluralistic security community, but one could hardly be established without rising transactions, interactions, and interdependence which would require shared norms and habits, extensive pathways of cooperation, formal rules, and organizations. How could all that emerge without concrete manifestations of the cooperative behavior pledged and involved? Both symbols and institutionalized expressions of community's values, and thus of the community, would be needed. Here MIs don't just facilitate cooperation, they embody and give visible expression to it.

This takes us back to Väyrynen's reference to institutions as valuable not as shapers of behavior so much as 'expressions of more fundamental changes in ideas, values, and norms'. The solution they offer is community building, and while institutions are facilitators and modest contributors they are prime indicators that vital community building has occurred in other ways. When this fails to prevent war it is not the fault of the institutions but of deficiencies in the underlying community building. As Miller notes on collective security, arrangements for intervening have not worked well but they have promoted rising acceptance in world affairs of aggressive warfare as unacceptable – this powerful norm is their major contribution.[43]

Two cases

In sum, institutions manifest and embody underlying norms and behavior that allow states to constitute a peaceful community; thus they create and maintain peace as an integral component of the necessary norms and behavior. But they do not maintain peace in the sense that when a powerful government disregards the foundations of the community they can either deter it or enforce the peace. That sounds clear enough.

However, there are two plausible objections. Perhaps institutions *are* an integral part of creating a durable international order because they actually constrain the powerful. A good example might be the community building in the North Atlantic area. The contrary objection would be that MIs are not necessary for stable peace in an international system. A good example here is the recent history of the East Asian regional system. We can consider each case in turn.

MIs appear to have been very important in community building to eliminate war among Western nations and this has deeply influenced thinking about institutions. While NATO kept the Soviets out it also functioned as a community, building important links among states which had often been enemies and had fought each other just a few years before. Also designed to make cooperation profound and war very unlikely were the early components of what became the European Union. And when the Cold War ended, security considerations helped incite another surge to deepen integration and enlarge NATO and EU membership. The Western community extended much further through the World Bank, the IMF, GATT, and OECD. Beneath all the organizational activity was an emerging mega-society of common values translated into norms of interstate behavior and rules embracing high levels of cooperation.

We should remember that the Soviet bloc tried to develop in a parallel fashion, creating MIs and insisting that a socialist community's common norms and rules would transcend traditional international relations. Soviet bilateral military arrangements with Eastern European states were supplemented by the Warsaw Pact, and economic cooperation tending toward integration was pursued via COMECON. Thus in both halves of Europe there were efforts to build communities as the correct basis for ending major warfare.

As we know, the Eastern European effort failed while the West's triumphed. The Soviet-dominated arrangements were discredited and abandoned along with the bloc and the USSR itself, largely because bloc members had limited confidence in the proclaimed norms and there was no record of achievement comparable to the

West's in operating an effective community. Thus the bloc was held together by force on several occasions and failed when Moscow would no longer do that; it was a marginal 'community'.

Western institutions made a significant contribution to ending war among the members and a recent analysis suggests how and why. Finding parallels with other durable postwar international orders, Ikenberry argues that the crucial step taken by the US was creating MIs that *constrained itself* along with the others. That made American power more acceptable, producing a community that appeared much more legitimate and thus endured: 'the lesson of American order building in this century is that international institutions have played a pervasive and ultimately constructive role in the exercise of American power.'[44]

Notice that institutions did this without deterrence and enforcement; there was actually no specified institutional capability for keeping peace *among* the members. It was not supposed to be necessary. Even having to try to deter war among the core members would have been deemed a disastrous failure of the community. The only occasions where it was necessary concerned members, Greece and Turkey, peripheral enough that the community was not called into question. Instead, the MIs operated by embodying and helping manage construction and elaboration of a vast multilayered community, which led to a pluralistic security community and, in Western Europe, an integrated community.

Several features of this effort were probably vital. Driving much of the West's effort was a common external threat, and simultaneously (partly for reasons of security) the common and serious economic task of recovery and development. The importance of hanging together in NATO was clear, while the US and others took the lead in driving a collective approach to economic recovery the others came to embrace. It is often suggested, typically by realists, that the West's achievements in multilateralism grew from these necessary burdens. Cooperation was in everyone's interest and therefore represented no fundamental change in international politics.

Alternatively, the cooperation represented an advanced multilateralism.[45] Going beyond simple cooperation, it has the following features:

1   A set of generalized principles as the basis for cooperation.
2   A sense among participants of indivisibility, of constituting a community.
3   An expectation of diffuse reciprocity.

The West's generalized principles included such things as treating an attack on one as an attack on all, and most-favored-nation treatment in trade. What defined the community was the nations to which the principles applied, and their sense of community was embodied in those principles. Expectations that the community would endure allowed members to settle at times for modest short run payoffs in the expectation of much larger long run benefits. This made resolving conflicts easier; agreement did not always have to fit with everyone's efforts to maximize specific gains. Expectations of diffuse reciprocity readily supported the creation of institutions, including organizations empowered to decide, over some members' disagreements, in keeping with generalized principles.

Another vital factor was the widespread presence of democracy. Particularly in a world where democracy, having survived the rise of Fascism, seemed under serious attack from another quarter, the appeal of extensive association with other democracies had enormous appeal. That made building a Western community far easier and the result much more durable. When the end of the Cold War posed new challenges in Europe, that community was able to move effectively to begin extending itself eastward and draw on its immense appeal throughout the rest of the continent.

The resulting cooperation has produced rising interdependence via enormous interactions. People in the West ceased to live in relatively closed national communities. They came to share values, many cultural elements, economic interpenetration, extensive military cooperation, even a common language of sorts. This forced elaborations of rules and practices and their interpretation and coordination by organizations; in turn, the organizations benefited from the interactions and common perspectives. The result was transformation of the regional international system through the end of the Cold War and the ensuing enlargement of the West.[46]

Another relevant element has received less attention than it should. Remember that trust in these arrangements *was never complete*. European members constantly worried that the US would some day return to isolationist ways; Europeans often reassured themselves on this not by citing the transatlantic community but a US national interest in preserving Europe from Soviet control. Once that argument no longer applied the fear reappeared. And why not – some Americans have always questioned the wisdom of continued direct involvement in European security. Meanwhile, for years Americans saw the US as the linchpin in the transatlantic community – without it Europe would fall back into classic quarrels and rivalries – a view reinvigorated by events in Yugoslavia in the 1990s. Europeans were also never certain that the old Germany would not reappear, or that the web of values and institutions would indefinitely prevent war.

Thus another vital element in community building was *insurance against failure*. American leadership of NATO was seen as insurance against a renewed drive for German dominance. NATO's integrated planning and command arrangements were to subsume West German forces under a broader command. British and French nuclear weapons were promoted as providing security if US deterrence ever failed or was withdrawn. Above all, Europeans expanded integration as the most reliable escape from traditional national conflicts, boosting it at key turning points rather than relying only on more multilateralism. The goal was to embed Germany in a highly integrated community, an objective German officials shared:

> We wanted to bend Germany into a structure which practically obliges Germany to take the interests of its neighbors into consideration. We wanted to give our neighbors assurances that we won't do what we don't intend to do anyway.[47]

The real insurance against major war for many Europeans was to keep building integration. This gives us several features of Western multilateralism to choose from in trying to explain why it was successful, and there are others. Perhaps all this was possible mainly because of American hegemony, particularly its liberalist character. What if the proponent of staunch realism, insisting on defense in all directions and holding itself apart from many significant institutional arrangements had been West Germany rather than France? Maybe what was important was that the nations involved were nearly all democracies. We don't know. We don't know with certainty what conditions were necessary or helpful. We can't be certain that the transatlantic community will last. We know Europeans have placed their bets on integration, and some analysts envision a tough rivalry between the US and the EU in the future.

What we can say is that after the collapse of the Soviet bloc the steps taken to make the rest of Europe peaceful were derived from the West's experience.[48] European integration has been deepened and enlarged, with plans for more. NATO has been enlarged by new members and by links with associates in the rest of Europe. As a result when NATO imposed on Serbia and the Bosnian Serbs in the name of European security so many other states cooperated with NATO that it resembled a collective security arrangement at work. Eastern Europeans have lined up to be members of the West. The Organization for Security and Co-operation in Europe (OSCE) is the overarching expression of common norms and rules that extend far beyond international interactions to democratization, protection of human rights, and the development of market economies.

Thus we have explanations for these developments but are far from closure. We cannot say how to duplicate this kind of community elsewhere. It seems to have been a very complicated process, and many have suggested it is time- or culture-bound and cannot be duplicated elsewhere. More importantly for this chapter, we cannot say exactly how important such a multilateral complex is for avoiding war. After all, the incidence of major war has dropped elsewhere too. Perhaps multilateral institutions are not as invaluable as the transatlantic experience might suggest. To elaborate on this we briefly consider another case.

For most of the twentieth century East Asia displayed traditional, and traditionally violent, international politics. Imperialist clashes culminated in Asia's portion of World War II, followed by national liberation wars, other violent domestic struggles, and Cold War conflicts – major fighting in China, Korea, Cambodia and Vietnam, lesser but nasty violence in Indonesia, Malaysia, and Thailand and between the Thais and Vietnamese, Indonesians and Malaysians, Vietnamese and Chinese, the Chinese and Soviets, etc. The region saw alliances, arms build-ups, crises, ideological divisions, and a huge superpower military presence. Even Japan, which maintained limited military forces and avoided displaying 'normal' great-power aims and ambitions, was widely assumed to be lying in wait, soon to pursue hegemony again.

But in the early 1970s the regional system began to change.[49] Over the next three decades nearly every serious dyadic conflict was significantly eased: talks were held, interactions expanded greatly, serious issues were resolved or cooled or at least set aside, cooperative arrangements expanded, and the general level of tension declined. In the Sino-Soviet dispute huge military concentrations and border clashes gradually gave way to negotiated demarcations, major troop pullbacks, normal trade, big arms sales, and a modest Moscow–Beijing association. In the Sino-American dispute enmity was replaced by cooperation and normalization of relations; trade and American investment in China vastly expanded, and there was some cooperation on arms control and the problem of North Korea. In the China–Taiwan dispute the US agreed that Taiwan is part of China, China and Taiwan mounted huge economic interactions, people began flowing across the straits, and the two governments negotiated at long range on the issue.

In the Southeast Asian disputes the parties eventually resolved or set aside their conflicts and moved into ASEAN, successful political cooperation to help manage the international environment, rising economic interactions, pursuit of a free trade zone, and establishment of the Asian Regional Forum for top-level discussions about security. In the two Koreas dispute the intense rivalry eventually eased a bit with agreement in 1991 on basic principles for relaxing tensions, and more with the emergence of extensive aid to North Korea in the late 1990s, the US pursuit of a modest engagement and the ROK sunshine policy, and a North–South summit conference in 2000. The US suspended confrontation with Pyongyang over the North's nuclear weapons ambitions and tried hard for elimination of the North's missile program. Pyongyang became the largest recipient of American aid in Asia. Even when the North Korean nuclear phoenix reappeared, the result was Northeast Asia's most impressive effort at multilateral security management to date.

Meanwhile, Japan and Russia went from low-level conflict to a much more normal relationship with periodic high-level meetings and extensive discussions about the shape of a possible Kuriles settlement. The same could be said, more or less, about the China–Vietnam border dispute, the China–Indonesia conflict, the development of Japanese relations with China, the progression of American–Vietnamese relations. This was facilitated by, and contributed to, regional economic interactions which produced some of the most remarkable growth rates in history. Vast trade and investment between the US and East Asians were gradually augmented by significant intra-Asian flows that boosted economic interdependence – between Japan and all of its neighbors, between Korea and China, between Taiwan and its neighbors.

How do we explain all this? Certainly not by citing multilateral institutions. In the East Asian system today there are disagreements about basic values, little institutionalization, and considerable suspicions of a realist nature among the members:

- China fears the US will push hegemony to the point of containment.
- The US fears China will seek regional hegemony and some Americans call it a 'strategic competitor'.

- The US believes its military presence, not an emerging community, determines regional stability.
- China and Korea have deep-seated fears of Japan's long-term intentions.

While there are some emerging rules of behavior they are not firmly rooted in a strong sense of community and sturdy common norms. The available multilateral organizations – ASEAN, ARF, APEC – are not imposing. The only alliance arrangement is the US bilateral wheel-and-spokes pattern.

In short, the East Asian system achieved a large improvement in its security situation, making major war unlikely after years of significant fighting and serious great-power crises, but not via anything like the transatlantic model. This contradicts past analyses which claimed little could be done without multilateralization. For example:

> [In the Asia-Pacific region] it was not possible to construct multilateral institutional frameworks there in the immediate postwar period. Today, the absence of such arrangements inhibits progressive adaptation to fundamental global shifts. . . . Thus, whereas today the potential to move beyond balance-of-power politics in its traditional form exists in Europe, a reasonably stable balance is the best that one can hope to achieve in the Asia-Pacific region.[50]

Analysts frequently suggest that significant development of MIs would help consolidate the progress made and ensure a more secure future, a position to which the US subscribes. This may be true. But the *initial* progress was made without a unifying element like the Cold War, among states that were mostly not democratic, without big cuts in their armed forces, and among economies clinging to neo-mercantilism. In short, neither the circumstances nor the broad liberalist recipe associated with the Western model seem to be prerequisites for major progress, at least initially, away from traditional international politics.

In a sense this is good. To make major war reliably unlikely would be very difficult if, regionally or globally, the steps taken in the transatlantic system had to be replicated. There is no evidence they can be taken in the Middle East, or South Asia, at least not any time soon. But it may be that they are not necessary, at least not initially. How nice.

On the other hand, this suggests there is less to the impact of MIs than is typically believed by all but the realists. Why? What explains the East Asian achievements? Several possibilities deserve consideration. Perhaps the East Asian case is a temporary conjunction of national interests and eventually progress will unravel and traditional international politics will come roaring back. A recurring concern in analyses of the system is that it is late nineteenth century Europe all over again: a group of states undergoing rapid development and quickly expanding national wealth and capabilities will experience surges in nationalism that heighten territorial disputes and competition over status, culminating in a systemwide brawl or great-power clashes over dominance.

An alternative view, more favorable to MIs, is that while the region displays few common norms, rules, and organizations for system management, many relevant elements are partly established at the global level and work from there to shape behavior in East Asia. There is the impact of the WTO, or the demonstration in the Gulf War of a norm (plus enforcement) against blatant aggression. On the other hand, the chief conclusion the Chinese seem to have drawn from the Gulf War, Bosnia, and Kosovo is that newly established norms mainly favor and are manipulated by the US and its allies at China's expense.

Another view is that East Asian progress on security is due to the power of domestic 'liberalizing coalitions', elites and leaders who, in pursuit of their own and national interests, espouse liberalization of national economic policies for vigorous participation in the world economy, and domestic political, economic, and social liberalization to make a breakthrough to rapid development.[51] In foreign policy liberalizing coalitions in power downplay confrontation and conflict in favor of building a stable international environment good for national modernization. One implication is that political and economic liberalization together drive foreign policy liberalization, curbing national foreign policy assertiveness and relaxing conflicts abroad so as to get on with development.

Still another view is that political liberalization is not necessary to start the process, that the key is devotion to export-led modernization and a related foreign economic policy. The states that initiated the transformation of East Asian international politics were not necessarily liberal at home. South Korea, Taiwan, Indonesia, and China (now possibly North Korea) started looking for rapid development to strengthen authoritarian rule and national competitiveness. Opening up to participation in the global economy was not necessarily intended to lead to domestic liberalization.

While political liberalization may gradually occur in the end, regardless of what was intended, the crucial point would be that moderating foreign policies and mitigating conflicts can get under way and make real progress without a prior or parallel liberalization of the political systems. Even a regional international system with uneven liberalization in human rights, democracy, and media freedom may still see a cluster of countries simultaneously seeking to ease international tensions and provide a stable international environment.

Again, the Western route to reducing major wars may not be the only one and thus multilateral institutions may not need to be well developed for this purpose. While they may become more important later on they are not crucial at the outset.

Conclusions

Multilateral institutions exist, and can be expanded, that can prevent or repress many lower-level kinds of warfare. They can supply mediation, conflict resolution, and peace building. They can also provide the deterrence and enforcement needed to prevent some wars. However, since the military might is provided by the members and the great powers are responsible for much of it, there are always powers that can be almost impossible for a multilateral arrangement to successfully coerce.

This means that MIs are most valuable for curbing major wars in contributing to installation of communities in which willingness to use war shrinks toward the vanishing point. This is how they have played a very important role in the transatlantic regional system during the Cold War and now in the further expansion of the Western community into Eastern Europe. They have expressed or symbolized the existence of a successful community of states in terms of security, and in this way they have enhanced security. They have facilitated transparency and interdependence. They have handled crises. Within their flexible frameworks nations have been able to adapt to even startling changes in the transatlantic system.

However, it seems possible to start to move an international system beyond traditional international politics, shrinking major wars, without elaborate multilateral institutions in place. The example of the East Asian system is instructive; great powers and lesser states, given suitable incentives within a favorable environment, may be able to go a long way to reduce the chances of major war (and other wars) with only modest recourse to MIs. It does seem that to curb major wars within a traditional system, or to arrive at strong communities of states complete with sound multilateral institutions, it is imperative that the great powers operate in harmony. If true then MIs are not a crucial intervening variable, at least initially. Multilateral institutions may turn out to be as much a product of the waning of major war as its producer.

Notes

1 I. L. Claude, Jr, *Swords Into Plowshares* (New York: Random House, 1956).
2 Recent books on international governance, for example, say very little about security management concerning major wars. See J. S. Nye and J. D. Donahue (eds), *Governance in a Globalizing World* (Washington, DC: Brookings, 2000) or M. Hewson and T. J. Sinclair (eds), *Approaches to Global Governance Theory* (Albany: State University of New York Press, 1999).
3 M. Mandelbaum, 'Is Major War Obsolete', *Survival*, 40, 4 (1998–9), pp. 28–40. On classifying wars see J. A. Vasquez, *The War Puzzle* (Cambridge: Cambridge University Press, 1993), pp. 51–85. The Korean War illustrates the difficulties. It had huge consequences and many casualties but was not a 'major' war by almost anyone's sense of these things.
4 Japan lacks the military capabilities of a global great power; as yet China lacks the reach or global spectrum of interests to be one; Russia is a regional power (at best) given its limited economic, military, and cultural reach. All three are global powers mainly by custom and in anticipation of what they could become.
5 Treating casualties and other consequences as making war 'major' is widespread; for example see E. A. Cohen, 'The Major Consequences of War', *Survival*, 41, 2 (summer 1999), pp. 143–6. Often analysts object to disregarding internal wars when they involve massive casualties and destruction.
6 To Mandelbaum an Indo-Pakistani nuclear war would not be major. See M. Mandelbaum, 'Learning to be Warless', *Survival*, 41, 2 (1999), pp. 149–52.

7   J. G. March and J. P. Olsen, 'The Institutional Dynamics of International Political Orders', *International Organization*, 52, 4 (1998), p. 948.

8   J. J. Mearsheimer, 'The False Promise of International Institutions', *International Security*, 19, 3 (1994/5), p. 8. It is hard to distinguish MIs from regimes, and not much reason to do so. Compare the above with Keohane on regimes: 'institutions with explicit rules, agreed upon by governments, that pertain to particular sets of issues in international relations', see R. Keohane, *International Institutions and State Power: Essays in International Relations Theory* (Boulder: Westview Press, 1989), p. 4; and see the discussion in A. Hasenclever, P. Mayer and V. Rittberger, *Theories of International Regimes* (Cambridge: Cambridge University Press, 1997).

9   MIs are not always specified via multilateral agreements; in some cases they are proliferating bilateral agreements with parallel clauses. Only about 5 percent of international agreements are multilateral. See M. Simai, *The Future of Global Governance* (Washington, DC: US Institute of Peace Press, 1994), p. 266.

10 G. A. Raymond, 'International Norms: Normative Orders and Peace', in J. A. Vasquez (ed.), *What Do We Know About War* (Lanham: Roman & Littlefield, 2000), pp. 281–97.

11 See R. Väyrynen's chapter in this volume, Chapter 10.

12 F. V. Kratochwil and J. G. Ruggie, 'International Organization: A State of the Art on an Art of the State', *International Organization*, 40 (1986), p. 760.

13 Hence comparisons have been drawn with the difficulty of getting members of legislatures to cooperate. L. Martin and B. Simmons, 'Theories and Empirical Studies of International Institutions', *International Organization*, 52, 4 (1998), pp. 729–57.

14 D. S. Geller and J. D. Singer, *Nations at War: A Scientific Study of International Conflict* (Cambridge: Cambridge University Press, 1998), p. 1.

15 K. J. Gantzel and T. Schwinghammer, *Warfare Since the Second World War* (London: Transaction, 2000), p. 89.

16 Often nuclear deterrence was described in bipolar balance of power terms. But over time it became deterrence-generated systemic management that included much cooperation and mutual restraint. Fear of deterrence instability generated superpower efforts to control clients on starting or fighting wars, prevent nuclear proliferation, and limit their own involvements in regional conflicts. It led to arms control on proliferation, deployments, accident controls, crisis management, verification arrangements, and nuclear testing. Deterrence became a multilateral institution for containing major wars. P. M. Morgan, *Deterrence Now* (Cambridge: Cambridge University Press, 2003).

17 On the difficulties and possibilities of cooperation in international politics see A. A. Stein, *Why Nations Cooperate: Circumstances and Choice in International Relations* (Ithaca: Cornell University Press, 1990).

18 K. A. Oye, 'Explaining Cooperation Under Anarchy: Hypotheses and Strategies', in K. A. Oye (ed.), *Cooperation Under Anarchy* (Princeton: Princeton University Press, 1986), pp. 1–24; R. Axelrod and R. O. Keohane, 'Achieving Cooperation Under Anarchy: Strategies and Institutions', in Oye (ed.), ibid., pp. 226–54.

19 It is plausible that nuclear deterrence still discourages war, especially major war. But great powers see little worth fighting about (with each other) these days so the deterring going on is modest.

20 G. Downs and K. Iida, 'Assessing the Theoretical Case Against Collective Security', in G. Downs (ed.), *Collective Security Beyond the Cold War* (Ann Arbor: University of Michigan Press, 1994), pp. 17–39.

21 Simai, *The Future of Global Governance*, p. 297.

22 Debate about how deterrable those states will be fuels missile defense efforts, for example.

23 For instance, Modelski depicts systemwide war as a selection process for a hegemon that then provides peace and development. That led him to look for a functional equivalent,

a way to select world powers peacefully. G. Modelski, *Long Cycles in World Politics* (Seattle: University of Washington Press, 1987).

24 R. Gilpin, *War and Change in World Politics* (Cambridge: Cambridge University Press, 1981).

25 P. Kennedy, *The Rise and Fall of the Great Powers: Economic Change and Military Conflict from 1500 to 2000* (New York: Random House, 1987).

26 Keohane, *International Institutions and State Power*; Martin and Simmons, 'Theories and Empirical Studies of International Institutions'.

27 J. G. Ruggie, 'Multilateralism: The Anatomy of an Institution', in J. G. Ruggie (ed.), *Multilateralism Matters: The Theory and Praxis of an Institutional Form* (New York: Columbia University Press, 1993), pp. 1–47; Kratochwil and Ruggie, 'International Organization; F. V. Kratochwil, *Rules, Norms, and Decisions: On the Conditions of Practical and Legal Reasoning in International Relations and Domestic Affairs* (Cambridge: Cambridge University Press, 1989); G. Flynn and H. Farrell, 'The CSCE and the "Construction" of Security in Post-Cold War Europe', *International Organization*, 53, 3 (summer 1999), pp. 505–35; M. N. Barnett and M. Finnemore, 'The Politics, Power, and Pathologies of International Organizations', *International Organization*, 53, 4 (autumn 1999), pp. 699–732.

28 M. Finnemore and K. Sikkink, 'International Norms Dynamics and Political Change', *International Organization*, 54, 4 (1998), pp. 887–917.

29 B. A. Simmons, 'Compliance With International Agreements', in N. W. Polsby (ed.), *Annual Review of Political Science, Volume I 1998* (Palo Alto: Annual Reviews, 1998), pp. 75–93.

30 P. F. Diehl, J. Reifschneider and P. R. Hensel, 'United Nations Intervention and Recurring Conflict', *International Organization*, 50, 4 (autumn 1996) pp. 683–700; E. B. Haas, 'Collective Conflict Management: Evidence for a New World Order?', in F. Kratochwil and E. D. Mansfield (eds), *International Organization: A Reader* (New York: HarperCollins, 1994), pp. 237–57; R. A. Coate and D. J. Puchala, 'Global Policies and the United Nations System: A Current Assessment', in Kratochwil and Mansfield (eds), ibid., pp. 257–70.

31 A. Roberts, 'The Crisis in UN Peacekeeping', in C. A. Crocker, F. O. Hampson and P. Aalt, *Managing Global Chaos: Sources of and Responses to International Conflict* (Washington, DC: US Institute of Peace Press, 1996), pp. 297–319.

32 S. Metz, 'The U.N. After the Cold War: Renaissance or Indian Summer?', in H. H. Almond, Jr and J. A. Burger (eds), *The History and Future of Warfare* (The Hague: Kluwer Law International, 1999), pp. 859–82.

33 B. Russett, J. Oneal and D. R. Davis, 'The Third Leg of the Kantian Tripod for Peace: International Organizations and Militarized Disputes, 1950–85', *International Organization*, 52, 3 (1998), pp. 441–67.

34 W. J. Durch, 'The United Nations and Collective Security in the 21st Century', in H. H. Almond, Jr and J. A. Burger (eds), *The History and Future of Warfare* (The Hague: Kluwer Law International, 1999), pp. 827–59.

35 R. Wedgwood, 'Regional and Subregional Organizations in International Conflict Management', in C. A. Crocker, F. O. Hampson and P. Aall (eds), *Managing Global Chaos: Sources of and Responses to International Conflict* (Washington, DC: US Institute of Peace Press, 1996), pp. 275–85.

36 For some analysts a concert is always power balancing but it depends. It can be arranged to avoid power balancing, although that is not a natural pattern.

37 Keohane, *International Institutions and State Power*.

38 'NATO: What Have You Done For Me Lately?' Earl Grey Memorial Lecture by the NATO Secretary General, 16 February 2001. Distributed at iipmag@hq.nato.int

39 'NATO in the 21st Century', Millennium Year Lord Mayor's Lecture by the NATO Secretary General, 20 July 2000. Distributed at iipmag@hq.nato.int

40 L. H. Miller, 'The Idea and Reality of Collective Security', *Global Governance*, 5, 3 (1999), p. 325; for an opposing view see Downs and Iida, 'Assessing the Theoretical Case Against Collective Security'.

41 The Kupchans argue that collective security can provide so much stability that challenges or disruptive conflicts rarely arise. C. A. Kupchan and C. A. Kupchan, 'Concerts, Collective Security, and the Future of Europe', *International Security*, 16, 1 (1991), pp. 114–61; C. A. Kupchan and C. A. Kupchan, 'The Promise of Collective Security', *International Security*, 20, 1 (1995), pp. 52–61. Other MIs might have a similar effect.

42 Because states are autonomous but without war or serious conflicts, confirming the liberal claim that vicious conflict is not inherent in international politics.

43 Miller, 'The Idea and Reality of Collective Security'.

44 G. J. Ikenberry, *After Victory: Institutions, Strategic Restraint, and the Rebuilding of Order After Major Wars* (Princeton: Princeton University Press, 2001), p. 273.

45 Ruggie, 'Multilateralism'.

46 B. Buzan, C. Jones and R. Little, *The Logic of Anarchy: Neorealism to Structural Realism* (New York: Columbia University Press, 1993), pp. 66–84.

47 Cited in R. Jervis, 'Realism in the Study of World Politics', *International Organization*, 42, 4 (1998), pp. 971–91.

48 See P. M. Morgan, 'Getting the "Liberalist" Transition Under Way: The Experience of the East Asian Regional International System', *The Korean Journal of Defense Analysis* XI, 2 (1999), pp. 5–34.

49 Ibid.

50 Ruggie, 'Multilateralism', p. 4.

51 E. Solingen, *Regional Orders at Century's Dawn: Global and Domestic Influences on Grand Strategy* (Princeton: Princeton University Press, 1998).

8

NORMATIVE
TRANSFORMATIONS IN
INTERNATIONAL RELATIONS
AND THE WANING
OF MAJOR WAR

Hendrik Spruyt

Introduction: Was there really a Long Peace?
Will it last?

Since 1945 the world's great powers have been at relative peace. Despite fears that the Cold War would spiral out of control to end in nuclear annihilation, a period of a Long Peace has prevailed.[1] This relative tranquility among the great powers in the last decades invites the question whether such peace will continue in the near future. More specifically, one might ask whether the number of interstate wars between the major powers, and the likelihood of hegemonic wars has declined, and whether we should read a long term trend into this decline of interstate conflict. If so this would repudiate the expectations of realism that international relations show great continuity in the perpetual jockeying for position and advantage. The Long Peace might be more than a temporary historical aberration.

The end of bipolarity and the rise of new great powers such as China give the question particular salience. After all, periods of structural change and the rise of hegemonic contenders have historically correlated with major wars.[2] However, if the past fifty years are evidence of a generalizable trend, then such changes in relative power distribution need not be the harbinger of conflict ahead. But if the reasons for the Long Peace are particularistic to the configuration of the postwar decades, one will likely see a return to the types of policies that realists emphasize. Rising powers will thus attempt to alter the status quo, and dominant incumbents will seek to block such ambitions.

I believe that the international environment today differs fundamentally from that of earlier epochs. Compared to earlier centuries of major power contests, it seems undeniable that the frequency of interstate war has declined in certain regions of the world. At one time the great powers seemed locked in perpetual war. During the seventeenth century Poland was only at peace one year out of three. England

and France were at war half the time. Spain waged war virtually every year in that century.[3] This is not to say that long periods of peace have never occurred before, as evinced by the nineteenth century concert system.[4] As Paul Schroeder argues in this volume there might be other incidences of extended periods of tranquility.[5] However, the very fact that such instances are cited as deviations from the historical trend of warring states suggests that periods of long peace are worth examining. Such isolated historical examples of tranquility amidst an ocean of conflict do not constitute evidence of a benign international system.

Many scholars have similarly noted the diminishing propensity for war among the great powers. Mueller suggests that states have learned from history and their violent past. Rosecrance argues that many states have opted for gains through trade rather than war.[6] Many states today, particularly in Europe, North America, and Latin America, exist in zones of peace. Thus while perhaps not all actors have forsaken interstate war, large parts of the globe have developed peaceful modes of coexistence.

This chapter will specifically argue that certain types of war have become less prevalent. That is, the likelihood of major power war (the dependent variable) has diminished. A strategically rational state will face considerable material costs and normative constraints should it attempt to engage in wars of conquest and empire. One might argue this is based on the available empirical evidence of the post-World War II era, but I believe there are also *a priori* reasons why this is the case. In other words, certain *casi belli* have become less prevalent for all states, due to broad systems level changes.

Without gainsaying the critical importance of material factors in any explanation – indeed I would argue that it is impossible to account for the decline in the likelihood of major power war without describing the impact of nuclear weapons and the changes in military technology – this chapter intends to explore whether ideational changes and normative constraints have played any causal role in this process. Some of the other authors in this volume, e.g. Martin van Creveld and T. V. Paul (Chapters 4 and 5), discuss the material changes after the Second World War. As Paul suggests, the likelihood of a premeditated nuclear attack has steadily diminished these last decades. This chapter, by contrast, examines whether changes in ideas, beliefs, norms, or more broadly changes in the *mentalité collective*, have played an independent and additional causal role in mitigating the propensity to engage in interstate war.

This chapter thus does not attribute primacy to either material interests or beliefs. Beliefs will often determine which interests actors pursue, and even how actors perceive their interests.[7] But material factors and structural necessities (such as state survival) will equally determine whether such beliefs get a foothold on elite and public imagination. For example, the spread of political liberal ideas and the principle of sovereign territoriality no doubt influenced nationalist demands in the colonies. But the acceptance of these ideas depended on material circumstances (such as relative decline of the European metropoles). In short, both need to be studied in tandem, and their causal linkages need to be elucidated.

I submit that two key ideational shifts occurred, which have diminished the likelihood of major power war because they delegitimized conquest and annexation and made such policies more costly. The global extension of international legal sovereignty and the spread of economic liberalism, the independent variables of this study, have imposed higher costs and fewer gains on territorial acquisition by force.[8] Consequently, imperialism and territorial aggrandizement, till the middle of the twentieth century perfectly acceptable policy options, no longer appear in most states' repertoires, even if they have the material means to pursue such options. Contemporary spheres of influence are not the same as yesterday's empires.

Although primarily driven by utilitarian calculations in the first instance, the sovereignty norm is now accepted as a taken-for-granted script.[9] It influences the terms of international interactions both as social practice and as moral precept.

The spread of international economic liberalism has also transformed state calculations of self-interest.[10] However, contrary to the spread of sovereignty as a constitutive rule of international relations, economic liberalism remains contested. While it for the moment has gained considerable foothold among many states (the number of members of the World Trade Organization, the WTO, exceeds 140), states continue to show degrees of variation in the extent that they accept liberal economic doctrine. Indeed, some continue to reject economic liberalism outright, and within virtually every state some domestic sectors oppose international openness. Thus while it may constitute a set of utilitarian conventions that most states are willing to support, economic liberalism does not constitute a taken-for-granted script.

The spread of political liberalism, which Huntington has described as the 'third wave of democracy', has paralleled this diffusion of economic liberalism.[11] The democratic peace literature in particular has taken this premise to heart. I leave this genre of literature aside in this chapter partially because it has already received considerable attention. Moreover, and more importantly, the objective in this chapter is not to examine the premise that democratic states are less conflictual, either monadically or dyadically, but to examine specifically whether utilitarian conventions exist prohibiting territorial conquest and empire that constrain *both* authoritarian and democratic states.[12]

I begin with a discussion of how one should examine the causal impact of norms and beliefs. I subsequently suggest how certain policy options for the great powers, such as the violation of juridical sovereignty and the pursuit of empire, have become less viable. The two subsequent parts of this chapter demonstrate how sovereignty and economic liberalism have spread in international behavior. I go on to suggest that sovereignty is well established and for most actors forms a constitutive rule of international relations, while economic liberalism remains contested. The conclusion reiterates how these two sets of beliefs have diminished the likelihood of conflict in the post-World War II decades, and why we should expect them to continue to do so in the decades ahead.

A methodology for studying norms based explanations

Many discussions on the causal impact of norms fail to clarify how the causal connections actually work, and they often resemble tautologies. Behavior is explained by the purported existence of certain norms, whose existence is then in turn derived from the observed behavior. Sometimes ideas serve merely as a convenient explanation for any residual behavior not well explained by materialist accounts. A more powerful account of the causal impact of ideas and norms needs, first, to distinguish among the various types of norms that might have a causal impact. It needs, furthermore, an exposition of the process of diffusion. Why are certain norms invoked but not others? What explains their appeal to elites and masses? In short, a norms based explanation requires both an account of the particular content of normative claims (are they moral or utilitarian in nature?) and an account of the diffusionary process.

One can distinguish the content of normative claims in three types: norms that act as moral rules; norms that establish social role patterns and taken-for-granted scripts; and norms that serve instrumental purposes, which I will call utilitarian conventions. Norms as moral rules create guidelines to distinguish right from wrong actions and behaviors.[13] Norms do not derive from exogenous interests but independently determine preferences and behaviors. Norms as social roles establish structural constraints and opportunities. They form scripts. Socialization into the existing script is a prerequisite for entry and recognition.[14] Norms are ontologically independent. They do not derive from other exogenously postulated interests. Finally, utilitarian norms establish conventions, reveal information, and reduce transaction costs.[15] Contrary to the first understandings, norms do not inform preferences. Ontologically they derive from other exogenously postulated interests.

These distinctions resemble March and Olson's separation between logics of consequences, norms that are largely appropriated on utilitarian grounds and logics of appropriateness, norms that establish moral criteria.[16] But, I argue, while this distinction is theoretically justifiable, the two different logics blend in practice. Norms based on purely utilitarian calculations, logics of consequences, may, over time, assume a taken-for-granted character. What at a given juncture might be justified on strategic grounds becomes, at a subsequent stage, part of the environment that presents given social conditions to new entrants. When individuals create networks of particular role patterns those same patterns present themselves as structural features to others. In this vein Durkheim speaks of social facts that are no less real than material variables.

Recent research on decision-making similarly suggests a closer connection between these two logics than is sometimes acknowledged. Robert Jervis thus suggests that, 'although rationalism does not see the interactive process operating as profoundly as this, far from being starkly opposed to constructivism, in a related area the two need to be combined'.[17] Actors, far from continuously searching through a repertoire of choices and opportunities, instead tend to rely on rules of thumb. Previously established routines thus operate as the inputs for the subsequent articulation of interests and preferences. For example, the articulation of anti-slavery norms might have been partially (although not necessarily completely) inspired by instrumental calculations. The French, for example, believed that British policy aimed to weaken France's colonial position in the Americas. Nevertheless, once the utilitarian norm spread (due to British hegemony, the incentive of local political entrepreneurs to support the anti-slavery drive, etc.), the existence of that normative framework over time presented itself as a *fait accompli*. Subsequent members of the international community no longer engaged in the evaluation of the costs and benefits of slavery but took the prohibition as a factor that raised the costs of slave production. And over yet a longer time span, the prohibition has become part of a system of logics of appropriateness.

The process through which norms diffuse has three dimensions. First norms are more likely to spread if they are internally consistent and externally compatible. Does the normative claim constitute an isolated admonition or does it form part of a much larger normative edifice (such as precepts following from a religious doctrine)? Does the norm conflict with already accepted normative frameworks?

This alone will not assure diffusion. Norms require champions. Are there incentives for political entrepreneurs to advocate those particular norms over others?[18] These entrepreneurs will have to override collective action problems and run the risks.[19] Similar to Max Weber's charismatic leader, such entrepreneurs suggest new avenues and possibilities.

Finally, the success of new norms will depend on their interaction with the larger systemic environment. How does the international system reinforce or weaken the normative claims put forward by social groups, rulers, and states?[20]

This proposed method of analysis, based on differentiating norms by content and on analyzing their process of diffusion, might be applied to an important set of cases of interstate war: imperialistic wars of territorial conquest and annexation. Imperialism created two strands of interstate war. Most obviously, imperialism meant conflict between two independent entities, one trying to subjugate the other. Cores expanded into peripheries. Imperialism also raised the prevalence of interstate war between the cores themselves. In the perceived zero-sum struggle for territorial aggrandizement, gains to the one automatically implied losses for the other core countries. Struggles between cores and peripheries thus correlated with conflicts between cores.[21]

Norms, belief systems, and the end of empire

Two leading scholars in the field, David Lake and Stephen Krasner, have in their recent works suggested that states often choose to violate the sovereignty of other actors, and that powerful actors (states or rulers) will choose whatever option best serves their interest. Their works dovetail with a large body of literature that emphasizes material reasons rather than normative accounts. While there is much truth in their accounts, I will argue that the options for great powers have diminished and that material factors alone do not tell the whole story.

In his recent work David Lake notes how states have a variety of means at their disposal to pursue security and economic gains.[22] On one end of the spectrum states may choose to be self-reliant. A state that opts for unilateralism (not to be confused with isolationism) forgoes ties with other states and relies on internal balancing and its own resources to protect its vital interests. States may also choose to pool resources in varying degrees of vertical integration. Alliances leave states considerable autonomy, whereas spheres of influence, and ultimately empire, diminish the room for independent decision-making by the weaker state. While Lake, by his own admission, focuses on material factors that affect the costs and benefits of the various options, and uses this framework to explain the variation in American security policy in the twentieth century, his model has broad applicability.

Stephen Krasner's recent historical study, like Lake's work, takes largely a materialist line of inquiry in examining the institution of state sovereignty.[23] More specifically, he argues that while many profess to adhere to the principle of state sovereignty, they often violate the principle in practice. Distinguishing between international legal sovereignty (the recognition by other states that one is a legitimate actor entitled to engage in international relations) and Westphalian sovereignty (which locates ultimate decision-making power with the government of a territorially defined unit), he argues that both principles, and particularly Westphalian sovereignty, are often violated. The principle, he argues, constitutes an example of 'organized hypocrisy'. Such infractions of sovereignty may be based on contractual relations, such as the relinquishing of sovereignty to multilateral institutions, or by imposition and coercion by a stronger power.

Both Lake and Krasner buttress their arguments with careful analysis of the historical record, and any glancing overview of imperial history will no doubt confirm that violations of sovereignty have been ubiquitous and commonplace.[24] Throughout modern history, the European states have expanded their reach without qualm. The Scramble for Africa in the late nineteenth century, the last territorial wave of annexation, completed the process. Stated more broadly, materialist interests have often overridden normative claims that the sovereignty of others should be respected.

Closer inspection of the contemporary record, however, suggests that a fundamental shift has occurred. The 'menu of choice' for the great powers, whether for material or ideological reasons, has been more constrained since the mid-twentieth century. In Krasner's own account recent violations of international legal sovereignty have been relatively modest. Thus while greater powers have sometimes curtailed the decision-making power of specific states (Westphalian sovereignty), the principle that territorial sovereignty is a constitutive rule in international relations is widely respected.

Moreover, one might object, contra Krasner, that contractual infringements of Westphalian sovereignty, the ability to autonomously make decisions free from external oversight, are not really infringements at all if the sovereign government itself makes the decision to relinquish such authority.[25] Indeed, the very ability of states to contract as equals in international agreements in fact reinforces the very notion of juridical equality and sovereign prerogative. Even the European Union, sometimes adduced as an example that contravenes international legal sovereignty in that ultimate jurisdiction on certain issues has been contracted out to Brussels, is distinct from the violations of the nineteenth and early twentieth centuries. This transfer of authority occurs by contract rather than by imposition. Ultimate decision-making authority resides with states.[26]

This leaves then the cases in which sovereign governments have been subjected to external authority against their will. Here the historical evidence of the twentieth century, certainly since 1945, surely shows that the most flagrant violations of sovereignty, colonialism and empire, have become far less prevalent, and delegitimized. If at one time, great powers could speak of a manifest destiny, indeed a moral burden, to subject other states and cultures, the same cannot be said today. Witness the painstaking attempt by Russians and Han Chinese to denote their polities as multinational states, to avoid the approbation attached to the term 'empire', and to delegitimize claims for independence within their polities. If violations of sovereignty can occur by coercion, then imperialism must surely constitute the most blatant negation of the principle. That form of violating sovereignty has become very rare. And the denial of equal juridical status to independent polities, which was commonplace in the pre-twentieth century by designating other non-developed polities as secondary and inferior, no longer forms part of international practice. Sovereignty has spread globally.

One may frame this in terms of Lake's analysis. If at one point empire and conquest constituted policy options on a par with any other option (unilateralism, alliances, etc.), one might question whether this still holds. The very fact that the two superpowers refrained from outright territorial annexation suggests that either the material or ideological environment had prohibitively raised such costs. Some policy options have become less viable.

No doubt a variety of material factors mattered in bringing this about. But changes in belief systems also affected cost–benefit calculations both in the metropoles as well as the periphery. Robert Jackson suggests one possible normative explanation. Invoking logics of appropriateness, he argues that the West European states could no longer reconcile metropolitan democracy with imperial hierarchy. From their own volition they withdrew.[27]

But Jackson's argument remains unsatisfactory. Empirically, many of the West European states faced few moral quandaries regarding their right to control their colonies.[28] The logics of consequences, which suggested that colonies still provided benefits and prestige, overrode logics of appropriateness, which suggested that empire was no longer legitimate – at least at that historical juncture. Instead, the peripheries were the ones to successfully champion the sovereignty principle, both domestically to organize their societies against imperial metropoles, and internationally to gain external support. Moreover, non-democracies as well – Portugal, and more recently, the Soviet Union – have surrendered their informal and formal empires. What norms or beliefs might have operated across democratic and non-democratic cases alike? The spread of two sets of beliefs has mitigated the tendency to engage in territorial conquest and expansion: the principle of territorial sovereignty and liberal economic doctrine.

The extension of territorial sovereignty

For all the talk about 'whither the state', the principle that governments are sovereign within fixed territorial parameters and have no higher authority beyond such borders remains as strong as it has been before. Indeed, arguably the last decades have fortified rather than weakened the principle. The debates surrounding the 'retreat of the state' largely focus on the ability of governments to act autonomously, what Krasner calls independence sovereignty. Interdependence and globalization are said to have eroded the state's autonomy, although the evidence is far from conclusive.[29] For many others the state's autonomy remains intact.

Even more importantly the issue of state autonomy is distinct from the principle of international legal sovereignty, the principle that internationally recognized actors are the constitutive elements of the international system. Such sovereignty has been widely respected. Indeed, international legal sovereignty, and the prohibition against violating such sovereignty by force, has increased in scope and force. Prior to the full extension of international legal sovereignty, polities that were not granted such status could legitimately be claimed by the colonial powers without contravening the principle in general. This lowered barriers for metropolitan countries to subject peripheral areas. Such is no longer the case. Why and how has this principle spread?

The internal consistency and external compatibility of the sovereignty claim

Territorial sovereignty in the modern era has had few alternatives to contend with. In the West, rival logics of organization such as universal empire and theocracy (both of which recognize no logical but only practical delimitation of their authority) had in effect been defeated by the middle of the seventeenth century. The gradual extension of public authority further augmented domestic hierarchy and the monopoly of the sovereign as the conduit for external contacts.[30] In other words claims to sovereign rule by new states in the wake of World War II built upon a solid historical foundation.

The principle also proved perfectly compatible with other sets of beliefs that had emerged in the West and had spread as well, such as democracy and market capitalism. The demand for popular sovereignty required only that sovereigns govern by the consent of their citizens. It did not alter the principle that sovereigns governed supremely within their territories, devoid from higher external authority.

Nor did territorial sovereignty contravene principles of market capitalism. On the contrary, by some accounts territorial sovereignty proved a prerequisite for efficient international markets. The extension of the market beyond the confines of any one political authority proved conducive to competition, and controlled the rent seeking behavior of autocrats that occurred in universal imperial settings, in which traders and businesspeople had few exit options. Capitalism thus developed in the fragmented state system of Europe rather than in the larger, universalistic empires of the Middle East and the Orient.[31]

Moreover, new states that wished to receive sovereign status could easily be subsumed in such a system.[32] Traditional universal empires, by contrast, such as the Roman, Ming China, or Tokugawa Japan, could not logically recognize other polities as equals since this would contravene the very basis of authority upon which that empire rested (as a unique and privileged entity). Sovereignty, in other words, is not a zero-sum game, and the club of constitutive units of a state system is not exclusive.

Strategic interests in expanding the principle of territorial sovereignty

Territorial sovereignty thus constitutes a particular mode of structuring international relations – which belies the common sense interpretation of anarchy. By locating authority at the domestic level, positive international law rests on the consent of territorial sovereigns (i.e. as multilateral agreements of juridical equals) rather than on the transnational authority of pope or emperor or some exogenous fountain head as divine law. It further serves to differentiate international private actions from international public agreements.

The European and developed powers thus had functional reasons to abide by sovereignty. Contrary to the common perception that anarchy entails the absence of societal rule, international anarchy itself is a socially constructed and mutually agreed pattern of governance. Domestic and international realms are clearly differentiated and trans-territorial claims are delegitimized. International sovereignty at once formalizes anarchy, in demarcating different spheres of authority, and at the same time enables sovereigns to construct international arrangements to facilitate market transactions and other agreements.[33] States are not antithetical to markets.

Metropoles themselves also started to extend the principle to other areas. Led by the United States after World War I, the principle of self-determination served to dissolve the multi-ethnic Austrian-Hungarian and Turkish empires, and to strip Germany of its overseas territories. While not granting all these areas equal juridical status, the European colonial powers could not very well expound self-determination as a pretext for dissolution of their enemies' territories, only to substitute that with rule of their own. New juridical categories, as the mandate, needed to be invented.[34]

The Montevideo Convention of 1933 allowed the European victors to finesse the point for some time. The Convention listed as the critical components of statehood: the specification of territorial borders, the presence of a permanent population, the ability to conduct diplomatic relations with other states, and the capability to govern its citizens. In the inter-war years, and for some time after World War II, the last criterion served as a justification to deny some polities and secessionist movements the right to sovereign status.[35] But the seeds for extension of sovereignty to the former colonies had already been sown.

In the post-World War II decades the superpowers became the most ardent advocates for full extension of the principle across the globe. They rejected the prerequisite criterion of effective self-governance and courted aspiring nationalist leaders to support the West or the East. Consequently the United States became a catalyst propelling the European powers to withdraw. Sumner Wells at the State Department and President Roosevelt had led the way; the US would not fight World War II merely to recompose the European colonial empires. America's post-war policy followed along similar tenets. Even the Soviet Union supported the extension of the principle to diminish the influence of the Western colonial powers. Over time, that very principle became the catalyst for nationalist movements within the Soviet Union itself.

Aspiring political leaders in would-be independent states thus had incentives to abide by such constitutive rules. This held not only throughout the early modern era in Europe, but also in the newly emerging states of the twentieth century. Despite momentary claims appealing to pan-Arabism, or pan-Turkic sentiments, or the shared interests of the worldwide proletariat, political leaders of new states clearly recognized that they had vested interests to perpetuate and insisted on territorial sovereignty as the prevailing norm.[36]

The principle of territorial sovereignty also functioned as a convenient mobilizing force of opposition.[37] Nationalists did not challenge the principle by resorting to pre-colonial concepts of organization. On the contrary, they largely accepted the artificial territorial demarcations handed down by their imperial masters and merely replaced the previous metropolitan government. In Africa, for example, political elites did not resort to tribal or ethnic justifications for rule but constructed new states along the territorial boundaries of the metropolitan powers, and they based their claims to authority on sovereign, territorial precepts, despite their dramatically different historical legacy.[38] (Although once these rulers did establish independence, they might very well have favored certain ethnic groups over others.)

Reinforcement from the international environment

The systemic environment reinforces these strategic incentives to abide by territorial sovereignty in several ways. International organizations and international public law have enshrined the principle as a precondition for mutual recognition. Sovereignty requires not merely the passive recognition of one's own status, it logically entails that one reciprocally extend that principle to second and third parties.[39] Respect for territorial sovereignty thus forms an explicit injunction in the United Nations charter and delineates appropriate state behavior.

Moreover, should a state choose to violate another state's legal sovereignty then such behavior will signal to other states that the predatorial state does not abide by the rules that govern interactions in general. A threat to one state thus transforms to a threat against others, and states that are not immediately threatened will counteract the violation. A predatorial state will consequently have difficulty convincing third parties of its limited aims. If, for example, Iraq violates Kuwaiti sovereignty, it potentially threatens the sovereignty of others, such as Saudi Arabia, as well. A Chinese takeover of Taiwan will be interpreted as signaling intentions beyond Chinese–Taiwanese relations. Violation will thus lead to overextension and counter-reaction – the mobilization of an offsetting alliance.[40] Breaking a fundamental rule of international practice will come at a price.

In this sense the sovereignty principle works as a systemic condition beyond bilateral relations. If it merely operated at the bilateral level, respect for sovereignty of another state might (as the logic of the security dilemma tells us) invoke aggression. Niceness will beget hostility. Conversely, understood as a broader principle, the disregard of sovereignty as a constitutive principle will precipitate reactions in multiple actors. The disregard of sovereignty to pursue gains through territorial conquest will in turn make many other states feel less secure and thus make the mobilization of a counter-alliance all the more likely.

Even if a state's own sovereignty has not been violated it will also have an incentive to curtail violations because such infringements of the rule may cascade. While violations on the margin might not erode the general rule, outright territorial takeover by one sovereign state of another threatens the norm to far greater extent. If the US or any of the other great powers would countenance a takeover of one Middle East state by another, other aspiring regional hegemons might be tempted to do something similar.

Respect for sovereignty thus allows actors to engage in long term cooperative behavior, while violators of the norm will distrust one another since each one of the latter group must fear for its own survival. Following Axelrod's explanation of how small sets of actors who abide by norms that enhance their ability to engage in iterative behavior can overcome larger groups, the sovereignty norm will become more entrenched over time.[41] The group of adherents will grow at a faster rate than the group of violators. The cumulative effect produces lock-in and path dependence.[42]

In sum, individual strategic calculations and overall environmental dynamics create *a priori* reasons why states will be reluctant to contravene territorial sovereignty. The sovereignty principle remains robust, and continues to operate at the systemic level.

The victory of liberal economic doctrine

The extension of territorial sovereignty to all parts of the globe corresponded with a second major development: the victory of liberal economic ideology. Prior to the last decades of the twentieth century, nothing indicated that economic liberalism would assume the paradigmatic status it now enjoys. While Britain as an early industrializer opted for private sector governance and liberal trade, later developers found little merit in free trade, open door policies, and laissez-faire. Instead, they opted for government intervention at home and abroad, trade barriers, and exclusivist economic zones. When hard pressed, as during the recession of the 1930s, even liberal Britain resorted to distinctly non-liberal policies such as imperial preference schemes. Whereas liberal doctrine sees opportunities for joint gains, and diminishes the need for exclusive control over foreign markets, mercantilists see relative gains and protected, colonial markets. Marxism of course confronted both mercantilist and liberal capitalists alike. For Marxists too, economic interaction, at least between socialist and capitalist states, amounted to a zero-sum contest. The reasons for the victory of economic liberalism and the consequences of that victory thus require some explanation.

Consistency and compatibility

Liberalism partially caught on because the liberal economic ideology appeared increasingly consistent with other objectives. First, mercantilism had lost its credibility in the wake of the Great Depression. American politicians in particular had learned the lessons of the Smoot Hawley tariffs.[43] Mercantilist protection by any of the leading capitalist economies could only lead to countervailing practices by other economies with disastrous results.[44] Despite rearguard action by isolationists the internationalists won the debate in America during the war. The US would no longer pass the buck on hegemonic leadership of the international economy, and would not again lead a slide to international protectionism.

Moreover, during the Second World War, theorists and policy-makers alike came to link the retreat to mercantilism with the outbreak of the war. The State Department thus early on developed plans to rebuild the post-war world on the principle that free trade and world peace were inextricably linked.[45] Those premises continued to guide American actions during the depths of the Cold War. As Deputy Assistant Secretary Beale described it, 'the broad objective of US foreign economic policy is identical with that of our general foreign policy'.[46]

Providing the final piece to this framework, the United States linked free trade with sovereignty and democracy in the colonial territories. Initially the US alone believed that support for decolonization, and thus the reduction of imperial preferences, was instrumental in averting communist encroachment on the colonies. But it soon convinced London that its best bet lay in managing the transition to independence rather than to fight it outright. In other words, free trade came to be linked with independence for the colonies, democratization, and the fight against communist expansion.

Strategic incentives to adopt liberalism

Despite the linking of economic liberalism with many other desirable objectives, the ideology would not have taken hold if it were not for the utilitarian calculations of political rulers. American politicians had a variety of motives to seek the spread of liberal economic ideals. As said, they had been persuaded by the negative fall out of their tariff policies of the 1930s. But they also sought to expand their trade to Europe and the colonies. For sure, not all colonies had been closed to American trade and investment. The Netherlands had tried to insulate the Indies but lacked the power to resist American pressure, particularly by its oil companies. Britain too had long permitted liberal trade into its colonies. Even France had various bilateral deals with the colonies, allowing some of them, such as Morocco and Tunisia (but not Algeria) to trade with other states.[47] However, in the 1930s the imperial metropoles had resorted to colonial preferences to guarantee markets in view of the declining overall patterns of trade. And after the war some voices in London, Brussels, and particularly in Paris, saw their post-war economic salvation in con-tinued colonial domination and renewed imperial preferences. The denial of sovereignty to the periphery thus correlated with renewed interest in mercantilist practices, which threatened to re-create the zero-sum politics of the inter-war period when territorial control over peripheral markets was deemed essential for great powers. The Americans, by contrast, advanced a different joint gains alternative: extension of sovereignty through decolonization, and liberalization of closed markets – diminishing the need for territorial control over preferred markets in the first place.

It quickly became obvious to European elites that retrenching to imperial lines could not substitute for American support. Thus, France, arguably the most vocal critic of American and even British policies, soon had to accept Washington's lead. If in 1945 the French could still claim to stand toe to toe with the greatest powers, financial crises in the next few years necessitated that it move away from revitalizing imperial preference schemes.[48]

Washington played one trump card in particular: the threat to withhold Marshall Aid. The threat to withhold such aid from the Netherlands made it surrender its colonial pretensions in the East Indies in 1949. The French financial situation in 1947 similarly required the French to depend for the vast majority of investment capital on the US and rely heavily on Marshall Aid receipts to aid beleaguered budgets. Under those conditions, political elites in Europe could hardly resist American dictates to embark on a more liberal economic course.

Increasingly, European elites also came to realize that their calculations regard-ing the benefits of empire might be mistaken. Often they simply assumed that the colonies yielded a net gain over costs. All such calculations, or what passed as calculations, showed that the imperial holdings yielded greater gains than costs. Such estimates, however, did not take opportunity costs into account. As it turned out investments at home in fact correlated with increased productivity and increased trade. Thus when the Dutch had to abandon the East Indies in 1949, fearing that 10 percent of the Dutch workforce would lose their jobs, they found instead that their economy grew at an explosive pace in the decade thereafter.[49] Similarly, the French initially refused to entertain any thought about costs possibly exceeding benefits in the immediate post-war world. When Raymond Aron raised the question for Indochina in 1945 he was resolutely ignored, and posing the question for Northern Africa was simply unimaginable.[50] By 1958, however, the editor of *Paris*

Match could argue that fighting for Algeria simply cost more than it was worth. The Dutch experience since 1949 now became evidence for the French that colonial retreat, not empire, could be the engine for growth.

The calculations of communist elites similarly evolved. While the authoritarian rulers of these countries of course hardly anticipated handing over the reins of their authority to any domestic opposition, it became increasingly clear that the early rate of economic growth could not be maintained without serious reforms. A variety of these were thus tried within Eastern Europe and the Soviet Union. Of all the experiments, the models focusing on decentralization and greater local responsibility met with the greatest success. Some elites thus had good reason to champion economic reforms. But economic decentralization contradicted central party guidance. Hence, reformist elites and old line party administrations continuously clashed. Some of these reformist sentiments gradually spread to the top, and ultimately culminated in the demise of the communist system itself.[51]

Reinforcement from the international environment

Systemic conditions further reinforced these elite calculations. Over time these conditions defeated not only imperial pretensions in the West, but they exerted even greater pressures on the communist states. In the initial stages of expanding economic liberalism, American hegemony proved to be a key variable. Albert Hirschman's parsimonious explanation for the victory of Keynesianism – he argues simply that American hegemony led to its adoption by its allies – holds equally for economic liberalism.[52] American leadership in Bretton Woods and in forging the various rounds in the General Agreement on Tariffs and Trade (GATT), with incentives and penalties mixed with sufficient escape clauses, led to a dramatic increase in the number of countries willing to join the GATT and later the WTO.

This diffusion of liberal ideals mixed with increasing levels of international trade and financial flows. Globalization in turn put pressure not only on protectionist governments in the West, but ultimately they strained even the most isolated countries within the international economy. As the club of liberal trading states expanded the opportunity costs increased for remaining outside this framework.[53] Liberal economic doctrine created a cascade effect.

The effects of globalization eventually hit the non-market economies as well. Indeed, the absence of meaningful price mechanisms exacerbated the socialist states' ability to deal with the changes in the global economy. Particularly the trade in resources poorly reflected real world prices.[54] Thus the Soviet Union tended to export natural resources below world market prices, for which it received over-valued finished goods from its East European allies.[55] Within the internal empire overall terms of trade worked against Russia, even though some of the greatest beneficiaries of the transfer system, such as the Central Asian states, believed they were being exploited.[56] In short, the overall system increasingly penalized those not part of the global liberal trading scheme.

Utilitarian conventions or social scripts?

The argument developed in this chapter largely looks at the role of utilitarian conventions, logics of consequences, in diminishing the likelihood of great power conflict. It thus acknowledges the important role of material factors in altering the policies of the great powers since World War II. Might one nevertheless make a case that these logics of consequences might shade into logics of appropriateness? Might utilitarian conventions become taken-for-granted scripts? There are several reasons to believe this might be so, and arguably this has occurred with regard to the sovereignty principle.

First, strategic utilitarian calculations are imperfect models of complex behavioral patterns. A broad range of scholarship has pointed out that the assumptions of utility maximizing individuals stretches empirical reality. Satisficing behavior, perceptions and misperceptions, are critical elements in explaining actual choices. Recent scholarship in economics has similarly started to abandon the simple models of economic behavior.[57] New behavioral economics shows how existing social categories frame strategic choices.

More fundamentally, societal rules of the game operate as collective knowledge. Individuals in pursuing optimal outcomes, for example through iterated interaction in Prisoner's Dilemmas, will not be able to achieve their desired outcome without knowledge of the particular social context. In this sense, utilitarian conventions established at an earlier point with particular interests in mind, become at later stages of history the collective background knowledge that informs preferences and choices and that makes cooperation possible.

Consequently, over time, logics of consequences tend to become logics of appropriateness. They are perceived not merely as rules of expediency, but as widely shared understandings of behaviors that produce beneficial effects, and they become rules that are morally desirable.

The principle of territorial sovereignty blurs the distinction of logics of consequences and logics of appropriateness. The principle fundamentally informs the calculations of political elites. Few, if any, secessionist movements deny the validity of the principle. Indeed, their highest ambitions are to be recognized as an element of the Westphalian system.

Whether economic liberal beliefs have booked such a resounding victory appears less likely. While many states, and private actors within them, accept the dictates of international market pressures and the diminished role for the state in seeking economic advantages, many others challenge that sentiment. Even within the leading liberal states, domestic pressures may demand protection from foreign encroachment. And while few would advocate a return to imperial preference schemes, the prospect of defensive regional blocs is not that remote that it can be relegated to the realms of impossibility. Many rulers and populations in developing and transitioning countries continue to question the merits of laissez-faire, either as a strategy for domestic development or as a strategy for international interaction. The East Asian state interventionist alternative comes to mind.

Conclusions: Will peace between the major powers last?

I have argued that one prevalent form of major war, conflict resulting from the pursuit of territorial conquest and annexation, has become less probable. The pursuit of territorial aggrandizement and empire has become largely obsolete on utilitarian as well as moral grounds. Two sets of beliefs and normative practices have brought this about. First, the global extension of sovereignty has curtailed previously common policies of annexation and imperialism. While theoretically such policies are available to the great powers, as Krasner and Lake suggest, in practice the international system and multilateral organizations have delegitimized the naked exercise of force to gain territory. Sovereignty has become more entrenched in the post-World War II era.[58]

Second, the ascendance of liberal economic beliefs has also diminished the likelihood of major power conflict. Among the capitalist powers, it diminished the zero-sum nature of economic competition. Without the closed borders of imperial preferences, access for one state did not entail a commensurate denial of access for another. Fair field and fair play thus diminished the need for metropolitan powers to annex territories by force and the necessity to deny those areas to rivals.

Among the protagonists of the Cold War, the spread of economic liberalism undercut the primary impetus for the Cold War in the first place: the antagonism between two modes of economic production and property rights. As the communist elites themselves lost confidence in the millenarian promises of a victory of communism, the populations of their countries could hardly be expected to maintain the level of sacrifice necessary to keep the Cold War going. Economic liberalism, moreover, with its emphasis on decentralization, could not be reconciled with the privileged position of the party and restricted property rights.

In sum, the victory of economic liberalism heralded the defeat of rival philosophies that viewed economic interaction as a contest and a zero-sum game, making conflicts inevitable. Potential markets needed to be controlled to guarantee exports for the metropole while denying such territories to contending great powers. Economic liberalism, by contrast, emphasized the possibilities for joint gains, while simultaneously diminishing the need for territorial control over potential markets. But, unlike the principle of sovereign territoriality, it is not uncontested. It has yet to become a taken-for-granted script. Economic liberal ideas are regulative rather than constitutive rules.

What does this chapter imply about expectations for the future? How robust will the Long Peace and ideational constraints on territorial conquest be? I would argue that the respect for territorial sovereignty and the victory of economic liberalism are particularly well entrenched in Europe and the Americas. But what are, for example, the prospects of conflict between a rising authoritarian China and other great powers? What to make of Chinese–Japanese tensions, or Indian–Pakistani rivalry?

The preceding argument does not mean that great power conflict has become obsolete altogether. Wars have many precipitating factors. I have argued that one cause of war has become less prevalent. But it has been an important cause in the past, and the fact that it has declined since 1945 bodes well for the future. Consider the various conflicts between the great powers over the past century or so. Many of these conflicts were at least partially instigated by attempts to redress territorial borders by force, to annex territories, and to achieve economic gains. German dissatisfaction with French and British imperial gains prior to World War I sparked German expansion in Africa (Cameroon, German East Africa, Togo, South West Africa), as well as in the Pacific, and led to tensions with France and Britain. Italian ambitions in Ethiopia and Somalia similarly sparked French and British concerns. Various imperial ambitions about who would fill the power vacuum in the Balkans played perhaps the most critical role of all. In the Orient, Japan similarly joined the imperial game, bringing it into conflict with China (1894) and Russia (1905). Security motives intermeshed with mercantilist economic ambitions in the inter-war period. Italy attempted to develop Libya to make it economically profitable.[59] Germany saw in the Balkans a key region to obtain resources and sell its finished products. Japan attempted to build a Greater East Asian Co-Prosperity Zone.[60]

Does the counterfactual apply? That is, if the principle of territorial sovereignty and economic liberalism had been well established would those wars not have occurred? Too many other variables matter to allow us to draw such a firm conclusion. However, the likelihood of conflict would arguably diminish. First, if sovereignty had been well established, challenges to the international status quo would have been less easy to conceal. In the absence of a clear firebreak between legitimate and illegitimate territorial annexation (international practices then differentiated at least four categories of states and diverse degrees of sovereignty), Germany, Japan, and Italy could more readily claim, in the lead-up to World War II, that they merely followed time honored traditions. Japan could thus argue that its policies were no different from those of the Western powers. Germany suggested that it simply sought to redress inequitable outcomes of the World War I settlement. In the contemporary international environment, by contrast, with sovereignty uniformly granted, challenges to the status quo will be more transparent.

Secondly, if territorial control had not meant economic exclusion, then other actors would have had less reason to see the territorial gains of others as economic losses to themselves. Economic success would not have required territorial expansion. A rising Germany in the 1890s need not have feared that it had arrived too late on the international economic scene. Similarly, while the mercantilist choices of the 1930s led colonial powers to see their economic salvation in the periphery, exclusion from this colonial domain meant secondary status for other ambitious great powers. Had liberal trade survived, the appeal of economic nationalism would likely have diminished.

My argument is thus far from being merely a historical retrospective. With sovereignty and economic liberalism relatively robust, future conflicts will not be sparked by the pursuit of naked territorial conquest and zero-sum economic calculations. Relative shifts in power in decades ahead are less likely to lead to the policies that realists predict. American unilateralism need not spark balancing behavior by its erstwhile allies or rising states. Adherence to territorial sovereignty means they have less reason to fear for their own security than great powers did at other times in history. It also means that non-status quo powers that violate the principle will be at loggerheads with the vast majority of states. Imperialists, in today's environment, walk alone. Economic liberalism will allow competition in economic spheres without precipitating conflict. In this sense the likelihood of great power war has indeed declined.

One should, however, be cautious in applying the thesis that major power conflict has waned to specific bilateral relations. Asking whether China and Japan might be constrained from going to war, or whether conflict between India and Pakistan will be impossible, because of the extension of sovereignty and economic liberalism, must recognize the subtleties of such hypothetical and counterfactual explorations.

First, the argument that major power conflict has declined is a probabilistic statement, and must, therefore, be compared to the historical record. Given the frequency and repetitive pattern of major power conflicts in the past, the last half century must be considered a significant deviation from past practices. A singular event, such as say a possible clash between India and Pakistan over Kashmir, does not disprove the thesis, nor does the absence of conflict between two specific major powers alone constitute sufficient corroboration.

Consequently, the argument presented here has largely been a deductive one. I do not extrapolate from a singular case or by case comparison whether war will be more or less likely. Instead, I suggest *a priori* reasons why major powers will be less likely to pursue certain types of war. Rationalist governments will have fewer incentives to pursue territorial annexation than they have in the past.

Moreover, trying to predict whether great powers will be more or less likely to engage in conflict in the future will naturally have to take many variables into account. The presence of nuclear weapons, the relative power of both states, dynamic trends in the distribution of power, domestic institutions, the possibility of miscalculation, will all factor into the equation. A plethora of counterfactual scenarios could be developed. All such factors will operate side by side with ideational and normative constraints.

The question to ask is whether counterfactually great power behavior would look different if economic liberalism and sovereignty had not become pre-eminent. The normative argument gains particular saliency when focusing on great power versus small power relations. Here, realism should hold sway, and hence, these sets of relations constitute tough cases for the normative argument. In the past, significant power imbalances have precipitated great powers to expand territorially and seek exclusive economic zones. This indirectly brought them into conflict with other great powers, fearful that the expanding state had acquired too much. In the current environment, however, great powers are constrained from doing so. Counterfactually, without sovereignty established and imperialism at bay, and without a permissive economic environment, a Chinese takeover of Taiwan would be far more likely.

Indeed, such a hypothetical scenario applies to relations between the great powers as well. If a rising China today were confronted with imperial powers at its borders that had staked out exclusive economic zones for themselves by denying sovereignty to many other Asian states, the likelihood of a Pacific contest would increase dramatically. Chinese ascendance would resemble Japanese modernization and growth a century ago with similar consequences. The international system today, however, makes such calculations in Beijing far less likely.

Acknowledgment

I would like to thank Dale Copeland and Raimo Väyrynen for helpful comments and suggestions on an earlier draft.

Notes

1 J. Gaddis, 'The Long Peace: Elements of Stability in the Postwar International System', in S. Lynn-Jones and S. Miller (eds), *The Cold War and After* (Cambridge: MIT Press, 1994); J. Mueller, 'The Essential Irrelevance of Nuclear Weapons: Stability in the Postwar World', in Lynn-Jones and Miller (eds), ibid. (Cambridge: MIT Press, 1994).

2 R. Gilpin, *War and Change in World Politics* (Cambridge: Cambridge University Press, 1981); J. Goldstein, *Long Cycles* (New Haven: Yale University Press, 1988); Rasler and Thompson have described the correlation between hegemonic wars and relative shifts in power. See K. Rasler and W. Thompson, 'War Making and State Making', *American Political Science Review*, 79, 2 (1985), pp. 491–507.

3 G. Parker, *Europe in Crisis: 1598–1648* (Ithaca: Cornell University Press, 1979), p. 73.

4 For the particular conditions behind this period of extended peace, see E. V. Gulick, *Europe's Classical Balance of Power* (New York: W.W. Norton, 1955); R. Jervis, 'Security Regimes', in S. Krasner (ed.), *International Regimes* (Ithaca: Cornell University Press, 1983).

5 See P. Schroeder's chapter in this volume, Chapter 1.

6 Mueller, 'The Essential Irrelevance of Nuclear Weapons'.

7 For a strong version of the influence of ideas, see M. Blyth, 'Any More Bright Ideas? The Ideational Turn of Comparative Political Economy', *Comparative Politics*, 29, 2 (1997), pp. 229–50; R. Price, 'A Genealogy of the Chemical Weapons Taboo', *International Organization*, 49, 1 (1995), pp. 73–103; R. Price, 'Reversing the Gun Sights: Transnational Civil Society Targets Land Mines', *International Organization*, 52, 3 (1998), pp. 613–44; K. Sikkink, 'The Power of Principled Ideas: Human Rights Policies in the United States and Western Europe', in J. Goldstein and R. Keohane (eds), *Ideas and Foreign Policy* (Ithaca: Cornell University Press, 1993), pp.139–70.

8 For discussions of the concept of sovereignty, see F. H. Hinsley, 'The Concept of Sovereignty and the Relations Between States', in W. Stankiewicz (ed.), *In Defense of Sovereignty* (New York: Oxford University Press, 1969); A. James, *Sovereign Statehood* (London: Allen & Unwin, 1986); S. Benn, 'Sovereignty', *The Encyclopedia of Philosophy*, Vol. 7/8 (New York: Macmillan, 1967), pp. 501–5.

9 The concept of 'taken-for-grantedness' is clarified in P. DiMaggio and W. Powell, 'The Iron Cage Revisited: Institutional Isomorphism and Collective Rationality in Organizational Fields', *American Sociological Review*, 48 (1983), pp. 147–60.

10 For Tetlock this would constitute a change in beliefs regarding particular cause and effect relations, see G. Breslauer and P. Tetlock (eds), *Learning in U.S. and Soviet Foreign Policy* (Boulder: Westview Press, 1991). For the general spread of

international economic transactions and liberalism, see R. Keohane and H. Milner (eds), *Internationalization and Domestic Politics* (New York: Cambridge University Press, 1996).

11 S. Huntington, 'Democracy's Third Wave', in L. Diamond and M. Plattner (eds), *The Global Resurgence of Democracy* (Baltimore: Johns Hopkins University Press, 1996).

12 Miriam Elman surveys a variety of the literature in her introduction in M. Elman (ed.), *Paths to Peace: Is Democracy the Answer?* (Cambridge: MIT Press, 1997). See also William Thompson's discussion in this volume, Chapter 9.

13 Finnemore similarly distinguishes between norms as rule-like prescriptions and as moral statements. M. Finnemore, 'International Organizations as Teachers of Norms: The United Nations Educational, Scientific, and Cultural Organization and Science Policy', *International Organization*, 47, 4 (1993), p. 566. Goldstein and Keohane use the term 'principled beliefs' for the latter category. J. Goldstein and R. Keohane (eds), *Ideas and Foreign Policy* (Ithaca: Cornell University Press, 1993), p. 9.

14 See for further discussion of the concepts of taken-for-grantedness and social scripts, DiMaggio and Powell, 'The Iron Cage Revisited'; and N. Abercrombie, 'Knowledge, Order and Human Autonomy', in J. Hunter and S. Ainlay (eds), *Making Sense of Modern Times* (London: Routledge & Kegan Paul, 1986), pp. 11–30; M. Finnemore, 'Norms, Culture and World Politics: Insights from Sociology's Institutionalism', *International Organization*, 50, 2 (1996), pp. 325–47.

15 For a utilitarian view of norms, see G. Garrett and B. Weingast, 'Ideas, Interests, and Institutions: Constructing the European Community's Internal Market', in J. Goldstein and R. Keohane (eds), *Ideas and Foreign Policy* (Ithaca: Cornell University Press, 1993), pp. 173–206.

16 J. March and J. Olsen, *Rediscovering Institutions* (New York: Free Press, 1989), pp. 22–4.

17 R. Jervis, 'Realism in the Study of World Politics', *International Organization*, 52, 4 (1998), p. 978.

18 I discuss this proposed strategy of research in greater detail in H. Spruyt, 'The End of Empire and the Extension of the Westphalian System: The Normative Basis of the Modern State Order', *International Studies Review*, 2, 2 (2000), pp. 65–92.

19 For the strategic dimensions in championing certain ideas in terms of supply and demand, see J. Snyder and K. Ballentine, 'Nationalism and the Marketplace of Ideas', *International Security*, 21, 2 (1996), pp. 5–40.

20 For a discussion of how norms might emerge in international politics, see, *inter alia*, Finnemore, 'International Organizations as Teachers of Norms'; J. Ikenberry and C. Kupchan, 'Socialization and Hegemonic Power', *International Organization*, 44, 3 (1990), pp. 283–315; Price, 'A Genealogy of the Chemical Weapons Taboo'; Price, 'Reversing the Gun Sights'; N. Tannenwald, 'The Nuclear Taboo: The United States and the Normative Basis of Nuclear Non-Use', *International Organization*, 53, 3 (1999), pp. 433–68.

21 Some of the best recent accounts are M. Doyle, *Empires* (Ithaca: Cornell University Press, 1986); J. Snyder, *Myths of Empire* (Ithaca: Cornell University Press, 1991); C. Kupchan, *The Vulnerability of Empire* (Ithaca: Cornell University Press, 1994).

22 D. Lake, *Entangling Relations: American Foreign Policy in Its Century* (Princeton: Princeton University Press, 1999).

23 S. Krasner, *Sovereignty: Organized Hypocrisy* (Princeton: Princeton University Press, 1999).

24 See Doyle, *Empires* for a discussion of imperial motives and policies.

25 See also Philpott's evaluation of Krasner's work in D. Philpott, 'Usurping the Sovereignty of Sovereignty?', *World Politics*, 53, 2 (2001), pp. 297–324.

26 Moravcsik and Garrett both argue that political elites had strategic, self-interested

motives to push for the EU. A. Moravcsik, 'Negotiating the Single European Act', *International Organization*, 45, 1 (1991), pp. 19–56; G. Garrett, 'International Cooperation and Institutional Choice: The European Community's Internal Market', *International Organization*, 46, 2 (1992), pp. 533–60.

27 R. Jackson, 'The Weight of Ideas in Decolonization: Normative Change in International Relations', in J. Goldstein and R. Keohane (eds), *Ideas and Foreign Policy* (Ithaca: Cornell University Press, 1993), pp. 111–38.

28 Spruyt, 'The End of Empire and the Extension of the Westphalian System' discusses this at greater length.

29 For the argument that state autonomy is still significant, see P. Doremus (ed.), *The Myth of the Global Corporation* (Princeton: Princeton University Press, 1998).

30 H. Spruyt, *The Sovereign State and Its Competitors* (Princeton: Princeton University Press, 1994); J. Thomson, 'State Practices, International Norms, and the Decline of Mercenarism', *International Studies Quarterly*, 34, 1 (1990), pp. 23–48.

31 D. North, *Structure and Change in Economic History* (New York: W.W. Norton, 1981); Spruyt, *The Sovereign State and Its Competitors*; R. Unger, *Plasticity into Power* (New York: Cambridge University Press, 1987).

32 For a variety of ways that rule may be organized non-territorially or as a non-sovereign entity, see F. Kratochwil, 'Of Systems, Boundaries, and Territoriality: An Inquiry into the Formation of the State System', *World Politics*, 39, 1 (1986), pp. 27–52.

33 Spruyt, *The Sovereign State and Its Competitors*.

34 R. Betts, *Uncertain Dimensions* (Minneapolis: University of Minnesota Press, 1985), pp. 62–3.

35 Thus Britain employed a 'prerequisites model' to deny Indian nationalist ambitions till World War II.

36 See G. Gause, 'Sovereignty, Statecraft and Stability in the Middle East', *Journal of International Affairs*, 45, 2 (1992), pp. 441–69 on the Middle East. See also various essays in M. Mandelbaum (ed.), *Central Asia and the World* (New York: Council on Foreign Relations Press, 1994), which argue that Pan-Turkic affinities in Central Asia have been overstated.

37 Spruyt, 'The End of Empire and the Extension of the Westphalian System'.

38 R. Emerson, *From Empire to Nation* (Cambridge, Mass.: Harvard University Press, 1967); J. Herbst, 'The Creation and Maintenance of National Boundaries in Africa', *International Organization*, 43, 4 (1989), pp. 673–92.

39 For the reciprocal nature of sovereignty, see A. Giddens, *The Nation-State and Violence* (Berkeley: University of California Press, 1987). Giddens thus suggests that international agreements and treaties in fact strengthen rather than weaken the principle of sovereignty.

40 For a conceptual discussion of overextension, see Snyder, *Myths of Empire*.

41 R. Axelrod, 'The Emergence of Cooperation among Egoists', *American Political Science Review*, 75, 2 (1981), pp. 306–18; R. Axelrod, *The Evolution of Cooperation* (New York: Basic Books, 1984); R. Axelrod, 'An Evolutionary Approach to Norms', *American Political Science Review*, 80, 4 (1986), pp. 1095–112.

42 For the logic of path dependence and lock-in, see P. David, 'Clio and the Economics of QWERTY', *American Economic Review*, 75 (1985), pp. 332–7; S. Krasner, 'Sovereignty: An Institutional Perspective', in J. Caporaso (ed.), *The Elusive State* (Newbury Park: Sage, 1989).

43 J. Goldstein, *Ideas, Interests, and American Trade Policy* (Ithaca: Cornell University Press, 1993).

44 K. Oye, 'The Sterling–Dollar–France Triangle: Monetary Diplomacy 1929–1973', in K. Oye (ed.), *Cooperation Under Anarchy* (Princeton: Princeton University Press, 1986); and C. Kindleberger, *The World in Depression 1929–1939* (Berkeley: University of California Press, 1983) discuss the logic of beggar thy neighbor economic policies.

45   W. Kimball, *The Juggler* (Princeton: Princeton University Press, 1991) demonstrates Roosevelt's antagonism to imperial preference zones and colonialism.

46   *Foreign Relations of the United States, 1958–1960, Vol. IV, Foreign Economic Policy* (Government Printing Office, 1992), p. 214.

47   J. Marseille, *Empire Coloniale et Capitalisme Français* (Paris: Albin Michel, 1984).

48   This is a constant theme throughout the essays in R. Paxton and N. Wahl (eds), *De Gaulle and the United States* (Oxford: Berg Publishers, 1994).

49   For accounts of Dutch decolonization, see J. A. van Doorn, *Indische lessen* (Amsterdam: Uitgeverij Bert Bakker, 1995); J. A. van Doorn, 'The Dutch–Indonesian Conflict and the Persistence of the Colonial Pattern', *The Netherlands Journal of Social Sciences*, 31, 2 (1995b), pp. 153–71; H. W. van den Doel, *Het Rijk van Insulinde* (Amsterdam: Prometheus, 1996); A. Maddison, 'Dutch Income In and From Indonesia, 1700–1938', *Modern Asian Studies*, 23, 4 (1989), pp. 645–70; A. Maddison, 'Dutch Colonialism in Indonesia: A Comparative Perspective', in A. Booth, W.J. O'Malley and A. Weidemann (eds), *Indonesian Economic History in the Dutch Colonial Era* (New Haven: Yale University South East Asian Studies, 1990).

50   M. Kahler, *Decolonization in Britain and France* (Princeton: Princeton University Press, 1984) provides a fine account of the differences in the decolonization policies of Britain and France. See also I. Lustick, *Unsettled States, Disputed Lands* (Ithaca: Cornell University Press, 1993); T. Smith, *The Pattern of Imperialism* (New York: Cambridge University Press, 1981).

51   For a discussion of the various economic reforms that were tried in the post-Stalin period, see P. Toumanoff, 'Economic Reform and Industrial Performance in the Soviet Union: 1950–1984', *Comparative Economic Studies*, 29, 4 (1987), pp. 128–49.

52   A. Hirschman, 'How the Keynesian Revolution was Exported from the United States, and Other Comments', in P. Hall (ed.), *The Political Power of Economic Ideas* (Princeton: Princeton University Press, 1989).

53   See Richard Baldwin's explanation of regional integration. R. Baldwin, P. Haaparanta and J. Kiander, *Expanding Membership of the European Union* (New York: Cambridge University Press, 1995). As the number of members within a free trading region increases, the costs of exclusion go up.

54   J. Frieden and R. Rogowski, 'The Impact of the International Economy on National Policies', in R. Keohane and H. Milner (eds), *Internationalization and Domestic Politics* (New York: Cambridge University Press, 1996).

55   V. Bunce, 'The Empire Strikes Back: The Transformation of the Eastern Bloc from a Soviet Asset to a Soviet Liability', *International Organization*, 39, 1 (1985), pp. 1–46.

56   K. Dawisha and B. Parrott, *Russia and the New States of Eurasia* (New York: Cambridge University Press, 1994); B. Rubin's chapter in M. Mandelbaum (ed.), *Central Asia and the World* (New York: Council on Foreign Relations Press, 1994).

57   For an overview of some of the literature in the new behavioral economics, see M. Rabin, 'Psychology and Economics', *Journal of Economic Literature*, 36 (1998), pp. 11–46.

58   Kahler also makes this point. See M. Kahler, 'Empires, Neo-Empires, and Political Change: The British and French Experience', in K. Dawisha and B. Parrott (eds), *The End of Empire?* (Armonk: M. E. Sharpe, 1997), pp. 286–312. See also Zacher, who notes that there have been few sovereignty violations in recent decades. M. Zacher, 'The Territorial Integrity Norm: International Boundaries and the Use of Force', *International Organization*, 55, 2 (2001), pp. 215–50.

59   Betts, *Uncertain Dimensions*.

60   On the German economic strategy for the Balkans in World War II, see A. Hirschman, *National Power and the Structure of Foreign Trade* (Berkeley: University of California Press, 1945).

Part IV

LONG-TERM PERSPECTIVES ON MAJOR WAR

9

THE DEMOCRATIC PEACE
AND CIVIL SOCIETY AS
CONSTRAINTS ON MAJOR
POWER WARFARE

William R. Thompson

Asking whether the democratic peace and civil society arguments foretell the waning of major power warfare is not unlike asking whether European infantry and cavalry could have defeated Asian infantry and cavalry in the 1500s. This latter question arose recently on a world history web-list and lends itself to a variety of answers: yes, no, maybe. The basic problem is that whatever the perceived advantages and liabilities of European and Asian armies in the 1500s, in the sixteenth century they rarely clashed as armies east of the Ottoman Empire. In the absence of much in the way of real world tests of the proposition that one region's armies were inferior/superior to the other's, any definitive answer is rather problematic.[1] In the case of the democratic peace and major power warfare, the problem is not so much the absence of a trial-at-arms but rather the failure of two sets of explanations to meet on common ground very often. Students of the democratic peace and civil society explanations privilege unit-level explanations – in which the unit is either, respectively, a dyad of two state actors or a national society. The explanatory outcome tends to focus on a reduced probability of interstate conflict. The problem, however, is that most (but certainly not all) students of major power warfare privilege systemic-level explanations over unit-level explanations and the explanatory outcome is that major power warfare tends to become more or less likely given the advent of an appropriate context. If that appropriate context excludes the regime type transformations on which the democratic peace arguments focus, the two sets of explanations for conflict pass by one another not unlike two planes on a dark night that manage to avoid collision by sticking to different, predetermined altitudes. At best, they may brush alongside each other but not much more 'damage' is done.

Moreover, 'interstate conflict' certainly overlaps with major power warfare but it is not quite the same thing. Major power warfare is a special subset of the larger category of interstate conflict. What characterizes or influences the larger category need not apply to the specialized subset. To think otherwise runs the risk of engaging in ecological fallacy. To assess whether the democratic peace/civil society arguments should affect the likelihood of major power warfare, it is necessary to ascertain whether, or to what extent, domestic transformations of regime type and the number of autonomous societal actors are likely to influence the systemic contexts thought to be conducive to major power warfare. That is an exercise that is rarely if ever accomplished in a direct fashion.

In this chapter, I will first lay out what students of major power warfare choose to focus upon and then do the same for democratic peace and civil society arguments. The task then becomes one of attempting to integrate them better than has been the case in the past. I attempt this by modifying Rosecrance's (1987) trading state theory into a more explicitly evolutionary argument about ongoing transformations in war/peace and trade/development. Once this task is performed, the simple answer that emerges can be summarized in the following way. If the democratic peace and civil society arguments are correct, and that is not an assumption that should be adopted too quickly, major power war should become extinct as soon as the transformations associated with democratization and civil society have worked their magic on the political systems and societies of all current and future major powers. One would also have to disallow the possibility of institutional and societal reversals once these transformations are achieved. But until all major powers are transformed and can no longer revert to some previous status, some possibility of major power warfare will persist. On the other hand, if the modified trading state theory is on the right track, regime type and societal transformations are wrapped up in a complex of changes taking place in military, political, and economic spheres that do suggest major power warfare is on the wane for reasons other than solely regime type transformations. But, as long as there remains some possibility of such warfare, one also needs to keep in mind that while major power warfare has become less frequent, it also has become increasingly more lethal and planet-wide in scale and scope. Such a development should work against future iterations but it does not guarantee it.

The transformations that appear to be underway move slowly and unevenly. It may easily take much, if not all, of the twenty-first century, to see if we are genuinely out of the major power warfare 'woods.'

Major power warfare

Major power warfare is about wars involving the confrontation of two or more antagonistic major powers. Non-major powers may also be involved but the presumption is that wars involving the strongest powers are somehow more significant than those involving relatively weaker states. The amount of economic resources that can be mobilized, the lethality of the weaponry arsenals that can be introduced into combat, the geographical scale of the combat, the stakes that are involved, and the societal impacts of the warfare all tend to be manifested in greater respects in major power warfare than in non-major power warfare. This is all the more the case if the warfare involves all of the major powers as bipolarized opponents – the ultimate form of major power warfare.

Table 9.1 lists the number of war onsets involving the confrontation of major powers by century since the 1490s. The first column lists all wars in which at least one great power was aligned against another great power. The second column lists the number of war onsets, variously called 'general,' 'hegemonic,' 'global,' 'world,' or 'systemic wars' by different authors, involving the participation of all great powers as opponents. Neither column contains large numbers. Wars between major powers have been relatively rare and have become increasingly so – although one could argue, presumably, that the 'trend' in the second column could be subject to various interpretations. However one reads the frequency of major power warfare in the modern era, though, there has been no new outbreak of such combat in the last half century. Nor is there any strong expectation of such an outbreak in the near future.

Putting aside momentarily the question of whether major power warfare is becoming (has become?) an extinct institution, how are these periodic onsets of warfare to be explained? It is of course quite possible to explain them just as one might explain any other type of interstate warfare. Vasquez (1996, 1997), for instance, accounts for major power warfare in terms of territorial conflicts, rivalries, arms races, and hard-liner decision-makers. In this school of thought, the more extensive, major power wars are explained by the facilitative presence of a conducive structural environment (a multipolar, bipolarized system in which neither bloc has preponderance) and incentives to join ongoing wars. Alternatively, Snyder (1991) traces all or most foreign policy machinations including major power warfare to domestic political struggles. To be sure, we have access to a complex and extensive array of conceptual materials for elucidating the etiology of warfare, ranging from biological impulses through psychological pathologies to national attributes and structural change in the international system. Yet it is the last category – structural change in the international system – to which students of major power warfare, even Vasquez, are most likely to be drawn. The reason for this is that it is the major powers that are the primary agents in the construction of systemic

Table 9.1 The frequency of major power warfare

Century	Wars involving two or more major powers as opponents	Wars involving all of the major powers as opponents
1495–1599	27	2
1600–1699	17	3
1700–1799	10	4
1800–1899	6	1
1900–1999	6	2

Sources: Column 1 is based on Levy (1983). Column 2 is based on the candidate wars put forward by Gilpin (1981), Modelski (1984), Wallerstein (1984), Midlarsky (1984), and Levy (1985). My thanks to Paul Schroeder for noticing a typographical error in an earlier version of this table.

structure. For instance, their relative capabilities determine the distribution of relative positions known as polarity.[2] A very high concentration of capabilities centered in a single major power is unipolarity. Bipolarity is characterized by two major powers roughly in positional parity and no others as close competitors. Multipolarity involves three (tripolarity) or more major powers possessing some share of relative capabilities beyond some minimal threshold. Similarly, their alignments determine the extent to which the system is polarized. The usual range varies between one extreme of bipolarization in which all major powers are aligned on one of two opposing sides to the opposite extreme – the absence of polarization tendencies – in which no major powers are aligned with any other.

Polarity and polarization need not be the only attributes that define a system's structure, but they are certainly among the most popular ones in the study of major power warfare. Entire schools of thought (for example, neorealism) have been developed utilizing polarity as one of the prime explanatory movers.[3] Debates continue over whether bipolarity or multipolarity are more conducive to warfare propensities.[4] Many analysts are content to leave it at that – not so much the continuing debate but the question of whether one type of distribution is more dangerous than another. Still, the next logical question is what drives positional change? Whatever the dangers associated with various distributions of power, what is it that leads to changes in these static distributions? What is (are) the dynamic(s) of system change?

The most popular prime movers include population growth, economic growth in general, or technological change in particular. These are hardly mutually exclusive choices. Population growth and/or technological change can lead to general economic growth, just as general economic growth can lead to population growth and technological change. Yet all states are unlikely to experience the same rate of growth simultaneously. Some become bigger, more technologically proficient, and wealthier faster than others. In this respect, it is uneven development rates that lie at the root of the most intensive major power conflict. New major powers must force their way into a systemic structure that was created prior to their advent to elite status. Established major powers can choose to accommodate the demands and preferences of the new arrivals or they can choose to ignore their claims to a share of the privileges associated with high rank and power.[5]

It is always possible that new powers will remain passively meek and not complain about their treatment by the old guard. It is perhaps equally possible that the old guard will not feel threatened by the newcomers to elite status and do everything required to appease their demands. However, neither possibility is very probable. As a consequence, structural change enhances the probability of major power conflict and warfare.

Precisely how it does so remains contested. One argument (Rasler and Thompson, 1994, 2000a) envisions two types of major powers that create two different structures, one global and the other regional. The global system focuses on long-distance, commercial transactions and its elite are the leading industrial and commercial powers that rely on capabilities of global reach to protect their interests and to project their influence. Intermittent technological change sets the rhythms for this global system and the most successful technological pioneer tends to assume the roles of lead economy and global system leader (Modelski and Thompson, 1996).[6] Yet since the foundation for systemic leadership is not finite, it waxes and wanes according to the leader's ability to monopolize continuing technological innovation and capabilities of global reach. Accordingly, global systemic leadership is strong at one point and then erodes as others catch on and catch up with the leader's position.

The principal regional system may encompass the home bases of some of these global powers but it also contains large land powers that compete for territorial expansion and regional hegemony. Population growth and conventional and technologically induced economic wealth are important movers at the regional level. Given the proximity of threats and opportunities, armies are the primary coercive instrument of choice of the land powers

The two systems do not move at the same pace. In particular, a regional challenger is most likely to emerge when the global system's power structure is less con-centrated. The declining global leader must then cobble together a coalition to suppress the explicit threat posed by an aspiring regional hegemon. In the process of defeating the regional hegemon, but not solely due to that feat, the global system becomes more highly concentrated and may also acquire new leadership. The power concentration of the principal regional system, on the other hand, is coerced into becoming less focused on the aspiring regional hegemon until or unless a new challenger emerges. Between 1494 and 1945, western Europe played the role of principal region. After 1945, the scope of the principal region expanded to encompass all of Eurasia (Rasler and Thompson, 2001b).

However, most analysts do not subscribe to the notion that more than one systemic structure is in play. They work with a single hierarchy in which one possible dynamic (power transition) is whether lower ranked powers are both dis-satisfied and catching up with higher ranked powers (Organski and Kugler, 1980; Väyrynen, 1983; Houweling and Siccama, 1991; Kim, 1992; Tammen et al., 2000). As the point of transition in relative capability nears, conflict becomes more prob-able. Another dynamic interpretation focuses instead on the preemptive behavior of a declining leader (Copeland, 2000) or on the relative power cycle conflict between a newly emerging power and a state that has its ascending, relative trajectory thwarted by the newly emerging state (Doran, 2000). In these cases, the frustrated power is apt to attack the source of its decline if decision-makers feel that an attack may prevent continued or projected decline. Still another scenario is envisioned by the revival of classical realism's emphasis on malign expansionary threats with unlimited war aims (Schweller, 1994; Kydd, 1997; Kupchan, 1997; Rasler and Thompson, 2001a). Should such a threat emerge in any structural context, although an anarchic structure, of course, is always assumed, it is likely to be opposed by a coalition of likely targets of the expansion.

While these dynamics are clearly not the same, in large part because they are embedded in differently perceived structures, they are not ambiguous about the nature of the problem or the identity of the source of utmost threat. In the first case, it is the aspiring hegemon of the principal regional system (once western Europe, now Eurasia) that clashes with the declining global system leader and its coalition.[7] In the second case, it is the dissatisfied, number two power catching up to the system's declining dominant power. In the third case, it is the leading state or one of its near-competitors that turns on a newly emerging threat to its position in hopes of staving off further relative decline. In the fourth case, it is a revisionist power seeking to maximize its power and control. All variations identify a structural change dynamic in which a threat emerges to the status quo (precisely whose status quo and how it is structured is what is contested) that must be suppressed to salvage that status quo. The irony is that coercive attempts to salvage a status quo usually result in an altered status quo anyway. But the victors would probably admit that the new status quo is still preferable to the status quo that would have emerged if the victors had instead been the vanquished.

Thus, the 'bottom line' for many students of major power warfare is whether an explicit and serious threat to the structural status quo is emerging and how other powers are likely to respond to it. We are not talking about minor threats to the status quo, such as the Fidel Castros or Saddam Husseins who are viewed as troublemakers but who do not have the capability to change the system substantially. The Napoleons and the Hitlers who combine ambition and capability are a different matter. They do have the capability to radically change the existing system because they are perceived as possessing the ambition to do so and because they appear to have access to resources that might be able to bring about major structural alterations unless they are stopped. These are the circumstances that bring about the serious major power warfare. Lesser bouts of major power warfare usually involve more restricted conflicts over relative position and other values being contested as in the Franco-Prussian or Russo-Japanese wars that were about territorial control, spheres of influence, and the improving position of one of the combatants.

The question is whether transformations in domestic political systems and their implications for transformations in world politics spell the extinction of positional concerns that lead to intensive conflict. Structural change presumably will continue no matter what political transformations are wrought. But will the consequences of structural change continue to be worth fighting about on occasion?

The constraints of the democratic peace and civil society

The approaches that might be pursued in specifying 'democratic peace' constraints can be reduced to two generic categories. The minimalist approach involves taking the 'democratic peace' term at its face value. Democratization of political regimes leads to reduced conflict at least among democracies even if we are not quite sure why. The maximalist approach involves the consideration of some ten or more complexes of variables, all ostensibly intertwined, that currently appear to be linked to the prospects of greater peace and security.[8] Since it seems unlikely that democratization alone is up to the burden of transforming the world and its international politics, I will take the maximalist path in this chapter. The ten complexes to be discussed will be labeled for present purposes as community norm building, civil society, electoral punishment, transparency/signaling, economic growth and development, economic interdependence, external threat, external status quo satisfaction, external institutional support, and systemic leadership. No single complex is viewed as sufficient to explain the 'democratic peace.' Nor are any of them mutually exclusive. The problem is the opposite. They all seem so excessively intertwined that analytical disaggregation is difficult.

One of the main democratic peace explanations involves the construction of interstate communities predicated on shared values, institutions, and culture (Deutsch *et al.*, 1957; Maoz and Russett, 1993; Russett, 1998; Ray, 1995; Weart, 1998). Democracies are said to be characterized by norms of nonviolence in political contestation. Electoral losers surrender gracefully knowing that they can always renew the contest in the next election. Electoral winners refrain from persecuting the defeated side knowing that they may not be victorious the next time around. As a consequence, democratic populations and politicians, in particular, are schooled in avoiding violent solutions to their political differences. Negotiated outcomes involving some degree of compromise are the expected or standard method of operation. Consequently, two democracies, sharing this type of political culture, will expect that their mutual interstate differences will be treated similarly. Violent solutions will be avoided (Dixon, 1993, 1994). Mediation and negotiation should prevail (Raymond, 1994). As the democratic community expands, a zone of peaceful, inter-democratic interactions emerges.[9]

The 'civil society' argument(s) is a societal-oriented and highly normative variation on the democratic culture idea. Democratic politics are easier to bring about and maintain if non-political spheres of human interaction are also democratic in operation (Dahrendorf, 2000). One thing to look for is a psychological predisposition toward long-term procedures for advancing private interests. If one believes that current losses can be turned around in the future, moderation, trust, tolerance, and restraint in dealing with the demands of others are more likely (Maddison, 1998: 115–16). The existence of independent associations that can be utilized to pursue private interests is another critical prerequisite. If all social institutions are highly centralized, there is little room for, and likelihood of, change. There is also less likelihood that groups will be able to contest powerful institutions (the state, churches, economic corporations) and carve out space for private rights and autonomy. The combination of moderation, tolerance, and voluntary organizations thus creates a liberal culture that can reinforce a liberal political system. Such a cultural context also creates an environment in which further improvements toward liberalization can be attained. Yet it is conceivable and historically demonstrated that the agencies of civil society and the state need not act as checks on one another's relative power. Trentmann (2000), for instance, notes that nineteenth century nationalism and imperialism were popular foci for British and German civil societies. Hence, the development of civil societies can lead to variable outcomes depending on historical context. Put another way, the emergence of a civil society can work to constrain political decision-makers but it also can be mobilized to intensify interstate rivalries and conflict.

The other main explanation for the democratic peace emphasizes institutional constraints on decision-makers in democracies. Democratic decision-makers periodically are subjected to the discipline of electoral contests in which they can be punished for engaging in rash foreign policy adventures or merely for presiding over costly external combat (Bueno de Mesquita, Siverson, and Woller, 1992; Bueno de Mesquita and Siverson, 1995; Thompson, 1995). Whether they win or lose these external combats, voters remember the economic and physical sacrifices and penalize the decision-makers thought to be responsible. Democratic politicians are perfectly aware of this potential retribution and, in order to avoid it and maintain their posts, they will evade opportunities for its exercise. Even if they are not always mindful of electoral punishment, democratic decision-makers are thought to be institutionally handicapped in foreign affairs. They often need authorization from other elected bodies (e.g., legislatures) to go to war. They will also need a relatively high degree of domestic consensus to be able to mobilize resources for external combat. Unless a democratic state is actually attacked, these types of support may be difficult to create. In any event, they will usually take time to cultivate. All of these considerations suggest that democratic decision-makers will need to be more cautious than their autocratic counterparts in committing to foreign policies involving violence and coercion. Ultimately, they are constrained in one way or another by the average citizen's dislike for risk, death, and economic sacrifices.

The transparency/signaling cluster is related to the electoral punishment cluster. Transparency draws attention to the difficulties democracies experience in cloaking their intentions (Kydd, 1997). If decision-makers require institutional and popular support for their activities, they must engage in public discussions of motivation and intentions. Secret arrangements or public deceptions are apt to boomerang once brought to light and may lead to audience costs (Fearon, 1994) and electoral punishment. If democracies must be relatively more public in announcing their intentions, the signals they send are more likely to be congruent with those publicized intentions. External opponents should be able to read these signals with less chance of misinterpretation – although it may also make democracies more vulnerable to attacks at different points of the electoral cycle (Gaubatz, 1991). Democratic decision-makers should also be more able to demonstrate resolve and make lasting commitments because allies and adversaries can assume that what they are being told is sincere and not duplicitous (Siverson and Emmons, 1991; Gaubatz, 1996). Resolve is good for communicating deterrent threats that may prevent the need to escalate to violence. Lasting commitments are good for enduring alliance arrangements which can augment capability against external threats.

The economic growth explanation has developed at least three tracks. The older track (Lipset, 1959, 1994) argues that economic growth reduces inequalities and diffuses resources, including more wealth and education, to individuals throughout the economy. As individuals become more affluent and educated, they will insist on greater participation in the political system. They will also demand property rights and the rule of law. They should also become more tolerant of minority rights. All of these tendencies should be expected to promote democratization. A second track (Barro, 1997) argues for a reciprocal effect. Democratized political systems should experience greater economic growth because they are less prone to capricious governmental intervention in the economy and violation of property rights. The most recent variant (Przeworski *et al.*, 2000) to emerge argues that democratization does not require antecedent economic development to come about, but if a democracy is to survive, some minimal level of economic development is a prerequisite. Accordingly, economic development supports democratization even if it does not cause it.

Closely related to the economic growth arguments is the emphasis on the peaceful implications of economic interdependence (Oneal and Russett, 1997, 1999; Russett, 1998). Economic growth and development are likely to lead to greater economic interdependence. Greater economic interdependence is also thought to benefit further economic growth and development. Equally important, however, is the probability that increased economic interactions across borders will create and expand domestic pressures for avoiding the disruption of those interactions. External conflict tends to disrupt and distort trading patterns. As a consequence, people whose livelihoods depend on uninterrupted trade should be expected to lobby for decisions that avoid serious interruptions in their businesses. Another way of looking at this is that economic interdependence should expand the size of foreign policy 'doves' and 'soft-liners.' Autarky, on the other hand, should be associated with 'hawks' and 'hard-liners' in a two-way causation scheme. 'Hawks' and 'hard-liners' will prefer to reduce their dependency on the outside world so that they are better able to cope with external threats. A reduced dependency on the outside world also means that there are fewer incentives to lobby for maintaining the existing pattern of international interactions.

The external threat argument (Seeley, 1886; Hintze, 1975; Finer, 1975; Tilly, 1975; Almond, 1990; Midlarsky, 1995; Thompson, 1996; Rasler and Thompson, 2000b; Colaresi and Thompson, 2001b) suggests that to some extent the democracy → peace relationship needs to be reversed. The relative absence of external threat is conducive to the initial emergence of democratic practices. A high degree of external danger encourages hierarchical centralization of authority to deal with foreign threats. Individual and minority privileges tend to be superseded by the overriding need to thwart the intentions of malignant external opponents. Thus, 'nasty' neighborhoods can forestall the development of democratization. They can also erode it once it has developed. Moreover, external threats can also affect economic development by increasing the actual and opportunity costs of national security preparations and engagement in external conflict. If the economic development argument(s) is right, these economic costs should also reverberate in the political system's proclivity for more open practices. Therefore, if 'nice' neighborhoods facilitate and support the emergence and maintenance of democracy, to what extent are those same 'nice' neighborhoods responsible for the ostensible democratic peace outcome? The answer might range from all to none, with the most likely probability falling somewhere in between.

The external institutional support dimension (Huntington, 1991; Przeworski et al., 2000) is straightforward. Democracies have a vested interest in encouraging the development of democracy elsewhere. They need allies to defeat autocratic foes. They also wish to nip autocratic foreign policies in the bud so to speak by encouraging more democratization in former and continuing autocracies. Thus, democracy begets more democracies to the extent that democracies support and lobby for democratization. As the size of the democratic community expands, pressures for continued democratization in less democratic territory should also expand. These pressures are likely to be manifested in the foreign policy practices of democracies and also in the international institutions they create and control. A reverse spiral effect can also be imagined. As the size of the democratic community shrinks, it should be increasingly difficult to stem internal and external pressures to autocratize in order to respond to a deteriorating economic and political environment at home and abroad.

The external status quo explanation (Lemke and Reed, 1996; Tammen et al., 2000) focuses on the likelihood that democracies are more likely to support the existing status quo than to be revisionists. To the extent that democracies have been wealthy and powerful for some time, they are likely to be beneficiaries of existing structural arrangements. To the extent that democracies are firmly embedded in economic interdependencies, they are apt to value the maintenance of existing arrangements as most useful for advancing their interests. Turmoil threatens wealth, stability, peace, and community. The point here is that supporters of the status quo are less likely to be the agents of disruption and conflict. Again, then, some portion of the democratic peace outcome may be attributable to a disinclination to rock the international boat in the first place.

Finally, the tenth complex of variables is based on the premise (Modelski and Perry, 1991; Modelski, 1990; Thompson, 2000) that the modern history of democracy can be traced to a considerable extent to the emergence of small trading states on the fringe of western Europe, the success of which created a succession of global system leaders committed to increasingly democratic political practices (i.e., Venice, the Netherlands, Britain, and the United States). The early commercial specialization encouraged the development of domestic political systems emphasizing limited governmental intervention in the economy, general constraints on governmental behavior, and an inclination toward the usually nonviolent rotation of competing groups of political elites. These practices set the foundation for subsequent movements toward expanded franchises and political rights which, in turn, established formulas for success and emulation by the rest of the world. In this respect, democratization depended (and depends) on the successes of the global system leaders.[10] This dependence is most dramatically observed in the intermittent battles between coalitions of democracies and expanding autocracies in global warfare. The point is not that the democratic coalitions were exclusively composed of democracies. They have not been. Nor is the point that global warfare is solely about the relative merits of democracy versus various types of autocracy (aristo-cratic, fascist, communist). However, the more democratic side has triumphed consistently in these battles. If it had not, the world would be a different place and undoubtedly characterized by less democracy rather than more. In general, then, the democratization of the global system leaders encourages the democratization of other states in the system through external institutional support, just as the same system leaders also stimulate economic growth and development, and create and defend the existing status quo against external threats.

Two planes passing in the night?

Both sets of arguments – why major power wars come about and how the demo-cratic peace has emerged – are about the transformation of the international political–economic and military system. Yet the major power focus, in some respects, is the more all-encompassing one even though the questions it raises may seem more narrow. Structural change brings about major power war and it is structural change that is most manifested at the elite level of world politics. The democratic peace argument(s) address structural change as well but the emphasis is more selective. Some states and dyads qualify for these transformations while others do not. Some states and dyads are moving to a different, less conflictual way of interacting with some of their competitors. But the emphasis must always be on the *some*. As long as some important competitors remain relatively outside the influence of the zone in which the transformations are believed to be taking place, there remains some possibility of 'old-fashioned,' structural change-induced conflict over relative positions in the system hierarchy.

This is not to say that there is no overlap whatsoever in the two sets of arguments. There are some points of contact – the two planes do not pass in the night totally unscathed. They scrape but they do not collide. The strength of systemic leadership is one overlapping feature. Strong systemic leadership facilitates economic growth, democratization, and community building at least among the states satisfied with the status quo. Weak leadership does the opposite. Weak leadership also encourages militarized challenges of the systemic pecking orders (both regionally and globally). One could also argue that transformations within the democratized zone make it easier for states outside the zone to act predatorily. If democracies are more constrained than autocracies, the advantage in taking the initiative would seem to lie in the autocratic court. This advantage may be outweighed by the advantage democracies – or at least some democracies – have exhibited in mobilizing coali-tions and superior resources. Yet this advantage only comes to the fore after war has broken out, not before.

There is another way in which the two sets of arguments implicitly overlap. It is captured well by Gleditsch and Hegre's (1997; see as well Rasler and Thompson, 2001a) idea that the systemic relationship between the spread of the democratic peace and reduced conflict is nonlinear. They point out that as democratic dyads become more pacific, mixed dyads (democracies versus autocracies) become more conflictual. Why this increase in conflict occurred can be interpreted in different ways. They did not absolutely have to become more conflictual but there was some probability that they would given the differences in political, economic, ideological, and geopolitical orientations. The more autocratic states were not simply more autocratic. They also were slower to develop economically. They retained or formulated ideologies (imperial aristocracies, fascism, and communism) that were antithetical to the survival of democracy. These same autocracies, moreover, tended to be large continental powers with a proclivity toward threatening to dominate the principal region (western Europe or Eurasia) of the world system.

Thus, as democratization spreads (and before it diffuses maximally), the risks of certain kinds of conflict actually increase rather than decrease. If this seems counterintuitive, one need only consider a five-actor system. With one democracy, there are four mixed dyads. With two democracies, there are six mixed dyads. With three democracies, there are still six mixed dyads. Only after one reaches four democracies does the number of mixed dyads begin to decline back to four. The odds of major power warfare need not be identical to the number of mixed dyads within the major power subsystem. But there has definitely been some relationship over the past few centuries. There is no reason to assume that this rough relationship will disappear in the near future.

The argument says nothing about the relative capabilities of the imagined five actors. If the nondemocratic holdouts are very weak, the nonlinear dyadic mathematics of democratization may not matter. But if there are powerful, nondemocratic holdouts that also feel threatened by the democracies (and vice versa) or that feel dissatisfied with the international status quo crafted by the democracies, the nonlinearity is something to keep in mind. Only when almost all, or all, of the system is transformed, do the formal odds of substantial conflict begin to decline.

Indeed, this emphasis on system transformation is suggestive. What we need are not static interpretations of the democratic peace (two democracies will avoid intensive conflict) or major power war (there will always be power transitions that lead to intensive major power conflict). We need more dynamic theorizing. Rosecrance's trading state theory offers one very useful take on this problem. It is both dynamic and it integrates processes involving increased cooperation and warfare. It needs more work for our present purposes but, drawing on some of the arguments that have already been discussed, the presentation of the modifications is a fairly manageable task.

A modified trading state theory

Richard Rosecrance's (1987) trading state model, with some appropriate major and minor tweaks here and there, provides a good synthetic theoretical explanation for ongoing developments in political economy and conflict. Rosecrance begins with an emphasis on two strategies. One is labeled 'military–political' and is focused on states that base their relative power on how much territory is controlled. Territorial expansion is useful both for establishing independence and self-sufficiency, as well as for improving one's competitive standing in the struggle for international primacy. Given the probability of resistance to territorial expansion gambits and the competition for primacy, occasional bouts of warfare are a likely outcome as competitors determine how far they can expand.

The second strategy is referred to as the 'trading state' approach. Trading states do not seek self-sufficiency and regard such a goal as inefficient. Some division of labor is preferred, with differentially endowed economies occupying various specialized niches, and the strong likelihood of increasing dependence on trading partners is accepted as par for the course. Trading states also avoid the temptations of territorial expansion in preference for a concentration on domestic economic development and trade relationships which are apt to be interrupted by warfare.

Rosecrance envisions a situation in which decision-makers are constantly choosing between these strategies. Neither strategy is entirely mutually exclusive and, historically, most states have opted for some combination. However, with some notable exceptions, the modal combined strategy has given greater weight to the military–political route than to the trading option. One exceptional era is attributed to the outstanding success of British industrial and naval prowess in the mid-nineteenth century. For a few decades, a trading world characterized by decreasing barriers to trade and increasing interdependence began to emerge only to be terminated as World Wars I and II brutally returned the systemic emphasis to military–political issues. The trading world 'experiment' resumed only after 1945, this time with German and Japanese exemplars leading the way.

Several changes had taken place prior to and by the second half of the twentieth century to make the expansion of the trading world feasible. A series of industrial revolutions beginning in the late eighteenth century altered the demand for natural resources needed to fuel industrialization. Since few developing states possessed access to these resources at home, their economic dependence on obtaining the commodities through trade increased. The same industrial revolutions reduced transaction costs as transportation on land, sea, and through the air became less costly and faster. Then, too, the most successful industrializers developed production capacities that exceeded the demands of their home markets. The cultivation of, and continued access to, foreign markets became increasingly critical to sustaining domestic growth and employment. Perhaps ironically, the ballooning size of the international system after decolonization and the independence of many small and weak states in the former third world also left most of these new states with few choices but to pursue economic development and trade over territorial expansion. Economic independence was never a real option for the newly independent states.

At the same time, the costs of warfare had risen, while the probable payoffs from winning wars had declined. Technological advances in military weaponry meant that force could be projected at greater distances and with greater lethality but with little improvement in the ability to defend the home base. Vulnerability to attack therefore had increased even as the cost of military preparations had escalated immensely. If military conflicts were increasingly likely to be highly destructive, conquering some target that would be destroyed in the process began to lose some of its appeal. Even more of the appeal was lost if the victor was also likely to be destroyed in the process. Even if maximum destructiveness could somehow be avoided, conquered populations had become increasingly resistant to being absorbed readily into the victor's territorial domain.

In general, the costs of military–political strategies had risen enormously, and especially after 1945. Fortuitously, the costs of economic development and trade were declining as the barriers to trade were being whittled away in the increasingly prosperous, postwar era. Decision-makers, faced with rising military–political costs and declining trading costs, made the rational choice and opted for participation in the expanding trading world. Substantial defections from the military–political world might have occurred after World War I – the war to end all wars. But as long as a few aggressors remained and even fewer defenders were prepared to restrain their aggression, the inter-war years and World War II had to first be experienced to give the trading world approach its strongest opportunity to thrive after 1945. Only ideological conflict and differences in domestic political constitutions persisted in suggesting some benefits might be attained via warfare and military–political strategies.

Now for the tweaking – several elements are missing from Rosecrance's theory. Fortunately, inserting them is not difficult because Rosecrance was focused on a very important process in world politics and hits much of it right on target. What is missing? The answers are evolution, a greater emphasis on historical systemic processes, especially systemic leadership and eclipsed contenders (as opposed to national choices), and some role for democratization.

The last element is the easiest of the three to insert. If Rosecrance had published his thesis a few years later, he probably would have inserted it himself. As it is, he leaves an explicit opening when he notes (1987: 27) that one of the domestic features facilitating participation in the trading world was merchant autonomy to freely participate in external networks of exchange. Barriers to trade had to be avoided domestically as well as internationally. Not surprisingly, early trading states had been characterized by merchant participation in politics and while these earlier forms (e.g., Venice, the Netherlands) were more accurately described as merchant oligarchies, they did help establish a republican tradition that clearly contrasted with aristocratic formulae and contributed to subsequent democratization efforts by making a case for limited state intervention in internal processes. Domestic economic development also tends to expand the proportion of a population with sufficient resources to expect and to demand some form of participation in political decision-making. An emphasis on Rosecrance's trading strategy thus tended to encourage democratization. Accordingly, the first wave of democracies initially restricted the extent of participation to property holders above a certain threshold and then gradually expanded the scope of franchise inclusion by lowering the threshold. But one could say that groups of people were more likely to be enfranchised as they became regarded as important contributors to economic development and/or threats to domestic stability that was conducive to economic development.

We know from a large number of studies that economic development is an albeit imperfect predictor of democratization. Emphasizing economic development and trade as the predominant national strategy is therefore likely to facilitate democratization. Put another way, the most successful trading states are also likely to be highly democratic. One could easily imagine a causal sequence that resembled the following:

$$economic\ development \rightarrow trade\ interdependence + democratization \rightarrow$$
$$democratic\ peace$$

That is, economic development leads to expanded trade participation and democratization, which leads consequently to reduced conflict within democratic dyads, especially to the extent that they are developed economically and also economically interdependent. That is precisely what Mousseau (2000) and Hegre (2000) find empirically and argue substantively.

But other interpretations are also tenable. Rosecrance's own argument is actually driven by the ratio of net costs associated with war and trade. As the war/trade costs ratio rises (war becomes more costly and trade less costly), more states adopt trading strategies that include avoiding the costly disruptions of intense conflict as much as possible. Disruptions raise the costs of war and trade simultaneously. From this perspective, economic development, trade interdependence, and democratization are to a large extent outcomes of strategy selection processes – not necessarily their antecedents. That is to say that we should expect economic development, trade interdependence, and democratization all to be correlated with more pacific international relations of various sorts, but that the first three do not necessarily cause or produce the more pacific international relations. It is perceptions of the net costs of war and trade that drive the more pacific outcome in Rosecrance's theory.

A second missing element that is also fairly easy to insert or simply make more explicit is the notion of evolution.[11] How states interact in international relations is not static. It is subject to change and transformation as features of the environment change and as actors undergo change. One possible focus in evolutionary arguments is that it is strategies per se that evolve. Actors choose different strategies (or have them thrust upon them) to deal with different types of policy problems. As environments and actors change, so too do their perceived policy problems. In terms of the Rosecrance argument, one of the important things that evolves in international relations is the predominant strategy. Is international relations characterized by territorial expansion, constant threats and the need to resort to independent self-help, and intermittent warfare as the realists would have it? Or, is international relations characterized by an economic division of labor that stresses cooperative exchange, interdependence, and development as the liberals would have us believe? Rosecrance is arguing that we appear to be evolving from a realist world toward a liberal world as more states abandon the strategies predominant in the former and adopt the strategies predominant in the latter. From his perspective, international relations are evolving primarily because of trends in changes in the net costs of war making and economic development/trading.

But there is a third missing element. Rosecrance couches his argument in a Westphalian genesis story. He might have argued that these war/trading options have been available as long as people have been engaged in war and trade. That would take us back at least 9,000 years and no doubt even longer. But while Rosecrance makes some mention of Genoan/Venetian activities in the Mediterranean and Spanish/Portuguese activities in the rest of the world – all taking place before 1648 and the Treaty of Westphalia that ended the Thirty Years War – his historical script really begins in the mid-seventeenth century and the European institutionalization of the myth of state sovereignty (i.e., legal independence). From 1648 to 1945, with some deviation in the mid-nineteenth century, international relations strategies approximated the political–military end of the continuum. After 1945, strategies began to move toward the trading end of the dualistic behavioral spectrum as the world became more interdependent.

Of course, another reason for Rosecrance's late-blooming interpretation of trading strategies is that he requires traders to eschew conflict and attempts at market monopoly. If earlier trading states mixed considerable elements of coercion into their efforts to acquire and control external markets, these precocious manifestations of trading orientations do not count as the real thing. But that stance denies any possibilities of evolution within each of the principal strategies. A great deal of evolution occurred within the political–military strategy, given changes in offensive and defensive military technology and organizational formats (e.g., city-states, empires, nation-states). Without such evolution, it is unlikely that the costs of warfare would have eventually exceeded the perceived benefits. Why deny the same types of evolutionary processes to the trading strategy world in which the use of coercion became gradually more intermittent or at least more subtle. Market monopolies, however, are still very much sought by firms.

The Westphalian assumptions thus ignore or suppress an important aspect of duality in world politics. As western Europe and some of its states moved to the center of the world system after 1500, some of these increasingly central states sought to disentangle themselves from European affairs to better focus on controlling American and Asian trade with Europe. Portugal, the Netherlands, and England sought as much as possible to keep some distance from territorial conflicts in Europe. Ultimately, as in the case of their prototypical predecessor, Venice, the first two in this trio were unsuccessful. They were invaded and conquered by Spain and France, respectively but not before establishing a record as early trading state behavior prior to the Treaty of Westphalia. Rosecrance would dispute this characterization. The difference of opinion reduces to how one views Portuguese, Dutch and English coercive tactics outside of Europe. If Portugal, the Netherlands, and England chose to specialize in African, Asian, and American conquests, how does that distinguish them from Spanish activities in the Americas or Spanish and French expansion efforts in Europe? Rosecrance presumably would say there is no difference as long as the emphasis was on territorial expansion as opposed to trade. Yet Portuguese, Dutch, and English agents in long-distance trade always began with the premise that territorial conquest should be avoided as much as possible. The gradual acquisition of first bases and then political–military control adjacent to the bases in ever-increasing scale was neither entirely premeditated nor did it represent successful strategy. Many imperial acquisitions were rightly regarded as drains on profit-making in trade but ones that somehow could not be avoided. The Portuguese were usually too weak to penetrate very far inland. The Dutch essentially were bankrupted by the success of their initially reluctant efforts to control Indonesia. The English were more successful after they lost their first empire but in the process they also became something other than what they had started out as. One can speculate whether the British might have been more likely to have retained their industrial lead, or at least a leading role in technological change, in the absence of an extensive empire to fall back on.

Whether one speculates or not, there is a lineage of trading states in the history of contemporary (which corresponds to the last 500 years) European international relations. They engaged in predatory behavior outside of Europe but, within Europe, they tended to conform to Rosecrance's trading strategy unless or until attacked by the 'military–political' powers of continental Europe. And attacked they were to the extent that one can describe their interactions as a dissynchronized oscillation (Rasler and Thompson, 1994). One leading military–political power built up its strength on land and aspired to regional hegemony. Regional hegemony threatened the global trading network. A coalition of trading states and land powers, led by the leading trading state/maritime power would successfully suppress the threat every hundred years or so (1494–1517, 1585–1608, 1688–1713, 1702–1815, and 1914–45). The outcome was a concentration of power in the global system devoted primarily to the management of long-distance commerce and a deconcentration of power on land in the leading region of the system. As the global concentration of power eroded, new challengers (Spain, France, and Germany, in that order) were encouraged to try their hand at European hegemony up to 1945. Four hundred and fifty years of this increasingly destructive process exhausted the potential for coercive hegemonies in western Europe. Since 1945, the process appears to have moved to a larger regional focus – Eurasia.

Very much a part of this interpretation is the emphasis on systemic leadership at the global level which gradually grew stronger until Britain could lead a movement for free trade in the mid-nineteenth century that impresses Rosecrance as the first era of trading strategy predominance. But earlier system leaders also had advanced organization schemes and strategic doctrines, but with less impact on behavior or pertaining to a more limited geographical scope. One reason is that the earlier leaders had to rely on leadership resource platforms built on gains from long-distance trade. The nineteenth century British had this commercial edge in addition to their lead in industrial technology.

Yet the British nineteenth century 'experiment' did not end the succession of system leaders. One of the more puzzling features of the Rosecrance interpretation is the placement of the late twentieth century United States in the 'political–military' world. How one ignores the US lead in establishing a postwar regime for the management of political economy questions in emulation of the earlier British experiment is difficult to explain. Even more difficult to account for is the lack of appreciation for the role of the system leader as the world's lead economy. That is, the world's most successful exemplar of technological innovation and the rewards these pioneering innovations bestow in terms of a head start over all other economies. As a consequence, the most successful trading state becomes the system leader. It does not matter if the system leader's economy is so large that trade is not (at least initially) a large proportion of its economy. No matter the size of their exports and imports, system leaders virtually reorganize the trading world along lines reflecting their preferences, interests, and strengths because, for a time, they are the predominant trading state.

The absence of leadership in the Rosecrance version is all the more odd since relatively weak states often need protection from remaining predators so that they can pursue trading strategies. This protection, especially after 1945, was clearly organized by the United States. It allowed, among other things, Germany and Japan to redevelop their economies for trading purposes. Other small trading states, such as the Benelux states, also enjoyed considerable protection in the most recent era of international politics. All states do not enjoy free choice in the strategies they pursue. Most do what they can given their resources and opportunities. But if the external threats are much greater than they can manage on their own resources, a security shield can be very helpful in creating safe niches to pursue cooperative strategies. Britain did some of this shielding on a very selective basis in the mid-nineteenth century; the United States did much more in the second half of the twentieth century. In this respect, shifts to different predominant strategies rely on Pax Britannicas and Pax Americanas that are created by system leaders to preserve the world orders they construct after successfully defeating the last hegemonic challenge.

Another major reason for not overlooking system leadership is its crucial role in generating the economic basis for eras of increasing interdependence. System leaders lead in a variety of areas. They control the system's lead economy which generates pioneering innovations in commerce and industry. These hard and soft technological innovations bring about paradigmatic shifts in how economies are structured and how they interact. They produce new products, increase supply and demand for trade, and lower transaction costs (e.g., steamships, railroads, jet engines). The ability to outproduce all other economies gives the leader substantial incentives to take the lead in reducing barriers to trade that the lead economy no longer needs. Yet system leaders can maintain their edges only for finite periods. Other economies catch up by adapting and often improving upon the pioneering technology of the leader. Trading interdependence is especially encouraged by these periods of catch-up and increased specialization. Then, too, lead economies, also for a time, become the system's primary source for investment capital and loans. All of these factors are critical to spirals of interdependence and lowered costs of trade. Without them, economic processes would be fairly static and characterized only by the slow-moving, incremental change enshrined in equilibrium analyses.

One last missing element deserves some consideration. As in other cases of 'missing elements,' it is not altogether absent from the Rosecrance framework. Rosecrance (1987: 18) acknowledges that trading strategies are often chosen by states that no longer are competitive in the political–military world. There is more to it than just a casual correlation. The ongoing transformation of international relations reflects the fact that a number of contenders for power and position have been defeated, exhausted, and eclipsed in the last 500 years of European international relations. Spain, the Ottoman Empire, Sweden, Denmark, Austria, France, Italy, Germany, Japan, and Britain have all dropped from the list of main contenders. Most recently, Russia may finally have dropped out permanently as well. Of course, some of these states could return to the front ranks but none seems close to doing so in the very near future. If you remove or declaw the most powerful territorial expanders from the system, the transformational opportunities for that system expand immensely. Their removal or demotion does not mean that small states will not attempt to emulate the failed great powers. But the level of pervasive threat is much less and that should facilitate (without guaranteeing) the expansion of alternative strategies. It is not simply the costs of warfare that have changed. The entry costs for engaging in competitive warfare have also escalated. Combined with the fortunes of past wars, few states can afford to compete any more. Moreover, most of the past major contenders for power and position have been eclipsed along the way by larger, stronger, and/or wealthier states. Thus, costs and strategies have evolved. So, too, have the thresholds for successful competition in military–political competition. Very few potentially elite players for the twenty-first century survive. Most of the past's political–military dinosaurs have either died or been transformed into birds.

So here we have a theory that combines a number of ingredients: dual and dueling strategies, power, territorial expansion, economic development, military costs, barriers to trade, systemic leadership, democratization, and interdependence – all subject to evolutionary change and transformation. What drives this theory? Rosecrance is quite right to emphasize the costs of warfare and trade but they represent only part of the story. Systemic leadership, waves of technological innovation, and centuries of warfare and elite attrition have played and continued to play crucial roles as well. The story is sufficiently complex that we might do well not to worry too much about what variable, if any, lies at the root of the complicated web.[12] For instance, the costs of warfare have been driven upward in a ratchet-like fashion by centuries of largely European warfare.[13] The costs of trade have been reduced by the development of new products and lowered transaction costs that have both been the outcome of technological and economic development, driven, in turn, by successive system leaders.[14] It has been empirically demonstrated (Thompson and Reuveny, 1998) that even tariffs are more a function of economic growth than the other way around. It is unlikely that a case for any single variable, such as democratization, economic development, or economic interdependence, can be made that sustains the whole ensemble of ongoing transformations. What should matter most is whether all of these variables are working together in the predicted direction.

More specifically, however, we are also alerted to the likelihood of transformations that may be underway. We should be looking for mixtures of military–political and trading elements because neither 'world' is predominant. If we are in flux, moving from the predominance of military–political strategies toward the predominance of trading strategies, analyses should be picking up manifestations of both types of orientation simultaneously. Over time, the manifestations of military–political strategic predominance should be waning while the effects of trading strategy predominance could be waxing. But this waxing and waning need not be monotonic. The older orientations can reassert themselves; the newer orientations can stumble. We may also be in flux – caught between two worlds – for some time to come.

We also need to keep in mind that this transition is likely to work in a highly uneven geographical pattern. Two nuclear-armed states face much higher warfare costs than two conventionally armed states. Two economically developed states, other things being equal, should find trade more attractive than two lesser developed states. We know that there are pockets of affluence, democratization, and high military capability and vast areas of slow economic development, autocracy, and limited military capability. The relative attractiveness of the dual strategies is unlikely to be the same in areas characterized by markedly different wealth and military strength distributions. Heterogeneity, therefore, breeds unevenness in the degree to which one or the other of the two strategies is preeminent. This unevenness is compounded further by the transitional shifts in appreciations for the dual strategies. In sum, we should not always expect clear outcomes that are easy to comprehend if the world that we are trying to interpret is in the process of being transformed. Until or unless the transformation process is 'completed,' we should look for and anticipate mixed signals, both spatially and temporally.[15]

Alternative futures

Of course, future forecasts depend on choices among alternative scenarios. One scenario, the maximal diffusion of the democratic peace/trading strategy throughout the planet, in the next half century is possible but seems unlikely. The most probable holdouts, China and perhaps a Russia which is likely to vacillate in its experimentation with democratization and trading strategies, happen to be major powers. They are also reasonably well situated, at least geographically, to contest for Eurasian predominance. The only other conceivable, entirely new, major power contender for Eurasian position in the twenty-first century is India. There are also old west European and east Asian contenders (Germany/EU and Japan) that might be expected to improve their relative economic and military positions in the coming half century. The point is that the current, sole surviving superpower, the United States, is not likely to retain its lead unchallenged indefinitely into the future. Should its relative position decay – something that is almost inevitable even if the US does retain its lead economy status for several more decades – a prospect that is hardly inevitable, the conditions that have encouraged serious major power warfare in the past could be upon us once again. As long as there is significant variance in the appreciation for the relative attractions of the dual strategies, the possibility of a relapse into a concerted emphasis on politico-military strategies is not out of the question.

A variation on this scenario involves pointing to the unprecedented absence of major power rivalries since the late 1980s. In the absence of threatening rivalries and rivals, conflicts are much less likely to escalate to war. That is a generalization that can be and has been documented (Rasler and Thompson, 2001c; Colaresi and Thompson, 2002a, 2002b). However, here again, the fact that the termination of the US–Soviet and Soviet–Chinese rivalries almost simultaneously and not coincidentally took place does not mean that they and other major power rivalries might not reemerge.[16] One has the impression that the United States and China have been very close to acknowledging a strategic rivalry relationship.[17] The United States and Russia may not be too far behind, depending perhaps on how long their common interests in suppressing threats from Islamic fundamentalists can prolong the process. Decision-makers have been cautious in the post-Cold War era about admitting perceptions of threat. But the caution may not persist indefinitely.

Another scenario that is popular is that the advent of nuclear weapons has altered the prospects of major power warfare, putting aside the effects of all other transformations. This is a hypothesis that is difficult to dismiss easily. The costs of major power warfare in which both sides are armed with nuclear weapons and prepared to use them would be so high that one could argue that reasonable or rational decision-makers would find such warfare unthinkable (Mueller, 1988; Kayser, 1990; Waltz, 1993). However, there are several problems with this hypothesis that caution us to think of it as a hypothesis and not as a well-established fact. First, we really have no idea whether the possession of nuclear weapons deters aggression. Cold War warriors were quick to point to the 1945–89 record in which neither the Soviet Union nor the United States attacked the other overtly. But we still lack evidence that either side intended to attack the other side and decided not to because of the potential horrors of nuclear war. In the absence of such evidence, it is possible to interpret the relative absence of major power war during the Cold War in several alternative ways.

Second, there is some tendency for decision-makers to start wars with the premise that some weapons will not be utilized. Sometimes this works and sometimes it does not. Neither side intended to bomb cities from the air in World War II but it did not take long for that reluctance to be pushed aside. Alternatively, poison gas has been used sparingly since World War I. The point is that prewar intentions about what is appropriate and what is not can change in the midst of war. Third, while the horrors of nuclear warfare cannot be downplayed, they did not prevent Cold War professional military planners from contemplating and planning for their utilization in the event that war did break out. There were also professional military planners who were prepared to accept the losses anticipated in a nuclear exchange.

Third, the continuing post-mortems of the Cuban Missile Crisis suggest luck can make a difference. If we were all lucky in 1962, there is no guarantee that we will be equally lucky in a similar situation in, say, 2032. There is also the very strong possibility that the types of structural change outlined in major power warfare arguments simply had not advanced sufficiently far in 1962. If facilitative environments assist 'luck' – both good and bad – the odds of worse luck may or may not advance with continued structural change.

None of these observations deny the occurrence of significant transformation along the lines of the democratic peace/trading strategy predominance in selected parts of the world. The likelihood of major power warfare, and the relative probability of interstate war for that matter (Holsti, 1996) do appear to be waning, especially in the North. Presumably, these and other transformations will continue to spread, although not necessarily at the same speed as before. The easier cases to transform may already have undergone conversion to more pacific strategies of international competition. For that matter, all of the conversions are not likely to stick. Democratization and economic development proceed in waves, not straight lines. Surges in democratization and economic development have tended to be followed by some relapses into autocracy and/or economic depression. The cycling of these phenomena is likely to continue. If there also prove to be inherent limitations to the diffusion of modern economic development, democratization, and threat termination and deescalation, as seems likely, the attainment of maximal diffusion must be projected well into the future. In this environment of uneven development, both sets of arguments can be correct simultaneously. The democratic peace/trading strategy argument, ultimately, only becomes incompatible with the arguments for major power warfare when the transformations associated maximally with the democratic peace idea have diffused throughout the entire planet. Until or unless that point is attained, we can have a partially evolving democratic peace/ movement toward the predominance of trading strategies *and* some continued possibility of major power warfare. The latter possibility may be quite remote today and tomorrow as well. Thirty years down the road could be a very different story.

But, imagine an even more distant future in which the trading strategy ostensibly has triumphed completely over the political–military strategy. Everyone pursues a trading strategy and no one has much appreciation for the attractions of political–military strategies. Would such a transformation imply the eradication of any possibility of major power warfare? The answer is no. Some possibility could persist for several reasons. One reason is that making predictions in situations of evolving transformations is tricky. Stable and simple parameters facilitate prediction. If the parameters are experiencing mutation and/or involve multiple processes, it is not easy to forecast what will emerge with any great precision.

A second reason for caution is that Rosecrance's theory emphasizes two variables – the net costs or benefits of war and trade. When you have a monovariate theory that predicts that democratic dyads lead to greatly reduced probabilities of intensive conflict, the theory's anticipated conflict implications for a world in which all dyads are democratic are fairly straightforward. Yet, even though the lethality of warfare has increased enormously, even Rosecrance leaves some wiggle room for circumstances that might favor high perceived benefits from war. He mentions ideological differences and different political structures. But trading environments need not remain characterized by relatively benign divisions of labor forever.[18] At least, they certainly have not in the past. States lower on the technological gradient aspire to upward mobility. States near the top of the economic 'food chain' may not wish to settle for second place. States at the top may not choose to experience relative decline gracefully. Mix in periodic shocks to the trading world in the form of world depressions, resource and fuel shortages, environmental deterioration, different mixes of philosophy about state and corporation alliances, tendencies toward trading bloc formations, and/or waves of destabilizing, radical technological innovations – all of which might be expected in an exclusively liberal, trading world. Some reevaluations of the net benefits of the war/trade ratio, even if all political and economic systems are structured similarly, might be anticipated from time to time if the perceived costs and benefits associated with the war/trade ratio prove to be more significant than regime type in explaining trends in conflict.

Hence, we can all hope that major power war will go the way of the wooly mammoth or the saber-toothed tiger. But, theoretically (whether one emphasizes regime type, the costs of war and trade, economic development and interdependence, all of the above, or some other mix of factors), it is not clear that we have grounds to assume that such a probable eventuality will occur soon or smoothly. World politics has yet to experience sufficient transformation to guarantee the elimination of major power war. And even when the world has experienced sufficient transformation, we may still find that people will find things to fight about, given the right sort of conducive environment. Evolutionary processes do not merely shift actors and their strategies from one static category to another. They are ongoing processes of change in which the 'dust never quite settles.' We may choose to impose static outcomes such as the democratic peace analytically but that does not mean that evolving environments, actors, and their strategies will pay much heed. And because continuing evolution seems a good bet, clearcut predictions of what will happen, when, and where in world politics need to be advanced cautiously.

Notes

1 On the other hand, Portuguese infantry were not very successful in the 1500s in Morocco, Ethiopia, or along the coasts of southern Africa.

2 For a discussion of the polarity and polarization concepts, see Rapkin *et al.* (1979). Schweller's (1998) emphasis on the special instability of tripolarity and Copeland's (2000) argument that declining leaders act differently in bipolar versus multipolar settings are the latest entries in this subfield.

3 The central statement of structural realism which places so much emphasis on the statics of polarity is Waltz (1979).

4 A summary of the debates over polarity and warfare can be found in Kegley and Raymond (1994).

5   There are a number of approaches that rely on uneven development to explain systemic warfare. Compare, for instance, Gilpin (1981), Wallerstein (1984), Kennedy (1987), Organski and Kugler (1980), Modelski and Thompson (1996), Chase-Dunn and Podobnik (1999), Knutsen (1999), and Boswell and Chase-Dunn (2000).

6   Of course, there are a number of other approaches that utilize long waves of technological change as the main carrier of economic change underlying periodic major power warfare. See Väyrynen (1983), Goldstein (1988, 1991), Boswell and Sweat (1991), Pollins (1996), Chase-Dunn (1989), and Boswell and Chase-Dunn (2000).

7   See as well my five-variable model identifying most probable challengers in Thompson (1997, 2000).

8   Many, but not all, of the ten complexes can be identified at least implicitly in Chan (1997).

9   Initially, the argument for increasingly peaceful interactions was restricted to dyadic relations between democracies, but the consensus (see, among others, Benoit, 1996; Rummel, 1995; Russett and Starr, 2000; Ray, 2000) seems to be moving in the direction of democracies acting monadically in more peaceful ways than nondemocracies.

10 The successes of the democratic system leaders are not quite the same thing as the argument that democracies tend to be more successful in war (Lake, 1992; Stam, 1996). However, the former probably has much to do with the outcomes supporting the latter.

11 The types of explicitly evolutionary arguments I have in mind are illustrated by Modelski (1996, 2000, 2001), Cederman (1997), and the chapters found in Thompson (2001).

12 Along similar lines, Modelski (2000) argues that political, economic, and cultural developments in global-level processes are nested within each other. Rather than focus on one variable 'causing' another, global-level processes coevolve as reciprocal influences on one another.

13 Rasler and Thompson (1983, 1985, 1989) and Thompson and Rasler (1999) empirically demonstrate the effect of wars on state revenues and expenditures, public debts, and army size.

14 Reuveny and Thompson (2001) demonstrate that the system leader's technological innovation drives its aggregate economic growth and that both the leader's innovation and aggregate economic growth drive world economic growth.

15 One contemporary illustration of mixes is authoritarian governments attempting to liberalize their economic systems and democratic governments with managed economies. Presumably, there are tensions within these systems working toward reconciling the frictions of opposed logics by having one strategy predominate. But there is no reason to assume that these mixed cases cannot exist for some indefinite period of time. Much the same can be said about external (political–military vs. trading) orientations. They have coexisted, albeit not peacefully, for several hundreds of years already.

16 See Thompson (2001) for a theoretical explanation of the termination of the Sino-Soviet rivalry that could also be extended to account for the US–Soviet case.

17 The China Problem of the twenty-first century – how to accommodate China's likely ascent in relative power – may come to resemble the German Problem of the late nineteenth and first half of the twentieth century. For various views on this question, see, among a number of others, Nathan and Ross (1997), Bernstein and Munro (1998), and Swaine and Tellis (2000).

18 How benign the division of labor appears most definitely depends on where one fits into the scheme of things. The idea that a particular division of labor is beneficial and that all should accept their assigned role complacently would appeal most to those actors who benefit most from the status quo.

References

Almond, Gabriel A. (1990) *A Discipline Divided: Schools and Sects in Political Science.* Newbury Park, Calif.: Sage.

Barro, Robert J. (1997) *Determinants of Economic Growth: A Cross-Country Empirical Study.* Cambridge, Mass.: MIT Press.

Benoit, Kenneth (1996) 'Democracies Really are More Peaceful (In General).' *Journal of Conflict Resolution* 40: 636–57.

Bernstein, Richard and Ross H. Munro (1998) *The Coming Conflict with China.* New York: Vintage.

Boswell, Terry and Christopher Chase-Dunn (2000) *The Spiral of Capitalism and Socialism.* Boulder, Colo.: Lynne Rienner.

Boswell, Terry and Mike Sweat (1991) 'Hegemony, Long Waves and Major Wars.' *International Studies Quarterly* 35: 123–49.

Bueno de Mesquita, Bruce, Randolph M. Siverson, and Gary Woller (1992) 'War and the Fate of Regimes: A Comparative Analysis.' *American Political Science Review* 86: 638–46.

Bueno de Mesquita, Bruce and Randolph M. Siverson (1995) 'War and the Survival of Political Leaders: A Comparative Study of Regime Types and Political Accountability.' *American Political Science Review* 89: 841–53.

Cederman, Lars-Erik (1997) *Emergent Actors in World Politics.* Princeton, NJ: Princeton University Press.

Chan, Steve (1997) 'In Search of Democratic Peace: Problems and Promise.' *Mershon International Studies Review* 41 (Supplement 1): 59–91.

Chase-Dunn, Christopher (1989) *Global Formation: Structures of the World-Economy.* Cambridge, Mass.: Blackwell.

—— and Bruce Podobnik (1999) 'The Next World War: World-System Cyclical Trends,' in Volker Bornschier and Christopher Chase-Dunn, eds, *The Future of Global Conflict.* Thousand Oaks, Calif.: Sage.

Choucri, Nazli, Robert C. North, and Susumu Yamakage (1992) *The Challenge of Japan: Before World War II and After.* New York: Routledge.

Colaresi, Michael and William R. Thompson (2002a) 'Strategic Rivalry, Protracted Conflict, and Crisis Behavior.' *Journal of Peace Research* 39: 263–87.

—— (2002b) 'Hot Spots or Hot Hands? Serial Crisis Behavior, Escalating Risks, and Rivalry.' *Journal of Politics* 64: 1175–98.

—— (2003) 'The Economic Development–Democratization Relationship: Does the Outside World Matter?' *Comparative Political Studies* 36: 381–403.

Copeland, Dale C. (2000) *The Origins of Major War.* Ithaca, NY: Cornell University Press.

Dahrendorf, Ralf (2000) 'Foreword,' in Fran Tonkiss, Andrew Passey, Natalie Fenton, and Leslie C. Helms, eds, *Trust and Civil Society.* New York: St Martin's Press.

Deutsch, Karl W., Sidney A. Burrell, Robert A. Kann, Maurice Lee, Jr, Martin Lichtenman, Raymond E. Lindgren, Frances L. Loewenheim, and Richard W. Van Wagenen (1957) *Political Community and the North Atlantic Area: International Organization in the Light of Historical Experience.* New York: Greenwood.

Dixon, William J. (1993) 'Democracy and the Management of International Conflict.' *Journal of Conflict Resolution* 37: 42–68.

—— (1994) 'Democracy and the Peaceful Settlement of International Conflict.' *American Political Science Review* 88: 14–32.

Doran, Charles F. (2000) 'Confronting the Principles of the Power Cycle: Changing Systems Structure, Expectations, and War,' in Manus Midlarsky, ed., *Handbook of War Studies II*. Ann Arbor: University of Michigan Press.

Fearon, James D. (1994) 'Domestic Political Audiences and the Escalation of International Disputes.' *American Political Science Review* 88: 577–92.

Finer, Samuel E. (1975) 'State and Nation-Building in Europe: The Role of the Military,' in Charles Tilly, ed., *The Formation of National States in Western Europe*. Princeton, NJ: Princeton University Press.

Gaubatz, Kurt T. (1991) 'Election Cycles and War.' *Journal of Conflict Resolution* 35: 212–44.

—— (1996) 'Democratic States and Commitment in International Relations.' *International Organization* 50: 109–39.

Gilpin, Robert (1981) *War and Change in World Politics*. New York: Cambridge University Press.

Gleditsch, Nils Petter and Havard Hegre (1997) 'Peace and Democracy: Three Levels of Analysis.' *Journal of Conflict Resolution* 41 (2): 283–310.

Goldstein, Joshua S. (1988) *Long Cycles: Prosperity and War in the Modern Age*. New Haven, Conn.: Yale University Press.

—— (1991) 'A War-Economy Theory of the Long Wave,' in Niels Thygesen, Kumaraswamy Velupillai, and Stefano Zambelli, eds, *Business Cycles: Theories, Evidence and Analysis*. New York: New York University Press.

Hegre, Havard (2000) 'Development and the Liberal Peace: What Does It Take to Be a Trading State?' *Journal of Peace Research* 37: 5–30.

Hintze, Otto (1975) *The Historical Essays of Otto Hintze*. New York: Oxford University Press.

Holsti, Kalevi J. (1996) *The State, War, and the State of War*. Cambridge: Cambridge University Press.

Houweling, Henk and Jan Siccama (1991) 'Power Transitions and Critical Points as Predictors of Great Power War: Toward a Synthesis.' *Journal of Conflict Resolution* 35: 642–58.

Huntington, Samuel P. (1991) *The Third Wave: Democratization in the Late Twentieth Century*. Norman: University of Oklahoma Press.

Kayser, Carl (1990) 'Is War Obsolete?' *International Security* 14: 42–64.

Kegley, Charles W., Jr and Gregory Raymond (1994) *A Multipolar Peace? Great Power Politics in the Twenty-First Century*. New York: St Martin's Press.

Kennedy, Paul (1987) *The Rise and Fall of Great Powers*. New York: Random House.

Kim, Woosang (1992) 'Power Transitions from Westphalia to Waterloo.' *World Politics* 45: 153–72.

Knutsen, Torborn (1999) *The Rise and Fall of World Orders*. Manchester: University of Manchester Press.

Kupchan, Charles A. (1997) ' Regionalism and Europe's Security: The Case for a New Mitteleuropa,' in Edward A. Mansfield and Helen V. Milner, eds, *The Political Economy of Regionalism*. New York: Columbia University Press.

Kydd, Andrew (1997) 'Sheep in Sheep's Clothing: Why Security Seekers Do Not Fight Each Other.' *Security Studies* 7: 114–54.

Lake, David A. (1992) 'Powerful Pacifists: Democratic States and War.' *American Political Science Review* 86: 24–37.

Lemke, Douglas and William Reed (1996) 'Regime Types and Status Quo Evaluations: Power Transitions Theory and the Democratic Peace.' *International Interactions* 22: 143–64.

Levy, Jack S. (1983) *War in the Modern Great Power System, 1495–1975*. Lexington: University Press of Kentucky.

—— (1985) 'Theories of General War.' *World Politics* 37: 344–75.

Lipset, Seymour M. (1959) 'Some Social Requisites of Democracy: Economic Development and Political Legitimacy.' *American Political Science Review* 53: 69–105.

—— (1994) 'The Social Requisites of Democracy Revisited.' *American Sociological Review* 59: 1–22.

Maddison, G.B. (1998) *The Political Economy of Civil Society and Human Rights*. London: Routledge.

Maoz, Zeev and Bruce M. Russett (1993) 'Normative and Structural Causes of Democratic Peace, 1946–1986.' *American Political Science Review* 87: 624–38.

Midlarsky, Manus I. (1984) 'Some Uniformities in the Origin of Systemic War.' Paper presented at the annual meeting of the American Political Science Association, Washington, DC, September.

—— (1995) 'Environmental Influences on Democracy: Aridity, Warfare and a Reversal of the Causal Arrow.' *Journal of Conflict Resolution* 39: 224–62.

Modelski, George (1984) 'Global Wars and World Leadership Selection.' Paper presented at the second World Peace Science Society Congress, Rotterdam, the Netherlands.

—— (1990) 'Enduring Rivalry in the Democratic Lineage: The Venice–Portugal Case,' in William R. Thompson, ed., *Great Power Rivalries*. Columbia: University of South Carolina Press.

—— (1996) 'Evolutionary Paradigm for Global Politics.' *International Studies Quarterly* 40: 321–42.

—— (2000) 'World System Evolution,' in Robert A. Denemark, Jonathan Friedman, Barry K. Gills, and George Modelski, eds, *World System History: The Social Science of Long-term Change*. London: Routledge.

—— (2001) 'Evolutionary World Politics: Problems of Scope and Methods,' in William R. Thompson, ed., *Evolutionary Interpretations of World Politics*. New York: Routledge.

—— and Gardner Perry III (1991) 'Democratization in Long Perspective.' *Technological Forecasting and Social Change* 39: 23–34.

—— and William R. Thompson (1989) 'Long Cycles of Global War,' in Manus Midlarsky, ed., *Handbook of War Studies*. Boston, Mass.: Unwin Hyman.

—— (1996) *Leading Sectors and World Power: The Coevolution of Global Economics and Politics*. Columbia: University of South Carolina Press.

Morgan, T. Clifton and Sally Howard Campbell (1991) 'Domestic Structure, Decisional Constraints, and War: So Why Kant Democracies Fight?' *Journal of Conflict Resolution* 35: 187–211.

Mousseau, Michael (2000) 'Market Prosperity, Democratic Consolidation, and Democratic Peace.' *Journal of Conflict Resolution* 44: 472–507.

Mueller, John (1988) *Retreat from Doomsday: The Obsolescence of Major War*. New York: Basic Books.

Nathan, Andrew J. and Robert S. Ross (1997) *The Great Wall and the Empty Fortress*. New York: W.W. Norton.

Oneal, John R. and Bruce Russett (1997) 'The Classical Liberals Were Right: Democracy, Interdependence and Conflict, 1950–85.' *International Studies Quarterly* 41: 267–93.

—— (1999) 'The Kantian Peace: The Pacific Benefits of Democracy, Interdependence, and International Organizations, 1885–1992.' *World Politics* 52 (1): 1–37.

Organski, A.F.K. and Jacek Kugler (1980) *The War Ledger*. Chicago, Ill.: University of Chicago Press.

Pollins, Brian M. (1996) 'Global Political Order, Economic Change, and Armed Conflict: Coevolving Systems and the Use of Force.' *American Political Science Review* 90: 103–17.

Przeworski, Adam, Michael E. Alvarez, Jose A. Cheibub, and Fernando Limogi (2000) *Democracy and Development: Political Institutions and Well-Being in the World, 1950–1990*. New York: Cambridge University Press.

Rapkin, David P., William R. Thompson, with Jon Christopherson (1979) 'Bipolarity and Bipolarization in the Cold War Era: Conceptualization, Measurement and Validation.' *Journal of Conflict Resolution* 23: 261–95.

Rasler, Karen and William R. Thompson (1983) 'Global Wars, Public Debts and the Long Cycle.' *World Politics* 35: 489–516.

—— (1985) 'War Making and State Making: Governmental Expenditures, Tax Revenues, and Global Wars.' *American Political Science Review* 79: 491–507.

—— (1989) *War and State Making: The Shaping of the Global Powers*. Boston, Mass.: Unwin Hyman.

—— (1994) *The Great Powers and Global Struggle, 1490–1990*. Lexington: University Press of Kentucky.

—— (2000) 'Global War and the Political Economy of Structural Change,' in Manus Midlarsky, ed., *Handbook of War Studies II*. Ann Arbor: University of Michigan Press.

—— (2001a) 'Malign Autocracies and Major Power Warfare: Evil, Tragedy and International Relations Theory.' *Security Studies* 10: 46–79.

—— (2001b) 'Structural Change and Democratization in the Major Power Subsystem: Some Systemic Puzzles of the Democratic Peace.' Unpublished ms.

—— (2001c) 'Rivalries and the Democratic Peace in the Major Power Subsystem.' *Journal of Peace Research* 38: 657–83.

—— (2004) 'The Democratic Peace and the Sequential, Reciprocal, Causal Arrow Hypothesis.' *Comparative Political Studies* 37: 879–908.

Ray, James Lee (1995) *Democracy and International Conflict: An Evaluation of the Democratic Peace Proposition*. Columbia: University of South Carolina Press.

—— (2000) 'Democracy: On the Level(s), Does Democracy Correlate with Peace?' in John A. Vasquez, ed., *What Do We Know About War?* Lanham, Md.: Rowman & Littlefield.

Raymond, Gregory A. (1994) 'Democracies, Disputes and Third Party Intermediaries.' *Journal of Conflict Resolution* 38: 24–42.

Reuveny, Rafael and William R. Thompson (2001) 'Leading Sectors, Lead Economies, and Their Impact on Economic Growth.' *Review of International Political Economy* 11 (November).

Rosecrance, Richard (1987) *The Rise of the Trading State: Commerce and Conquest in the Modern World*. New York: Basic Books.

Rousseau, David, Christopher Gelpi, Dan Reiter, and Paul Huth (1996) 'Assessing the Dyadic Nature of the Democratic Peace, 1918–1988.' *American Political Science Review* 89: 512–33.

Rummel, Rudolph (1995) 'Democracies ARE Less Warlike Than Other Regimes.' *European Journal of International Relations* 1: 457–79.

Russett, Bruce M. (1998) 'A Neo-Kantian Perspective: Democracy, Interdependence and International Organizations in Building Security Communities,' in Emanuel Adler and Michael Barnett, eds, *Security Communities*. Cambridge: Cambridge University Press.

—— and Harvey Starr (2000) 'From Democratic Peace to Kantian Peace: Democracy and Conflict in the International System,' in Manus Midlarsky, ed., *Handbook of War Studies II*. Ann Arbor: University of Michigan Press.

Schweller, Randall L. (1994) 'Bandwagoning for Profit: Bringing the Revisionist State Back In.' *International Security* 19: 72–107.

—— (1998) *Deadly Imbalances: Tripolarity and Hitler's Strategy of World Conquest*. New York: Columbia University Press.

Seeley, John R. (1886) *An Introduction to Political Science*. London: Macmillan.

Singer, J. David, Stuart Bremer, and John Stukey (1972) 'Capability Distribution, Uncertainty and Major Power War, 1820–1965,' in Bruce Russett, ed., *Peace, War and Numbers*. Beverly Hills, Calif.: Sage.

Siverson, Randolph and Juliann Emmons (1991) 'Birds of a Feather: Democratic Political Systems and Alliance Choices in the Twentieth Century.' *Journal of Conflict Resolution* 35: 285–306.

Snyder, Jack (1991) *Myths of Empire: Domestic Politics and International Ambitions*. Ithaca, NY: Cornell University Press.

Stam, Alan (1996) *Win, Lose or Draw: Domestic Politics and the Crucible of War*. Ann Arbor: University of Michigan Press.

Swaine, Michael and Ashley J. Tellis (2000) *Interpreting China's Grand Strategy: Past, Present, and Future*. Santa Monica, Calif.: Rand.

Tammen, Ronald L., Douglas Lemke, Carole Alsharabati, Brian Efird, Jacek Kugler, Allan C. Stam III, Mark A. Abdollahian, and A.F.K. Organski (2000) *Power Transitions: Strategies for the 21st Century*. New York: Chatham House.

Thompson, William R. (1995) 'Foreign Policy, the End of the Cold War, and the 1992 Election,' in Bryan D. Jones, ed., *The New American Politics: Reflections of Political Change and the Clinton Administration*. Boulder, Colo.: Westview.

—— (1996) 'Democracy at Peace: Putting the Cart Before the Horse?' *International Organization* 50: 141–74.

—— (1997) 'The Evolution of Politico-Economic Challenges in the Active Zone.' *Review of International Political Economy* 4: 286–318.

—— (2000) *The Emergence of the Global Political Economy*. London: UCL Press/Routledge.

——, ed. (2001) *Evolutionary Interpretations of World Politics*. New York: Routledge.

—— and Karen Rasler (1999) 'War, the Military Revolution(s) Controversy, and Army Expansion: A Test of Two Explanations of Historical Influences on European State Making.' *Comparative Political Studies* 32: 3–31.

—— and Rafael Reuveny (1998) 'Tariffs and Trade Fluctuations: Does Protectionism Matter as Much as We Think?' *International Organization* 52 (spring).

Tilly, Charles (1975) 'Reflections on the History of European State Making,' in Charles Tilly, ed., *The Formation of National States in Western Europe*. Princeton, NJ: Princeton University Press.

Trentmann, Frank (2000) 'Introduction: Paradoxes of Civil Society,' in Frank Trentmann, ed., *Paradoxes of Civil Society: New Perspectives on Modern German and British History*. New York: Berghahn Books.

Vasquez, John (1996) 'The Causes of the Second World War in Europe: A New Scientific Explanation.' *International Political Science Review* 17: 161–78.

——— (1997) 'The Evolution of Multiple Rivalries Prior to the Second World War in the Pacific,' in Paul Diehl, ed., *The Dynamics of Enduring Rivalries*. Urbana: University of Illinois Press.

Väyrynen, Raimo (1983) 'Economic Cycles, Power Transitions, Political Management and War Between the Major Powers.' *International Studies Quarterly* 27: 389–418.

Wallerstein, Immanuel (1984) *The Politics of the World-Economy*. Cambridge: Cambridge University Press.

Waltz, Kenneth (1979) *Theory of International Politics*. Reading, Mass.: Addison-Wesley.

——— (1993) 'The Emerging Structure of International Politics.' *International Security* 18: 45–73.

Weart, Spencer (1998) *Never at War: Why Democracies Will Not Fight One Another*. New Haven, Conn.: Yale University Press.

10

CAPITALISM, WAR, AND PEACE

Virtual or vicious circles

Raimo Väyrynen

Introduction

Does capitalism produce war, peace, both, or neither? Do different varieties of capitalism have a different relationship with war and peace? How were the earlier modes of production, especially feudalism, converted into capitalism and how did that transition affect the nature and frequency of wars? How did the break-through and evolution of capitalism interact with the transformation of political systems, especially the rise of the modern state, and how did that interaction shape warfare?

There is no consensus, either academic or political, on these issues; instead, different theories and opinions abound. This reflects the pivotal nature of the key concepts of this chapter; i.e. capitalism, war, and peace to whose complex rela-tionships every major social theory has tried to find answers. The problem for a scholar of the field is not the lack of original material or existing research; to the contrary, there is plenty of them both. The challenge is rather to find a theoretical and historical framework that would help to define these key concepts and specify their relationships that seem to have mutually reinforcing and contradictory elements.

The basic assertion of this chapter is that capitalism has two complementary political aspects: aggressive and peaceful. Which one of these faces we see, depends on the prevailing phase of the capitalist economy and its relationship to political power, especially state power. Thus, in abstract, capitalism is neither aggressive nor peaceful as such, but the prevalence of these features depends on the historical conditions. The general conclusion of the chapter is that, today, capitalism is becom-ing more conducive to peace than war. In fact, we may be witnessing the coming of the new era of capitalist peace in major-power relations.

Social and historical research utilizing the concept of the production mode has too easily opted for a materialist perspective. True, the mode of production conveys the idea that the functioning of a society is primarily determined by the relation-ship between its economic and political systems, and the level of technological capabilities. A key issue concerns the way politics affects the definition of property rights. One of the main bones of contention has concerned the relative impor- tance of the market versus reciprocal and redistributive economic systems. In the course of time, it has become clear that human history cannot be divided into neat periods on the basis of the distinction between markets and society, and private and public ownership. Both in the past and today, they are in reality parallel and intertwined; the real difference may be the extent any of them is converted into an ideology to serve particular ends.[1]

The sole emphasis on the mode of production leads easily to truncated materialist interpretations of reality. Thus, there can be, for instance, feudal, absolutist, capi- talist, and socialist wars, each of them having their specific political and military characteristics. In some respects, this approach has its merits, but it should not be taken too far. In addition, one has to consider the 'idea of war' for the reason that war always follows rules that cannot be decided unilaterally, but they are based on formal and informal moral or utilitarian understandings. Ultimately, the idea and rules of war are interrelated: there is an 'intimate connection between the very concept of war and the kinds of rules which might be set down for their conduct'.[2] Moreover, ideas and rules of war are not detached from the social structure and organization. In fact, the idea of war may even offer the 'ultimate link between armed forces and society' informing us how these forces reflect the society in which they are situated, but are never synonymous with it.[3]

To understand the nature of this 'ultimate link', both the material realities and intellectual constructs of war have to be considered. On the material side, war relates to the nature of feudalism, its transformation into capitalism, the evolution of the varieties of capitalism, and the opposition provided by its various counter- ideologies.[4] At the risk of oversimplification, I would like to suggest the following historical succession of various politico-economic modes of production: feudalism, absolutism, merchant capitalism, industrial capitalism, and digital capitalism. These modes, of course, have some historical overlap which make the points of transition from one system to another particularly interesting.

These varieties of production mode shape the institutions, instruments, and strategies of war. They are dependent, among other things, on the material capability and the political governance of the society. Yet, this is not the whole story; although they are hardly able to provide full accounts of shifts from one mode of warfare to another, ideas can also have an independent impact. Thus, to state that 'changing intellectual construction of peace and war decisively shapes the construction of military power' is probably exaggerated. One is on firmer ground if it is admitted that 'economic, military, and political realities establish outer limits on the possible'.[5]

This chapter is based on the assumption that the key factor in each production mode is how strongly the economic resources and political control are concentrated in the society. In feudalism, economic resources were deconcentrated and so were the opportunities of political control, although kings made efforts in this direction. The transition from feudalism to absolutism meant obviously a strong centralization of political power to the hands of the sovereign which was gradually matched by the concentration of economic power as well. On the other hand, the emergence of merchant capitalism provided a counterpoise to absolutism by relying on decentralized economic power and in politics a compromise between early democracy and monarchical tendencies. Industrial capitalism brought these tendencies together by recentralizing the capitalist mechanism, but permitting in most countries the rise of its democratic nemesis. Finally, in digital capitalism economic power is becoming deconcentrated again, while the political control remains, by and large, democratic.

A simple message of this typology is that the degree of the political and economic control of national societies and the international system changes over time. It can be asserted that different historical combinations of political and economic governance produce different frequencies and outcomes in terms of peace and war. My main hypothesis is that the absolutist systems are most prone to major wars, often wars of aggression, while digital capitalism and feudalism suffer the least from severe, protracted wars (although these modes may be beset by other forms of violence). After absolutism, industrial capitalism is the most war-prone system and merchant capitalism comes soon behind it.

This typology is, however, at least in one critical respect too simple as it overlooks the different methods to appropriate resources. There are two basic modes of appropriation: rent-seeking and profit-seeking. In the simplest form, rent-seeking is based on the private access to resources conferred either by tradition or political privilege. It can be either legal or illegal and practiced routinely or by the resort to extortion and coercion; if the use of force is pervasive, one can speak of rent-seizing and predation. While rent-seeking is commonly regarded as an unproductive appropriation of assets as it does not generate new innovation and investment, profit-seeking is usually seen as a method to generate new resources by investment and employment of wage labor that creates surplus through the market.

Schematically, one can think that feudalism is based on rent-seeking and capitalism on profit-seeking. This means that as rent-seeking has coercive aspects, it is directly related to the prevalence of military force in feudal societies, while profit-seeking capitalism is more civilized and peaceful. This is, indeed, the view taken by several theorists of capitalist and industrial peace – such as Herbert Spencer, Thorstein Veblen, and Joseph Schumpeter – who claim that warfare in the capitalist era has been due to the militaristic legacies of feudalism and absolutism. Such neat distinctions do not seem to be historically justified, however. Historians are increasingly concluding that feudalism cannot be equated with coercive production, but it coexisted with the market mechanism, while the breakthroughs of capitalism and industrialism have not eliminated rent-seeking activities, but rather redefined their nature.[6]

Rent-seeking is obviously more common in centralized political systems in which a political authority, often also controlling economic resources, is able to redistribute rights to seek or seize rents. On the other hand, in decentralized systems, especially if politics and economics are separated from each other, profit-seeking becomes the dominant mode to obtain surplus. Centralization of power in absolutism obviously meant that the ruler had power to maintain peace in his realm, but also had access to resources to wage wars with other rulers for territory and booty. Neither the state nor the market is usually completely subordinated, but they need each other; capitalism cannot triumph without the support of the state, but the state also needs the resources generated by the market. According to Braudel, 'the modern state was one of the realities which capitalism had to navigate, by turns helped or hindered' by it, but it was 'seldom if ever solely in control'.[7] This leads to the suggestion that neither capitalism nor state alone create aggressive policies, but it is their particular combination that is most destructive.

Compared with absolutism, economic power in merchant capitalism was denationalized but it remained connected with the state interests, although in a less explicit way. The decrease in state power also helped to establish a better balance between the state and the society. This suggests that there were relatively few civil wars under merchant capitalism and most major wars were fought for the control of the transportation routes and market shares. The difference between absolutism and merchant capitalism is related to the distinction that Charles Tilly makes between 'coercion-intensive' and 'capital-intensive' modes of state-making (these strategies can also be called, respectively, territorialist and capitalist). Territorialism has a fixed and capitalism a mobile view of the world.[8] Finally, both feudalism and digital capitalism are based on the political and economic deconcentration which leads one to assume that interstate warfare in these systems is relatively rare and violence is more sporadic and decentralized (although feudalism is inherently more violent than digital capitalism).

Feudalism

The nature of the feudal system

Institutionally, the key characteristic of feudalism is the dispersal of power manifested in the existence of multiple, competing sovereigns: 'pre-modern sovereignty was fragmented and contested.'[9] The feudal society was vertically segmented; each king had personal ties with the nobles who, in turn, extracted rent from the peasants. Another key feature of feudalism was that, until at least the thirteenth century when market relations and proto-industrial production started to spread, land was by far the most important resource. Feudalism did not abhor trade and it permitted the expansion of towns, but both the rural nobility and urban elites saw markets primarily as a source of rents rather than of profits. Due to the barriers to the growth of productivity of land, the feudal society was economically stagnant which tended to push it to periodic crises when the environmental conditions deteriorated.[10]

Therefore, the only means of expansion in the feudal system, the 'lordly strategies of reproduction', was either to intensify rent-seizing from the peasants or the colonization of new lands. The latter could happen either by the peaceful reclamation of land or military conquest. The intensification of the exploitation was not easy because peasants were potentially independent and the nobles did not have any automatic access to their produce save by using coercion and extortion. In other words,

> mere property rights to land were meaningless if they did not include authority over the people who cultivated it, because peasants possessed their means of subsistence and were therefore under no internal compulsion to rent from or work for the lord to survive.[11]

The nobles faced the risk of peasant revolts or the dilemma of the stationary bandit; rationally, they should tax peasants only to the point where their long-term income was maximized.[12]

The colonization of new lands was possible only if the king was commanding a military force that was effective enough to defeat his peers in war. In addition, the colonization of land required that peasants were willing to move and start tilling it which also limited the options available to the feudal lords.[13] The nature of land as a relatively scarce and divisible commodity helped to intensify the competition for it. The rules of the game were not fixed, however, and they could be altered by forging new coalitions. For instance, the king could try to protect the peasants against the feudal lord, also creating in that way an alternative base for military recruitment which was further expanded by the growth and pauperization of the rural surplus population.[14]

In sum, the expansion and appropriation of land was in the very core of feudalism which helps to explain why feuding was so recurrent in the late medieval and early modern times. Over time, the growing autonomy of peasants permitted their political mobilization, fueled by the shrinking margin of subsistence due to the population growth and the scarcity of land. This forced the nobility to intensify coercion to extract enough rent from the peasants, i.e. they ceased to behave as a stationary bandit. As Kriedte notes, the result was the growing separation of production and appropriation which called, in turn, for more violent measures to continue to redistribute resources in the old way.[15]

Contrary to the simple view that feudalism did not have any state structures, Mann dates the emergence of 'coordinating states' to 1155.[16] This is roughly consonant with the view that in the early twelfth century states started to become more centralized.[17] The feudal state was, however, weak in its infrastructural power and logistical reach, and thus unable to control effectively any large territories. Schwartz notes that the feudal system was composed of microeconomies whose effective range was about twenty miles. This limited the efforts of kings to centralize political power and thus control the nobility and the peasants.[18]

In such a system, 'the powers of the ruler were feeble and indirect' and there was no single agency in the control of the system.[19] This could not but affect the relations between the king and the nobility which were characterized both by cooperation and defection. They both needed each other; as the king had only limited political power and the nobility was unable to fully control the peasants, they had to stick together to maintain the feudal system. The king and the nobility both benefited from that system, but they had also to calculate constantly their relative costs and benefits. In fact, the kings remained so autonomous that their mutual relations have been compared with anarchic interstate relations.[20]

Decentralization was reinforced by the military system which was based on castles that provided protection against the enemy. The weaponry of the cavalry was geared to serve the individual status of the knight rather than systemic military functions. Thus, the very nature of feudalism created an obstacle to the centralization of power.[21] In medieval Europe, the dispersal of political power and the weakness of the state contributed positively to economic dynamism and the expansion of trade.[22] For example, the production of arms was dispersed in small units and depended more on the local artisan traditions than political power.[23]

The political organization of feudalism grew out of the interrelated military needs of protection and conquest. In fact, the main purpose of feudalism was military; it provided a method of recruitment and a hierarchy in which the capacity of the king to wage war depended on his ability to cajole and persuade the nobles to join the campaign in the hope of personal privileges and booty.[24] On the other hand, the nobles needed the king for military reasons as they were usually too weak to defend themselves alone against enemy attacks. The military protection provided by the king was a mixed (impure) public good as he could either extend it to all lords or allocate it selectively to only those who had shown political loyalty.

The tenet of feudalism is summarized well by Koht who concludes that it was a result of military needs and social conditions in a weak state whose people still lived mostly in a natural economy. For a while, the contradictions could be checked by the cooperation of the king and the nobles, growing exploitation of the peasants, and the gradual centralization of the state.[25] However, the monetization of the economy started to erode the feudal system. It increased the circulation of money and raised prices – especially during the rapid inflation of 1180–1220 – which contributed to growing social polarization, especially in cities. Skills in the countryside became more specialized, improving, in turn, the chances for commercial interaction with the growing urban centers. This structural change was, however, slow and contained built-in tensions and even violence as feudal lords tried to tie peasants to the manor by coercion.[26]

The king stressed his protective functions to justify the levying of taxes and other means to appropriate a higher share of the existing wealth which prompted protests and revolts by the peasants. On the other hand, the income of the lords from their land remained, in the absence of money taxes, fixed which, due to the rising prices of tradable goods, spelled major economic problems for them. In effect, the monetization of the economy came to the rescue of the kings who had lost much of their political power to the local lords.[27] Thus, in this view, commercial capitalism helped temporarily to save the limited political centralism of the feudal era and paved the way to the transition to both capitalism and absolutism. On the other side, the centralization of political and legal power under feudalism reduced the costs of protection and transaction and encouraged market integration.[28]

Feudalism and war

A key military aspect of feudalism was the emergence of a hereditary warrior class, with its own code of behavior. Membership in the class of mounted knights required wealth to which only the landed elite had access. Dismounted men served and protected the knight rather than formed an organized infantry. To retain the military primacy of the knight, the bulwark of the feudal order, various norms were enacted to protect him; thus, the church banned in 1139 the use of a crossbow among the Christians, a ban that was repeated in Magna Carta in 1215.[29] Feudal warfare was localized and defensive installations were built to protect the populations and strategic points against other feudal armies and raiders, in particular the Saracens, Vikings, and Magyars.[30]

Gradually, the feudal advantages in warfare were eroded. The longbow and the crossbow, together with a stronger infantry, started to pose an increasing threat to the mounted knight as could be seen in the battle of Courtrai in 1302. The defensive dominance of the infantry redefined both the battlefield and the social order as its members came from lower social orders.[31] In addition, the fortresses became so strong that siege warfare was not often able to overcome the protection provided by them. The introduction of primitive artillery changed the balance a bit, but castles and fortifications around cities could still be strengthened to regain some of the lost defensive power. In fact, urban sieges and the defense against them, instead of mass battles, became a common form of warfare from the thirteenth century.[32] The military functions of fortifications were the main thing, but they were also useful in protecting the economic assets of the community. The wealth of the Northern Italian cities makes it comprehensible why they pioneered new technologies of fortification, especially *trace italienne*.[33]

The monetization of the economy had multiple consequences for feudal warfare. The vassalic obligation to serve in the lord's army started to decline from the middle of the twelfth century and service for pay became more common. The spread of money into the economy commercialized the military organizations.[34] The relationship between the economy and the military is well illustrated by the case of England where payment for the soldiers became common from the twelfth century on. To be able to finance their lengthy wars, the kings had to constantly borrow money, usually from Italian bankers and merchants. The payment of these loans was possible only by taxing wool exports heavily or giving the bankers direct access to the customs duties in selected harbors. Lending money to royal warriors was, however, a risky business and several financial companies were brought down by their inability to pay back the loans.[35]

The greater availability of money made it also possible for kings to hire mercenaries led by professional soldiers. Mercenary armies were a part of the more general process of commercialization in which the military enterprise and the early market system were merged into one. On the other hand, the need to raise taxes to pay for the *condottieri* (*condotte*=contract) strengthened the emerging state for which they provided an increasingly stable military force.[36] From the fourteenth century on, mercenaries ceased to be individual warriors and they were organized into 'free companies'. Their hiring was not possible, however, without the access of the king to large amounts of capital. The commercialization of medieval war reached its peak in Italy where the city states hired *condottieri* to serve both in the cavalry and the infantry. The business acumen of their leaders distinguished the mercenaries from the traditional feudal warriors, but in many respects battles were still characterized by the dominance of the defense and the emphasis on the proper rules of fighting.[37]

The weakness of the central state and its permanent fiscal crisis meant that organized mercenary bands could wield significant power over society. This created a strong opposition to mercenaries and pressure to integrate them more closely into the society. In Italy, the need to finance and control the *condottieri* strengthened regional territorial states which became, in turn, increasingly hostile to each other.[38] The medieval decentralization of power created a situation in which wars were intermittent, consisting of series of clashes rather than of pitched battles; warfare was a 'multitude of skirmishes, sieges, raids, burnings, encounters and battles'.[39] This was partly due to the scarcity of resources that were needed to keep the army in fighting condition for any extended period of time. Yet, some battles were cruel and bloody, reflecting the general lack of restraints on violence in the medieval society.[40]

Medieval warfare went through several stages which successively increased the intensity, size, and costs of wars. The 1290s was one of the turning points when the growing reliance on the infantry and gunpowder started to require bigger armies and more money. Associated with the 'general crisis' of feudalism and, in the 1340s, the Black Death, the expansion of war had devastating consequences.[41] The crisis was due to a vicious circle in which stagnant economies and epidemic-ridden societies were subjected to heavier taxation to raise resources needed in warfare.

Again from the fifteenth century on, the political and technological nature of warfare started to change. One influential study of historical revolutions in military affairs (RMA) dates the first revolution to the period of 1450–1530, manifested in the increasing use of artillery and firearms.[42] Technological change has also been used to explain the historical reversal in the sixteenth and the seventeenth centuries of the military balance between the European and the non-European centers of power, including the Mongols and the Turks. The RMA also prompted the colonization of the non-European areas.[43]

By the early sixteenth century, the aggregate number of troops grew at least ten-fold compared with the fifteenth century and armies also became more permanent. These military changes demanded more economic resources than the stagnant feudal system was able to raise.[44] The growing size of armies was a cause for the expansion of the state to provision war. This happened both by taxing citizens and acquiring implements of war from the market place. Military innovations were stimulated both by the commercialization of the economy and the competitive and decentralized nature of European politics in which states needed new weapons to prevail over each other and gain military advantage over the non-European power centers.

Transitions from feudalism

The crisis of feudalism had major consequences for European societies as it catalyzed a dual transition, both to capitalism and absolutism; the former increased the dynamism of the economy and the latter centralized political power.[45] Wallerstein in particular argues that the crisis of feudalism pushed the development towards merchant capitalism which assumed global proportions and became in the sixteenth century a 'capitalist world system'.[46] The other transition theory focuses on the rise of modern states which were often absolutist in nature.

There are three main explanations of the transition from feudalism to absolutism. The first theory postulates that to preserve the feudal mode of production, the nobility had to strengthen the coercive power of the state to control the peasant production. The second theory sees the transition as the first step to the victory of capitalism. From the sixteenth century on, the rising bourgeoisie started to share power with the nobility, although it was seldom strong enough to gain a full victory. Finally, the third theory regards absolutism as the start of the movement to state-centric politics. As a result, the state became a more autonomous agent which was further strengthened by interstate rivalries.[47]

In the military field, the new fiscal and technological requirements posed by large permanent armies support the statist interpretation, though international rivalries did not produce any uniform model of modern state. For instance, absolutist and constitutional states in early modern Europe differed significantly from each other. It appears that the traditional nobility was the main loser, even in absolutist states; the technological revolution had destroyed its old military justification and the spread of the market mechanism undermined its material basis. For instance, in Prussia there is a close connection between the decline of the *Landadel* and the rise of the state and modern warfare.[48]

This leaves the statist and capitalist theories of state-building as the key contenders. Capitalism made inroads to most parts of Europe when the Dutch trading operations started to expand in the late sixteenth century. The rise of merchant capitalism had its own impact also on the nature and scale of military operations. Elsewhere, markets and trade created new economic resources which the feudal agriculture had been incapable of generating. On the other hand, especially in non-constitutional states, the market and the bourgeoisie remained subordinated to the monarch and the nobility aligned with him.

State-making and war

Absolutist rule means the government of a monarch who has only a limited accountability to the nobility, the clergy, and the peasants. The rise of absolutism in Europe was linked both with the transition to the money economy and with state formation. As long as the economic exchanges were based on barter, there was only a limited base to set up larger, centralized political units. The transition to monarchical rule was started by the gradual formation of medieval states in the thirteenth century and the rise of the Italian states in the fifteenth century. This development was in no small measure due to the intermittent warfare; in particular, the Hundred Years War contributed to state formation in England and France.[49]

There appears to be a consensus that the first breakthrough of the combined forces of state and market capitalism took place towards the end of the fifteenth century. The economy became monetized helping the central state to raise taxes and acquire more military, administrative, and fiscal power.[50] The state needed money as it had to finance new and more expensive military technologies. However, the concentration of arms industries went in tandem with the growth of the state only in shipbuilding, while decentralization continued to characterize the production of the weaponry for land warfare.[51]

Together with the need to regulate the emerging capitalism, the needs of warfare and military technology expanded the state power.[52] Thus, the consolidation of the territorial state in France has been explained by a new alliance between the monarch and burghers. The royal rule permitted the expansion of the monetized economy which, in turn, created a more networked and coherent economy and gave to the monarch access to new financial resources which could be used then for warfare.[53] This view suggests that early capitalism and the needs of warfare were the motors of state-building in Europe.

This perspective has been put in doubt by those who focus on the impact of interstate competition as the main reason for both military innovation and state-building. In other words, 'the multi-polar European state system led to an increase in militarization, for reasons of both attack and defence' which, in turn, meant that a 'stable long-term public debt became imperative for the more belligerent states'.[54] Theorists of fiscal–military states consider them complex and powerful organizations which rose in the sixteenth century at the expense of traditional authorities and ended up competing with each other. A country that failed to build up a strong central power was defeated in European rivalries. Victorious fiscal–military states could emerge both in constitutional and absolutist states.[55] If such a state is considered the main agent of war, the implication is that both republican and monarchical governments can be prone to war.[56]

This view casts some doubt on the claim that there are two dominant modes of development: the capitalist and the coercive. In the former, the state is weak and the capitalist interests rule, while the latter has a strong state headed by an absolutist ruler. In addition to Tilly, this view has been adopted by those who place property rights in the center of their explanation. Those countries, especially France and Spain, which had strong confiscatory governments, violating private property rights, declined. On the other hand, if the country had a relatively weak, representative government, it created, by respecting private property, incentives to invest in economic production.[57]

Thus, to understand the process of state-making in early modern Europe, and its economic and political consequences, we have at least three different possibilities: (a) the *Eigendynamik* created by the military revolution, (b) the spread of market capitalism and property rights associated with it, and (c) the external and internal challenges to the central power. My view is that the state-building process was primarily a response to internal challenges to the state power and the efforts by other states to strengthen their power. The expansion of the armies and the introduction of new military technologies were tools of state-building, but this does not have independent explanatory power. From the late fifteenth century to the middle of the seventeenth century, capitalism was still subordinated to state power which benefited from the monetization of the economy as it helped to finance the fiscal–military state.

Putting the emphasis on the external and internal politico-military dynamics of state-building helps to account for several things. For instance, it makes comprehensible the economic profitability, until at least the eighteenth century, of the protection provided by governments for economic activities. Lane in particular has argued that the use of violence by the state produced a protection rent that was, overall, beneficial for economic development (although it probably had adverse distributional consequences). This was especially the case if the state could increase the rent by reducing the protection costs or increasing those of the adversary.[58] The primacy of the politico-military dynamics also helps to explain the anomaly mentioned above: the representative, market-oriented governments did not have weaker militaries, as often alleged, but all kinds of states, including the liberal ones, started to build permanent armies and navies. The rise of the fiscal–military states in Northwestern Europe and their mutual rivalries helps, for example, to explain their rise as maritime powers to challenge the established centers of naval power in the Mediterranean.[59]

England

The case of England is often considered unique; strong monarchical rule had old roots there, while the nobility was weaker and often aligned with commercial interests. The monetization of the economy in the sixteenth century brought into the orbit of economic circulation not only towns, but also parts of the countryside. The rise of the money economy was mostly due to the expansion of the wool trade and the conversion of the enclosed land from a feudal fief into private property. In contrast to the continental pattern, the upper class in the countryside gained, because of their commercial links, enough economic power to keep the monarchy at bay.

The case of England has been used as evidence of how capitalism can emerge from feudalism only if the 'despotic' power of the state remains relatively weak, permitting the separation of private and public interests from each other. There is an intimate relationship between the commercial class structure, weak state power, market-friendly legislation, and maritime orientation in trade and geopolitics. Although there was a monarch at the top of the state, it should be ultimately controlled by the interests of the commercial and civil society. In fact, Hobbes laid the groundwork for a social order in which sovereign individuals would replace the inherited class, thus shifting the source of legitimacy from the aristocracy to the people.[60]

This interpretation is, however, at odds with the fact that the total revenue of the government started to increase significantly from the 1670s on as England developed features of a fiscal–military state.[61] Paradoxically, this seems to have been possible because the state in England had become centralized earlier than its continental counterparts. It had thus been able to 'provide the security and uniformity upon which trade and industry could be based'. The merchants and industrialists continued to check by political means the royal ambitions to enhance the state power.[62] True, the English system also retained dynastic features, but to distinguish it from the continental 'vertical absolutism', where the monarch forged relations with subaltern groups to control the nobility and the clergy, it has been called 'horizontal absolutism'. In that system, the ruler's control of the army and the church did not necessarily diminish the bargaining power of the landed gentry and the parliament.[63]

The slow evolution of the state system on the continent allowed in England the internationally oriented coalition to keep the state weak, but yet operational. Thus, the weakness of other major powers helped the British ascent to economic and political predominance.[64] The liberal combination of class, state, and international orientation was not destroyed even by the first industrial revolution as it was based on textiles and other light industries. They did not require extensive capital investment and hence a strong state to extract from the society the resources needed.[65]

The coalition of social forces in the countryside was stable; not even the Civil War resulted in a major transfer of landed property from one class to another. As Barrington Moore, in reference to this war, concludes: 'the connection between the enclosing landlord and the bourgeoisie was close and intimate. . . . The outcome of the struggle was an enormous if still incomplete victory for an alliance between parliamentary democracy and capitalism.' Thus, in England, commercial and landed interests were blended together, using the parliament as the instrument of politics. The coalition of the upper classes provided a counterweight to royal power and paved the way to the capitalist breakthrough.[66] In England, the relative weakness of monarchy and the growth of capitalism were associated both with the structure of its economy and the insular geopolitical location.

The European continent

On the continent, the transition from feudalism to absolutism took place in quite different conditions. Its key feature was the pivotal role of agriculture that permitted the feudal legacy to linger on much longer. In continental Europe, the importance of land ownership has prompted material accounts for state formation. It has been considered a result of the fight between the kings and feudal lords for land and power in which one group tried to force the other out of the game. Thus, states on the continent were established by successful monopolization of coercive, territorial power.[67]

The emphasis on territorial monopoly misses, however, the incomplete and variable nature of control on the continent. For instance, the French territory was divided into separate commercial and rural societies. The Atlantic ports were parts of the global trading networks and had only limited contacts with the agricultural hinterland. The port communities had a close relationship with the monarchy through which political protection was exchanged for financial support. The rural society was, in turn, fragmented into small feudal units over which the government had ultimately control.[68]

The French case hints at the difficulties in building a fiscal–military state in the face of resistance from feudal forces. In France, the transition to absolutism was slow and the feudal institutions remained alive for a long time. The direct interest of the nobility in commercial agriculture was limited; they preferred to extract the peasants' surplus. Politically, the nobility became an appendix of the royal bureaucracy, funding its demands for war and luxury through the purchase of offices ('tax farming'). Until the French Revolution, the autonomy of the city burghers was limited; instead of developing new commercial enterprises, they joined the royal coalition.[69]

Thus in France absolutism was strong, while market relations remained, especially in the countryside, weak. The dominance of the royal court, *dominium regale*, and the semi-feudal nature of the agriculture made the capitalist transition difficult. The French economy remained centered on the state which extracted, by the help of the nobility, resources from the peasants and the merchants involved in commercial operations. The main aim of the king was to retain his autonomy to fight wars; therefore, in France, 'absolutist monarchs, war, institutional change, and the budget could not be separated'.[70]

Obviously, the economic systems in absolutist and republican states differ, but they do not form stark contrasts. Absolutist tendencies were everywhere, but they were organized differently. The mode of political governance could not alone assure that the state always had money available when a war broke out. Neither can one argue that one system was market-based and the other state-centric as both systems were based on a mixture of state and market. In republican states there were political groups who derived their resources from market operations and who could not be sidelined in decision-making. In absolutist–mercantilist systems there were also markets, but their development was regulated from the political center.

Absolutist mercantilism strengthened the state in its competition with other states, and its ruler internally vis-à-vis the society. Money itself was not thought to have any independent, productive value. Mercantilism hoarded gold and silver for a war chest by sucking up financial surplus available in the world market where the supply of money was always restricted. In France, the kings, handled by Colbert and Richelieu, licensed foreign trade companies and, to provide them with goods to sell, established manufactures for the production of textiles, arms, and various luxury items. According to the dominant thinking, trading companies could succeed only if there was a strong merchant fleet to carry goods and the navy to protect its operations. Therefore, Colbert embarked on an active maritime policy which also propped up France's capacity to compete for colonial possessions. In his famous view, 'commerce is the wellspring of finance, and finance is the sinew of war'.

In sum, the mercantilist policy helped to construct a national economic infrastructure and a strong military establishment which made France in the eighteenth century a center of innovations in military operations and administration. These innovations were also national responses to the humiliations suffered by the French armies on the European battlefields.[71] On the other hand, the mercantilist absolutism was able to create neither an independent and productive market system nor a capitalist class as happened in England and the Netherlands, the main competitors of France.[72]

The concentration of political and economic power was also reflected in the large-scale construction of fortresses. During the reign of Louis XIV, the emerging military science and public resources were brought together by Vauban who conducted an ambitious fortification plan to protect France.[73]

The nature of Prussian absolutism was quite different; it was bureaucratized and militarized. As a rule, the ruler was not as central as, for instance, in Petrine Russia, but the state power was used by the increasingly strong and effective bureaucracy. Its independence and power is indicated by Rosenberg's description of the Prussian bureaucracy as a self-governing public service class and autonomous political machine which collected taxes, primarily from the urban population, to finance the administrative and military needs. This account neglects, however, the central role of the landowners (*Junkers*) who de facto shared the sovereignty with the king and controlled administration at lower levels and whose support was needed to start a war. However, the impoverishment of the landowners, as a result of wars in the seventeenth century, tended to increase the power of the king and his bureaucracy.

To ward off liberalism, social life in Prussia was governed by strict rules and religion played a disciplinary role. The regimented nature of the society made it unnecessary to listen to the voice of the people.[74] In the late eighteenth century, limited urban capitalism got support in the countryside as new crops and techniques of cultivation started to commercialize the agriculture. The breakthrough happened in the aftermath of the Napoleonic wars when the collapse of the old absolutist order permitted the transformation of the *Junkers* from semi-feudal to commercial farmers.[75]

Both absolutism and mercantilism were purported to be rational doctrines in the service of state interests. The state must be above the parochial interests and be unfailingly able to administer the political and military activities, and collect money to finance them. To succeed, mercantilism and absolutism required the education of the bureaucratic elite to manage the state in the same way as engineers carry out technical projects. Ideally, absolutism thus combined mercantilism and technocratic bureaucracy to run 'rational' national projects under the leadership of the ruler. In reality, however, patronage was commonplace in recruiting the administrators and, with the partial exceptions of Russia and perhaps Prussia, even the absolutist king was constrained by the actions of the estates.[76]

Absolutism and war

The emergence of absolutism had obvious implications for the nature and frequency of war. The states were prepared to maintain large permanent armies both in peace and war to protect and expand their interests. The dynastic nature of the state meant that its key concern was the control of the territory whose size was a measure of the power acquired at the expense of other rulers.

It is not easy to say when the era of absolutism started, peaked, declined, and ended. For instance, Luard terms the period 1400–1559 the age of dynasties, the period 1559–1648 is one of religions, while in 1648–1789 the age of sovereignty prevailed. In his view, each of these periods had their own characteristic wars.[77] Both Glete and van Creveld consider the middle of the sixteenth century a turning point after which government became more centralized and absolutist. In addition, van Creveld suggests that during the period 1648–1789 the state was increasingly used as an instrument of politics and war.[78] In other words, we may speak of two periods in which the ruler's dynastic power was first converted into an absolutist system, i.e. 1550–1648, and then from that system gradually into a sovereign state, i.e. 1648–1789.

The problem of religious wars can perhaps be solved by noting that they were, in effect, an element in the consolidation of the absolutist rule within states and the organization of the states system around them.[79] In fact in 1559–1648 slightly over one half of the total 112 wars were civil wars in which religion was often the key bone of contention. In religious conflicts, the control of territory and property was also often a central aspect suggesting that they were associated with the process of state formation. The growing importance of economic causes is hinted at by the fact that some wars were fought over rights of trade and navigation.[80]

Dynastic claims on territories became a major cause of war; for instance, in 1648–1713 territory was the most contentious issue in the interstate rivalries. It was involved in generating war in over half of the cases. Many conflicts during this period were wars of succession, but often in name only; the real reason for dynastic conflicts was the effort to acquire control of the territory and in that way shape the balance of power.[81] Thus, territorial control became a key element in the emerging balance-of-power system by which the European states started to arrange their mutual relations, especially from the eighteenth century on. Absolutism and the balance of power became complementary to each other; centralized state power was needed to keep the adversaries in check and make quick decisions demanded by power politics.[82]

Wars in Northern Europe from the middle of the sixteenth century to the beginning of the eighteenth century confirm these patterns. Up and until at least the Thirty Years War, the dynastic struggles between Denmark, Sweden, Poland, Russia, and German principalities were a key reason for wars. Over time, the dynastic conflicts were replaced by or blended with religious motives and, in particular, territorial expansion and the concern with the balance of power.[83]

The nature of the absolutist armies

A key feature of the absolutist armies was their growing size and permanence, and their increasingly standardized and professionalized nature which directly shaped the character of warfare by increasing its organization and destructiveness. The single most important change was the new capacity of the infantry to increase the power of its fire. This change undermined the role of the cavalry whose relative costs were also becoming much higher than those of the infantry. Yet, the political and military traditions continued to assign to the cavalry a tactical role which was defended by saying that it could still provide some offensive advantages.[84]

Standardization of the military concerned the weaponry, training, and tactics. Technical advances, including the spread of bayonet-armed muskets, and the standardization of weapons increased their reliability and firepower. The introduction of systematic drill improved, in turn, the maneuverability of troops and their ability to operate in battle formations. The ideal was, as McNeill points out, that soldiers should 'become replaceable parts of a great military machine just as much as their weaponry'. In sum, standardization contributed to the improved management and control of the armies, although constraints on effective large-scale military operations still remained formidable.[85]

Another important new feature of the armies was their professional and disciplined nature. The challenge was to turn uneducated recruits into a capable fighting force. This task was accomplished by a new approach to officer training and the extension, especially in Prussia, of civilian bureaucratic control over the armies. In fact, Prussia and France spearheaded the professional revolution in military affairs converting the feudal military into a political symbol and coercive resource for the absolutist state. With good reason, Howard characterizes that era as the 'wars of the professionals'.[86]

Yet, one should not overemphasize the role of the state as the only source of change in weaponry and military doctrines. In effect, there are at least three reasons to look outside the absolutist state to find an adequate explanation for the military changes during the *ancien régime*. The first one is the scarcity of economic resources available to the ruler. Ferguson points out that the effort to close the gap between the money available in the state treasury and the costs of war is one of the key stories of history.[87] The financial constraint favored small and short wars, but this preference was contradicted by the permanent rivalries among the dynastic states and the growth of the armies themselves. Luard has shown that from the middle of the sixteenth to the middle of the seventeenth century, wars became shorter, more costly, and more lethal than earlier.[88]

The military spending had the heaviest toll in France where the state was bankrupted several times due to wartime debts. In France and Prussia, the payment of loans taken and taxes levied to finance war was a serious burden on the state budget, while it was slighter in England.[89] Thus, the dynastic states did not necessarily have resources to wage war as they would have liked.

On the other hand, the modernization of the military did not happen only in absolutist states. While France and Prussia carried out important military reforms in the seventeenth century, the Dutch actually started the modernization movement in the late sixteenth century. The long war of independence against Spain (1568–1648) created the need to reorganize the military forces and the onset of economic growth provided resources for them. In fact, the Netherlands developed a flexible, but strong fiscal–military state. Maurice of Nassau, who launched the reforms, created a military force which was characterized by 'intelligent leadership, unquestioning obedience, loyalty to the unit, and improvements in tactical employment and movement'.[90]

The Dutch military reform turned out to be so successful that it was imitated by another commercial republic, England (and a more absolutist Sweden). The Dutch and the English may have liked Maurice's reforms for the same reason; at least in the Netherlands, the emphasis on discipline and loyalty was motivated by domestic social pressures which emphasized the safety of the civilians against any harassment by the soldiers. The Dutch wanted a small, effective, and well-equipped military force that was firmly under the civilian political control.[91]

Thus, the second military revolution since the late sixteenth century, centered on the infantry and firepower, took place under the influence of two opposite tendencies. It was motivated on the one hand by the political and military ambitions of the absolutist rulers and, on the other hand, commercial republics that had access to skills and technology to professionalize the military force. Thus, the second RMA was not a uniform process, but was bifurcated to serve different and even contradictory interests.

The third factor warning against an excessive focus on the absolutist state is a kind of privatized, even parasitic market system that expanded in the provisioning and recruitment of the growing military forces. The military market had two key groups of actors: the officers and the suppliers. The kings turned to wealthy landowners, who raised their own troops and commanded them in return for monetary payment. Mercenaries added their share to the commercialization and privatization of war. The suppliers of weapons, uniforms, food, horses, and fodder came also increasingly from the landed aristocracy.[92]

Sombart even sees the origins of modern industry in the needs of war. In general, he suggests that the political focus on the destruction of war has blinded historians from the fact that wars have also had major economic effects. Building on that premise, Sombart shows that the establishment of the modern mass army did, in reality, pave the way to the consolidation of modern capitalism by propping up textile, metal, and other industries. He stresses especially the expansion of shipbuilding due to the military demand. Commercial demand would never have been strong enough to launch the industry in the way it emerged in the sixteenth and seventeenth centuries.[93] While the Dutch military shipbuilding was partly in private hands, it was in most countries under state control, in particular after the navies became permanent factors in military establishments.[94] This line of argument is consistent with the general suggestion that the adverse economic effects of warfare in the absolutist era have been exaggerated[95] and that in several respects wars in the eighteenth century had positive economic and technological consequences.[96]

In conclusion, absolutism was no doubt an important force shaping the nature and use of the military force. Absolutist politics over territory and other dynastic claims were a major cause of war after Westphalia till the French Revolution. However, even if it was the 'Age of Reason', armies and weapons were not necessarily used in a rational manner; the prevalence of dynastic and bellicist values, and the search for *gloire*, strongly shaped the decisions to go to and conduct war.[97] The relevance of absolutism seems to favor Tilly's account: 'coercive intensive mode', in which rulers extract societal resources and build massive military structures, is prone to warfare.

This is, however, only one aspect of the story. Political absolutism and mercantilism have never been able to destroy completely markets and private initiatives. Merchants might have been integrated in statist economic and commercial policies, but they also retained their own identity and interests. In addition, even war itself was, in part, a private enterprise which the ruler was unable to conduct on his own. The supply for war gave for the landed nobility a new type of economic role which, together with the commercialization of agriculture, opened up the capitalist road.

According to standard geopolitical thinking, territorial land powers are aggressive, while trading states are promoters of peace. My analysis leads, however, to a somewhat different observation: absolutist territorial states have a penchant for the acquisition of national power, but they are not destined to go to war. On the other hand, the commercial powers can also develop a fiscal–military state. To capture the roots of war, one should look carefully at the economic and social structure of societies and the ways in which they fuel and restrict war. In a geopolitical analysis, the territorial–maritime cleavage should be correlated with the domestic structures and the dynamics of changing power relations alignments.[98]

Commercial capitalism

Ideologies of trade and peace

In early modern Europe, the emergence of the market was historically concomitant with the rise of the state-centric political system, although their balance varied. By the late seventeenth century, commercial capitalism had started to expand from bilateral ties between the trading companies and their outposts to a more integrated world economy and colonialism. At about the same time, a shift took place in naval strategies which became, by the Seven Years War in the 1750s, costly transoceanic enterprises.[99] These two trends, commercial and naval expansionism, were closely intertwined. Naval power was used to protect global trade relations and thus the accumulation of capital. The objective was both to safeguard one's own trade and increase, by privateering if needed, the protection costs of the competitors.[100] Though economic interests were in command of this process, they could not prosper without the military protection of the cross-cultural trade.

Obviously, the link between naval and commercial power did not go unnoticed among the intellectuals of the time. They detected the tendency to establish international monopolies that combined economic and military power objectives.[101] As monopolies had a violent aspect, it was natural that observers grappled with the critical question of whether international trade contributes to peace or war. Often the answer was 'war', but there were others who concluded that commerce is the best friend of peace.

Thus, Montesquieu discusses at length international commerce and its effects. He suggests that 'commerce is related to constitution' and that monarchies are less inclined to become involved in trade. Yet he defended the opposite view: 'the true maxim is to exclude no nation from one's commerce without great reasons.' Therefore, Montesquieu is opposed to mixing up the conduct of commerce with the activities benefiting the state. If things are organized freely and fairly, 'the natural effect of commerce is to lead to peace', while the 'total absence of commerce produces the banditry'. Montesquieu has, moreover, an important qualification to this thesis: 'the spirit of commerce unites nations', but among the individual merchants trade leads to rivalry.[102]

Adam Smith, of course, also advocated the doctrine that economic freedom leads to social and political improvement. However, he is more circumspect than Montesquieu in extolling the virtues of international trade. He notes, for instance, how military power can be used to hinder the trade of other states. Yet, commerce is useful as it brings in new resources to society and, together with manufacturing, 'introduce[s] order and good government'. Trade does not provide, though, an adequate basis for economic development that must be based on productive agriculture. National independence is also continuously threatened by the barbarian nations; they are 'naturally superior' to a 'civilized nation' which can defend itself 'only by means of a well-regulated standing army'. In the best liberal tradition, Smith is concerned about the danger posed by such an army to liberty. This risk can be avoided, however, if 'the military is placed under the command of those who have the greatest interest in the support of the civil authority'.[103]

In sum, one cannot consider Smith as an unqualified advocate of a commercial peace; rather he emphasizes the political foundations of international trade, its real but limited benefits, and the need for vigilance against foreign military threats. Smith's contribution is to stress the importance of freedom from old bondage which permits individual initiative whose protection may well need military strength.

Immanuel Kant also pondered the impact of commerce on the political relations between states. His comments reflected the view that trade between nations must be founded on cosmopolitan law and the principle of universal hospitality. Kant declares his belief that the 'spirit of commerce' will 'sooner or later take hold of every nation'. As commerce 'cannot coexist with war', 'money power' and the 'human inclination' toward it become forces promoting peace. Moreover, 'civil freedom' and commerce reinforce each other as the 'state's power in external relations will also decline'. For Kant these observations were only a practical conviction and he hesitated to ascribe to them deeper theoretical reasons.[104]

Standard accounts of the peaceful nature of capitalism refer to its rational and utilitarian character that helps to subjugate aggressive political and military passions. This is the key argument developed by Hirschman who suggests that, since the eighteenth century, the passion for profit, 'money-making as a calm passion', has been used to control non-pecuniary, and often aggressive passions. Thus, capitalist interests can help to tame society and control individual and collective passions. In Hirschman's view, the breakthrough of capitalism increased predictability and interdependence and, through the expansion of trade, created more cohesive national communities, and helped to avoid wars between them.[105]

The views of the key liberal thinkers about the relationship of liberalism and peace/war were more circumscribed than it is often assumed. Smith, and even Kant, saw the need to maintain military forces as long as there existed aggressive states in the system. The utilitarian interests in production and trade created an inclination toward peace, but it hardly could be guaranteed before a more effective international law and the moral improvement of individuals made progress.[106]

The development of commercial capitalism

The commercial capitalism of the eighteenth century can be considered a factor of peace, but only in limited historical, geographical, and political contexts. In other respects, due to the interdependence of naval and trade operations, violence and commerce, capitalism can be also seen as a factor of war.

Commercial capitalism moved in the sixteenth century from Italy to the coastal cities of Northwestern Europe. Trade was conducted – in Amsterdam, Antwerp, London, and other port cities – by the emerging mercantile bourgeoisie. This class created a society with its own norms and culture, promoted economic legislation and political stability, and developed new financial institutions which provided powerful instruments of influence. The development of ship and navigation technologies by maritime hegemonies – from Portugal through the Netherlands to England – reduced the hazards of overseas trade, made transportation more profitable, and thus increased the return on the capital invested. In fact, each hegemon was able to defeat its predecessor by more advanced means of shipping and navigation.[107]

The Dutch Republic provides a prime example of how private interests are a centerpiece in commercial capitalism. It was based on political and religious liberty which made the urban merchants favor international peace and stability. John de Witt was a key figure in consolidating the Republic and eroding the power of the military and the clergy which were more anxious than the merchants to acquire territories. The winning system accorded priority to productivity, innovation, and freedom of economic activity. These virtues made the Dutch Republic the entrepôt center of global trade supported by the strong merchant fleet, effective financial system, and growing manufacturing industries.[108]

The 'benign' interpretation of commercial capitalism views the Dutch Republic as an effective economic and political construct which produced a 'Golden Age' in culture and a global source of prosperity. As a small and peaceful country, the Dutch hegemony was not feared by other states which were more concerned about the political and military designs of England and France.[109] In an important corrective, Glete admits that the Dutch Republic was a bourgeois state, but also a fiscal–military one which had both a strong army and navy. Its expansionism was not only commercial, but also based on robust military power; it had mercantilist but not territorialist aspects.[110]

Rather than being an exception, the Republic was merely different among the commercial powers of the seventeenth and eighteenth centuries. Its status is evidenced by the global economic and military reach of its leading trading companies, Verenigde Oostindische Compagnie (VOC) and Westindische Compagnie (WIC).[111] They were chartered both to trade and wage war, especially in the Americas, Southern Africa, and parts of Asia. The shipping lanes of the companies became lifelines of the Dutch empire, carrying both rich and commodity trades, and slaves. Amsterdam's political and commercial elites were anchored in the overseas trade and enriched themselves at the expense of the peripheries.[112]

In fact, one should not assume that the military and economic functions of absolutist and commercial states were as differentiated as they are today. For instance, one cannot easily distinguish piracy and commerce from each other.[113] The 'malign' interpretation of commercial capitalism stresses the role of military coercion in the global economic accumulation. Coercion was used extensively to extract silver and other valuables from the colonies. As much of the long-distance trade was in luxury goods, piracy and buccaneering became profitable professions. Thus vigilant military protection was needed to make sure that the profits from colonial trade did not go to line the pockets of others than those financing it in Amsterdam and London.[114]

One can conclude that the rise of merchant empires thus continued a European union of trade and warfare which had its origins in the Italian maritime empires. The war on land was integrated with the war business at sea, and it is often very difficult to separate them.[115] There was, indeed, 'a European union of trade and warfare', not only because economics and politics were integrated, but also because naval battle was the most Eurocentric form of warfare. True, naval battles were waged in all parts of the world, but the adversaries were, until quite recently, practically always European powers.

There has been a simmering debate among historians on whether strategic or economic causes dominated the naval warfare. The answer may be, however, simply that at first commercial interests dominated and, due to the relative weakness of states, naval units were funded by the merchants; military protection costs were a normal business expense. However, the technical development of shipping, the expansion of fleets, and the bureaucratization of their management made it by the end of the seventeenth century virtually impossible for the individual capitalists, or even trading companies, to bear the rapidly growing costs. As the state took over the funding of the navies, it started to conduct more strategic tasks, such as power projection. In other words, the supposedly capital-intensive mode of mobilization could also lead to wars of conquest and protection.[116]

Another view argues that the causes of war are geopolitical, but they also have a business aspect. Merchants are rational; when they anticipate that war is approaching, they start buying and storing necessities and wait for the prices especially of foreign goods to go up during the war. War profiteering was easy for the Dutch because of their strong control of the trading networks and Amsterdam's entrepôt role.[117]

Commerce and war

Several authors have used the theory of commercial capitalism to account for the causes of wars among the leading European powers in the seventeenth and eighteenth centuries. Wars were fought about the control of colonies and the sea lanes to make sure that profits would continue to flow.[118] Obviously, the answer is more complex than that; wars cannot be traced back simply to the accumulation logic of the commercial capital, but their motives contain also territorial ambitions and geopolitical reasons.

Yet, a systematic study of the issues generating wars concludes that in 1648–1713 commerce and navigation were present in 36 percent of wars; as such it was the second most common factor after territorial conflicts. In 1715–1814, commerce and navigation remained the second most important issue behind wars, but its relative importance declined in comparison to the territorial and boundary problems.[119] This is a reason to assume that during the second half of the seventeenth century and the early eighteenth century naval power was used often to secure commercial gains. In fact, the era from the Thirty Years War to the French Revolution was the only period in which European powers were fighting wars for the possession of colonies and for reasons of trade.[120]

Naval wars can be connected with the hegemonic cycles of the powers. Thus the Anglo-Dutch wars of 1652–4, 1665–7, and 1672–4 all had commercial motivations. The Dutch hegemony was peaking, while England's international position was slipping. In London, an effort was made to resist the Dutch leadership by building up the state and resorting to mercantilistic policies. The essence of these wars was about trade; the Dutch tried to keep the sea routes to Amsterdam open, while the English tried to close them. The Dutch were victorious in these naval wars and the terms of peace achieved in the Treaty of Breda in 1667 were the culmination of their hegemony.[121] However, this development prompted England and France to rebuild their navies to help them to beat the Dutch Republic in the mercantilistic game.

The gradual shift in international power relations left the Dutch on the sidelines and refocused military rivalries on the Anglo-French dyad until the 1760s when British hegemony became uncontested. During this era, warfare entered a new phase; first, it became increasingly global in scope and, second, naval and land battles became intertwined in these global wars. The maritime and continental military schools, articulating opposing economic and strategic interests, became differentiated from each other. These tendencies were manifested, in various ways, in the Nine Years War of 1689–97, the War of the Spanish Succession in 1702–13, the War of Austrian Succession in 1740–8, and the Seven Years War in 1756–63.

Commercial interests continued to generate wars both in colonies, as can be seen in the French and Indian War in North America, and in the efforts to control sea lanes. Their impact started to decline toward the end of the eighteenth century, however, for two reasons. Although economic factors were involved in European wars, for instance in the War of Austrian Succession, they were increasingly fueled by the struggle for the balance of power (in which succession crises played a role). The growing supremacy of the British fleet meant that no other power was able to engage it directly. This is evidenced by the shift in French naval strategy from *guerre d'escadre* to *guerre de course* in which commerce raiding replaced the traditional fleet battles. The French strategic interest started also to acquire a more continental flavor. Britain emerged as the leading global power.[122]

Industrial capitalism

Concentration and war

There is a common and well-founded view that the era of absolutist states, linked with mercantilist economic policies, was a fertile breeding ground for interstate wars, especially of the dynastic type. I have argued above that the commercial competition between the leading European powers had a rather similar effect. Especially after the construction and financing of the navies were increasingly taken over by the state, the distinction between conservative land powers and liberal maritime powers, and their characteristic external policies, started to lose its relevance.

This suggests that the centralization of political power to a ruling elite, striving to expand its territorial and colonial holdings, is an omen for continuing warfare between major powers. In other words, the concentration of resources and decision power within nations, especially major powers, is more critical in the explanation of war than, for instance, specific political and economic characteristics of the states concerned. On the other hand, international commerce is not alone able to save peace, in particular if the economic power is concentrated in a small group of wealthy traders who share the control of the state with the political elite.

A conventional view is that the growth of the industrial power per se increases the propensity for major war as it poses a potential security threat to other powers that have also to acquire new implements of war to be able to defend themselves. The industrialization of war was, of course, assisted by the spread of mass

261

production and new scientific breakthroughs in the period preceding World War I. The military–industrial revolution of the post-Napoleonic era was complemented by nationalistic and managerial revolutions that were both facilitated by the access to new means of communication.[123] The combined effect of these three revolutions was a more concentrated and effective military.

In addition, the dissemination of technologies and industries across borders created a transnational form of capitalism and permitted the rise of new non-European powers equalizing international power relations. McNeill stresses the political importance of these technological and industrial trends which were accompanied by the rise of politicized command economies and the strive for national unification in hitherto splintered countries. Their impact on the prospect for war was mediated by the concentration of the military command and arms production to fewer, pivotal actors.[124]

In sum, the concentration of technological capabilities and their management rather than industry as such seems to have been a decisive cause of war. This line of thinking is summarized well in the observation that the 'nineteenth century was a hundred years' war against smaller polities of all kinds in favor of unification, centralization, and consolidation; and that the twentieth century was an eighty years' war between the giants created in the nineteenth century'.[125]

How can peace be made sustainable in the industrial age? There appear to be two main roads to peace: (a) either the lust for territory, and thus for war, is diluted by setting up a liberal republic in which non-territorial interests dominate and/or (b) one should decentralize the economy by tearing down those economic hierarchies that habitually enlist the government to protect and promote their interests in foreign markets. Both of these ideas favor transnational instead of national interests. As neither political absolutism nor centralized commercial capitalism are conducive to a stable peace, one should try to replace dynastic political interests by capitalist ones and, as a part of this process, eliminate the vestiges of mercantilist economic power.

These assumptions lead authors to advocate an industrial peace or a capitalist peace. The former idea distinguishes from each other the 'militant' and 'industrial' societies, to use Spencer's terms. In militant societies, the traditional values of glory and greatness dominate and lead frequently to wars that are motivated by the interests of the old agricultural, even feudal, elites. These 'pre-modern' influences have been assumed to push states, especially the continental dynastic states, on the path to war. This idea was adopted by Mayer who, in accounting for World War I, argues that the 'pre-modern' elements were not only an empirical fact in most European societies, but their very essence contributed to the outbreak of the 'Great War'. Though these societies were not feudal, the *ancien régime* had so much influence that its idea of territoriality dominated the European societies and pushed them to war. In Mayer's view, the most critical factor in the war's outbreak was the contradiction between the aristocratic nature of the officer corps and the rural background of the soldiers on the one hand and the availability of modern, industrial technologies of destruction on the other.[126]

This conclusion grows out of a venerable intellectual tradition in which the rational industrial society, and the passion for work and economic gain, sublimate aggressive instincts. As in the old adage, leisure and, even worse, laziness, are the seedbeds of vice; in this case, war. The idea of an industrial peace grew out of the economic transformation that the European countries went through in the nineteenth century. It created a wave of optimism that the aggressive legacies of feudalism and absolutism can now be overcome by a rational and industrious approach to the economy.

As Aron has shown, the pedigree of the rational industrial peace starts from Saint-Simon's and Comte's positivism and progresses through the Social Darwinism of Spencer and Sumner, ending up in the praise of capitalism by Schumpeter and the emphasis on industrial values by Veblen.[127] Leaving out the pioneers of the theory, one can start from Schumpeter, a founder of the non-Marxist theory of imperialism. He views imperialism as an 'objectless . . . unlimited forcible expansion' fueled by atavistic interests and values of absolutism and the feudal element behind it. Imperialism is definitely not the highest stage of monopoly capitalism, as Lenin argued, but the last gasp of the dying dynastic–feudal order.

Schumpeter considers that feudalism leads to absolutism, while there is a break between absolutism and capitalism that derives its strength from the victory of bourgeois values. The firewall between absolutism and capitalism makes it possible to attribute imperialism and warfare to the feudal/absolutist nexus of society. Imperialism is due to 'atavism in social structure and in individual, psychological habits of emotional reaction' that have been carried over from the previous era to the new liberal society where they carved a niche for themselves.

In addition, Schumpeter attributes the cause of imperialism and warfare to 'export monopolism' which is a wrong kind of capitalism. It arises from the domestic concentration of economic power into trusts and monopolies, the establishment of protective tariffs, forced exports to foreign markets, and economic aggression in general. Thus, capitalism is anti-imperial and peaceful only if it avoids excessive concentrations of power and too close an alliance with the political elites, especially those looking back to the past.[128]

As an aristocrat, Schumpeter was skeptical of the role of industry in the promotion of peace which he saw as more likely in a civilized, bourgeoisie society. In that regard, Veblen had a different view; he believed that the internalization of industrial values of thrift and precision, what he called 'workmanship', will help to create a better and a more peaceful society. He made an explicit distinction between 'business' and 'industry'; the former was geared to unproductive speculation and even fraud, while the latter is a product of the 'machine process'. For Veblen, war is due to the predatory behavior of social entities that have access to surplus resources which can be converted into weapons and other instruments of expansion.

'Business' is not usually warlike, because it is too pleasure-seeking to go through the ordeal of battle. The real threat to peace comes from the dynastic groups that are remnants of the old feudal and absolutist societies, and the dynastic states controlled by these groups. Veblen regards pre-World War I Germany as the most clear-cut example of a dynastic state, but also places Japan in the same category. After some equivocation, he concludes that international trade can be a peace-producing factor, but only after appropriate political conditions are met.[129]

Both Schumpeter and Veblen tend to see the causes of war, and the conditions of peace, as a struggle between two competing historical tendencies. For Schumpeter, the contradiction is between atavistic and bourgeois social values, and for Veblen between the values of the bourgeois 'leisure class' and industrial 'workmanship'. Schumpeter sees this struggle in linear terms, hoping that bourgeois capitalism will win, although he becomes increasingly pessimistic for its future as totalitarian tendencies spread in the world. This pessimism also signifies for him a shift from commercial pacifism toward political realism.[130] Veblen's view of the relationship between business and industry is more complex and, in a way, dialectical.

The authors discussed above consider capitalism and industry progressive and rational forces to overcome the detrimental effects of political absolutism and economic mercantilism on peace. Another strand of thinking pointing in the same direction is the idea of financial peace advocated explicitly by Karl Polanyi. He attributes the 'Hundred Years' Peace' of 1815–1914 to financial interests and especially to the gold standard that ultimately helped to stabilize international relations after the 1870s. In his view, peace was possible because of the 'triumph of pragmatic capitalism' and the establishment of 'peaceful business as universal interest'. Peace was also maintained by the balance-of-power system; a super-structure 'erected upon and partly worked through the gold standard'.

Obviously, Polanyi's view of the nineteenth century system was not entirely benign. First, high finance had nothing against 'any number of minor, short, or localized wars. But their business would be impaired if a general war between the Great Powers should interfere with the monetary foundations of the system.' Like Schumpeter and Veblen, Polanyi also recognized the power of the 'cartel of dynasts and feudalists', but he thought that modern financial interests could contain them.[131]

The importance of finance in capitalism was first theoretically formulated by Hilferding whose *Finanzcapital* (1910) both Bukharin and Lenin utilized in their later theories of imperialism. Hilferding linked the rise of finance capital and economic concentration closely with each other, even to the point that, in his view, a 'general cartel' would dominate the entire production in every major capitalist country. He saw financial power as a means for imperialism to expand territorially and enclose the conquered area by protective tariffs that facilitate the exploitation of colonies by national monopolies. The international economic expansion and enclosure required the support of the state whose political control became, thus, pivotal. Hilferding considered war a likely result of imperialism; he did not believe in peaceful transitions, but expected violent, revolutionary social convulsions.[132]

However, Hilferding did not consider finance capital – which for him meant the combination of credit and industrial capital – to be the main cause of the coming war. The critical reason for interstate competition was the barriers to protect financial spheres of interest. If political barriers to financial and economic internationalization could be torn down, peace rather than war would take hold in international relations. This interpretation of Hilferding seems to be justified; in fact, he opposed the establishment of a protectionist Mitteleuropa, based on Austro-German cooperation, and advocated in 1914–15, in its stead, the promotion of free trade and the establishment of a league of nations as the safest road to peace.[133]

Hilferding represented one strand of imperialism theory in the pre-World War I debates. Another theorist, Hobson, especially in his book *Imperialism: A Study* (1902), saw the roots of war in the expansion of foreign investment and the military competition it stimulated. In some writings, Hobson was close to the idea that economic interdependence between independent states is the best guarantee of peace.[134] In fact, both Cobden and Hobson traced war and imperialism to the concentrations of economic power rather than capitalism itself. Cobden's ideal society was composed of small independent producers who develop strong mutual ties within and across national borders. The enemies of this small-scale liberal economic order were the large industrial conglomerates and the big landowners whose power was based on extra-market resources and instruments. Cobden favored the transition from feudal agriculture to industrialism, but with a human face. In Britain, this change required, in his view, the gradual withdrawal from the empire and the building up of a peaceable society on self-governing markets.[135]

In assessing the theories of capitalist and industrial peace, we have to contrast the cultural and political impact of industrialization on the one hand and the effects of the technological changes on the other. Contrary to Sombart and Mumford, there are reasons to support the Veblenian view that industrialization has peace-producing effects; it tends to mobilize people economically, organize them to work, and demand punctuality, but also encourage them to expand their horizons and demand their political rights. Industrialization creates a basis for both the capitalist organization of work and the political mobilization of masses. Neither of these changes leads automatically to any specific political consequences, but they open up new historical opportunities.

The sad history of the twentieth century shows that industrialization and mass mobilization do not necessarily produce peace. In fact, this period can be written as a history of close interaction between warfare, arms race, and the dominance of managerial economies, whether socialist, national socialist, or capitalist.[136] Thus, the degree of domestic concentration in economic and political power can be a critical mediating variable between industry and war. Yet, this conclusion appears to simplify the reality too much. First, the international conditions must change in such a manner that the outward thrust of domestic power becomes possible. Such changes include the breakdown of the effective gold standard and the balance of power after World War I.

Yet, the interaction of new resources, declining opportunity costs, and the concentration of political control cannot account for the movement toward the total war. In addition, there must be a shift in the dominant intellectual and popular mentality from peace to war. The breakthroughs in military technology from the middle of the nineteenth century prompted the rise of an autonomous, conservative officer corps which came to idealize machine warfare as a modern way of fighting. These officers combined a technocratic view of war with an anti-material view of society; a combination that was conducive to the rise of the cult of violence[137] and even proto-fascist political ideologies. Social Darwinism provided – in Britain, Germany, and the US – a way to assimilate these ideas into a single political doctrine.

Such fascist elements have been identified in the thinking of, for instance, Jünger and Fuller. Jünger envisioned a calculated synthesis of man and machine which would be built on the integration of the workers and the military (*Arbeiterstaat*), sidelining the weak bourgeois elements in society. This ideology had considerable influence in Nazi Germany. Fuller strived to develop a universal theory of war in which mechanical warfare had pride of place. The future 'model army' would combine the advances in science with mass industrial production making the tank the dominant weapon system on the battlefield. This would require, in turn, mass mobilization for total war and a new emphasis on patriotic values.[138] Obviously, the view about the correlation of the technical novelty and military effectiveness can be seen in the air war doctrines of Douhet and Mitchell.

No doubt industrialization of warfare has contributed significantly to the destructiveness, effectiveness, and velocity of military operations. The destructive effects of industrial war had already been witnessed in the Crimean War in the 1850s and in the material superiority of the North in the US Civil War of 1861–5. The impact of new technologies was also visible in the German Blitzkrieg operations against Austria, Denmark, and France in the 1860s and the 1870s,[139] but it was only in World War I that machine warfare became the dominant element. But was this development due to the capitalist element of industrialization? Engels would probably answer affirmatively. Armaments are not instruments created by the military, but they reflect in each society the level of the development of the productive forces; the 'methods of warfare . . . prove to be dependent on material, that is, economic conditions'. In Engels' analysis an interesting thing is that he does not attribute militarism to capitalism, but rather to the technological level of the society.[140]

Perhaps, indeed, capitalism and militarism can be separated from each other and war considered a result not of capitalism or socialism per se, but a consequence of industrialization that concentrates power in the state and the limited economic elite. In this case, militarism and warfare can be brewed both in capitalist and socialist societies provided that their popular control is restricted. Before World War I, 'national populations were more confined within cages whose relations with other national cages were defined not by the people as a whole, but first by private state and military elites, second by the nationalists'.[141]

In developing the concept of the mode of warfare as separate from the mode of production, Kaldor suggests that there is no endogenous relationship between capitalism and warfare; on the contrary, there is the 'possibility of warfare as a cancerous growth within capitalism'. In socialism, both production and warfare are aspects of the state activity, while in capitalism they have started to diverge from each other and even become competing forms of activities. This may create a tension between capitalism and warfare.[142] Kaldor thinks that this tension is solved by occasional wars, but I rather believe that the solution is achieved by distancing capitalism from warfare undermining its essence: the accumulation and redistribution of capital. Moreover, as Thompson and Kaldor argue, nuclear weapons have made modern war an 'exterminist mode of production'.

The history of technological arms races suggests that they are fueled by a combination of technological advances and competitive major-power relations. It seems that military crises and wars between major powers are related to their mutual competition and transitions from one leading economic sector to another, and the technological capabilities fostering these rivalries. This takes us back to the importance of interstate relations; preparations for war require the existence of a competitive multi-state system which was in existence even before capitalism emerged. The rivalries built into this system, together with power concentrations within societies, are the true cause of militarism and warfare, not their economic or political constitution.[143] Therefore, the explanations that warfare is a result of modernity or 'illiberal unconsciousness' are inadequate unless they are connected with the intra- and interstate conditions.[144]

The mutual reinforcement of the state and the military was very obvious in the Soviet Union: the centralized one-party state was an almost ideal breeding ground for the construction of massive technological systems by which one could orbit the earth and fire intercontinental missiles. In the United States, the involvement in the strategic arms race with the Soviet Union was compatible with the corporate centralization which sprang originally from the regulated war economy. The leading corporations of the 1950s and the 1960s were those that had the central role in running the 'arsenal of democracy' during World War II. It appears that military-driven and market-driven reasons for corporate concentration reinforced each other, probably to the detriment of the US national economy. The moment of truth came in the 1970s when it became apparent that the US can remain the leading economic and military power only if it is able to restructure its civilian economy to improve its productivity and international competitiveness by moving from the regulated Cold War economy to the liberal economy.

Digital capitalism

The era of digital capitalism started with the great technological transformation of the US industrial system in the 1970s which also had pivotal political and economic consequences; first of all, the decentralization of economic activities and the growing separation of the state and the market from each other. Economic decentralization refers here primarily to the restructuring of corporate activities, fostered by the development of new information technologies. This has resulted in the rise of flexible production models, network enterprises, and strategic alliances between firms all of which have a strong transnational flavor. On the downside is the decline of vertical organizations both in the private and public spheres.[145]

The globalization of economic activities has also redefined the relationship between the market and the state. Historically, they have been growing together in an interdependent relationship. It has not been fully severed today, and the market and the state still need each other. However, the disjuncture between transnational markets and national states has become more pronounced than it has ever been, save perhaps the heyday of the gold standard. A main result of this disjuncture is that the state has limits to mobilizing resources for political and military projects. Neither are firms able to bring together their resources from various transnational sources even if they would like to do so. In the contemporary world, both the state power and the market power are increasingly dispersed; it is difficult to see that they could be caged simultaneously by any major powers to fight each other.

The transition to digital capitalism and the strengthening of the transnational market structures have become an impediment to major interstate wars; (post)-modern capitalism has an increasingly peaceful flavor. True, weapons producers benefit from the growing military outlays and the orders of more precision-guided munitions, but for most other corporations a major war would mean an economic disaster as it would tear apart their transnational business networks. Few corporations would survive if they had to confine their activities to the domestic markets. Neither would the traditional military aggression pay for a post-industrial, market-oriented state which is built on transnational, economic interactions.[146]

New technologies, globalization, and corporate structures will not end, of course, all warfare, but it will become more polarized. There will be high-tech wars fought by the leading industrialized countries, especially the United States, against various 'evil' and 'rogue' states and the low-tech violence within developing countries. These two types of war do not necessarily have a connection with each other. The international system of the industrial countries approximates a security community, while turmoil continues in the South: 'for the military–industrial powers, it is the state of peace that will dominate, for the military–rural powers, it will be the state of war.'[147] There continues to be more war in developing countries.

More exact and easily accessible digital information permits more flexible and effective, and even less destructive operations. The new battlefield is littered with ground sensors and flying micro-sized intelligence devices or unmanned aircraft used to trace the enemy movements. Pilotless aircraft can drop bombs and the soldiers on the ground can use their global positioning system (GPS) equipment to call for air strikes on enemy positions. Both the new methods of intelligence and precision weapons rely on digital technologies which are changing the nature of war, especially in asymmetric conflicts in which the opponent is unable to respond to the technological superiority. In asymmetric conflicts, getting 'special forces on the ground early dramatically increases the effectiveness of an air campaign'. In Afghanistan, the operation of special forces was 'the first U.S. cavalry attack of the twenty-first century'.[148]

The military technology is shifting from platforms to information systems which permit a greater reliance on remote-launched weapons. The debate on the implications of these technical changes for the nature of warfare will continue. It is too early to jump to any final conclusion, but it looks as though the emerging mode of warfare relies more on individual portable technologies, which are linked back to the lethal firepower deriving its destructiveness from accuracy. Sociologically, this mode of warfare has been called post-heroic and devoid of nationalistic hatred, and even as human in the sense that there is a deliberate effort to avoid casualties both among one's own soldiers and the civilians on the opposing side.[149]

This is not, however, the whole truth. In another type of asymmetric war tanks and bulldozers are used to destroy the communal infrastructure of the opponent. In more symmetric wars, matches and machettes can kill large numbers of people. On the other side, rapid advances in information, laser, and other technologies also open up the possibility of the large-scale technological militarization of the world. There are reasons to fear that the new technical opportunities will not only lead to the deployment of new missile defense technologies, but an extensive militarization of space in general.

Conclusion

The main aim of this chapter has been to develop a historical interpretation of the changes in the nature of warfare associated with the transitions from one mode of production to another. A key idea has been that, rather than the mode of production, the degree of economic and political concentration within it has been the most important factor accounting for war. Obviously, war also has a cultural dimension; it manifests the values and ideas of each society.

In feudal societies, both economic and political power were dispersed. Kings made efforts to concentrate power in their hands, but they never quite succeeded in this effort. In the fragmented feudal society warfare was intermittent, but mostly a series of disconnected matches in which the draw was a common outcome. The transition from feudalism pointed in several different directions. The rise of the urban merchants and other bourgeoisie meant that the emerging capitalism was quite decentralized and did not provide a material basis for wars of attrition or other prolonged military encounters. On the other hand, the transition from feudal political rule to dynastic states and fiscal–military states, and, ultimately, absolutism created entirely new concentrations of politico-military power.

Historically, capitalism and state tend to have developed in tandem. The financial needs of warfare have demanded the establishment of centralized political structures to collect taxes and convert them into arms and troops. Centralization was also needed in the conduct of large military operations and the command of increasingly complex military technologies. Thus, modern politics cannot be comprehended without considering its military roots, or in Tilly's classic formulation 'war made the state, and the state made the war'.[150] War could be financed only by taxing citizens and/or borrowing money from financiers. Thus, the 'fiscal state' and warfare have been closely intertwined, and debt became a means of power politics, and a source of economic crises, as Marx, Veblen, and Weber have recognized in their writings. Taxation for war has, in turn, been linked with the rise of absolutism. The military revolutions and the growing financial requirements of warfare helped to destroy the medieval monarchy and feudalism in the sixteenth and seventeenth centuries.

The centralization of political power interacted with the concentration of political power. The mercantilist policies of absolutist rulers merged political and economic power and created a lethal combination of resources that the rulers could use for warfare. Conventional wisdom suggests that the trading states have had weaker state structures than territorial states and were, therefore, less likely to engage in wars of aggression. This is not necessarily true, though; in fact, both territorial and trading states can have strong state structures, but in a different way. The trading states have been more democratic, but in critical elite sectors power has been often heavily concentrated. In effect, not a single important liberal author has denied the ultimate centrality of state power for successful capitalism. As Hall points out, 'capitalist freedom . . . depends upon the presence of a strong government'. The capitalist societies are pluralistic in nature and have, therefore, different sources of power which point 'perhaps miraculously, in the same direction'.[151]

Both territorial absolutism and merchant capitalism were extensively engaged in warfare. This is consistent with Arrighi's observation that, from the standpoint of war and peace, the most important transition was not from feudalism to capitalism, but 'from scattered to concentrated capitalist power'.[152] This observation leads one to suspect the argument that capitalist states are necessarily more peaceful than authoritarian ones. The empirical record indicates rather that they have both fought wars, but of different kinds. Their ideas of war have been different; in the drive to expand and control one looks to steppe and the other to ocean.

The transition to the industrial era meant that the economic resources became more concentrated. The new industrial capabilities provided an infrastructure to develop new weapons systems. Yet, the technological and financial demands of warfare increased so rapidly that even the main powers had difficulties in mobilizing adequate resources for warfare; therefore, wars tended to become prolonged and indecisive.[153] Some industrial wars became total wars, but the new mobile capabilities also provided to one state such an edge, as they did to Germany against France in 1870–1, that wars remained short and limited. Moreover, the rise of nationalism shaped the idea of war; first the national mobilization increased the destructiveness of warfare, but with the democratization of nationalism it started to constrain war.

Finally, globalization and the electronic revolution have decentralized the economy and diffused the centers of power that may have an interest in going to war. Democratic transitions have also kept politics decentralized which augurs a more peaceful future. The remaining problem is the same as during the age of merchant capitalism: despite political democracy, some elite segments, especially in great powers, have so much concentrated power that they can fight wars that are made in the image of the digital revolution.

This analysis sees the decentralization of economic and political power as a key to peace provided that a proper international framework of governance is created to support the market and democracy.[154]

Notes

1 This point is developed further by K. Polanyi, *The Great Transformation: The Political and Economic Origins of Our Times* (Boston: Beacon Press, 1957).

2 I. Clark, *Waging War: A Philosophical Introduction* (Oxford: Clarendon, 1988), pp. 23–30.

3 G. Best, 'Editor's Preface', in B. Bond, *War and Society in Europe in 1870–1970* (Suffolk: Fontana, 1984), pp. 8–9.

4 Different stages of capitalism are discussed, for example, in J. Baechler, *The Origins of Capitalism* (Oxford: Basil Blackwell, 1975); and M. Beaud, *A History of Capitalism* (New York: Monthly Review Press, 1983).

5 E. Rhodes, 'Constructing Peace and War: An Analysis of the Power of Ideas to Shape American Military Power', *Millennium*, 24, 1 (1995), pp. 54–9.

6 I. Wallerstein, 'The West, Capitalism, and the Modern World-System', in T. Brook and G. Blue (eds), *China and Historical Capitalism: Genealogies of Sinological Knowledge* (Cambridge: Cambridge University Press, 1999), pp. 17–19, 27.

7 F. Braudel, *Civilization and Capitalism 15th–18th Century*, Vol. II: *The Wheels of Commerce* (tr. by S. Reynolds) (New York: Harper & Row, 1986), pp. 553–5. See also G. Arrighi, *The Long Twentieth Century: Money, Power, and the Origins of Our Times* (London: Verso, 1994), pp. 10–13.

8 C. Tilly, *Coercion, Capital, and European States, AD 990–1990* (Oxford: Basil Blackwell, 1990). As Arrighi points out, these strategies are not alternatives, but capitalist resources can be converted to acquire a territorial empire. Arrighi, *The Long Twentieth Century*, pp. 33–4.

9 S. R. Epstein, *Freedom and Growth: The Rise of States and Markets in Europe, 1300–1750* (London: Routledge, 2000), pp. 12–16.

10 Ibid., pp. 49–52.

11 B. Teschke, 'Geopolitical Relations in the European Middle Ages: History and Theory', *International Organization*, 52, 2 (1998), pp. 339–41.

12 M. Olson, *Power and Prosperity: Outgrowing Communist and Capitalist Dictatorships* (New York: Basic Books, 2000), pp. 6–9.

13 Wallerstein, 'The West, Capitalism, and the Modern World-System', pp. 30–1.

14 E. L. Jones, *The European Miracle: Environments, Economies, and Geopolitics in the History of Europe and Asia* (Cambridge: Cambridge University Press, 1981), pp. 131–3.

15 P. Kriedte, *Spätfeudalismus und Handelskapital: Grundlienien der europäischen Wirtschaftsgesichte vom 16.bis zum Ausgang des 18. Jahrhunderts* (Göttingen: Vandenhoeck & Ruprecht, 1980), pp. 9–15.

16 M. Mann, *The Sources of Social Power*, Vol. I: *A History of Power from the Beginning of A.D. 1760* (Cambridge: Cambridge University Press, 1986), pp. 416–17.

17 P. Contamine, *War in the Middle Ages* (tr. by M. Jones) (Oxford: Basil Blackwell, 1980), pp. 41–3.

18 H. M. Schwartz, *States versus Markets: The Emergence of a Global Economy*, 2nd edn (New York: St Martin's Press, 2000), pp. 13–16.

19 Mann, *The Sources of Social Power*, pp. 390–3. See also H. Spruyt, *The Sovereign State and Its Competitors* (Princeton: Princeton University Press, 1994), pp. 36–8.

20 N. Elias, *State Formation and Civilization: The Civilizing Process*, Vol. 2 (Oxford: Basil Blackwell, 1982 [1939]), pp. 57–65. For a different view on the medieval state, see Teschke, 'Geopolitical Relations in the European Middle Ages', pp. 342–4.

21 R. L. O'Connell, *Of Arms and Men: A History of War, Weapons, and Aggression* (Oxford: Oxford University Press, 1989), pp. 87–9.

22 Mann, *The Sources of Social Power*, pp. 407–9.

23 F. Braudel, *The Structures of Everyday Life*, Vol. 1: *The Limits of the Possible* (New York: Harper & Row, 1981), pp. 380–1.

24 Ransom and booty were common spoils of war that started, toward the end of the Middle Ages, to become regulated; for instance, there was increasing concern about their fair distribution, see P. Contamine, 'The Growth of State Control: Practices of War, 1300–1800: Ransom and Booty', in P. Contamine (ed.), *War and Competition between States* (Oxford: Clarendon, 2000), pp. 163–78.

25 H. Koht, *Driving Forces of History* (New York: Atheneum, 1968), pp. 66, 86–90.

26 Kriedte, *Spätfeudalismus und Handelskapital*, pp. 24–7 and Mann, *The Sources of Social Power*, pp. 411–12.

27 This interpretation relies primarily on Elias, *State Formation and Civilization*, pp. 8–9, 15–22.

28 See Epstein, *Freedom and Growth*, pp. 147, 167.

29 O'Connell, *Of Arms and Men*, pp. 89–97 and 103.

30 For analyses of medieval warfare, see O'Connell, *Of Arms and Men*, pp. 84–123; M. Howard, *War in European History* (Oxford: Oxford University Press, 1976), pp. 1–19; and A. Jones, *The Art of War in the Western World* (Oxford: Oxford University Press, 1987), pp. 127–34, *passim*.

31 C. J. Rogers, 'The Age of Hundred Years War', in M. Keen (ed.), *Medieval Warfare: A History* (Oxford: Oxford University Press, 1999), pp. 136–60. Other observers suggest that during the period, instead of defense dominance, there was a 'fine balance between defensive structures and offensive weapons'; see R. L. C. Jones, 'Fortifications and Sieges in Western Europe *c.* 800–1450', in M. Keen (ed.), *Medieval Warfare: A History* (Oxford: Oxford University Press, 1999), pp. 163–85.

32 G. J. Ashwort, *War and the City* (London: Routledge, 1991), pp. 19–27. See also C. Duffy, *Siege Warfare: The Fortress in the Early Modern World 1494–1660* (New York: Barnes & Noble, 1979).

33 See Duffy, *Siege Warfare*, pp. 23–42 and W. H. McNeill, *The Pursuit of Power: Technology, Armed Forces, and Society since A.D. 1000* (Chicago: University of Chicago Press, 1982), pp. 89–95.

34 P. Contamine, *War in the Middle Ages*, pp. 77–101, 150–65.

35 R. W. Kaeuper, *War, Justice, and Public Order: England and France in the Later Middle Ages* (Oxford: Clarendon Press, 1988), pp. 32–62, 90–3.

36 McNeill, *The Pursuit of Power*, pp. 65–79.

37 Jones, *The Art of War in the Western World*, pp. 175–82 and T. Roppe, *War in the Modern World* (London: Collier Macmillan, 1962), pp. 19–28.

38 M. N. Covini, 'Political and Military Bonds in the Italian State System, Thirteenth to Sixteenth Centuries', in P. Contamine (ed.), *War and Competition between States* (Oxford: Clarendon Press, 2000), pp. 19–27.

39 Contamine, *War in the Middle Ages*, p. 31.

40 This is illustrated by the Battle of Agincourt in October 1415 as described in J. Keegan, *The Face of Battle* (New York: Barnes & Noble, 1993 [1976]), pp. 79–116.

41 Wallerstein, 'The West, Capitalism, and the Modern World-System', pp. 30–4; Epstein, *Freedom and Growth*, pp. 40–2; and Kaeuper, *War, Justice, and Public Order*, pp. 63–7, 88–9.

42 G. Parker, *The Military Revolution and the Rise of the West, 1500–1800* (Cambridge: Cambridge University Press, 1988).

43 R. L. Reynolds, *Europe Emerges: Transition towards an Industrial World-wide Society 600–1750* (Madison: The University of Wisconsin Press, 1982 [1961]), pp. 171–4 and J. Black, *War and the World: Military Power and the Fate of the Continents 1450–2000* (Suffolk: Fontana, 1998), pp. 10–17.

44 Contamine, *War in the Middle Ages*, pp. 165–72; F. Tallett, *War and Society in Early-Modern Europe, 1495–1715* (London: Routledge, 1992), pp. 4–13; cf. Mann, *The Sources of Social Power*, pp. 425–30.

45 Epstein, *Freedom and Growth*, pp. 52–5. Schwartz, *States versus Markets*, pp. 18–22, suggests that mercantilism is the 'hinge' between commercialization and state-building.

46 I. Wallerstein, *The Modern World System I: Capitalist Agriculture and the Origins of the World-Economy in the Sixteenth Century* (New York: Academic Publishers, 1974).

47 R. Lachmann, *Capitalists in Spite of Themselves: Elite Conflict and Economic Transitions in Early Modern Europe* (Oxford: Oxford University Press, 2000), pp. 95–9. See also Mann, *The Sources of Social Power*, pp. 476–7.

48 H. Barbera, *The Military Factor in Social Change*, Vol. 2 of *The State and Revolution* (New Brunswick: Transaction Publishers, 1998), pp. 231–3.

49 Kaeuper, *War, Justice, and Public Order*, pp. 117–33.

50 The interaction between capitalism and state-formation is captured by van Creveld: 'capitalism provided monarchy with financial muscle. Monarchy repaid its debt by providing capitalist enterprise with military protection'; M. van Creveld, *The Rise and the Decline of the State* (Cambridge: Cambridge University Press, 1999), p. 119. For a similar conclusion on England, see Mann, *The Sources of Social Power*, pp. 431–2.

51 J. Black, *European Warfare 1660–1815* (New Haven: Yale University Press, 1994), pp. 52, 55–9. See also Braudel, *The Structures of Everyday Life*, pp. 393–5.

52 This view has been advanced by Mann, *The Sources of Social Power*, pp. 445–6, 453–5 and, at length, B. Porter, *War and the Rise of the State: The Military Foundations of Modern Politics* (New York: Free Press, 1994).

53 Spruyt, *The Sovereign State and Its Competitors*, pp. 105–7.

54 M. Hart, 'The Emergence and Consolidation of the "Tax State"', in R. Bonney (ed.), *Economic Systems and State Finance* (Oxford: Clarendon Press, 1995), pp. 281–2.

55 J. Glete, *War and the State in Early Modern Europe* (London: Routledge, 2002), pp. 25–6, 28–30.

56 This runs counter to Montesquieu's maxim that 'the spirit of monarch is war and expansion; the spirit of republics is peace and moderation'; see Montesquieu, *The Spirit of Laws* (tr. by A. M. Cohler, B. C. Miller and H. S. Stone) (Cambridge: Cambridge University Press, 1989 [1748]), Part 2, Book 9, Chapter 2.

57 D. C. North, *Structure and Change in Economic History* (New York: W.W. Norton, 1981), pp. 146–57. This view is also adopted, with some minor modifications, by P. T. Hoffman and J.-L. Rosenthal, 'The Political Economy of Warfare and Taxation in Early Modern Europe: Historical Lessons for Economic Development', in J. N. Drobak and J. V. C. Nye (eds), *The Frontiers of the New Institutional Economics* (San Diego: Academic Press, 1997), pp. 31–55.

58 F. C. Lane, *Profits from Power: Readings in Protection Rent and Violence-Controlling Enterprises* (Albany: State University of New York Press, 1979).

59 J. Glete, *Warfare at Sea 1500–1650: Maritime Conflicts and the Transformation of Europe* (London: Routledge, 2000), pp. 60–9. For additional evidence, see Glete, *War and the State in Early Modern Europe*, pp. 30–8; and J. R. Bruijn, 'States and their Navies from the Late Sixteenth to the End of the Eighteenth Centuries', in P. Contamine (ed.), *War and Competition between States* (Oxford: Clarendon Press, 2000), pp. 69–98.

60 H. Caton, *The Politics of Progress: The Origins and Development of the Commercial Republic* (Gainesville: University of Florida Press, 1988), pp. 155–61.

61 P. K. O'Brien and P. A. Hunt, 'England, 1485–1815', in R. Bonney (eds), *The Rise of the Fiscal State in Europe, c. 1200–1815* (Oxford: Oxford University Press, 1999), pp. 53–100.

62 A. Macfarlane, 'The Cradle of Capitalism: The Case of England', in J. Baechler, J. A. Hall and M. Mann (eds), *Europe and the Rise of Capitalism* (Oxford: Basil Blackwell, 1988), pp. 185–203 (the quotation is on p. 201).

63 Lachmann, *Capitalists in Spite of Themselves*, pp. 99–100 and 118.

64 A. Zolberg, 'Origins of the Modern World System: A Missing Link', *World Politics*, 33, 2 (1981), pp. 253–81.

65 J. Kurth, 'Industrial Change and Political Change: A European Perspective', in D. Collier (ed.), *The New Authoritarianism in Latin America* (Princeton: Princeton University Press, 1975), pp. 330–3.

66 B. Moore, Jr, *Social Origins of Dictatorship and Democracy: Lord and Peasant in the Making of the Modern World* (Boston: Beacon Press, 1996), pp. 18–19, 29–30.

67 Elias, *State Formation and Civilization*, pp. 98–101. The role of violent struggles in the establishment of European states has also been stressed by Y. Cohen, B. Brown and A. F. K. Organski, 'The Paradoxical Nature of State Making: The Violent Creation of Order', *American Political Science Review*, 75, 4 (1981), pp. 901–10.

68 E. W. Fox, *History in Geographical Perspective: The Other France* (New York: Norton, 1971).

69 Moore, *Social Origins of Dictatorship and Democracy*, pp. 55–60. Also Lachmann, *Capitalists in Spite of Themselves* and van Creveld, *The Rise and the Decline of the State*, pp. 87–103 contrast England and France. The main difference between them seems to concern the outcome of the struggle between the royalty and the estates.

70 J.-L. Rosenthal, 'The Political Economy of Absolutism Reconsidered', in R. H. Bates *et al.*, *Analytic Narratives* (Princeton: Princeton University Press, 1998), pp. 64–108 (the quotation is on p. 77). On the complex relationship of taxation and warfare in France, see also R. Bonney, 'France, 1494–1815', in R. Bonney (ed.), *The Rise of the Fiscal State in Europe c. 1200–1815* (Oxford: Oxford University Press, 1999), pp. 123–76.

71 McNeill, *The Pursuit of Power*, pp. 161–6; J. Black, *Warfare in the Eighteenth Century* (London: Cassell, 1999), pp. 193–8.

72 Beaud, *A History of Capitalism*, pp. 35–40; Caton, *The Politics of Progress*, pp. 87–97; and I. Murat, *Colbert* (Charlottesville: University Press of Virginia, 1984), pp. 129–50.

73 H. Guerlac, 'Vauban: The Impact of Science on War', in P. Paret (ed.), *Makers of Modern Strategy: From Machiavelli to the Nuclear Age* (Princeton: Princeton University Press, 1986), pp. 64–90 and M. Parent, *Vauban: Un encyclopediste avant la lettre* (Paris: Berger-Levrault, 1982). Vauban pioneered an entire school of military science; see A. Gat, *The Origins of Military Thought from the Enlightenment to Clausewitz* (Oxford: Clarendon Press, 1989), pp. 25–53.

74 H. Rosenberg, *Bureaucracy, Aristocracy and Autocracy: The Prussian Experience 1660–1815* (Boston: Beacon Press, 1958). See also Barbera, *The Military Factor in Social Change*, pp. 234–8 and H. Schulze, *States, Nations, and Nationalism: From the Middle Ages to the Present* (tr. by William E. Yuill) (Oxford: Basil Blackwell, 1996), pp. 62–4.

75 T. Byres, *Capitalism from Above and Capitalism from Below* (London: Macmillan, 1996), pp. 75–80, 104–17.

76 Caton, *The Politics of Progress*, pp. 98–102 and Rosenthal, 'The Political Economy of Absolutism Reconsidered'.

77 E. Luard, *War in International Society: A Study in International Sociology* (New Haven: Yale University Press, 1986).

78 Van Creveld, *The Rise and the Decline of the State* and Glete, *War and the State in Early Modern Europe*.

79 Schulze, *States, Nations, and Nationalism*, pp. 40–1.

80 Luard, *War in International Society*, pp. 35–8, 93–9.

81 K. J. Holsti, *Peace and War: Armed Conflicts and International Order 1648–1989* (Cambridge: Cambridge University Press, 1991), pp. 47–52. See also Luard, *War in International Society*, pp. 47, 100–4.

82 Tallett, *War and Society in Early-Modern Europe*, pp. 17–20; and E. V. Gulick, *Europe's Classical Balance of Power* (New York: W.W. Norton, 1967 [1955]), pp. 68–9.

83 For evidence, see R. I. Frost, *The Northern Wars: War, State and Society in Northeastern Europe, 1558–1721* (London: Longman, 2000).

84 Black, *European Warfare 1660–1815*, pp. 39–41; and H. Strachan, *European Armies and the Conduct of War* (London: Allen & Unwin, 1983), pp. 16–18.

85 Jones, *The Art of War in the Western World*, pp. 267–72; Black, *European Warfare 1660–1815*, pp. 60–2; McNeill, *The Pursuit of Power*, pp. 125–43; and H. Delbrück, *The Dawn of Modern Warfare: History of the Art of War*, Vol. IV (Lincoln: University of Nebraska Press, 1990 [1920]), pp. 269–92.

86 Howard, *War in European History*, pp. 54–74. See also M. S. Anderson, *War and Society in Europe of the Old Regime, 1618–1789* (Leicester: Leicester University Press, 1988), pp. 24–32.

87 N. Ferguson, *The Cash Nexus: Money and Power in the Modern World, 1700–2000* (New York: Basic Books, 2001), pp. 23, 25.

88 Luard, *War in International Society*, pp. 35, 42, 47.

89 Van Creveld, *The Rise and the Decline of the State*, pp. 150–4.

90 Delbrück, *The Dawn of Modern Warfare*, pp. 155–71; G. Rothenberg, 'Maurice of Nassau, Gustavus Adolphus, Raimondo Montecuccoli, and the "Military Revolution" of the Seventeenth Century', in P. Paret (ed.), *Makers of Modern Strategy from Machiavelli to the Nuclear Era* (Princeton: Princeton University Press, 1986), pp. 34–45. See also P. Wilson, 'European Warfare 1450–1815', in J. Black (ed.), *War in the Early Modern World 1450–1815* (Boulder: Westview Press, 1999), pp. 192–6 and, on the fiscal military state, Glete, *War and the State in Early Modern Europe*, pp. 140–73.

91 J. Israel, *The Dutch Republic: Its Rise, Greatness, and Fall 1477–1806* (Oxford: Clarendon Press, 1995), pp. 267–71.

92 Anderson, *War and Society in Europe of the Old Regime*, pp. 45–56; and Black, *European Warfare 1660–1815*, pp. 87–92.

93 W. Sombart, *Krieg und Kapitalismus* (München: Verlag von Duncker & Humboldt, 1913). For the opposite conclusion that military preparations have prevented the full realization of technological potentialities, see J. Nef, *War and Human Progress: An Essay on the Rise of Industrial Civilization* (New York: W.W. Norton, 1963 [1950]), esp. pp. 65–88.

94 Bruijn, 'States and their Navies from the Late Sixteenth to the End of the Eighteenth Centuries', pp. 80–90.

95 The limited impact of the Seven Years War on the French economy has been documented in J. C. Riley, *The Seven Years War and the Old Regime in France: The Economic and Financial Toll* (Princeton: Princeton University Press, 1986).

96 McNeill, *The Pursuit of Power*; and P. Deane, 'War and Industrialization', in J. M. Winter (ed.), *War and Economic Development* (Cambridge: Cambridge University Press, 1975).

97 J. Black, *Why Wars Happen* (New York: New York University Press, 1998), pp. 86–103.

98 For such an analysis, see G. Liska, *Quest for Equilibrium: America and the Balance of Power on Land and Sea* (Baltimore: Johns Hopkins University Press, 1977). See also Glete, *War and the State in Early Modern Europe*.

99 Black, *Warfare in the Eighteenth Century*, pp. 106–7.

100 Lane, *Profits from Power*; and K. Pomeranz and S. Topic, *The World That Trade Created: Society, Culture, and the World Economy, 1400–The Present* (Armonk: M.E. Sharpe, 1999), pp. 147–78.

101 Braudel, *Civilization and Capitalism 15th–18th Century*, Vol. II, pp. 416–21.

102 Montesquieu, *The Spirit of Laws* (tr. and ed. by A. Cohler, B. C. Miller and H. S. Stone) (Cambridge: Cambridge University Press, 1989 [1748]), pp. 337–48.

103 A. Smith, *An Inquiry into the Nature and Causes of the Wealth of Nations* (ed. by E. Cannan) (Chicago: University of Chicago Press, 1976 [1776]), Book I, ch. 1, p. 25; Book III, ch. 4, pp. 432–45; and Book V, ch. 1, pp. 213–31. See also M. Doyle, *Ways of War and Peace: Realism, Liberalism, and Socialism* (New York: W.W. Norton, 1997), pp. 231–41; and M. Howard, *War and the Liberal Conscience* (Oxford: Oxford University Press, 1981), pp. 13–30.

104 I. Kant, 'Perpetual Peace', in H. Kainz (ed.), *Philosophical Perspectives on Peace: An Anthology of Classical and Modern Sources* (Athens: Ohio University Press, 1987 [1795]), pp. 65–86.

105 A. O. Hirschman, *The Passions and the Interests: Political Arguments for Capitalism before Its Triumph* (Princeton: Princeton University Press, 1977), pp. 56–76 and *passim*. J. A. Hall, *Liberalism: Politics, Ideology, and the Market* (Chapel Hill: University of North Carolina Press, 1987) also discusses, at some length, the role of interests and passions in liberal theory.

106 The historical integration of liberalism and realism is documented in I. Hont, 'Free Trade and Economic Limits to National Politics: Neo-Machiavellian Political Economy Reconsidered', in J. Dunn (ed.), *The Economic Limits to Modern Politics* (Cambridge: Cambridge University Press, 1990), pp. 41–120.

107 P. Hugill, *World Trade Since 1431: Geography, Technology, and Capitalism* (Baltimore: Johns Hopkins University Press, 1993), pp. 103–58.

108 Caton, *The Politics of Progress*, pp. 221–40.

109 This interpretation pervades S. Schama, *The Embarrassment of Riches* (New York: Alfred A. Knopf, 1987) and J. Israel, *Dutch Primacy in World Trade, 1585–1740* (Oxford: Clarendon, 1990). Later on, Israel adopted a broader view (Israel, *The Dutch Republic*). See also Lachmann, *Capitalists in Spite of Themselves*, pp. 159–64 on the formation of Dutch elites.

110 Glete, *War and the State in Early Modern Europe*, pp. 140–73. For a similar interpretation, see Arrighi, *The Long Twentieth Century*, pp. 140–2, 151–2 who stresses the strength of the Dutch coercive apparatus.

111 Wallerstein suggests that the distinction between benign and malign commercial capitalism cuts across Dutch society; the VOC was controlled by the peace-loving merchants of Amsterdam, while the warlike colonizers wielded power in the WIC; see I. Wallerstein, *The Modern World System II: Mercantilism and the Consolidation of the European World-Economy, 1600–1750* (New York: Academic Press, 1980), pp. 50–2. Pomeranz and Topik suggest that high protection costs of commerce, due in particular to VOC's wars against the Portuguese in Asia, accelerated the spread of risks by establishing joint stock companies (Pomeranz and Topic, *The World That Trade Created*, pp. 163–6).

112 For details, see Israel, *The Dutch Republic*, pp. 934–5.

113 For background, see J. Thompson, *Mercenaries, Pirates, and Sovereigns: State-Building and Extra-Territorial Violence in Early Modern Europe* (Princeton: Princeton University Press, 1994) and for a more systemic interpretation, see A. Perotin-Dumon, 'The Pirate and the Emperor: Power and the Law on the Seas, 1450–1850', in James Tracy (ed.), *The Political Economy of Merchant Empires* (Cambridge: Cambridge University Press, 1997), pp. 196–227.

114 T. Brady, Jr, 'The Rise of Merchant Empires, 1400–1700: A European Counterpoint', in James Tracy (ed.), *The Political Economy of Merchant Empires* (Cambridge: Cambridge University Press, 1997), pp. 148–55 and Pomeranz and Topic, *The World That Trade Created*, pp. 147–78.

115 Brady, 'The Rise of Merchant Empires', p. 153.

116 For detailed evidence, see especially J. Glete, 'Warfare at Sea 1450–1815', in J. Black (ed.), *War in Early Modern Europe 1450–1815* (Boulder: Westview Press, 1999),

pp. 25–52; and J. Glete, *Warfare at Sea*. Critical naval battles are described by P. Padfield, *Tide of Empires: Decisive Naval Campaigns in the Rise of the West*, Vol. 2: *1654–1763* (London: Routledge & Kegan Paul, 1982).

117 Braudel, *Civilization and Capitalism 15th–18th Century*, Vol. II, p. 419. For similar evidence on France, see Riley, *The Seven Years War and the Old Regime in France*, pp. 111–12, 118–20.

118 See, e.g., Kriedte, *Spätfeudalismus und Handelskapital*, pp. 145–50 and J. Siegelberg, *Kapitalismus und Krieg: Eine Theorie des Krieges in der Weltgesellschaft* (Münster: LIT Verlag, 1994), pp. 50–78.

119 Holsti, *Peace and War*, pp. 50, 52–4, 89 and 91–2.

120 Luard, *War in International Society*, pp. 104–6.

121 Wallerstein, *The Modern World System II*, pp. 75–81; and Padfield, *Tide of Empires*, pp. 23–6, 35–6, 115–17.

122 Wallerstein, *The Modern World System II*, pp. 245–51, 255–8; Black, *Warfare in the Eighteenth Century*, pp. 79–122; and Padfield, *Tide of Empires*.

123 M. S. Neiberg, *Warfare in World History* (London: Routledge, 2001), pp. 47–53.

124 McNeill, *The Pursuit of Power*; see also M. Pearton, *Diplomacy, War and Technology since 1830* (Lawrence: University Press of Kansas, 1983).

125 D. Livingston, 'Dismantling Leviathan', *Harper's Magazine*, 1824, May (2002), pp. 13–17.

126 A. Mayer, *The Persistence of the Old Regime: Europe to the Great War* (New York: Pantheon Books, 1981), esp. pp. 305–23.

127 R. Aron, *War and Industrial Society: August Comte Memorial Trust Lecture no. 3* (Oxford: Oxford University Press, 1958). John Nef reaches a similar conclusion: in the nineteenth century, there was a 'growing sentiment among the leaders of European thought that the rational powers of man, demonstrated tangibly by the remarkable increase of production were gradually getting control over violence and war'; see Nef, *War and Human Progress*, pp. 330–5, 340–4 (the quotation is on p. 333).

128 J. Schumpeter, 'The Sociology of Imperialisms', in R. Swedberg (ed.), *Joseph A. Schumpeter: The Economics and Sociology of Capitalism* (Princeton: Princeton University Press, 1991 [1919]), pp. 141–219. For an analysis of his contribution, see R. Väyrynen, 'Joseph A. Schumpeter on Imperialism and War: A Historical and Conceptual Inquiry', in Pauli Kettunen *et al.* (eds), *Jäljillä: Kirjoituksia historian ongelmista*, Vol. 2 (Turku: Aurora Books, 2000), pp. 91–122.

129 See especially T. Veblen, *Imperial Germany and the Industrial Revolution* (New York: The Viking Press, 1939 [1915]); and T. Veblen, *The Nature of Peace*, with a new introduction by W. J. Samuels (New Brunswick: Transaction Publishers, 1998 [1917]).

130 Here my emphasis is different from the interpretation provided by Doyle, *Ways of War and Peace*, pp. 241–8.

131 Polanyi, *The Great Transformation*, pp. 3–19, 264–6. An opposite, warlike view of the capitalists and 'political economists standing behind them' was provided in Britain by John Ruskin, see I. Melada, *Guns for Sale: War and Capitalism in British Literature, 1851–1939* (London: McFarland, 1983), pp. 28–34.

132 W. Smalldone, *Rudolf Hilferding: The Tragedy of a German Social Democrat* (Dekalb: Northern Illinois University Press, 1998), pp. 40–54.

133 Ibid., pp. 71–2. Later in his life – he died in a Nazi dungeon in Paris in 1941 – Hilferding (ibid., pp. 203–4) came to consider state power as an independent mover of international politics and suggested that many fundamental economic changes had been ushered in by the use of military force.

134 See H. C. G. Matthew, 'Hobson, Ruskin and Cobden', in M. Fredeen (ed.), *Reappraising J. A. Hobson: Humanism and Welfare* (London: Unwin Hyman, 1990),

pp. 11–30 and 31–53; and P. J. Cain, 'Variations on a Famous Theme: Hobson, International Trade and Imperialism, 1902–1938', in M. Fredeen (ed.), *Reappraising J. A. Hobson: Humanism and Welfare* (London: Unwin Hyman, 1990), pp. 11–30 and 31–53.

135 P. Cain, 'Capitalism, War and Internationalism in the Thought of Richard Cobden', *British Journal of International Studies*, 5, 2 (1979), pp. 229–47; and N. Edsall, *Richard Cobden: Independent Radical* (Cambridge, Mass.: Harvard University Press, 1986).

136 This is the key idea in McNeill, *The Pursuit of Power*, chs 9 and 10.

137 On the cult of violence before World War I, see Nef, *War and Human Progress*, pp. 404–10. A similar idea on the 'cult of offensive' has been suggested by J. Snyder, *Ideology of the Offensive: Military Decision Making and the Disasters of 1914* (Ithaca: Cornell University Press, 1984).

138 On Jünger and his influence, see A. Gat, *Fascist and Liberal Visions of War: Fuller, Liddell Hart, Douhet, and Other Modernists* (Oxford: Clarendon Press, 1998), pp. 81–103; and C. Coker, *War and the Illiberal Conscience* (Boulder: Westview, 1998), pp. 51–5. On Fuller, see Gat, *Fascist and Liberal Visions of War*, pp. 13–42; and B. H. Reid, *J. F. C. Fuller: The Military Thinker* (London: Macmillan, 1987).

139 The economic and technological background of wars in the nineteenth century is summarized well in E. Hobsbawm, *The Age of Capital 1848–1870.* (New York: Times Mirror, 1979).

140 F. Engels, *Anti-Dühring: Herr Eugen Dühring's Revolution in Science* (Moscow: Foreign Languages Publishing House, 1959), pp. 229–40.

141 M. Mann, *The Sources of Social Power*, Vol. II: *The Rise of Classes and Nation-States, 1760–1914* (Cambridge: Cambridge University Press, 1993), p. 754.

142 M. Kaldor, 'Warfare and Capitalism', in E. P. Thompson (ed.), *Exterminism and Cold War* (London: NLB, 1982), pp. 261–87. See also M. Mann, *States, War, and Capitalism: Studies in Political Sociology* (Oxford: Basil Blackwell, 1988), pp. 124–39.

143 This is the conclusion by Mann, *States, War, and Capitalism*, pp. 139–43.

144 Coker, *War and the Illiberal Conscience*. See also P. Lawrence, *Modernity and War: The Creed of Absolute Violence* (London: Macmillan, 1997).

145 These changes are described in detail by M. Castells, *The Information Age: Economy, Society and Culture*, Vol. I: *The Rise of the Network Society* (Oxford: Blackwell, 1996), pp. 152–72.

146 On that score I am in rough agreement with R. Rosecrance, *The Rise of the Virtual State: Wealth and Power in the Coming Century* (New York: Basic Books, 1998).

147 P. Virilio, 'Military Space', in J. D. Derian (ed.), *The Virilio Reader* (Oxford: Blackwell, 1998), pp. 22–8 (emphasis in the original). A similar conclusion on the agricultural periphery as the main site of future war has been reached by R. O'Connell, *Ride of the Second Horseman: The Birth and Death of War* (Oxford: Oxford University Press, 1995), pp. 241–2.

148 D. H. Rumsfeld, 'Transforming the Military', *Foreign Affairs*, 81, 3 (2002), pp. 20–32. See also B. Berkowitz, *The New Face of War* (New York: Free Press, 2002).

149 For such views, see E. N. Luttwak, 'Blood and Computers: The Crisis of Classic Military Power in Advanced Postindustrial Societies and the Scope of Technological Remedies', in Z. Maoz and A. Gat (eds), *War in a Changing World* (Ann Arbor: Michigan University Press, 2001), pp. 49–75; and C. Coker, *Humane Warfare* (London: Routledge, 2001).

150 Tilly, *Coercion, Capital, and European States, AD 990–1990* and Porter, *War and the Rise of the State*.

151 Hall, *Liberalism*, pp. 52–4.

152 Arrighi, *The Long Twentieth Century*, p. 11.

153 This was witnessed by the British mobilization crisis in 1914; see C. Trebilcock, 'War and the Failure of Industrial Mobilization: 1899 and 1914', in J. M. Winter (ed.), *War and Economic Development* (Cambridge: Cambridge University Press, 1975), pp. 139–64.

154 For a related, but different conclusion, see P. Bobbitt, *The Shield of Achilles: War, Peace, and the Course of History* (New York: Alfred A. Knopf, 2002).

11

THE CHANGING PROBABILITY
OF INTERSTATE WAR,
1816–1992

Marie T. Henehan and John Vasquez

Query

In recent years, there has been much attention focused on the possible waning of interstate war.[1] Much of this theorizing has resulted from the absence of a direct war among the major states, specifically the United States and the Soviet Union, during the Cold War.[2] While some have criticized the idea that the Cold War was a long peace, generally most scholars have accepted the absence of a war between the superpowers as an important indicator of peace at some level.[3] Instead, theoretical disagreement has turned on why such a long peace might have occurred. John Lewis Gaddis led the way in terms of outlining some possible answers.[4]

A good part of the debate focuses on whether the absence of a US–Soviet war was due to the efficacy of nuclear weapons or other factors, such as a repugnance toward total war brought about by the experience of the First World War (and reinforced by the Second), the ability to manage the nuclear rivalry through the creation of norms and rules, or the absence of the causal factors that bring about war.[5]

The first two positions (nuclear deterrence makes for peace and the experience of total war has resulted in the obsolescence of major war) both expect war to be on the wane, especially war among major states (see the chapters in this book). While predictions about the future always have a speculative quality and can only be tested by waiting to see whether they come true, it is possible to test the claim that major war has been on the wane by examining trends in warfare since 1816.

Several efforts have been attempted to do just this.[6] While the results differ somewhat depending on how war is (operationally) defined, what measures are employed and whether all wars or just those with major states on each side are examined, two trends appear to be suggested by the data: on the one hand, while the number of interstate wars in the post-1945 period is down from the number of wars in the 1914–1945 period, it is not down from the 1816–1914 period (the so-called 'one hundred years of peace').[7] This sort of analysis supports those who question the idea that warfare is permanently on the wane.

On the other hand, it is very clear that if one looks at the number of wars per nation-state, the number of interstate wars, as Holsti points out, has gone way down.[8] Whether one concludes, based on this sort of evidence, that war is on the wane turns on whether one thinks it is legitimate to count wars per nation-state, rather than wars in terms of their absolute number.

Quantitative scholars have in the past divided the number of wars or militarized disputes by system members (nation-states) on the assumption that more states make for more opportunities for war; therefore, to get an idea of the amount of warfare in a period, one must control for the number of states. In the post-World War II period, however, the assumption that more states would mean more war turned out not to be true. The independence of a number of colonies greatly increased the number of system members while the number of interstate wars seemed to remain about the same. Does this mean that war is on the wane? On a per nation-state basis, this is certainly the case, but in terms of the absolute number of all interstate wars, this conclusion is more difficult to infer.

In this analysis, we take a different tack in trying to answer the question in the hope that this approach might provide new evidence and a different perspective on the question. Instead of examining the number of wars, we look at the probability of war occurring in different historical periods during the post-Napoleonic era to see whether there is a trend toward the waning of major state warfare, as well as interstate war generally. To calculate the probability of war, we look at the probability that a given militarized interstate dispute will escalate to war.[9] Data on militarized interstate disputes (MIDs) and whether they escalate to war is available from the Correlates of War project.[10]

One way to see whether war is waning is to examine the overall (base) probability of a militarized dispute's escalating to war for 1816–1992 and compare it to the probability of war in the post-1945 period. War can be said to be on the wane or declining if the probability of MIDs escalating to war is significantly different in the periods before and after the Second World War.

Any single test of a proposition is always subject to problems of making inferences from limited evidence. If the above test shows that the probability of war in the post-1945 period is not significantly different from the earlier period or the period as a whole, then this would be serious evidence against the notion that war is waning. Conversely, if the test shows that war is, in fact, on the decline, this would not necessarily mean that war is on the wane, since there is an obvious counter-hypothesis to the one advocated by the waning-of-war proponents.

Those who maintain that war is on the wane argue that a fundamental political shift has occurred that has produced this effect and that it will be permanent or at least long lasting. Theoretically, we find this explanation troubling because it appears to be based on a progressive theory of history that sees history evolving to a time when all will be well and the major problems of humanity, including war, will be solved by human reason, science, and/or technology. Such theories reflect the assumptions and hopes of the Enlightenment.

Our view is closer to that of Foucault, who sees history as a set of discontinuities and not one of overall progress.[11] A counter-hypothesis, which we embrace, would suggest that there is no long-term secular trend, but that the probability of war changes over time depending on whether the factors promoting war or peace are present in a given era. If the latter is the case, then any trend in the post-1945 period might simply reflect a temporary decline in the probability of war. One way to see whether a recent decline in the probability of war is something new and fundamental (due to nuclear deterrence or the spread of democracy) and not simply one of a number of periods that have seen a reduction in the probability of war is to break down 1816–1992 into a set of periods based on some understanding of what would make for periods of peace.

A theory within peace research that helps identify such periods is the one that maintains that when major states attempt to establish rules of the game to manage their relations, the probability of war among them declines.[12] Using the judgment of historians, Wallensteen has provided a classification of periods from 1816 to 1976 in terms of whether major states have attempted to establish rules of the game.[13] His classification can be used to see whether when rules are present (which he refers to as states pursuing *universalist* policies) and when they are absent (which he refers to as states pursuing *particularist* policies), there is an effect on the probability of war. Since these rules are made by major states, it can be presumed that the rules will have the biggest impact on their own relations and the probability of their going to war with each other. Nevertheless, it is not unreasonable to expect the rules to have some spillover, if not direct relevance, to minor states, thereby having an effect on the probability of interstate war in general.

Thus, to address the question of whether war is waning, two sorts of tests will be conducted – first, one comparing the overall probability of an MID escalating to war in 1816–1945 with that in the post-1945 period, and second, a test comparing the probability of war in periods when rules are thought to be present and when they are absent. In order for the war-is-waning proposition to be accepted, at minimum, the post-1945 period must show a distinct decline in the probability of war. Even if it does, however, it may only reflect one of a number of periods that have seen a decline in war. If the latter proposition is true, then these periods of decline must be documented in the evidence. Identifying a series of periods when the probability of war declines suggests that any recent change in the probability may not be any more permanent than previous ones. While discussing the future always involves an element of speculation, what can be useful from such an analysis is an identification of the variables that are associated with a decline in the probability of war.

To this end, in addition to examining the probability of a militarized dispute escalating to war, the analysis will also introduce a control variable – the type of dispute: territorial, policy, or regime. Examining the type of dispute is important in that previous work has found that territorial disputes have a higher probability of going to war than disputes over regime or general foreign policy questions.[14]

We will begin by examining trends for interstate war in general, and then we will examine major state warfare (MM), as well as warfare between major and minor (Mm) states and war fought exclusively by minor states (mm). Major states will be distinguished from minor states by using the conventional identification in the Correlates of War project as to the status of states.[15] The following are defined as major states for the periods indicated: Austria (and later Austria-Hungary) (1816–1945), Prussia (and later Germany) (1816–1917, 1925–1945), Britain (1816–1992), Russia (1816–1916, 1922–1992), France (1816–1939, 1945–1992), Italy (1860–1945), Japan (1895–1945), United States (1898–1992), China (1950–1992). All other states are, by definition, minor states.[16] We have made no attempt to further refine the typology by distinguishing between regional powers and other minor states, mostly because such data are neither available nor easily created going back to 1816.[17]

Additional methodological questions will be addressed in the course of presenting the findings.

Findings on interstate war

Do the findings show that war is waning over time? To address this question, there must be some sort of benchmark. In a previous analysis, we found that the overall (base) probability of a dyadic militarized interstate dispute's (MID) escalating to war was 0.180 for the entire 1816–1992 period (464 dyadic disputes out of 2,576 escalate to war).[18] Of course, some types of disputes are much more war prone than others. As we expected, territorial disputes have a higher probability of going to war than the base probability and other types of disputes, with a probability of 0.324 (for territorial disputes) compared to 0.084 (for policy disputes), 0.123 (for regime disputes), and 0.224 (for 'other' disputes).[19] This overall base probability of war as well as the (conditional) probabilities of war for specific types of disputes can be used as a benchmark to see whether war is waning.

When the time period is split into two periods – 1816–1945 and 1946–1992 – some interesting results appear.[20] As shown in Table 11.1, the overall (base) probability of war in the 1816–1945 period is 0.296, but only 0.089 in the 1946–1992 period.[21] Of equal importance is that there is a sharp decline across the two periods in the probability that territorial disputes will escalate to war: from 0.475 (1816–1945) to 0.185 (1946–1992). While there is also a decline in the probability of policy and regime disputes escalating to war, these have comparatively low probabilities in each period – always below 0.170.[22]

The territorial explanation of war suggests additional inferences that can be made from Table 11.1 to assess the nature of this change in the probability of war.[23] It can be noted that in both periods (disregarding the small 'other' category) territorial disputes always have the highest probability of going to war – substantially higher than policy or regime disputes, as would be expected by the territorial explanation of war. This suggests that certain fundamental factors promoting the escalation of dyadic disputes to war have not changed between the periods. Further evidence supporting this conclusion is that, in both time periods, territorial disputes account for the bulk of the wars. In the early period, territorial disputes produce 65.4 percent

Table 11.1 The probability of interstate war: controlling for time period and type of dispute

	1816–1945		1946–1992	
		N* wars/N MIDs		N wars/N MIDs
Base	0.296	335/1,131	0.089	129/1,445
Territory	0.475	219/461	0.185	93/503
Policy	0.168	96/570	0.019	14/740
Regime	0.149	10/67	0.113	21/186
Other	0.303	10/33	0.063	1/16

Differences between time periods (1816 and 1946):

$$X^2 = 183.87 \quad p = 0.000$$

Differences among types of disputes within each period:

1816–1945	1946–1992
$X^2 = 151.65 \quad p = 0.000$	$X^2 = 126.89 \quad p = 0.000$

Note:
* Number of.

of the dyadic wars fought from 1816 to 1945 and in the post-1945 period they produce 72.1 percent of the dyadic wars, an even higher percentage.

Since territorial disputes still have the highest probability of going to war in the post-1945 period, it may be that what accounts for the reduction in the overall (base) probability of war is that the number of territorial disputes has been reduced in the second period; i.e. that the system has managed to keep a good number of territorial disputes off the agenda and this has made for more peace. This is in part the case. In the 1816–1945 period, territorial disputes constitute 40.8 percent of the total MIDs (461/1,131), but in the post-1945 period, territorial disputes constitute 34.8 percent of the total MIDs (503/1,445). While this is a noticeable shift, it is unlikely that this alone would reduce the probability of war for the period as a whole.

What seems to be going on in addition to reducing the number of territorial disputes is that they are handled in a way that actually makes them less likely to go to war. This decline in their probability of going to war from 0.475 to 0.185 has a large impact on making the overall (base) probability of war between the two periods go down. Thus, in the earlier period, there are 219 dyadic territorial MIDs that escalate to war out of a total of 1,131 MIDs, which constitutes 19.4 percent of the total MIDs. Conversely, in the later period, there are 93 dyadic territorial MIDs that escalate to war out of a total of 1,445 MIDs, which constitutes only 6.4 percent of the total MIDs. Something is happening in the post-1945 period that is making it less likely that territorial disputes will escalate to war, and this appears to be having a major impact on the reduction in the overall (base) probability of war going from 0.296 in 1816–1945 to 0.089 in 1946–1992.

Whatever the deeper reason for this shift, these numbers provide evidence that there has been a clear decline in the overall probability of war in the post-1945 period and a decline in the probability that the highly volatile territorial disputes will escalate to war. This evidence is consistent with the waning-of-war proposition and provides additional evidence for the proposition separate from simply counting the number of wars that break out per system member.

However, this difference between the two periods does not necessarily demonstrate a secular trend. It may be the case that the probability of war changes periodically and that this most recent period is simply one of many that have seen a decline in war and that it too will be superseded by a period with a high probability of war. To test this 'changing-probability-of-war' proposition, it is necessary to further break down the 1816–1945 period. If it is possible to find definite periods of peace that do not move in a secular trend, then the waning-of-war proposition will be undercut.[24] Conversely, if a definite secular trend is found, that will provide additional credence for the waning-of-war proposition.

Table 11.2 divides the entire 1816–1992 period into eight historical eras based on Wallensteen's (1984) classification of whether these periods were characterized by major states attempting to develop rules of the game to regulate and manage their relations: 1816–1848 (U)(Concert of Europe), 1849–1870 (P), 1871–1895 (U)(Bismarck's order), 1896–1918 (P), 1919–1932 (U)(League of Nations), 1933–1944 (P), 1945–1962 (P), 1963–1991 (U)(détente, end of the Cold War). The last year, 1992, is kept as the beginning of a separate period. The names of the periods are Wallensteen's and a (U) following a period indicates that Wallensteen sees this as a universalist period in which major states attempt to develop rules of the game, whereas a (P) indicates a particularist period.[25]

A perusal of Table 11.2 shows that the probability of war changes over time according to whether a period is labeled by Wallensteen as universalist or particularist. For example, in the first period – the Concert of Europe – the base probability of war is 0.151 (below the benchmark base probability for the entire 1816–1992 period of 0.180), but it then increases to 0.419 for the particularist period of 1849–1870, goes down again during Bismarck's order (1871–1895) to 0.118, up to 0.261 in the particularist period of 1896–1918, way down during the League of Nations era to 0.088, up during 1933–1944 to 0.470, but down during the particularist Cold War era to 0.104, and down further during the détente/end of the Cold War period to 0.087.

A logit analysis was run to see whether the probabilities were statistically significant from one period to another. The probability of war in a given period is always statistically significantly different from the probability of war in the period following it, with one exception. In other words, the difference between the probability of war for 1816–1848 (0.151) and the probability of war for 1849–1870 (0.419) is statistically significant. The one exception is for the two post-1945 periods. The probability of war in 1945–1962 of 0.104 is not statistically significantly different from the probability of war in 1963–1991 of 0.087.[26]

Table 11.2 shows that low probabilities of war are not new. They clearly follow Wallensteen's characterization of whether attempts have been made to establish rules of the game and norms among major states. The lowest probabilities of war

Table 11.2 The probability of interstate war: controlling for historical era (universalist vs. particularist) and type of dispute

1816–1848 (Universalist)		N* wars/N MIDs	1849–1870 (Particularist)		N wars/N MIDs
Base	0.151	14/93	Base	0.419	67/160
Territory	0.222	4/18	Territory	0.631	41/65
Policy	0.141	10/71	Policy	0.176	12/68
Regime	0.000	0/4	Regime	0.500	4/8
Other	—	—	Other	0.526	10/19
1871–1895 (Universalist)		N wars/N MIDs	1896–1918 (Particularist)		N wars/N MIDs
Base	0.118	14/119	Base	0.261	74/284
Territory	0.093	4/43	Territory	0.171	12/70
Policy	0.104	7/67	Policy	0.335	59/176
Regime	0.600	3/5	Regime	0.091	3/33
Other	0.000	0/4	Other	0.000	0/5
1919–1932 (Universalist)		N wars/N MIDs	1933–1944 (Particularist)		N wars/N MIDs
Base	0.088	13/148	Base	0.470	151/321
Territory	0.210	13/62	Territory	0.715	143/200
Policy	0.000	0/77	Policy	0.073	8/109
Regime	0.000	0/6	Regime	0.000	0/10
Other	0.000	0/3	Other	0.000	0/2
			1945–1962 (Particularist)		N wars/N MIDs
			Base	0.104	47/453
			Territory	0.170	39/229
			Policy	0.044	7/158
			Regime	0.016	1/62
			Other	0.000	0/4
1963–1991 (Universalist)		N wars/N MIDs			
Base	0.087	84/968			
Territory	0.208	56/269			
Policy	0.012	7/562			
Regime	0.160	20/125			
Other	0.083	1/12			

Note:
* Number of.

are associated with his universalist periods and the highest with his particularist periods. Indeed, all of the universalist periods have a probability of war lower than the benchmark base probability of war for the entire 1816–1992 of 0.180, and all but one of the particularist periods have a probability of war above that benchmark.[27]

Territorial disputes, however, are generally still the most likely to result in war, regardless of whether it is a universalist or particularist period. This is true in six of the eight periods. Regime disputes have the highest probability of going to war in 1871–1895, but the number of cases here is only five, with three going to war. Policy disputes have the highest probability of going to war in the World War I era.[28]

On the basis of these findings, periods of low probability of war should be more properly seen as intermittent historical periods during which certain norms have been worked out and prevail rather than some 'end of history' that has arrived. In this sense, it is more proper to speak of the changing probability of war rather than the waning of war per se. The probability of war has declined in the past only to return to high levels. The post-1945 period may simply be of this sort – a decline in the probability of war and not a permanent waning of war. One must remember that this is not the first time war has been seen as waning – one recalls the famous one hundred years of peace that ended in 1914 and the Wilsonian dream of the war to end all war.

The changing probability of war that has been documented in this analysis shows that there is no straightforward secular trend in the decline of war. The probability of war can go up and it can go down. If Wallensteen's measure of universalist and particularist periods is at all on the mark, at least some of this fluctuation is due to successful efforts to manage relations among major states.[29] On the basis of this hypothesis, it would be expected that the probability of war will decline when states have rules and norms (especially for dealing with territorial disputes) and will increase when they do not.[30] We now turn to see whether these general patterns are the same for major state warfare and other types of war.

Findings on major state war and other types of war

Most of the attention in the waning-of-warfare literature has focused on major state wars and not on war in general. Thus, recent events like the US war on Al Qaeda, the Taliban, and Iraq are not seen as an anomaly to the hypothesis because no major state is fighting against the US. Indeed, the absence of any major state taking the side of Afghanistan or willing to defend Iraq may be seen as evidence in favor of the idea that wars among major states have become undesirable. To test the waning-of-major-war hypothesis properly, it is necessary to restrict the sample to only disputes where major states are on each side.

Table 11.3 displays the findings on major–major (MM) disputes. The benchmark for this test, or base probability that they will escalate to war, is 0.246, which is a good deal higher than the 0.180 base probability for interstate war in general. This finding is consistent with previous research that shows that major states are more war prone than other states.[31] This implies that a waning of this type of war is going to be more difficult to achieve, and in a sense this is a more stringent test of the waning-of-war hypothesis.

As in the previous analysis, one way of testing whether war is declining is to split the sample at 1946. The probability of major state warfare before 1946 is 0.346

Table 11.3 The probability of war: controlling for time period, type of dispute,* and power status

Major–major (MM)

		1816–1992		N**MM wars/N MM MIDs
Base		0.246		60/244

		1816–1945		1946–1992	
		N MM wars/N MM MIDs			N MM wars/N MM MIDs
Base	0.346	53/153	0.077	7/91
Territory	0.617	29/47	0.100	3/30
Policy	0.228	23/101	0.065	3/46
Regime	0.000	0/3	0.067	1/15
Other	0.500	1/2	—	—

Major–minor (Mm)

		1816–1992		N Mm wars/N Mm MIDs
Base		0.206		214/1,040

		1816–1945		1946–1992	
		N Mm wars/N Mm MIDs			N Mm wars/N Mm MIDs
Base	0.282	172/610	0.098	42/430
Territory	0.560	116/207	0.284	25/88
Policy	0.142	51/358	0.022	6/268
Regime	0.053	2/38	0.159	11/69
Other	0.429	3/7	0.000	0/5

Minor–minor (mm)

		1816–1992		N mm wars/N mm MIDs
Base		0.147		190/1,292

		1816–1945		1946–1992	
		N mm wars/N mm MIDs			N mm wars/N mm MIDs
Base	0.299	110/368	0.087	80/924
Territory	0.357	74/207	0.169	65/385
Policy	0.198	22/111	0.012	5/426
Regime	0.308	8/26	0.088	9/102
Other	0.250	6/24	0.091	1/11

Notes:

  * Non-applicable cases not included.

** Number of.

while after 1945 it is only 0.077. This indicates a decline.[32] In fact, the drop in major state warfare is more dramatic than the decline of interstate war in general in that the probability of major war before 1946 is higher than the probability of war in general (0.346 vs. 0.296) and lower for the post-1945 period than for war in general (0.077 vs. 0.089). If MM disputes are generally more likely to escalate, but the incidence of escalation is decreasing, that is very significant.

As with war in general, Table 11.3 shows that there is a sharp decline in the probability of MM territorial disputes escalating to war, going from 0.617 in 1816–1945 to 0.100 in the post-1945 era. Nevertheless, in both periods, territorial disputes have the highest probability of going to war, disregarding the miscellaneous 'other' category. They also account for the most major state wars – 54.7 percent (29/53) in 1816–1945 – and tie with policy for the most wars (three out of seven each – 42.9 percent) in the period 1946–1992.[33]

Part of the reason that the post-1945 period is less war prone may be that there are simply fewer MM territorial disputes during this period – 30 after 1945 versus 47 before. However, since this is not a large difference, the major reason for the different base probabilities must be that territorial disputes that do occur simply do not escalate to war as frequently after 1945 as they do before, which implies that the territorial disputes that do occur between major states are handled in a manner that somehow reduces the probability of war.

Despite these findings that show a decline in major state warfare, this does not mean that major state war is permanently on the wane. This could be just a downturn that might subsequently give rise to an upturn. To see whether this is truly a trend, the two time periods need to be broken down into more refined categories. Table 11.4 does this for major state wars by employing the Wallensteen universalist and particularist periods used in Table 11.2. When this is done, it can be seen that periods of low probability of major state warfare have occurred in the past only to be followed by periods of high, and sometimes very high, major state warfare. There is a decline, then a rise, and then a decline, indicating that a rise could occur in the future in the next particularist period.

In the first period, 1816–1848, the probability of major state warfare is 0.125 (this is below the overall base probability of 0.246). In 1849–1870, the probability of major state warfare increases dramatically to 0.500; this is due to the wars of Italian and German Unification. This is followed by the extremely peaceful 1871–1895 era, with the probability of major war being only 0.059 (a probability lower than that in the Cold War up to 1962 and not very different from the probability of war in the détente/end of the Cold War era from 1963 to 1991). This period is then followed by the period leading up to the First World War. The League period, 1919–1932, does not have a single major state dispute that escalated to war, which gives it the lowest probability of major state war in the post-Napoleonic era. The League period also has the lowest number of major–major MIDs, with only nine. These two findings show that the League, although it was unable to prevent the Second World War, was successful for just over a decade, until the rise of militant regimes in Japan, Italy, and Germany. The 1930s and the period of the Second World War have one of the highest probabilities of major war, as expected. The Cold War bipolar period shows a sharp drop in the probability of major war, which drops even further after 1962 with the rise of détente (from 0.106 to 0.045).

As with the findings on interstate wars, the probability for major state warfare in a given period is generally statistically significantly different from the probability of war in the period following it. The only exception is again for the last two periods

Table 11.4 The probability of major state war (MM): controlling for historical era (universalist vs. particularist), type of dispute, and power status

	1816–1991		N* MM wars/ N MM MIDs**		
Base	0.246		60/244		

1816–1848 (Universalist)		N MM wars/ N MM MIDs	1849–1870 (Particularist)		N MM wars/ N MM MIDs
Base	0.125	2/16	Base	0.500	10/20
Territory	0.000	0/1	Territory	0.750	6/8
Policy	0.133	2/15	Policy	0.273	3/11
Regime	—	—	Regime	—	—
Other	—	—	Other	1.00	1/1

1871–1895 (Universalist)		N MM wars/ N MM MIDs	1896–1918 (Particularist)		N MM wars/ N MM MIDs
Base	0.059	1/17	Base	0.389	14/36
Territory	0.250	1/4	Territory	0.143	1/7
Policy	0.000	0/13	Policy	0.500	13/26
Regime	—	—	Regime	0.000	0/2
Other	—	—	Other	0.000	0/1

1919–1932 (Universalist)		N MM wars/ N MM MIDs	1933–1944 (Particularist)		N MM wars/ N MM MIDs
Base	0.000	0/9	Base	0.473	26/55
Territory	—	—	Territory	0.778	21/27
Policy	0.000	0/9	Policy	0.185	5/27
Regime	—	—	Regime	0.000	0/1
Other	—	—	Other	—	—

			1945–1962 (Particularist)		N MM wars/ N MM MIDs
			Base	0.106	5/47
			Territory	0.158	3/19
			Policy	0.133	2/15
			Regime	0.000	0/13
			Other	—	—

1963–1991 (Universalist)		N MM wars/ N MM MIDs			
Base	0.045	2/44			
Territory	0.000	0/11			
Policy	0.032	1/31			
Regime	0.500	1/2			
Other	—	—			

Notes:

 * Number of.

** There are 30 MIDs in 1992: 20 between minor states, 10 between major–minor, and 0 between major states.

starting respectively in 1945 and 1963, where the probabilities of major state warfare (0.106 and 0.045) are not significantly different. However, this conclusion holds only for the first and second periods (1816 and 1849) if the 0.10 significance level is taken as the benchmark, since $p = 0.063$.[34]

None of this shows an overall secular decline in the probability of war. There have been periods with lower probabilities of major state war before. What it does show is that the particularist Cold War period has the lowest probability of war among the particularist periods, reaching the low levels of war found in the universalist periods. Nonetheless, two of the three pre-1945 universalist periods have lower probabilities of major state warfare. Whatever it is that makes for a reduced probability of major state warfare in the bipolar Cold War era (through 1962) is not as potent as whatever reduced the probability of major war in 1871–1895 and 1919–1932.

Table 11.4, like Table 11.2, supports the changing-probability-of-war hypothesis over the waning-of-war hypothesis. It also shows that there is not a real difference in the pattern of major state warfare compared to interstate warfare in general. Declines and increases of each go hand in hand, which is not surprising. To the extent that one has confidence in Wallensteen's classification of universalist vs. particularist periods, the changing probability of war can be a function of the extent to which major states attempt to establish rules of the game and norms to manage their relations.[35] At any rate, this is a hypothesis worthy of further investigation, once a better measure of rules of the game can be developed.

One preliminary way to investigate this hypothesis is to compare the Cold War period of 1945–1962, which is generally seen as not having a common set of rules of the game shared by the US and the USSR, with the détente/end of the Cold War period, which is seen as trying to establish and live by such rules. The Cold War era has a probability of major state war of 0.106 and the détente/end of the Cold War period, which is characterized by attempts to make rules to manage relations, has a probability of war of 0.045. While the difference in these two probabilities is not statistically significant, they are in the right direction in that the universalist period is still lower.[36] This finding suggests that dividing the long Cold War peace into two eras – one with clear rules and one without – is consistent with the hypothesis that rules and norms make a difference.

Table 11.5 shows that wars between major and minor states, as well as minor state wars, also show a changing pattern in the probability of war rather than a waning-of-war pattern.[37] Interestingly, during the bipolar Cold War era, major–minor (Mm) disputes were the most likely to result in war (0.128 (for Mm) vs. 0.106 (for MM) and 0.084 (for mm)).

Nevertheless, despite the clear thrust of the findings, there is some slight evidence in favor of the waning-of-war hypothesis, and this is portrayed in Table 11.6. This table presents the base probability of war and the conditional probability of war for territorial disputes for each of the universalist and particularist periods. What is most interesting is that the probability of war seems to decline generally for universalist periods, but it goes down and up for particularist periods.

Table 11.5 The probability of major–minor and minor–minor war: controlling for historical era (universalist vs. particularist) and power status*

Major–minor (Mm)

1816–1991

Base probability		N* Mm wars/N Mm MIDs
0.208		214/1,030

Universalist periods			Particularist periods		
Base probability	N Mm wars/N Mm MIDs		Base probability	N Mm wars/N Mm MIDs	
0.175	10/57	1849–1870	0.464	32/69	
0.102	5/49	1896–1918	0.212	36/170	
0.075	5/67	1933–1944	0.427	82/192	
		1945–1962	0.128	23/179	
0.085	21/247				

(Universalist rows: 1816–1848, 1871–1895, 1919–1932, 1963–1991)

Minor–minor (mm)

1816–1991

Base probability		N mm wars/N mm MIDs
0.149		190/1,272

Universalist periods			Particularist periods		
Base probability	N mm wars/N mm MIDs		Base probability	N mm wars/N mm MIDs	
0.100	2/20	1849–1870	0.352	25/71	
0.151	8/53	1896–1918	0.308	24/78	
0.111	8/72	1933–1944	0.581	43/74	
		1945–1962	0.084	19/227	
0.090	61/677				

(Universalist rows: 1816–1848, 1871–1895, 1919–1932, 1963–1991)

Notes:
* Table deletes missing non-applicable 'issues', also dropped in Table 11.3.
** Number of.

Table 11.6 Trends over time

Interstate war		
Universalist	Base probability	Conditional probability of territorial MID
1816–1848	0.151	0.222
1871–1895	0.118	0.093
1919–1932	0.088	0.210
1963–1991	0.087	0.208
Particularist		
1849–1870	0.419	0.631
1896–1918	0.261	0.171
1933–1944	0.470	0.715
1945–1962	0.104	0.170
Major–major		
Universalist	Base probability	Conditional probability of territorial MID
1816–1848	0.125	0.000
1871–1895	0.059	0.250
1919–1932	0.000	—
1963–1991	0.045	0.000
Particularist		
1849–1870	0.500	0.750
1896–1918	0.389	0.143
1933–1944	0.473	0.778
1945–1962	0.106	0.158
Major–minor		
Universalist	Base probability	Conditional probability of territorial MID
1816–1848	0.175	0.250
1871–1895	0.102	0.067
1919–1932	0.075	0.250
1963–1991	0.085	0.257
Particularist		
1849–1870	0.464	0.733
1896–1918	0.212	0.176
1933–1944	0.427	0.727
1945–1962	0.128	0.321
Minor–minor		
Universalist	Base probability	Conditional probability of territorial MID
1816–1848	0.100	0.222
1871–1895	0.151	0.083
1919–1932	0.111	0.190
1963–1991	0.090	0.211
Particularist		
1849–1870	0.352	0.481
1896–1918	0.308	0.174
1933–1944	0.581	0.667
1945–1962	0.084	0.117

Table 11.6 shows that there is a downward trend in the probability of interstate war, in general, during the universalist periods, going from 0.151 to 0.118 to 0.088 to 0.087 for each of the four periods.[38] No such trend emerges with particularist periods or territorial disputes. This indicates that rules of the game may have been effective in lowering the probability of war, but they have never been able to eliminate war, or, put another way, these rules themselves have waned and with their waning, war has arisen. Even so, the comparison across universalist periods shows that the two most recent periods seem to have been more effective in muting war.

The findings on major wars are a little more uneven, but they too show that universalist periods have a downward trend that might be consistent with a waning-of-war hypothesis (at least across universalist periods). The first period, the Concert of Europe era, has the highest probability of major state disputes escalating to war among universalist periods – 0.125 – but this is low compared to particularist periods. This then goes down to 0.059 in 1871–1895, and then down to 0.00 in the League period. This drop to 0 makes it impossible for the trend to continue to decline, and it goes up to 0.045 in the détente/end of the Cold War period, although it can be pointed out that this is still lower than the previous universalist period before the League of Nations era (i.e. 1871–1895).[39]

A comparison of the (conditional) probabilities of territorial disputes among major states escalating to war during universalist periods provides some insight as to why and how major states have lowered their probability of going to war. For three of the four universalist periods (1816, 1919, 1963), the probability of major state territorial disputes resulting in war was reduced to 0.00. For the League of Nations period, major states managed to avoid all territorial disputes amongst themselves. Territorial disputes in the other two periods (1816, 1871) were also infrequent (one and four, respectively).[40] The thrust of these findings suggests that a main reason for the lowered probability of major warfare may have something to do with keeping territorial disputes off the agenda. Indeed, there are only 25 territorial MIDs in the 101 universalist years compared to 61 territorial MIDs in the 75 particularist years.[41]

While keeping territorial disputes off the agenda is an important reason for the low probability of war, it is not the only reason. Learning how to manage those territorial disputes that cannot be kept off is also important.[42] The analysis shows that major states have been very successful in managing the territorial disputes they have in universalist periods. Only 1 of 25 of these territorial disputes goes to war (0.040) compared to 31 of the 61 territorial disputes (0.508) in particularist periods.

Further evidence on the efficacy of universalist periods managing territorial disputes between majors can be seen by comparing Table 11.2 with Table 11.4. Table 11.2 shows that for interstate war in general, in three of the four universalist periods and in three of the four particularist periods, territorial disputes are the most war prone. However, Table 11.4 shows that for major–major disputes, while territorial issues are the most war prone for three of the four particularist periods (1896–1918 being the exception), this is the case for only one of the four universalist periods. Furthermore, the probabilities are generally all low, except for the one case of regime disputes, with a very small N (one war/two disputes = 0.500).

The findings on major–minor disputes that escalated to war during universalist periods also show a downward trend. The probability of war goes from 0.175 to 0.102 to 0.075 to 0.085.[43] The last is the only deviation and probably indicates the absence of a decline, rather than an increase. The findings on minor state wars during universalist periods are the most inconsistent with the idea of a waning of war. Here, there is a downward trend only if one ignores the first period.[44] The classic Concert of Europe period greatly muted the probability of minor state wars. These low levels were not attained again until the League period.[45]

It should also be noted that the above findings suggest that a downward trend in the probability of major war and interstate war in general across universalist periods long pre-dates the nuclear era, so that nuclear deterrence should not be seen as the reason for the waning of major war.[46] Likewise, these findings suggest that a world of peace does not require a large number of democratic states.

Conclusion

The findings in this analysis have shown that, since 1945, there has been a decline in the probability of dyadic militarized interstate disputes (MIDs) escalating to war. The overall probability of MIDs escalating after 1945 is much lower than before. This is consistent with the waning-of-war proposition, but the analysis also shows that there have been other periods in the post-Napoleonic era during which the probability of war has declined only to increase again. The same has been found to hold for the highly war prone territorial disputes. These findings suggest that a more accurate description of the 1816–1992 period is to see it as one with changing probabilities of war, rather than one with an overall secular trend culminating in the waning of war.

Nevertheless, while there is no secular trend, some evidence has been uncovered from examining the probability of war that is not inconsistent with the waning-of-war proposition. This is evidence that shows that within universalist periods that have occurred, there has been a downward trend in the overall probability of interstate war in general since 1816, and, with relatively minor exceptions, in major state warfare as well. Unfortunately, these universalist periods of rules have always been superseded by periods in which the rules created by major states decay and war occurs. From this perspective, whether the current absence of war, especially among the major states, will last depends upon whether norms and rules remain shared.

Acknowledgment

Our thanks to Raimo Väyrynen for valuable comments and to Chris Leskiw for configuring the data. The research reported in this article was supported by the National Science Foundation (grant #SES-9818557). The sole responsibility for the analysis remains ours alone.

Notes

1 See J. Mueller, *Retreat from Doomsday: The Obsolescence of Major War* (New York: Basic Books, 1989); K. J. Holsti, *The State, War, and the State of War* (Cambridge: Cambridge University Press, 1996).

2 J. L. Gaddis, *The Long Peace: Inquiries into the History of the Cold War* (New York: Oxford University Press, 1987).

3 See M. Brecher and J. Wilkenfeld, 'International Crises and Global Instability: The Myth of the "Long Peace"', in C. Kegley (ed.), *The Long Postwar Peace* (New York: HarperCollins, 1991), pp. 85–104; and J. D. Singer, 'Peace in the Global System: Displacement, Interregnum, or Transformation?', in C. Kegley (ed.), *The Long Postwar Peace* (New York: HarperCollins, 1991), pp. 56–84.

4 Gaddis, *The Long Peace: Inquiries into the History of the Cold War*.

5 On nuclear weapons, see K. N. Waltz, *The Spread of Nuclear Weapons: More May Be Better*, Adelphi Paper No. 171 (London: Institute for Strategic Studies, 1981); M. van Creveld's chapter in this volume, Chapter 4; see also J. Mearsheimer, 'Back to the Future: Instability in Europe After the Cold War', *International Security*, 15 (1990), pp. 5–56. On the effect of the world wars, see J. Mueller, *Retreat from Doomsday*. On norms and rules, see A. L. George, *Managing U.S.–Soviet Rivalry: Problems of Crisis Prevention* (Boulder: Westview Press, 1983). On the absence of factors causing war, see A. F. K. Organski and J. Kugler, *The War Ledger* (Chicago: University of Chicago Press, 1980); J. A. Vasquez, 'The Deterrence Myth', in C. Kegley (ed.), *The Long Postwar Peace* (New York: HarperCollins, 1991), pp. 205–23.

6 See Holsti, *The State, War, and the State of War*; Holsti's chapter in this volume, Chapter 6; M. R. Sarkees and J. D. Singer, 'The Correlates of War Warsets: The Totality of War', paper presented at the annual meeting of the International Studies Association, Chicago, 21–24 February 2001; P. Wallensteen's chapter in this volume, Chapter 3.

7 See J. Vasquez, 'Mapping the Probability of War and Analyzing the Possibility of Peace: The Role of Territorial Disputes, Presidential Address to the Peace Science Society (International)', *Conflict Management and Peace Science*, 18 (Fall 2001), Figures 1 & 2, pp. 159–60.

8 Holsti, *The State, War, and the State of War*, pp. 21–8.

9 All probabilities reported in this study are actual probabilities and not predicted probabilities derived from logit models. The probabilities are derived by dividing the number of militarized interstate disputes that go to war by the total number of militarized interstate disputes. If any party in the MID goes to war, then each dyadic dispute is coded as having 'resulted in' a war escalation.

10 See D. M. Jones, S. A. Bremer and J. D. Singer, 'Militarized Interstate Disputes, 1816–1992: Rationale, Coding Rules, and Empirical Patterns', *Conflict Management and Peace Science*, 15 (Fall 1996), pp.163–213 for a description of the data.

11 M. Foucault, *The Archaeology of Knowledge* (New York: Pantheon Books, 1972).

12 P. Wallensteen, 'Universalism vs. Particularism: On the Limits of Major Power Order', *Journal of Peace Research*, 21, 3 (1984), pp. 243–57; see also C. W. Kegley, Jr and G. Raymond, 'Alliance Norms and War: A New Piece in an Old Puzzle', *International Studies Quarterly*, 26 (1982), pp. 572–95 and C. Kegley, Jr and G. Raymond, *When Trust Breaks Down* (Columbia: University of South Carolina Press, 1990); G. A. Raymond, 'International Norms: Normative Orders and Peace', in J. A. Vasquez (ed.), *What Do We Know about War?* (Lanham: Rowman & Littlefield, 2000), pp. 281–97; A. L. George, *Managing U.S.–Soviet Rivalry*; R. W. Mansbach and J. A. Vasquez, *In Search of Theory: A New Paradigm for Global Politics* (New York: Columbia University Press, 1981); J. A. Vasquez, *The War Puzzle* (Cambridge: Cambridge University Press, 1993), ch. 8.

13 Wallensteen, 'Universalism vs. Particularism'.
14 See J. Vasquez and M. Henehan, 'Territorial Disputes and the Probability of War, 1815–1992', *Journal of Peace Research*, 38, 2 (2001), pp. 123–38.
15 J. D. Singer, S. Bremer and J. Stuckey, 'Capability Distribution, Uncertainty, and Major Power War', in B. Russett (ed.), *Peace, War, and Numbers* (Beverly Hills: Sage, 1972), p. 22.
16 Some have argued that Germany and Japan should be elevated to the status of major states beginning in 1990 because of their economic capability. Since our analyses end in 1992, we have not seen the need to make this change, nor would such a minor change affect the statistical analysis.
17 One must also be wary of unconsciously classifying states as regional powers because they have fought in wars – e.g. Israel and Egypt, Iran and Iraq, India and Pakistan. While this is also a problem with major states, the problem is more manageable and the existing classification widely accepted.
18 Vasquez and Henehan, 'Territorial Disputes and the Probability of War', Table IB, p.128.
19 See ibid., pp. 127–31, for details.
20 The year 1946 is an obvious year to pick to capture the post-World War II period since it comes after the end of World War II and before 1947, which is often seen as the beginning of the Cold War. We have also kept 1992 in this aggregate comparison, even though the Cold War ends in 1991. When we later examine the Cold War specifically (in Table 11.2), we separate 1992 out.
21 As can be seen in Table 11.1, the difference in the probability of war in the two periods is statistically significant at the 0.000 level. The Yule's Q (not reported in the table) is –0.622.
22 'Other' has a higher probability, but a very small N (number of cases). Since it is a miscellaneous category, we do not think much emphasis should be placed on it. Elsewhere we present a detailed analysis of 'other' disputes. See Vasquez and Henehan, 'Territorial Disputes and the Probability of War', footnote 9, p. 129.
23 See Vasquez, *The War Puzzle*, ch. 4 for a discussion of the territorial explanation of war.
24 If one does not think that Wallensteen has validly measured the presence of rules of the game, his classification can still be used, since all that is needed to falsify one of the two propositions is any reasonable historical classification that shows either a change in the probability of war or a secular trend. Wallensteen, 'Universalism vs. Particularism'.
25 We have kept Wallensteen's demarcation of the Cold War period beginning at 1945, although we earlier split the period at 1946. Wallensteen, 'Universalism vs. Particularism'.
26 The logit analysis was run with robust standard errors, a dummy variable for each period, and the revision type variable (with non-applicable cases dropped) included in the model; 1992 was dropped. This resulted in 2,546 cases. The Z scores for each of the coupled periods (only start dates are given) are: 1816 & 1849 (4.029), 1849 & 1871 (–5.235), 1871 & 1896 (3.421), 1896 & 1919 (–4.898), 1919 & 1933 (6.969), 1933 & 1945 (–10.570), 1945 & 1963 (0.123 n.s.).
27 An analysis of the probability of war comparing all universalist periods with particularist periods (including 1992 as part of a universalist period) shows that the (conditional) probability of dyadic disputes escalating to war in universalist periods is 0.092 and for particularist periods 0.278. Interestingly, the one particularist period below the benchmark is the Cold War 1945–1962 period.
28 This is a function of the fact that the July 1914 dispute that escalates to World War I is coded in the data as a policy dispute between Austria-Hungary and Serbia.
29 Wallensteen, 'Universalism vs. Particularism'.
30 See Vasquez, *The War Puzzle*, ch. 8.
31 S. Bremer, 'National Capabilities and War Proneness', in J. D. Singer (ed.), *The*

Correlates of War II (New York: Free Press, 1980), pp. 57–82; S. Bremer, 'Who Fights Whom, When, Where, and Why?' in J. Vasquez, *What Do We Know about War?* (Lanham: Rowman & Littlefield, 2000), pp. 23–36.

32 The difference in the probability of major state warfare in the two periods is statistically significant at the 0.000 level; the Yule's Q = –0.728.

33 Table 11.3 also shows that major–minor and minor–minor territorial disputes have the highest probability of going to war in each period, but that this probability also declines quite a bit in the post-1945 era.

34 As before, a logit analysis was run with robust standard errors, a dummy variable for each period and the revision type variable (with non-applicable cases dropped) included in the model. This resulted in 244 MM cases. At times, 1919–1932 was dropped because it had no wars and logit drops perfect predictors. Also 1992 was dropped. The Z scores for each of the periods are: 1816 & 1849 (1.862, $p = 0.063$), 1849 & 1871 (–2.507), 1871 & 1896 (2.357), 1896 & 1919 (1919 perfect predictor, $p=0.000$), 1919 & 1933 (1919 perfect predictor, $p=0.000$), 1933 & 1945 (–3.464), 1945 & 1963 (0.994 n.s.).

35 Wallensteen, 'Universalism vs. Particularism'.

36 This finding also holds for interstate wars in general in that the probability of war is 0.104 in the Cold War era and 0.087 in the détente/end of the Cold War period (see Table 11.2), but again, the difference between the two probabilities of war is not statistically significant.

37 The difference in the probability of war in a given period from that following it for both Mm and mm is always statistically significant with the exception of the two post-1945 periods. For mm the difference between the 1871 and 1896 periods is significant at the 0.085 level.

38 The evidence for a trend is only slight in that each drop in the probability of war is not statistically significant. Thus, the first universalist period listed is not significantly different from the second period; i.e. the difference between 0.151 and 0.118 is not statistically significant. Nevertheless, the probabilities do decline. More solid evidence for a trend is evinced by the fact that the first period, starting in 1816, has a significantly different probability of war from the 1919 period (Z = 2.056, $p=0.04$) and the 1963 period (Z = –3.345, $p=0.001$). The Z scores for the universalist periods that follow each other are: 1816 & 1871 (–1.041), 1871 & 1919 (–0.966), 1919 & 1963 (0.545) (all n.s.). The logit run to generate these findings is the same as discussed previously.

39 The difference in the probability of war between 1816 & 1871 is not statistically significant (Z = 0.832), but those between 1871 & 1919 and 1919 & 1963 are ($p=0.000$). The difference between 1816 & 1919 is also statistically significant, but the difference between 1816 & 1963 is not.

40 The 1963–1991 period had 11 territorial disputes of a total of 44 MIDs – 25 percent.

41 These are respectively 0.248 territorial MID per universalist year and 0.813 territorial MID per particularist year. If one examines the percentage of territorial MIDs of the total MIDs, it is still the case that universalist periods have fewer territorial MIDs. In universalist periods, 29.07 percent (25/86) of the MIDs are over territory, whereas in particularist periods 38.61 percent (61/158) of the MIDs are over territory.

42 On the basis of these findings, each of these periods would make for interesting case studies in terms of trying to determine how territorial issues were handled by major states and how the general rules of the game they established were related to the main territorial issues of the time.

43 Again, none of these are statistically significant differences; the 1816 period is significantly different from the 1919 period (p=0.043).

44 None of these are statistically significant differences, and the 1816 period is not significantly different from the 1919 and 1963 periods.

45 Table 11.6 can also be used to get an idea of how well the various universalist 'regimes'

did in managing war among the different types of actors. The Concert of Europe period, for example, seems to do quite well in managing major state and especially minor state disputes, but not major–minor disputes. The last, however, may not have been the intent of the Concert. Rather it seems to be the case that the rules of the game of the Concert were aimed at permitting major states to fight wars against minor states without having to fear that a major state might come to the aid of the minor state. The League of Nations 'regime', by contrast, greatly reduces this type of war (cf. the Bismarckian period and détente, as well as the particularist bipolar Cold War era).

46 See van Creveld's chapter in this volume, Chapter 4.

CONCLUSION

Raimo Väyrynen

War, in one form or another, has been ubiquitous in human history. However, due to the existence of several modes of warfare and their fluctuations over time, it is very difficult to discover any robust historical trends in warfare. At a minimum, one should specify the type of violence one is looking at, i.e. whether the focus is on major-power wars, regional war complexes, external interventions, militarized disputes, civil wars, or large-scale communal violence. In addition, there is a need to distinguish between territorial, dynastic, religious, economic, and other types of war. The trends in these different types of war and violence are obviously pointing in different directions and there may even be trade-offs among them. Thus, it is argued in this volume that we may be witnessing the demise of the Prussian mode of warfare (which does not mean, of course, the end of all kinds of warfare).

This volume deliberately deals with major wars, and more specifically major-power wars, which involve the leading powers of the international, and in some cases regional systems. Such wars are large-scale political convulsions in international relations, produce extensive casualties, and usually have major political consequences. In fact, major-power or global wars are often seen as the birth pains of a new international order whose stability depends a lot on the strategic choices made by the victor(s) of the war. Historically, convulsive wars have expressed, however, different interests; the religious wars of the seventeenth century are quite different from the naval-trade wars of the eighteenth century which again can hardly be compared with the total wars of the twentieth century, or what seems to be an era of fragmented wars in the early twenty-first century.

There has been a tendency in the scholarship on war to trace historical trends that prove either the amelioration or the deterioration of the situation concerning warfare. We should have learned so far that general theories or statistical patterns are incapable of providing any consistent picture of warfare in the past and present, and even less in future international relations. Neither the long-term economic cycles, power-transition theories, nor perspectives on systemic crises are able to provide a robust and consistent explanation of the occurrence of major-power wars. These approaches are, at best, heuristic devices and approximations of reality by which we can try to make sense of the complexity of political and military history.

There is no consensus on whether the hypothesis about the historical fluctuations in the frequency of war or its waning is statistically more solid. Any conclusion about the rise, decline, or waxing of major-power wars hinges on the impact of the structural, economic, and normative background factors. This view departs from the notion that war itself is a (semi-)permanent instrument of statecraft in the conduct of international politics. War cannot be wished away simply by imposing a legal ban on it or condemning it in moral terms. In order to create a more peaceful world, the antecedents of war have to be modified. Depending on individual views, peace is the work either of justice, responsibility, or power. In other words, a more lasting peace has to be found from outside the peace–war nexus itself.

There is no single and simple strategy for doing this. Deep changes in the structure of international relations may produce conditions for more peace and stability, but they may also be conducive to the outbreak of new major-power war, sooner or later. In fact, a major contestation in the study of major-power war is taking place today between the structuralists and the pluralists. The structuralist approach refers primarily to those scholars who view political trends and events as results of the shifting power relations among states, in particular major powers. This approach has several strands, dubbed for instance as offensive and defensive realisms, which hold, in effect, quite different views on the relations between the polarities of power and other structural conditions, and the likelihood of major-power war. Moreover, there is the traditional realist approach that, while not neglecting structural power factors, assigns a greater role to the nature of foreign policy, i.e. benign and malign forms of statecraft, in accounting for major war.

The pluralist perspective is perhaps even more diverse. What unites its supporters is the view that to explain war, one has to consider multiple factors on different levels of analysis. In other words, war results, among other factors, from politics, technology, and culture. For instance, the Kantian view is pluralistic rather than singular in nature. It argues that to end war one has to combine moral improvement, domestic political transformation, and a commitment to international rules. Compared with the structuralist theories, the main missing factor in the Kantian analysis is the lack of an explicit theory concerning the balance of power.

The contributors to this volume are certainly aware of the importance of the structural conditions in determining the likelihood of international war. However, they seem to hold a consensus that the atrocities associated with the two world wars of the twentieth century, and other major wars, have not been results of a single structural logic. Instead, they have been consequences of ill-informed decisions and, in some cases, perverse ideologies and policies that have been chosen by unresponsive, even evil leaders.

In a larger historical context, peace is on the march but its progress is by no means assured. The 'long peace' of the nineteenth century did not last, but ended through a slow process of erosion. Now it is legitimate to ask whether another 'long peace', since World War II, can last or whether a relentless power struggle will ensue between, say, China and the United States. In fact, the failure or success of the accommodation of China to the evolving structure of international relations will be a key test of the hypothesis on the major-power peace. The reason for focusing on China is that, among the major powers, it has by far the most rapidly growing economy, non-democratic political leadership, and the historical ambition to be a center nation.

The growing degree of globalization in the world economy – including the gradual integration of China, India, and Russia in it – is an omen for a lesser likelihood for wars between major powers. However, the lessons from the gold standard before World War I suggest that even a tightly integrated world economy cannot provide for peace if it leaves the majority of people outside its benefits or creates an economic straitjacket that generates a political backlash. In this sense, peace is the work of equitable and flexible global governance that helps to redistribute the results of global economic integration to the hands of responsive governments and the citizens supporting them.

A main conclusion from the contributions to this volume is that institutional and normative changes make a difference. The gradual institutionalization of international law and the cascade of international norms, proscribing war and favoring peace, have changed international relations, perhaps for good. It is easy to both belittle and overrate the importance of 'soft' factors in determining peace and war. It is clear that international institutions and norms are not yet robust enough to provide an absolute barrier to the use of military force among the major powers. It is equally clear that the instruments embedded in the institutions of collective security and international law can fail, and may even be likely to fail, if a serious threat to international peace arises. Yet, international institutions have gained new relevance by setting up new normative standards, negotiation channels, and communication patterns.

In this context, one should single out for analysis both regional and global institutions. There is a trend toward the building of new regional security structures in the European Union, the African Union, the ASEAN, and elsewhere. These regional arrangements have different functions in terms of whether their main task is to keep peace within or outside the region; the EU deals with crises outside the region, while the AU has an intra-regional focus. In both cases, regional organizations seem, however, to be replacing some of the functions exercised previously by the United Nations.

It is important to keep in mind, though, that global and regional institutions are seldom stark alternatives to each other; in many crises, the possibilities of the United Nations to act are limited, partly because of the constraints imposed by the leading member states, and therefore the regional bodies have to bear the brunt. On the other hand, regional bodies often need the legitimation provided by the UN Security Council. Even single powers may find that, perhaps against their will, the global consent provided by the Council is a condition for their own effective action. This reflects, of course, a key dilemma in current international relations: national power matters a lot, but without a reasonable international consent it may turn out to be ineffective and even counterproductive.

However, one should focus more on the normative than instrumental aspects of international change. It is possible to argue that a new culture of peace is gradually emerging and spreading. It is not necessarily a traditional pacifist culture, but more ingrained in the prevalent democratic, institutional, and commercial practices. A domestic key to peace is to avoid the concurrent centralization of economic and political power in the hands of any one group in society. Decentralization of relevant power resources within a legitimate and stable political system is the best predictor of peaceful policies both at home and abroad.

It is a somewhat open question whether the centralization of economic or political resources is more conducive to war. Politics starts the war, but it cannot be waged effectively unless the government is able to capture the necessary financial resources to fund the troops and their weapons. Historically, the financial system seems to have been holding the keys to peace and war. Governments have usually needed either the consent of the parliament or help from private financial institutions to be able to sustain the sinews of war. Of course, they do not always deny their support, but choose to support war for ideological and other political reasons.

This perspective applies primarily to the established capitalist–democratic societies that have developed a commercial civilization and democratic practice that is unlikely to deteriorate into a violent civil strife. If these characteristics are shared by several states, it is realistic to believe that any major war among them is highly unlikely. The obvious conclusion from this stance is that while peace necessarily has an international aspect, it ultimately starts at home.

This observation can be challenged, though, by referring to weapons of mass destruction that may, moreover, be proliferating rather than being contained within a handful of privileged countries. There are two contrasting perspectives on nuclear weapons in the context of the debate on the possibility of major-power war. In one view, they are regarded as the ultimate weapon of destruction that nuclear weapon powers can use against each other in the event of a war among them. While the risk of nuclear war may be minimal today, it still is there as an existential possibility. In effect, the risk of nuclear war may be more likely among the regional powers, especially in South Asia and the Korean Peninsula, than the adversaries of the Cold War era. The unquantifiable factor is the potential access of terrorist organizations to various weapons of mass destruction.

The second perspective recognizes the existence of risk, but it puts more emphasis on the deterring and stabilizing effects of nuclear weapons in major-power relations. These two accounts may not be as contradictory as they look; nuclear weapons have no doubt had a deterring and preventing effect, not only in the US–Soviet relations of the past, but also in today's relations between India and Pakistan. Nuclear weapons are, however, a fragile instrument of peace and, therefore, cannot be relied upon as a dependable strategy for peace. There are even well-founded arguments that nuclear weapons, and deterrence built on them, have been a lesser factor in stabilizing great-power relations than, say, structural bipolarity or internal constraints.

In the North, interstate peace is due to the spread of market civilization and political democracy, rooted primarily in domestic conditions. In the South, the risk of violence is associated, in turn, with the lack of political power-sharing institutions, the absence of a predictable judiciary, and the prevalence of an imperfect, and even predatory economic system. In many a developing country, violence is endemic; it is practiced by various entrepreneurs of violence, ranging from black market dealers through criminal thugs and mercenaries to ethnic clan leaders. Their violent and predatory actions produce lasting political and economic instability and human suffering, even complex humanitarian emergencies. The issue for the international community, and even more so for the national societies, is how to deal with the 'remnants of war' as we have come to know them in international relations.

Various forms of communal violence are a real risk to the life and limb of many ordinary people in the South, but there is little danger that they will lead to big interstate wars and even less to a war between major powers. It is noted in this volume that especially in Africa and Latin America interstate wars have been rare and, if they have broken out, the result has not been a war of conquest or destruction of a sovereign country. It is even argued that the norm respecting territorial sovereignty is now more firmly rooted in international practice than perhaps ever before in history. For this reason, demands for a more active policy of humanitarian intervention have largely fallen on deaf ears.

The low probability of the escalation of local violence into major wars is, in part, due to the fact that the global peripheries have, in the post Cold War world, become increasingly disentangled from the relations between great powers. This suggestion holds some interest as in the past both wars and revolutions have had a propensity to spread from one country to another. Are we now perhaps entering a period in which the old patterns of emulation and imitation do not work as effectively as before? No doubt negative events in one country are reflected in neighboring countries, as we have witnessed, for instance, in Central America and West Africa, but these linkages are a far cry from the kind of 'macroproliferation' of ideologies that we witnessed in the 1930s or during the height of the Cold War.

An obvious counterargument to the claim that international peace is in the offing is that the leading powers, especially the United States, have recently been actively engaged in international military actions as part of the war on terrorism. The interventions in Afganistan and Iraq, supported by the 'coalitions of the willing', are a new face of great-power behavior, but they do not amount to a war between major powers. While there has been strong political opposition to the US intervention in Iraq, there have been no signs of international military measures against its policy. On the contrary, there has been a gradual, although somewhat reluctant evolution toward burden-sharing among the members of NATO to prop up the internal security in Iraq.

Consensus-building is perhaps the most difficult art of politics, including academic politics. Any queries concerning the future of war are, almost by definition, contested. This volume does not pretend to be able to predict the future. On the contrary, we recognize that many issues remain open, including even the definition and measurement of major war. However, as soon as we restrict the inquiry to a war between major powers, we can start a reasoned debate. Then we can begin asking whether the lack of major–major power war since 1945 is just a lull in the military confrontations between the leading powers, a passing period of a 'brief' peace, or a more profound tendency due to a combination of structural, political, and normative changes.

Those, like myself, who see the last six decades as a beginning of a much longer peace in major-power relations like to trace the roots of the present 'long peace' to the emerging trends, or maybe silent signals, emanating from World War I or even the Napoleonic wars. In other words, peace among the major powers has been in the making for a hundred or even two hundred years because of the gradual demise of religious, dynastic, and, more recently, territorial and statist reasons for going to war. As we well know, there have been major aberrations to this positive trend, both because of total(itarian) wars and great-power interventions, but yet the deeper trend has not been reversed for good.

Of course, it is possible to say that this version of history relies on a very optimistic reading of it. A more skeptical view would argue that the 'long peace' is 'long' only in a limited sense. The bipolar competition between the two nuclear powers during the Cold War created a 'cold peace' from the late 1940s till the early 1990s between the main adversaries and their allies. This period of relative stability was replaced in the 1990s, and beyond, by the structural unipolarity or the US hegemony (that is more or less the same matter). In this view, peace among major powers will hold as long as the US hegemony lasts. If it starts declining in a serious manner, a new global war may well ensue.

The spirit of this volume is that there are strong structural, institutional, and normative forces at work that give us hope about the possibility of avoiding the next big war. This is not, of course, guaranteed in any way as the conditions for a more durable peace among the major powers may fail to materialize; either the known forces of peace may prove inadequate or new causes and instruments of war may emerge. Any achievement or failure is, however, more of a result of political choice than of necessity; there is no structural logic leading to the next big war. In this volume, we have focused quite heavily on international factors fostering and preventing war among major powers. Yet, it seems to be fair to say that any war, and any peace, starts at home. Signs for hope include the growing domestic constraints against the large-scale use of military force, expanding transnational institutional and economic ties, and the deepening of a new, non-bellistic global culture.

BIBLIOGRAPHY

Abbé de Saint Pierre *A Scheme for Lasting Peace in Europe* (London: Peace Book, 1939 [1739]).

Abercrombie, N. 'Knowledge, Order and Human Autonomy', in J. Hunter and S. Ainlay (eds), *Making Sense of Modern Times* (London: Routledge & Kegan Paul, 1986), pp. 11–30.

Adler, E. and Barnett, M. (eds) *Security Communities* (Cambridge: Cambridge University Press, 1998).

Alderson, K. 'Making Sense of State Socialization', *Review of International Studies*, 27, 3 (2001), pp. 415–34.

Anderson, M. S. *War and Society in Europe of the Old Regime, 1618–1789* (Leicester: Leicester University Press, 1988).

Andrew, C. *Théophile Delcassé and the Making of the Entente Cordiale: A Reappraisal of French Foreign Policy, 1898–1905* (New York: St Martin's Press, 1968).

Angell, N. *The Great Illusion* (New York: G.P. Putnam's Sons, 1933 [1909]).

Arbatov, A. G. 'The Transformation of Russian Military Doctrine: Lessons Learned from Kosovo and Chechnya', *The Marshall Center Papers*, 2 (2000), pp. 1–62.

Aron, R. *War and Industrial Society. August Comte Memorial Trust Lecture No. 3* (Oxford: Oxford University Press, 1958).

Aronson, S. *The Politics and Strategy of Nuclear Weapons in the Middle East* (Albany: State University of New York Press, 1992).

Arrighi, G. *The Long Twentieth Century: Money, Power, and the Origins of Our Times* (London: Verso, 1994).

Ashley, R. K. *The Political Economy of War and Peace* (London: Frances Pinter, 1980).

Ashwort, G. J. *War and the City* (London: Routledge, 1991).

Axelrod, R. 'The Emergence of Cooperation among Egoists', *American Political Science Review*, 75, 2 (1981), pp. 306–18.

Axelrod, R. *The Evolution of Cooperation* (New York: Basic Books, 1984).

Axelrod, R. 'An Evolutionary Approach to Norms', *American Political Science Review*, 80, 4 (1986), pp. 1095–112.

Axelrod, R. and Keohane, R. O. 'Achieving Cooperation Under Anarchy: Strategies and Institutions', in Kenneth A. Oye (ed.), *Cooperation Under Anarchy* (Princeton: Princeton University Press, 1986), pp. 226–54.

Baechler, J. *The Origins of Capitalism* (Oxford: Basil Blackwell, 1975).

Bailey, S. D. *Prohibitions and Restraints on War* (London: Oxford University Press, 1972).

Bain, W. *Between Anarchy and Society: Trusteeship and the Obligations of Power* (Oxford: Oxford University Press, 2003).

Bajpai, K. 'India's Nuclear Posture after Pokhran II', *International Studies*, 37, October–December (2000), pp. 267–301.

Baldwin, R., Haaparanta, P. and Kiander, J. *Expanding Membership of the European Union* (New York: Cambridge University Press, 1995).

Barany, Z. 'Bulgaria's Royal Elections', *Journal of Democracy*, 13, 2 (2002), pp. 141–55.

Barbera, H. *The Military Factor in Social Change,* Vol. 2 of *The State and Revolution* (New Brunswick: Transaction Publishers, 1998).

Barbieri, K. *The Liberal Illusion: Does Trade Promote Peace?* (Ann Arbor: Michigan University Press, 2002).

Barkawi, T. and Laffey, M. 'The Imperial Peace: Democracy, Force and Globalization', *European Journal of International Relations*, 5, 4 (1999), pp. 403–34.

Barnett, M. N. and Finnemore, M. 'The Politics, Power, and Pathologies of International Organizations', *International Organization*, 53, 4 (autumn 1999), pp. 699–732.

Bean, R. 'War and the Birth of the Nation State', *Journal of Economic History*, 33, 2 (1973), pp. 203–21.

Beaud, M. *A History of Capitalism* (New York: Monthly Review Press, 1983).

Behnen, M. *Rüstung, Bündnis, Sicherheit: Dreibund und informeller Imperialismus, 1900–1908* (Tübingen: M. Niemeyer, 1985).

Benn, S. 'Sovereignty', *The Encyclopedia of Philosophy*, Vol. 7/8 (New York: Macmillan, 1967), pp. 501–5.

Berkowitz, B. *The New Face of War* (New York: Free Press, 2002).

Best, G. *War and Society in Revolutionary Europe* (London: Fontana, 1982).

Best, G. 'Editor's Preface', in B. Bond, *War and Society in Europe in 1870–1970* (Suffolk: Fontana, 1984).

Best, G. *War and Law since 1945* (Oxford: Clarendon Press, 1991).

Betts, R. *Uncertain Dimensions* (Minneapolis: University of Minnesota Press, 1985).

Betts, R. K. 'Systems for Peace or Causes of War? Collective Security, Arms Control, and the New Europe', *International Security*, 17, 1 (1992), pp. 5–43.

Black, J. *European Warfare 1660–1815* (New Haven: Yale University Press, 1994).

Black, J. *War and the World: Military Power and the Fate of the Continents 1450–2000* (Suffolk: Fontana, 1998).

Black, J. *Why Wars Happen* (New York: New York University Press, 1998).

Black, J. *Warfare in the Eighteenth Century* (London: Cassell, 1999).

Blackett, P. M. S. *The Military and Political Consequences of Atomic Energy* (London: Turnstile Press, 1948).

Blainey, G. *The Causes of War* (New York: Free Press, 1973).

Blair, B. G. *Strategic Command and Control: Redefining the Nuclear Threat* (Washington DC: The Brookings Institution, 1985).

Blair, B. G. *The Logic of Accidental Nuclear War* (Washington DC: The Brookings Institution, 1993).

Blair, B. G. *Global Zero Alert for Nuclear Forces* (Washington DC: The Brookings Institution, 1995).

Bluntschli, J. G. *Gesammelte kleine Schriften*, Vol. 2 (Nordlingen: Beck'sche Buchhandlung, 1879–81).

Blyth, M. 'Any More Bright Ideas? The Ideational Turn of Comparative Political Economy', *Comparative Politics*, 29, 2 (1997), pp. 229–50.

Bobbitt, P. *The Shield of Achilles: War, Peace, and the Course of History* (New York: Alfred A. Knopf, 2002).

Bonney, R. 'France, 1494–1815', in R. Bonney (ed.), *The Rise of the Fiscal State in Europe c. 1200–1815* (Oxford: Oxford University Press, 1999), pp. 123–76.

Bosworth, R. J. B. *Italy the Least of the Great Powers* (London: Cambridge University Press, 1979).

Bosworth, R. J. B. *Italy and the Approach of the First World War* (London: Macmillan, 1983).

Bracken, P. *The Command and Control of Nuclear Forces* (New Haven: Yale University Press, 1983).

Brady, T. Jr 'The Rise of Merchant Empires, 1400–1700: A European Counterpoint', in James Tracy (ed.), *The Political Economy of Merchant Empires* (Cambridge: Cambridge University Press, 1997), pp. 148–55.

Braudel, F. *The Structures of Everyday Life*, Vol. 1: *The Limits of the Possible* (New York: Harper & Row, 1981).

Braudel, F. *Civilization and Capitalism 15th–18th Century*, Vol. II: *The Wheels of Commerce* (tr. by S. Reynolds), (New York: Harper & Row, 1986).

Brecher, M. and Wilkenfeld, J. 'International Crises and Global Instability: The Myth of the "Long Peace"', in C. Kegley (ed.), *The Long Postwar Peace* (New York: HarperCollins, 1991), pp. 85–104.

Bremer, S. 'National Capabilities and War Proneness', in J.D. Singer (ed.), *The Correlates of War II* (New York: Free Press, 1980), pp. 57–82.

Bremer, S. 'Who Fights Whom, When, Where, and Why?', in J. Vasquez (ed.), *What Do We Know about War?* (Lanham: Rowman & Littlefield, 2000), pp. 23–36.

Breslauer, G. and Tetlock, P. (eds) *Learning in U.S. and Soviet Foreign Policy* (Boulder: Westview Press, 1991).

Brodie, B. (ed.) *The Absolute Weapons* (New York: Columbia University Press, 1946).

Brodie, B. 'The Atom Bomb as Policy Maker', *Foreign Affairs*, 27, 1 (1948), pp. 1–16.

Brosman, C. S. *Visions of War in France: Fiction, Art, Ideology* (Baton Rouge: Louisiana State University Press, 1999).

Brown, N. *The Future of Air Power* (New York: Holmes & Meier, 1986).

Browne, N. *Strategic Mobility* (London: Praeger, 1963).

Brubaker, R. 'Ethnicity without Groups', *Archives Européennes de Sociologie*, 43, 2 (2002), pp. 163–89.

Bruijn, J. R. 'States and their Navies from the Late Sixteenth to the End of the Eighteenth Centuries', in P. Contamine (ed.), *War and Competition between States* (Oxford: Clarendon Press, 2000), pp. 69–98.

Bull, H. *The Anarchical Society* (London: Macmillan, 1977).

Bunce, V. 'The Empire Strikes Back: The Transformation of the Eastern Bloc from a Soviet Asset to a Soviet Liability', *International Organization*, 39, 1 (1985), pp. 1–46.

Burkhardt, J. 'Die Friedlosigkeit der Frühen Neuzeit: Grundlegung einer Theorie der Bellizität Europas', *Zeitschrift für Historische Forschung*, 24, 4 (1997), pp. 510–74.

Burr, W. and Richelson, J. T. 'Whether to "Strangle the Baby in the Cradle": The United States and the Chinese Nuclear Program, 1960–64', *International Security*, 25, 1 (2000), pp. 54–99.

Buzan, B., Jones, C. and Little, R. *The Logic of Anarchy: Neorealism to Structural Realism* (New York: Columbia University Press, 1993).

Byres, T. *Capitalism from Above and Capitalism from Below* (London: Macmillan, 1996).

Cain, P. 'Capitalism, War and Internationalism in the Thought of Richard Cobden', *British Journal of International Studies*, 5, 2 (1979), pp. 229–47.

Cain, P. J. 'Variations on a Famous Theme: Hobson, International Trade and Imperialism, 1902–1938', in M. Fredeen (ed.), *Reappraising J. A. Hobson: Humanism and Welfare* (London: Unwin Hyman, 1990), pp. 11–53.

Carr, E. H. *The Twenty Years Crisis, 1919–1939* (New York: Harper Torchbooks, 1964 [1946]).

Carter, A. B., Steinbruner, J. D. and Zraket, C. A. (eds) *Managing Nuclear Operations* (Washington DC: The Brookings Institution, 1987).

Castells, M. *The Information Age: Economy, Society and Culture*, Vol. I: *The Rise of the Network Society* (Oxford: Blackwell, 1996).

Caton, H. *The Politics of Progress: The Origins and Development of the Commercial Republic* (Gainesville: University of Florida Press, 1988).

Cavallar, G. 'Kantian Perspectives on Democratic Peace: Alternatives to Doyle', *Review of International Studies*, 27, 2 (2001), pp. 243–7.

Ceadel, M. *Thinking about Peace and War* (Oxford: Oxford University Press, 1987).

Cederman, L.-E. 'Back to Kant: Reinterpreting the Democratic Peace as a Macrohistorical Learning Process', *American Political Science Review*, 95, 1 (2001).

Chan, S. 'Chinese Perspectives on World Order', in T.V. Paul and J. A. Hall (eds), *International Order and the Future of World Politics* (Cambridge: Cambridge University Press, 1999), pp. 197–212.

Cheema, Z. I. 'Pakistan's Nuclear Use Doctrine and Command and Control', in P. R. Lavoy, S. D. Sagan and J. J. Wirtz (eds), *Planning the Unthinkable: How New Powers will Use Nuclear, Biological and Chemical Weapons* (Ithaca: Cornell University Press, 2000), pp. 158–81.

Choucri, N. and North, R. C. *Nations in Conflict: National Growth and International Violence* (San Francisco: W.H. Freeman, 1975).

Choucri, N. and North, R. C. 'Lateral Pressure in International Relations: Concept and Theory', in Manus Midlarsky (ed.), *Handbook of War Studies* (Ann Arbor: University of Michigan Press, 1989).

Churchill, W. *In the Balance: Speeches 1949 and 1950* (Boston: Houghton Mifflin, 1951).

Clark, I. V. *Voices Prophesizing War* (Middlesex: Penguin, 1963).

Clark, I. *Waging War: A Philosophical Introduction* (Oxford: Clarendon Press, 1988).

Claude, I. L. Jr *Swords Into Plowshares* (New York: Random House, 1956).

Coate, R. A. and Puchala, D. J. 'Global Policies and the United Nations System: A Current Assessment', in F. Kratochwil and E. D. Mansfield (eds), *International Organization: A Reader* (New York: HarperCollins, 1994), pp. 257–70.

Cohen, A. 'Nuclear Arms in Crisis under Secrecy: Israel and the Lessons of the 1967 and 1973 Wars', in P. R. Lavoy, S. D. Sagan and J. J. Wirtz (eds), *Planning the Unthinkable: How New Powers will Use Nuclear, Biological and Chemical Weapons* (Ithaca: Cornell University Press, 2000), pp. 104–24.

Cohen, E. A. 'The Major Consequences of War', *Survival*, 41, 2 (1999), pp. 143–6.

Cohen, S. F. *Failed Crusade: America and the Tragedy of Post-Communist Russia* (New York: W.W. Norton, 2000).

Cohen, Y., Brown, B. and Organski, A. F. K. 'The Paradoxical Nature of State Making: The Violent Creation of Order', *American Political Science Review*, 75, 4 (1981), pp. 901–10.

Coker, C. *War and the Illiberal Conscience* (Boulder: Westview, 1998).

Coker, C. *Humane Warfare* (London: Routledge, 2001).

Contamine, P. *War in the Middle Ages* (tr. by M. Jones), (Oxford: Basil Blackwell, 1980).

Contamine, P. 'The Growth of State Control. Practices of War, 1300–1800: Ransom and Booty', in P. Contamine (ed.), *War and Competition between States* (Oxford: Clarendon Press, 2000).

Copeland, D. C. *The Origins of Major War* (Ithaca: Cornell University Press, 2000).

Covell, C. *Kant and the Law of Peace: A Study in the Philosophy of International Law and International Relations* (New York: St Martin's Press, 1998).

Covini, M. N. 'Political and Military Bonds in the Italian State System, Thirteenth to Sixteenth Centuries', in P. Contamine (ed.), *War and Competition between States* (Oxford: Clarendon Press, 2000).

Crawford, N. *Argument and Change in World Politics: Ethics, Decolonization, and Humanitarian Intervention* (Cambridge: Cambridge University Press, 2002).

Dahl, R. A. *Polyarchy* (New Haven: Yale University Press, 1971).

David, P. 'Clio and the Economics of QWERTY', *American Economic Review*, 75 (1985), pp. 332–7.

Davis, L. E. *Limited Nuclear Options: Deterrence and the New American Doctrine, Adelphi paper No. 121* (London: International Institute for Strategic Studies, 1976).

Dawisha, K. and Parrott, B. *Russia and the New States of Eurasia* (New York: Cambridge University Press, 1994).

Dawisha, K. and Parrott, B. (eds) *The End of Empire?* (Armonk: M. E. Sharpe, 1997).

De Lupis, I. D. *The Law of War* (Cambridge: Cambridge University Press, 1987).

Deane, P. 'War and Industrialization', in J. M. Winter (ed.), *War and Economic Development* (Cambridge: Cambridge University Press, 1975).

Delbrück, H. *The Dawn of Modern Warfare: History of the Art of War*, Vol. IV (Lincoln: University of Nebraska Press, 1990 [1920]).

Delmas, F. *The Rosy Future of War* (New York: Free Press, 1995).

Desch, M. C. 'War and Strong States, Peace and Weak States', *International Organization*, 50, 2 (1996), pp. 237–68.

Diehl, P. F., Reifschneider, J. and Hensel, P. R. 'United Nations Intervention and Recurring Conflict', *International Organization*, 50, 4 (autumn 1996), pp. 683–700.

DiMaggio, P. and Powell, W. 'The Iron Cage Revisited: Institutional Isomorphism and Collective Rationality in Organizational Fields', *American Sociological Review*, 48 (1983), pp. 147–60.

Doran, C. F. 'Power Cycle Theory of Systems Structure and Stability: Commonalities and Complementarities', in M. Midlarsky (ed.), *Handbook of War Studies* (Ann Arbor: University of Michigan Press, 1989).

Doran, C. F. *Systems in Crisis: New Imperatives of High Politics at Century's End* (Cambridge: Cambridge University Press, 1991).

Doremus, P. (ed.) *The Myth of the Global Corporation* (Princeton: Princeton University Press, 1998).

Downs, G. and Iida, K. 'Assessing the Theoretical Case Against Collective Security', in G. Downs (ed.), *Collective Security Beyond the Cold War* (Ann Arbor: University of Michigan Press, 1994), pp. 17–39.

Doyle, M. W. 'Kant, Liberal Legacies, and Foreign Affairs', *Philosophy and Public Affairs*, 12, 2 and 3 (1983), pp. 205–35 and 323–53.

Doyle, M. *Empires* (Ithaca: Cornell University Press, 1986).

Doyle, M. W. 'Liberalism and World Politics', *American Political Science Review*, 80, 4 (1986), pp. 1151–69.

Doyle, M. *Ways of War and Peace: Realism, Liberalism, and Socialism* (New York: W.W. Norton, 1997).

Drucker, P. 'The Global Economy and the Nation-State', *Foreign Affairs*, 76, 5 (1997).

Ducci, R. 'The World Order in the Sixties', *Foreign Affairs*, 43, 3 (1964), pp. 379–90.

Duchhardt, H. *Gleichgewicht der Kräfte, Convenance, Europäisches Konzert* (Darmstadt: Wissenschaftliche Buchgesellschaft, 1976).

Duchhardt, H. *Studien zur Friedensvermittlung in der frühen Neuzeit* (Wiesbaden, 1979).

Duchhardt, H. (ed.) *Rahmenbedingungen und Handlunsspielräume europäischer Aussenpolitik im Zeitalter Ludwigs XIV* (Berlin: Duncker & Humblot, 1991).

Duchhardt, H. (ed.) *Zwischenstaatliche Friedenswahrung im Mittelalter und früher Neuzeit* (Cologne: Böhlau, 1991).

Duchhardt, H. *Balance of Power und Pentarchie 1700–1785* (Paderborn: Schöningh, 1997).

Duffy, C. *Siege Warfare: The Fortress in the Early Modern World 1494–1660* (New York: Barnes & Noble, 1979).

Dülffer, J. *Vermiedene Kriege: Deeskalation von Konflikten der Grossmächte zwischen Krimkrieg und Erstem Weltkrieg (1865–1914)* (Munich, 1997).

Dunlop, I. *Louis XIV* (New York: St Martin's Press, 1999).

Durch, W. J. 'The United Nations and Collective Security in the 21st Century', in H. H. Almond, Jr and J. A. Burger (eds), *The History and Future of Warfare* (The Hague: Kluwer Law International, 1999), pp. 827–59.

Eberwein, W.-D. 'The Future of International Warfare: Toward a Global Security Community?', *International Political Science Review*, 16, 4 (1996), pp. 341–60.

Echevarria II, A. J. *After Clausewitz: German Military Thinkers before the Great War* (Lawrence: University Press of Kansas, 2000), pp. 85–91.

Edsall, N. *Richard Cobden: Independent Radical* (Cambridge, Mass.: Harvard University Press, 1986).

Ehrenreich, B. *Blood Rites: Origins and History of the Passions of War* (New York: Metropolitan, 1997).

Elias, N. *State Formation and Civilization: The Civilizing Process*, Vol. 2 (Oxford: Basil Blackwell, 1982 [1939]).

Elias, N. *The Civilizing Process: State Formation and Civilization* (Oxford: Basil Blackwell, 1982 [1939]).

Elman, M. (ed.) *Paths to Peace: Is Democracy the Answer?* (Cambridge: MIT Press, 1997).

Emerson, R. *From Empire to Nation* (Cambridge, Mass.: Harvard University Press, 1967).

Engels, F. *Anti-Dühring: Herr Eugen Dühring's Revolution in Science* (Moscow: Foreign Languages Publishing House, 1959).

Enthoven, A. *How Much is Enough? Shaping the Defense Budget, 1961–69* (New York: Harper & Row, 1971).

Epstein, J. 'Always Time to Kill', *The New York Review of Books*, 46, 17 (1999), pp. 57–64.

Epstein, S. R. *Freedom and Growth: The Rise of States and Markets in Europe, 1300–1750* (London: Routledge, 2000).

Eriksson, M., Wallensteen, P. and Sollenberg, M. 'Armed Conflict, 1989–2002', *Journal of Peace Research*, 40 (2003), pp. 593–607.

Esthus, R. *Double Eagle and Rising Sun: The Russians and Japanese at Portsmouth in 1905* (Durham: Duke University Press, 1988).

Etherington, N. *Theories of Imperialism: War, Conquest and Capital* (London: Croom Helm, 1984).

Evan, L. *War in International Society: A Study in International Sociology* (New Haven: Yale University Press, 1986).

Feiveson, H. A. (ed.) *The Nuclear Turning Point* (Washington DC: The Brookings Institution, 1999).

Ferenczi, C. *Aussenpolitik und Öffentlichkeit in Russland, 1906–1912* (Husum: Matthiesen Verlag, 1982).

Ferguson, N. *The Pity of War: Explaining World War I* (New York: Basic Books, 1999).

Ferguson, N. *The Cash Nexus: Money and Power in the Modern World, 1700–2000* (New York: Basic Books, 2001).

Fernandes, G. 'Presentation', *National Seminar on Challenges of Limited War*, New Delhi, Institute for Defense Studies and Analysis, 5–6, January 2000.

Figes, O. *A People's Tragedy: The Russian Revolution, 1891–1924* (New York: Jonathan Cape, 1997).

Finnemore, M. 'International Organizations as Teachers of Norms: The United Nations Educational, Scientific, and Cultural Organization and Science Policy', *International Organization*, 47, 4 (1993), pp. 565–97.

Finnemore, M. 'Norms, Culture and World Politics: Insights from Sociology's Institutionalism', *International Organization*, 50, 2 (1996), pp. 325–47.

Finnemore, M. and Sikkink, K. 'International Norms Dynamics and Political Change', *International Organization*, 54, 4 (autumn 1998), pp. 887–917.

Fletcher, J. *Violence and Civilization: An Introduction to the Work of Norbert Elias* (London: Polity Press, 1997).

Flynn, G. and Farrell, H. 'The CSCE and the "Construction" of Security in Post-Cold War Europe', *International Organization*, 53, 3 (summer 1999), pp. 505–35.

Forsberg, R. C. 'Socially-Sanctioned and Non-Sanctioned Violence: On the Role of Moral Beliefs in Causing and Preventing War and Other Forms of Large-Group Violence', in R. Stanley (ed.), *Gewalt und Konflikt in Einer Globalizierten Welt: Festschrift für Ulrich Albrecht* (Wiesbaden: Westdeutscher Verlag, 2001).

Förster, S. *Der doppelte Militarismus: Die Deutsche Heeresrüstungspolitik zwischen Status-Quo-Sicherung und Aggression 1890–1913* (Stuttgart: F. Steiner, 1985).

Foucault, M. *The Archaeology of Knowledge* (New York: Pantheon Books, 1972).

Fox, E. W. *History in Geographical Perspective: The Other France* (New York: W. W. Norton, 1971).

Franke, M. F. N. *Global Limits: Immanuel Kant, International Relations, and Critique of World Politics* (Albany: State University of New York Press, 2001).

Freedman, L. *The Evolution of Nuclear Strategy* (New York: St Martin's Press, 1981).

Frei, D. and Catrina, C. *Risks of Unintentional Nuclear War* (Totowa: Allanheld Osmun, 1983).

Frieden, J. and Rogowski, R. 'The Impact of the International Economy on National Policies', in R. Keohane and H. Milner (eds), *Internationalization and Domestic Politics* (New York: Cambridge University Press, 1996).

Friedman, T. L. *The Lexus and the Olive Tree* (New York: Random House, 2000).

Friedrich, C. *Inevitable Peace* (Cambridge, Mass.: Harvard University Press, 1948).

Friedrichs, C. R. *Urban Society in an Age of War* (Princeton: Princeton University Press, 1979).

Frost, R. I. *The Northern Wars: War, State and Society in Northeastern Europe, 1558–1721* (London: Longman, 2000).

Fukuyama, F. *The End of History and the Last Man* (New York: Avon Books, 1993).

Fuller, J. F. C. *The Conduct of War* (London: Eyre & Spottiswode, 1961).

Fuller, W. C. *Civil–Military Conflict in Imperial Russia, 1881–1914* (Princeton: Princeton University Press, 1985).

Gaddis, J. 'The Long Peace: Elements of Stability in the Postwar International System', in S. Lynn-Jones and S. Miller (eds), *The Cold War and After* (Cambridge, Mass.: MIT Press, 1994).

Gaddis, J. D. 'Conclusion', in J. D. Gaddis, P. H. Gordon, E. R. May and J. Rosenberg (eds), *Cold War Statesmen Confront the Bomb: Nuclear Diplomacy since 1945* (Oxford: Oxford University Press, 1999), pp. 260–71.

Gaddis, J. D. *The United States and the Cold War: Implications, Reconsiderations, Provocations* (New York: Oxford University Press, 1992).

Gaddis, J. L. *The Long Peace: Inquiries into the History of the Cold War* (New York: Oxford University Press, 1987).

Gaddis, J. L. *We Now Know: Rethinking Cold War History* (Oxford: Clarendon Press, 1997).

Ganev, V. I. 'Bulgaria's Symphony of Hope', *Journal of Democracy*, 8, 4 (1997), pp. 125–39.

Gantzel, K. J. and Schwinghammer, T. *Warfare Since the Second World War* (London: Transaction, 2000).

Garfield, D. *Punishment and Modern Society: A Study in Social Theory* (Chicago: University of Chicago Press, 1990).

Garrett, G. 'International Cooperation and Institutional Choice: The European Community's Internal Market', *International Organization*, 46, 2 (1992), pp. 533–60.

Garrett, G. and Weingast, B. 'Ideas, Interests, and Institutions: Constructing the European Community's Internal Market', in J. Goldstein and R. Keohane (eds), *Ideas and Foreign Policy* (Ithaca: Cornell University Press, 1993), pp. 173–206.

Garrity, P. J. 'The Depreciation of Nuclear Weapons in International Politics: Possibilities, Limits, Uncertainties', *Journal of Strategic Studies*, 14, 4 (1991), pp. 463–514.

Gat, A. *The Origins of Military Thought from the Enlightenment to Clausewitz* (Oxford: Clarendon Press, 1989).

Gat, A. *The Development of Military Thought: The Nineteenth Century* (Oxford: Clarendon Press, 1992).

Gat, A. *Fascist and Liberal Visions of War: Fuller, Liddell Hart, Douhet, and Other Modernists* (Oxford: Clarendon Press, 1998).

Gause, G. 'Sovereignty, Statecraft and Stability in the Middle East', *Journal of International Affairs*, 45, 2 (1992), pp. 441–69.

Geller, D. S. and Singer, J. D. *Nations at War: A Scientific Study of International Conflict* (Cambridge: Cambridge University Press, 1998).

George, A. L. *Managing U.S.–Soviet Rivalry: Problems of Crisis Prevention* (Boulder: Westview Press, 1983).

Geyer, D. *Der russische Imperialismus: Studien über den Zusammenhang von innerer und auswärtiger Politik, 1860–1914* (Göttingen: Vandenhoeck and Ruprecht, 1977).

Giddens, A. *The Nation-State and Violence* (Berkeley: University of California Press, 1987).

Gilpin, R. *War and Change in World Politics* (Cambridge: Cambridge University Press, 1981).

Given, J. B. *Society and Homicide in Thirteenth Century England* (Stanford: Stanford University Press, 1977).

Glaser, C. T. *Analyzing Strategic Nuclear Policy* (Princeton: Princeton University Press, 1990).

Gleditsch, N. P. *The Future of Armed Conflict* (Ramat Gan: The Begin–Sadat Center for Strategic Studies, 2003).

Glete, J. 'Warfare at Sea 1450–1815', in J. Black (ed.), *War in Early Modern Europe 1450–1815* (Boulder: Westview Press, 1999), pp. 25–52.

Glete, J. *Warfare at Sea, 1500–1650: Maritime Conflicts and the Transformation of Europe* (London: Routledge, 2000).

Glete, J. *War and the State in Early Modern Europe* (London: Routledge, 2002).

Gochman, C. S. 'Capability-Driven Disputes', in C. S. Gochman and A. N. Sabrosky (eds), *Prisoners of War? Nation-States in the Modern Era* (Lexington: Lexington Books, 1990).

Goldstein, J. *Long Cycles* (New Haven: Yale University Press, 1988).

Goldstein, J. *Ideas, Interests, and American Trade Policy* (Ithaca: Cornell University Press, 1993).

Goldstein, J. and Keohane, R. (eds) *Ideas and Foreign Policy* (Ithaca: Cornell University Press, 1993).

Gordon, E. J. and Troxel, L. 'Minority Mobilization Without War', Paper presented at the conference on Post-Communism and Ethnic Mobilization at Cornell University, 21–22 April 1995.

Gray, C. S. 'War Fighting for Deterrence', *Journal of Strategic Studies*, 7, 1 (1984), pp. 5–28.

Green, R. *The Naked Nuclear Emperor* (Christchurch: The Disarmament and Security Center, 2000).

Grotius, H. *de Jure Belli ac Pacis* (Amsterdam: Jansunium, 1632).

Guerlac, H. 'Vauban: The Impact of Science on War', in P. Paret (ed.), *Makers of Modern Strategy: From Machiavelli to the Nuclear Age* (Princeton: Princeton University Press, 1986), pp. 64–90.

Gulick, E. V. *Europe's Classical Balance of Power* (New York: W. W. Norton, 1955).

Gulick, E. V. *Europe's Classical Balance of Power* (New York: W. W. Norton, 1967 [1955]).

Gurr, T. R. 'Historical Trends in Violent Crime: A Critical Review of the Evidence', *Crime and Justice*, 3 (1981), pp. 295–353.

Haas, E. B. 'Collective Conflict Management: Evidence for a New World Order?', in F. Kratochwil and E. D. Mansfield (eds), *International Organization: A Reader* (New York: HarperCollins, 1994), pp. 237–57.

Habermas, J. 'Kant's Idea of Perpetual Peace, with the Benefit of Two Hundred Years' Hindsight', in J. Bohman and M. Lutz-Bachmann (eds), *Perpetual Peace: Essays on Kant's Cosmopolitan Ideal* (Cambridge: MIT Press, 1997).

Hall, J. A. *Liberalism: Politics, Ideology, and the Market* (Chapel Hill: University of North Carolina Press, 1987).

Hall, J. A. 'Peace, Peace At Last?', in J. A. Hall and I. C. Jarvie (eds), *Transition to Modernity: Essays on Wealth, Power, and Belief* (Cambridge: Cambridge University Press, 1992).

Halliday, F. *Revolution and World Politics: The Rise and Fall of the Sixth Great Power* (Durham: Duke University Press, 1999).

Hanson, V. D. *Carnage and Culture: Landmark Battles in the Rise of Western Power* (New York: Doubleday, 2001).

Hart, M. 'The Emergence and Consolidation of the "Tax State"', in R. Bonney (ed.), *Economic Systems and State Finance* (Oxford: Clarendon Press, 1995), pp. 281–2.

Hasenclever, A., Mayer, P. and Rittberger, V. *Theories of International Regimes* (Cambridge: Cambridge University Press, 1997).

314

Hegre, H. 'Development and Liberal Peace: What Does It Take To Be a Trading State?', *Journal of Peace Research*, 37, 1 (2000), pp. 5–30.

Hegre, H., Ellingsen, T., Gates, S. and Gleditsch, N. P. 'Towards a Democratic Civil Peace?', *American Political Science Review*, 95, 1 (2001), pp. 33–48.

Herbst, J. 'The Creation and Maintenance of National Boundaries in Africa', *International Organization*, 43, 4 (1989), pp. 673–92.

Hewson, M. and Sinclair, T. J. (eds) *Approaches to Global Governance Theory* (Albany: State University of New York Press, 1999).

Hinsley, F. H. 'The Concept of Sovereignty and the Relations Between States', in W. Stankiewicz (ed.), *In Defense of Sovereignty* (New York: Oxford University Press, 1969).

Hinsley, F. H. *Power and the Pursuit of Peace: Theory and Practice in the History of Relations between the States* (Cambridge: Cambridge University Press, 1963).

Hirschman, A. O. *The Passions and the Interests: Political Arguments for Capitalism Before Its Triumph* (Princeton: Princeton University Press, 1977).

Hirschman, A. *National Power and the Structure of Foreign Trade* (Berkeley: University of California Press, 1945, repr. 1980).

Hirschman, A. 'How the Keynesian Revolution was exported from the United States, and Other Comments', in P. Hall (ed.), *The Political Power of Economic Ideas* (Princeton: Princeton University Press, 1989).

Hitler, A., Cameron, N. (translator), Stevens, R. H. (translator) and Trevor-Roper, H. R. *Hitler's Table Talk 1941–1944* (Oxford: Oxford University Press, 1953).

Hobsbawm, E. *The Age of Capital 1848–1870* (New York: Times Mirror, 1979).

Hoffman, B. 'Terrorism Trends and Prospects', in I. O. Lesser (ed.), *Countering the New Terrorism* (Santa Monica: Rand Corporation, 1999).

Hoffman, P. T. and Rosenthal, J.-L. 'The Political Economy of Warfare and Taxation in Early Modern Europe: Historical Lessons for Economic Development', in J. N. Drobak and J. V. C. Nye (eds), *The Frontiers of the New Institutional Economics* (San Diego: Academic Press, 1997), pp. 31–55.

Hoffmann, S. 'Watch out for a New World Disorder', *International Herald Tribune*, 26 February 1991, p. 6.

Holloway, D. *Stalin and the Bomb* (New Haven: Yale University Press, 1994).

Holmes, R. L. *On War and Morality* (Princeton: Princeton University Press, 1989).

Holsti, K. J. *The State, War, and the State of War* (Cambridge: Cambridge University Press, 1996).

Holsti, K. J. *Peace and War: Armed Conflict and International Order, 1648–1989* (Cambridge: Cambridge University Press, 1991).

Hont, I. 'Free Trade and Economic Limits to National Politics: Neo-Machiavellian Political Economy Reconsidered', in J. Dunn (ed.), *The Economic Limits to Modern Politics* (Cambridge: Cambridge University Press, 1990).

Horowitz, D. L. *The Deadly Ethnic Riot* (Berkeley: University of California Press, 2001).

Howard, M. *War in European History* (Oxford: Oxford University Press, 1976).

Howard, M. *War and the Liberal Conscience* (Oxford: Oxford University Press, 1981).

Howard, M. 'A Death Knell for War?', *New York Times Book Review*, 30 April 1989, p. 14.

Howard, M. *The Lessons of History* (New Haven: Yale University Press, 1991).

Howard, M. *The Invention of Peace: Reflections on War and International Order* (New Haven: Yale University Press, 2000).

Howe, A. *Free Trade and Liberal England 1846–1946* (Oxford: Clarendon Press, 1997).

Hugill, P. *World Trade Since 1431: Geography, Technology, and Capitalism* (Baltimore: Johns Hopkins University Press, 1993).

Huntington, S. 'Democracy's Third Wave', in L. Diamond and M. Plattner (eds), *The Global Resurgence of Democracy* (Baltimore: Johns Hopkins University Press, 1996).

Huntley, W. L. 'Kant's Third Image: Systemic Sources of the Liberal Peace', *International Studies Quarterly*, 40, 1 (1996), pp. 56–7.

Hurrell, A. 'Kant and the Kantian Paradigm in International Relations', *Review of International Studies*, 16, 3 (1990), pp. 182–205.

Ikenberry, G. J. *After Victory: Institutions, Strategic Restraint, and the Rebuilding of Order after Major Wars* (Princeton: Princeton University Press, 2001).

Ikenberry, G. J. and Kupchan, C. 'Socialization and Hegemonic Power', *International Organization*, 44, 3 (1990), pp. 283–315.

Israel, J. *Dutch Primacy in World Trade, 1585–1740* (Oxford: Clarendon Press, 1990).

Israel, J. *The Dutch Republic: Its Rise, Greatness, and Fall 1477–1806* (Oxford: Clarendon Press, 1995).

Jackson, R. 'The Weight of Ideas in Decolonization: Normative Change in International Relations', in J. Goldstein and R. Keohane (eds), *Ideas and Foreign Policy* (Ithaca: Cornell University Press, 1993), pp. 111–38.

Jackson, R. *The Global Covenant: Human Conduct in a World of States* (Oxford: Oxford University Press, 2000).

Jackson, R. H. and Rosberg, C. G. 'Why Africa's Weak States Persist: The Empirical and the Juridical in Statehood', *World Politics*, 35 (1982), pp. 1–24.

Jackson, R. H. and Zacher, M. W. 'The Territorial Covenant: International Society and the Stabilization of Territories', Working Paper No. 15 (Vancouver: Institute of International Relations, University of British Columbia, 1997).

Jaggers, K. 'War and the Three Faces of Power: War Making and State Making in Europe and the Americas', *Comparative Political Studies*, 25, 1 (1992), pp. 26–62.

James, A. *Sovereign Statehood* (London: Allen & Unwin, 1986).

Jervis, R. 'Security Regimes', in S. Krasner (ed.), *International Regimes* (Ithaca: Cornell University Press, 1983).

Jervis, R. 'The Political Effects of Nuclear Weapons', *International Security*, 13, 2 (1988), pp. 28–38.

Jervis, R. *The Meaning of the Nuclear Revolution: Statecraft and the Prospect of Armageddon* (Ithaca: Cornell University Press, 1989).

Jervis, R. 'Realism in the Study of World Politics', *International Organization*, 52, 4 (1998), pp. 971–92.

Jervis, R. 'Theories of War in an Era of Leading-Power Peace', *American Political Science Review*, 96 (2002), pp. 1–14.

Joas, H. 'Die modernität des Krieges: Die Modernisierungstheorie und das Problem der Gewalt', *Leviathan*, 24, 1 (1996), pp. 13–27.

Johnson, P. 'Another 50 Years of Peace?', *Wall Street Journal*, 9 May 1955.

Jones, A. *The Art of War in the Western World* (Oxford: Oxford University Press, 1987).

Jones, D. M., Bremer, S. A. and Singer, J. D. 'Militarized Interstate Disputes, 1816–1992: Rationale, Coding Rules, and Empirical Patterns', *Conflict Management and Peace Science*, 15 (1996), pp. 163–213.

Jones, D. V. *Code of Peace: Ethics and Security in the World of Warlord States* (Chicago: Chicago University Press, 1989).

Jones, E. L. *The European Miracle: Environments, Economies, and Geopolitics in the History of Europe and Asia* (Cambridge: Cambridge University Press, 1981).

Jones, R. L. C. 'Fortifications and Sieges in Western Europe *c.* 800–1450', in M. Keen (ed.), *Medieval Warfare: A History* (Oxford: Oxford University Press, 1999).

Kacowicz, A. M. (ed.) *Stable Peace among Nations* (Lanham: Rowman & Littlefield, 2000).

Kaeuper, R. W. *War, Justice, and Public Order: England and France in the Later Middle Ages* (Oxford: Clarendon Press, 1988).

Kagan, D. *On the Origins of War and the Preservation of Peace* (New York: Doubleday, 1995).

Kahler, M. 'Empires, Neo-Empires, and Political Change: The British and French Experience', in K. Dawisha and B. Parrott (eds), *The End of Empire?* (Armonk: M. E. Sharpe, 1997), pp. 286–312.

Kahler, M. *Decolonization in Britain and France* (Princeton: Princeton University Press, 1984).

Kaldor, M. 'Warfare and Capitalism', in E. P. Thompson (ed.), *Exterminism and Cold War* (London: NLB, 1982), pp. 261–87.

Kaldor, M. *The Baroque Arsenal* (London: Abacus, 1983).

Kaldor, M. *New Wars for Old* (London: Pergamon, 1998).

Kaldor, M. *New and Old Wars: Organized Violence in a Global Era* (Stanford: Stanford University Press, 1999).

Kalyvas, S. N. '"New" and "Old" Civil Wars: A Valid Distinction?', *World Politics*, 54 (2001), pp. 99–118.

Kant, E. *Plan for a Universal and Everlasting Peace* (New York: Garland, 1973 [1796]).

Kant, I. 'Perpetual Peace', in H. Kainz (ed.), *Philosophical Perspectives on Peace: An Anthology of Classical and Modern Sources* (Athens: Ohio University Press, 1987 [1795]), pp. 65–86.

Kaplan, R. 'The Coming Anarchy', *The Atlantic Monthly*, 273 (1994), pp. 44–76.

Karl, D. J. 'Proliferation Pessimism and Emerging Nuclear Powers', *International Security*, 21, 3 (1996/97), pp. 87–119.

Kaysen, C. 'Is War Obsolete? A Review Essay', *International Security*, 14, 4 (1990), pp. 42–64.

Kazemzadeh, F. *Russia and Britain in Persia, 1864–1914: A Study in Imperialism* (New Haven: Yale University Press, 1968).

Keegan, J. *A History of Warfare* (New York: Knopf, 1993).

Keegan, J. *The Face of Battle* (New York: Barnes & Noble, 1993 [1976]).

Keeley, L. H. *War Before Civilization: The Myth of the Peaceful Savage* (New York: Oxford University Press, 1996).

Kegley, C. W. Jr (ed.) *The Long Postwar Peace: Contending Explanations and Projections* (New York: HarperCollins, 1991).

Kegley, C. W. Jr and Raymond, G. A. *How Nations Make Peace*. (New York: St Martin's Press, 1999).

Kegley, C. W. Jr and Raymond, R. 'Alliance Norms and War: A New Piece in an Old Puzzle', *International Studies Quarterly*, 26 (1982), pp. 572–95.

Kegley, C. W. Jr and Raymond, R. *When Trust Breaks Down* (Columbia: University of South Carolina Press, 1990).

Keiger, J. F. V. *France and the Origins of the First World War* (London: Palgrave Macmillan, 1983).

Kennedy, P. *The Rise and Fall of the Great Powers: Economic Change and Military Conflict from 1500–2000* (New York: Random House, 1987).

Keohane, R. *International Institutions and State Power: Essays in International Relations Theory* (Boulder: Westview Press, 1989).

Keohane, R. and Milner, H. (eds) *Internationalization and Domestic Politics* (New York: Cambridge University Press, 1996).

Khazanov, A. M. 'A State without a Nation? Russia after Empire', in T.V. Paul, G. J. Ikenberry and J. A. Hall (eds), *The Nation-State in Question* (Princeton: Princeton University Press, 2003), pp. 79–105.

Kimball, W. *The Juggler* (Princeton: Princeton University Press, 1991).

Kindleberger, C. *The World in Depression 1929–1939* (Berkeley: University of California Press, 1983).

Kissinger, H. A. *Nuclear Weapons and Foreign Policy: The Need for Choice* (New York: Harper & Row, 1957).

Knopf, J. W. 'Recasting the Proliferation Optimism–Pessimism Debate', *Security Studies*, 12, autumn (2002), pp. 41–96.

Knox, M. 'Conclusion: Continuity and Revolution in the Making of Strategy', in W. Murray, M. Knox and A. Bernstein (eds), *The Making of Strategy: Rulers, States, and War* (Cambridge: Cambridge University Press, 1994).

Knutsen, T. *The Rise and Fall of World Orders* (Manchester and New York: Manchester University Press, 1999).

Koht, H. *Driving Forces of History* (New York: Atheneum, 1968).

Koskenniemi, M. *The Gentle Civilizer of Nations: The Rise and Fall of International Law 1870–1960* (Cambridge: Cambridge University Press, 2001).

Kralev, N. 'Bush Approves Nuclear Response', *The Washington Times*, 31 January 2003.

Krasner, S. 'Sovereignty: An Institutional Perspective', in J. Caporaso (ed.), *The Elusive State* (Newbury Park: Sage, 1989).

Krasner, S. *Sovereignty: Organized Hypocrisy* (Princeton: Princeton University Press, 1999).

Kratochwil, F. V. 'Of Systems, Boundaries and Territoriality: An Inquiry into the Formation of the State System', *World Politics*, 39, 1 (1986), pp. 27–52.

Kratochwil, F. V. *Rules, Norms, and Decisions: On the Conditions of Practical and Legal Reasoning in International Relations and Domestic Affairs* (Cambridge: Cambridge University Press, 1989).

Kratochwil, F. V. and Ruggie, J. G. 'International Organization: A State of the Art on an Art of the State', *International Organization*, 40 (1986), pp. 753–75.

Kriedte, P. *Spätfeudalismus und Handelskapital: Grundlienien der europäischen Wirtschaftsgesichte vom 16. bis zum Ausgang des 18. Jahrhunderts* (Göttingen: Vandenhoeck & Ruprecht, 1980).

Kristensen, H. M. 'Nuclear Futures: Proliferation of Weapons of Mass Destruction and U.S. Nuclear Strategy', *BASIC Research Report*, March (1998), p. 10.

Kuehl, D. T. 'Airpower vs. Electricity: Electric Power as a Target for Strategic Air Operations', *Journal of Strategic Studies*, 18, 1 (1995), pp. 250–60.

Kunisch, J. *Staatsverfassung und Mächtepolitik: Zur Genese von Staatenkonflikten im Zeitalter des Absolutismus* (Berlin: Duncker & Humbolt, 1979).

Kupchan, C. A. *The Vulnerability of Empire* (Ithaca: Cornell University Press, 1994).

Kupchan, C. A. 'Hollow Hegemony or Stable Multipolarity?', in G. J. Ikenberry (ed.), *America Unrivaled: The Future of the Balance of Power* (Ithaca: Cornell University Press, 2002), pp. 68–97.

Kupchan, C. A. and Kupchan, C. A. 'Concerts, Collective Security, and the Future of Europe', *International Security*, 16, 1 (1991), pp. 114–61.

Kupchan, C. A. and Kupchan, C. A. 'The Promise of Collective Security', *International Security*, 20, 1 (1995), pp. 52–61.

Kurth, J. 'Industrial Change and Political Change: A European Perspective', in D. Collier (ed.), *The New Authoritarianism in Latin America* (Princeton: Princeton University Press, 1975), pp. 330–3.

Lachmann, R. *Capitalists in Spite of Themselves: Elite Conflict and Economic Transitions in Early Modern Europe* (Oxford: Oxford University Press, 2000).

Lake, D. *Entangling Relations: American Foreign Policy in Its Century* (Princeton: Princeton University Press, 1999).

Lambi, I. N. *The Navy and German Power Politics, 1862–1914* (Boston: Unwin Hyman, 1984).

Lane, F. C. *Profits from Power: Readings in Protection Rent and Violence-Controlling Enterprises* (Albany: State University of New York Press, 1979).

Lauterpacht, H. *International Law: A Treatise* (London: Longmans, 1947).

Lawrence, P. K. *Modernity and War: The Creed of Absolute Violence* (London: Macmillan, 1997).

Layne, C. 'The Unipolar Illusion: Why New Great Powers Will Rise', *International Security*, 17, 4 (1993).

Layne, C. 'Kant or Cant? The Myth of the Democratic Peace', *International Security*, 19, 2 (1994), pp. 5–49.

Lebow, R. N. *Nuclear Crisis Management: A Dangerous Illusion* (Ithaca: Cornell University Press, 1987).

Lebow, R. N. and Stein, J. G. 'Nuclear Lessons of the Cold War', in K. Booth (ed.), *Statecraft and Security: The Cold War and Beyond* (Cambridge: Cambridge University Press, 1998), pp. 71–86.

Lepsius, J. (ed.) *Die Grosse Politik der Europäischen Kabinette, 1871–1914* (Berlin: Deutsche Verlag Gesellschaft für Politik und Gesichte, 1927), 40 vols in 54 parts, XXII, pp. 9–19.

Levy, J. S. *War in the Modern Great-Power System, 1495–1975* (Lexington: University Press of Kentucky, 1983).

Levy, J. S. 'The Diversionary Theory of War: A Critique', in M. Midlarsky (ed.), *Handbook of War Studies* (Boston: Unwin Hyman, 1989), pp. 259–88.

Levy, J. S. 'Long Cycles, Hegemonic Transitions, and the Long Peace', in C. W. Kegley Jr (ed.), *The Long Postwar Peace: Contending Explanations and Projections* (New York: HarperCollins, 1991).

Levy, J. S., Walker, T. C. and Edwards, M. S. 'Continuity and Change in the Evolution of Warfare', in Z. Maoz and A. Gat (eds), *War in a Changing World* (Ann Arbor: University of Michigan Press, 2001).

Levy, Y. *The Other Army of Israel* [Hebrew] (Tel Aviv: Yediot Acharonot, 2003).

Lewis, G., Gronlund, L. and Wright, D. 'National Missile Defense: An Indefensible System', *Foreign Policy*, 117, winter (1999/2000), pp. 120–36.

Li, Q. and Sacko, D. 'The (Ir)Relevance of Militarized Interstate Disputes for International Trade', *International Studies Quarterly*, 46, 1 (2002), pp. 11–34.

Liddell Hart, B. H. *The Decisive Wars of History* (London: Faber & Faber, 1929), reprinted as *Strategy: The Indirect Approach* in 1946 and 1954 and as *Strategy* in 1967 and 1991.

Lieber, K. 'Grasping the Technological Peace: The Offense–Defense Balance and International Security', *International Security*, 25, 1 (2000), pp. 71–104.

Lifschitz, Y. 'Managing Defense After 2000', in H. Golan (ed.), *Israel's Security Web: Core*

Issues of Israel's National Security in Its Sixth Decade [Hebrew] (Tel Aviv: Maarachot, 2001), pp. 57–63.

Linden, R. H. 'Putting on Their Sunday Best: Romania, Hungary, and the Puzzle of Peace', *International Studies Quarterly*, 44, 1 (2000), pp. 121–45.

Lindqvist, S. *Nu dog du: Bombernas århundrade* (Stockholm: Norstedts, 1999).

Lipschutz, R. D. *After Authority: War, Peace, and Global Politics in the 21st Century* (Albany: State University of New York Press, 2000).

Liska, G. *Quest for Equilibrium: America and the Balance of Power on Land and Sea* (Baltimore: Johns Hopkins University Press, 1977).

Livingston, D. 'Dismantling Leviathan', *Harper's Magazine*, 1,824, May (2002), pp. 13–17.

Lorimer, J. *The Institutes of the Law of Nations* (Edinburgh: Blackwood, 1883–4).

Luard, E. *War in International Society: A Study in International Sociology* (New Haven: Yale University Press, 1986).

Luard, E. *The Blunted Sword: The Erosion of Military Power in Modern World Politics* (New York: New Amsterdam; London: I.B. Tauris, 1988).

Lustick, I. *Unsettled States, Disputed Lands* (Ithaca: Cornell University Press, 1993).

Luttwak, E. N. 'Blood and Computers: The Crisis of Classic Military Power in Advanced Postindustrial Societies and the Scope of Technological Remedies', in Z. Maoz and A. Gat (eds), *War in a Changing World* (Ann Arbor: Michigan University Press, 2001), pp. 49–75.

McDonald, D. M. *United Government and Foreign Policy in Russia, 1900–1914* (Cambridge, Mass.: Harvard University Press, 1992).

Macfarlane, A. 'The Cradle of Capitalism: The Case of England', in J. Baechler, J. A. Hall and M. Mann (eds), *Europe and the Rise of Capitalism* (Oxford: Basil Blackwell, 1988), pp. 185–203.

McGeorge, B. *Danger and Survival* (New York: Random House, 1988).

Mack, A. 'Civil War: Academic Research and the Policy Community', *Journal of Peace Research*, 39, 5 (2002), pp. 515–25.

McLean, D. *Britain and Her Buffer State: The Collapse of the Persian Empire, 1890–1914* (London, 1979).

McMahon, K. S. *Pursuit of the Shield: The U.S. Quest for Limited Ballistic Missile Defense* (Lanham: University Press of America, 1997).

Macmillan, S. M. 'Interdependence and Conflict', Mershon International Studies Review, 41, 1 (1997), pp. 33–58.

McNeill, W. H. *The Pursuit of Power: Technology, Armed Forces, and Society since A.D. 1000* (Chicago: University of Chicago Press, 1982).

Maddison, A. 'Dutch Income In and From Indonesia, 1700–1938', *Modern Asian Studies*, 23, 4 (1989), pp. 645–670.

Maddison, A. 'Dutch Colonialism in Indonesia: A Comparative Perspective', in A. Booth, W. J. O'Malley and A. Weidemann (eds), *Indonesian Economic History in the Dutch Colonial Era* (New Haven: Yale University South East Asian Studies, 1990).

Malozemoff, A. M. *Russian Far Eastern Policy, 1881–1904* (Berkeley: University of California Press, 1958).

Mandelbaum, M. *The Nuclear Revolution: Politics Before and After Hiroshima* (Cambridge: Cambridge University Press, 1981).

Mandelbaum, M. (ed.) *Central Asia and the World* (New York: Council on Foreign Relations Press, 1994).

Mandelbaum, M. 'Is Major War Obsolete', *Survival*, 40, 4 (1998–9), pp. 28–40.

Mandelbaum, M. 'Learning to be Warless', *Survival*, 41, 2 (1999), pp. 149–52.

Mandelbaum, M. *The Ideas That Conquered the World: Peace, Democracy, and Free Markets in the Twenty-first Century* (New York: Public Affairs, 2002).

Mann, M. *The Sources of Social Power*, Vol. I: *A History of Power from the Beginning of A.D. 1760* (Cambridge: Cambridge University Press, 1986).

Mann, M. *States, War, and Capitalism: Studies in Political Sociology* (Oxford: Basil Blackwell, 1988).

Mann, M. *The Sources of Social Power*, Vol. II: *The Rise of Classes and Nation-States, 1760–1914* (Cambridge: Cambridge University Press, 1993).

Mansbach, R. W. and Vasquez, J. *In Search of Theory: A New Paradigm for Global Politics* (New York: Columbia University Press, 1981).

Mansfield, E. 'The Concentration of Capabilities and the Onset of War', *Journal of Conflict Resolution*, 36 (1992), pp. 3–24.

March, J. G. and Olsen, J. P. *Rediscovering Institutions* (New York: Free Press, 1989).

March, J. G. and Olsen, J. P. 'The Institutional Dynamics of International Political Orders', *International Organization*, 53, 4 (1998), pp. 943–69.

Marseille, J. *Empire Coloniale et Capitalisme Français* (Paris: Albin Michel, 1984).

Marshall, M. G. and Gurr, T. R. *Peace and Conflict, 2003: A Global Survey of Armed Conflicts, Self-Determination Movements, and Democracy* (College Park: Center for International Development and Conflict Management, University of Maryland, 2003).

Martel, W. C. 'Deterrence and Alternative Images of Nuclear Possession', in T. V. Paul, R. Harknett and J. Wirtz (eds), *The Absolute Weapon Revisited: Nuclear Arms and the Emerging International Order* (Ann Arbor: University of Michigan Press, 1998), pp. 213–34.

Martin, B. *German–Persian Diplomatic Relations, 1873–1912* (The Hague: Mouton & Co.:'s-Gravenhage, 1959).

Martin, L. and Simmons, B. 'Theories and Empirical Studies of International Institutions', *International Organization*, 52, 4 (1998), pp. 729–57.

Mastanduno, M. 'A Realist View: Three Images of the Coming International Order', in T. V. Paul and John Hall (eds), *International Order and the Future of World Politics* (Cambridge: Cambridge University Press, 1999).

Mastanduno, M. 'Nuclear Weapons and US Grand Strategy Today', in D. G. Haglund (ed.), *Pondering NATO's Nuclear Options* (Kingston: Queens Quarterly, 1999), pp. 59–79.

Matthew, H. C. G. 'Hobson, Ruskin and Cobden', in M. Fredeen (ed.), *Reappraising J. A. Hobson: Humanism and Welfare* (London: Unwin Hyman, 1990), pp. 11–53.

Matthews, J. T. 'Power Shift', *Foreign Affairs*, 76, 1 (1997), pp. 50–66.

May, E. R. 'Introduction', in J. L. Gaddis, P. H. Gordon, E. R. May and J. Rosenberg (eds), *Cold War Statesmen Confront the Bomb: Nuclear Diplomacy since 1945* (Oxford: Oxford University Press, 1999), pp. 1–11.

Mayer, A. *The Persistence of the Old Regime: Europe to the Great War* (New York: Pantheon Books, 1981).

Mearsheimer, J. J. 'Back to the Future: Instability in Europe After the Cold War', *International Security*, 15 (1990), pp. 5–56.

Mearsheimer, J. J. 'The False Promise of International Institutions', *International Security*, 19, 3 (1995), pp. 5–49.

Mearsheimer, J. J. *The Tragedy of Great Power Politics* (New York: W. W. Norton, 2001).

Melada, I. *Guns for Sale: War and Capitalism in British Literature, 1851–1939* (London: McFarland, 1983).

Melzer, Y. *Just War* (Leiden: Sijthoff, 1975).

Mencken, H. L. *Prejudices: Second Series* (New York: Knopf, 1920).

Mendelsohn, J. 'NATO's Nuclear Weapons: The Rationale for No-first Use', *Arms Control Today*, July/August (1999), pp. 3–8.

Metz, S. 'The U.N. After the Cold War: Renaissance or Indian Summer?', in H. H. Almond, Jr and J. A. Burger (eds), *The History and Future of Warfare* (The Hague: Kluwer Law International, 1999), pp. 859–82.

Miller, B. 'Hot Wars, Cold Peace: An International–Regional Synthesis', in Z. Maoz and A. Gat (eds), *War in a Changing World* (Ann Arbor: University of Michigan Press, 2001), pp. 93–141.

Miller, B. 'The Global Sources of Regional Transitions from War to Peace', *Journal of Peace Research*, 38, 2 (2001), pp. 199–225.

Miller, J. D. B. *Norman Angell and the Futility of War: Peace and the Public Mind* (London: Macmillan, 1986).

Miller, L. H. 'The Idea and Reality of Collective Security', *Global Governance*, 5, 3 (1999), pp. 303–32.

Milward, A. S. *War, Economy and Society, 1939–1945* (Berkeley: University of California Press, 1977).

Mitchell, A. *Victors and Vanquished: The German Influence on Army and Church in France after 1870* (Chapel Hill: University of North Carolina Press, 1984).

Mlyn, E. 'U.S. Nuclear Policy and the End of the Cold War', in T. V. Paul, R. Harknett and J. Wirtz (eds), *The Absolute Weapon Revisited: Nuclear Arms and the Emerging International Order* (Ann Arbor: University of Michigan Press, 1998), pp. 137–66.

Modelski, G. *Long Cycles in World Politics* (Seattle: University of Washington Press, 1987).

Montesquieu, *The Spirit of Laws* (tr. and ed. by A. Cohler, B. C. Miller and H. S. Stone), (Cambridge: Cambridge University Press, 1989 [1748]).

Moore, B. Jr *Social Origins of Dictatorship and Democracy: Lord and Peasant in the Making of the Modern World* (Boston: Beacon Press, 1996).

Moravcsik, A. 'Negotiating the Single European Act', *International Organization*, 45, 1 (1991), pp. 19–56.

Morgan, P. M. *Deterrence: A Conceptual Analysis* (Beverly Hills: Sage Publications, 1977).

Morgan, P. M. 'Getting the "Liberalist" Transition Under Way: The Experience of the East Asian Regional International System', *The Korean Journal of Defense Analysis*, XI, 2 (1999), pp. 5–34.

Morgan, P. M. 'The Impact of the Revolution in Military Affairs', *The Journal of Strategic Studies*, 23, 1 (2000), pp. 132–61.

Morgan, P. M. *Deterrence Now* (Cambridge: Cambridge University Press, 2003).

Mott IV, W. H. *The Economic Basis of Peace: Linkages between Economic Growth and International Conflict* (Westport: Greenwood Press, 1997).

Mueller, J. *Retreat from Doomsday: The Obsolescence of Major War* (New York: Basic Books, 1989).

Mueller, J. 'The Essential Irrelevance of Nuclear Weapons: Stability in the Postwar World', in S. Lynn-Jones and S. Miller (eds), *The Cold War and After* (Cambridge, Mass.: MIT Press, 1994).

Mueller, J. *Quiet Cataclysm: Reflections on the Recent Transformation of World Politics* (New York: HarperCollins, 1995).

Mueller, J. 'The Escalating Irrelevance of Nuclear Weapons', in T.V. Paul, R. Harknett and

J. Wirtz (eds), *The Absolute Weapon Revisited: Nuclear Arms and the Emerging International Order* (Ann Arbor: University of Michigan Press, 1998), pp. 73–98.

Mueller, J. 'Epilogue: Duelling Counterfactuals', in J. L. Gaddis, P. H. Gordon, E. R. May and J. Rosenberg (eds), *Cold War Statesmen Confront the Bomb: Nuclear Diplomacy since 1945* (Oxford: Oxford University Press, 1999), pp. 272–83.

Mueller, J. *Capitalism, Democracy, and Ralph's Pretty Good Grocery* (Princeton: Princeton University Press, 1999).

Mueller, J. *The Remnants of War* (Ithaca: Cornell University Press, 2004).

Mueller, J. and Mueller, K. 'The Methodology of Mass Destruction: Assessing Threats in the New World Order', *Journal of Strategic Studies*, 23, 1 (2000), pp. 163–87.

Mumford, L. *Technics and Civilization* (San Diego: Harcourt Brace Jovanovich, 1963 [1934]).

Mumford, L. *The Pentagon of Power: The Myth of the Machine* (New York: Harcourt Brace Jovanovich, 1970).

Murat, I. *Colbert* (Charlottesville: University Press of Virginia, 1984).

Murray, W. and Knox, M. 'Thinking about Revolutions in Warfare', in M. Knox and W. Murray (eds), *The Dynamics of Military Revolution 1300–2050* (Cambridge: Cambridge University Press, 2001), pp. 1–14.

Myrdal, A. 'The High Price of Nuclear Arms Monopoly', *Foreign Policy*, 18, spring (1975), pp. 30–43.

Nadelman, E. A. 'Global Prohibition Regimes: The Evolution of Norms in International Society', *International Organization*, 44, 4 (1990), pp. 479–526.

National Academy of Sciences, Committee on International Security and Arms Control, *The Future of U.S. Nuclear Weapons Policy* (Washington DC: National Academy Press, 1997).

Nef, J. U. *War and Human Progress: An Essay on the Rise of Industrial Civilization* (New York: W. W. Norton, 1978 [1950]).

Neiberg, M. S. *Warfare in World History* (London: Routledge, 2001).

Nolan, J. E. *An Elusive Consensus: Nuclear Weapons and American Security after the Cold War* (Washington DC: Brookings Institution Press, 1999).

North, D. C. *Structure and Change in Economic History* (New York: W. W. Norton, 1981).

Nye, J. S. and Donahue, J. D. (eds) *Governance in a Globalizing World* (Washington, DC: Brookings Institution Press, 2000).

O'Brien, P. K. and Hunt, P. A. 'England, 1485–1815', in R. Bonney (ed.), *The Rise of the Fiscal State in Europe, c. 1200–1815* (Oxford: Oxford University Press, 1999), pp. 53–100.

O'Connell, R. L. *Of Arms and Men: A History of War, Weapons, and Aggression* (Oxford: Oxford University Press, 1989).

O'Connell, R. L. *Ride of the Second Horseman: The Birth and Death of War* (Oxford: Oxford University Press, 1995).

O'Hanlon, M. 'Star Wars Strike Back', *Foreign Affairs*, 78, November/December (1999), pp. 68–82.

Okamoto, S. *The Japanese Oligarchy and the Russo-Japanese War* (New York: Columbia University Press, 1970).

Olson, M. *Power and Prosperity: Outgrowing Communist and Capitalist Dictatorships* (New York: Basic Books, 2000).

Oren, I. and Hays, J. 'Democracies May Rarely Fight Each Other, but Developed Socialist States Rarely Fight At All', *Alternatives*, 22, 4 (1997), pp. 493–522.

Organski, A. F. K. *World Politics*, 2nd edn (New York: Alfred A. Knopf, 1968).

Organski, A. F. K. and Kugler, J. *The War Ledger* (Chicago: University of Chicago Press, 1980).

Overy, R. J. *The Air War 1939–1945* (London: Europa, 1980).

Overy, R. J. *The Nazi Economic Recovery 1932–1938* (London: Macmillan, 1982).

Owens, B. *Lifting the Fog of War* (New York: Farrar, Strauss, Giroux, 2000).

Oye, K. 'The Sterling–Dollar–France Triangle: Monetary Diplomacy 1929–1973', in K. Oye (ed.), *Cooperation Under Anarchy* (Princeton: Princeton University Press, 1986).

Oye, K. A. 'Explaining Cooperation Under Anarchy: Hypotheses and Strategies', in K. A. Oye (ed.), *Cooperation Under Anarchy* (Princeton: Princeton University Press, 1986), pp. 1–24.

Padfield, P. *Tide of Empires: Decisive Naval Campaigns in the Rise of the West*, Vol. 2: *1654–1763* (London: Routledge & Kegan Paul, 1982).

Paine, S. C. M. *Imperial Rivals: China, Russia, and Their Disputed Frontier* (Armonk and London: S. E. Sharpe, 1996).

Parent, M. *Vauban: Un encyclopediste avant la lettre* (Paris: Berger-Levrault, 1982).

Parker, G. *Europe in Crisis: 1598–1648* (Ithaca: Cornell University Press, 1979).

Parker, G. *The Military Revolution and the Rise of the West, 1500–1800* (Cambridge: Cambridge University Press, 1988).

Parker, G. (ed.) *The Thirty Years' War*, 2nd edn (New York: Routledge, 1997).

Paul, T.V. *Asymmetric Conflicts: War Initiation by Weaker Powers* (Cambridge: Cambridge University Press, 1994).

Paul, T. V. 'Nuclear Taboo and War Initiation in Regional Conflicts', *Journal of Conflict Resolution*, 39 (1995), pp. 696–717.

Paul, T.V. 'Great Equalizers or the Agents of Chaos? Weapons of Mass Destruction and the Emerging International Order', in T.V. Paul and J. A. Hall (eds), *International Order and the Future of World Politics* (Cambridge: Cambridge University Press, 1999).

Paul, T. V. *Power versus Prudence: Why Nations Forgo Nuclear Weapons* (Montreal and Kingston: McGill-Queen's University Press, 2000).

Paul, T. V. *States, Security Function and the New Global Forces* (Montreal: Group d'Étude et de Recherche sur la Securité Internationale/Research Group in International Security, Université de Montréal/McGill University, 2001, Note de Recherche/Working Paper 10).

Paxton, R. and Wahl, N. (eds) *De Gaulle and the United States* (Oxford: Berg Publishers, 1994).

Pearton, M. *Diplomacy, War and Technology since 1830* (Lawrence: University of Kansas Press, 1983).

Penn, W. *An Essay Towards the Present and Future Peace of Europe* (Hildesheim: Olms, 1983 [1699]).

Perotin-Dumon, A. 'The Pirate and the Emperor: Power and the Law on the Seas, 1450–1850', in James Tracy (ed.), *The Political Economy of Merchant Empires* (Cambridge: Cambridge University Press, 1997), pp. 196–227.

Pfaff, W. 'The Question of Hegemony', *Foreign Affairs*, 80 (2001), pp. 221–32.

Philpott, D. 'Usurping the Sovereignty of Sovereignty?', *World Politics*, 53, 2 (2001), pp. 297–324.

Picco, G. 'The UN and the Use of Force', *Foreign Affairs*, 73, 5 (1994), pp. 14–18.

Pick, D. *War Machine: The Rationalization of Slaughter in the Modern Age* (New Haven: Yale University Press, 1995).

Polanyi, K. *The Great Transformation: The Political and Economic Origins of Our Times* (Boston: Beacon Press, 1957).

Pollins, B. 'Conflict, Cooperation, and Commerce: The Effect of International Political Interactions on Bilateral Trade Flows', *American Journal of Political Science*, 33, 3 (1989), pp. 737–61.

Pollins, B. 'Does Trade Still Follow the Flag?', *American Political Science Review*, 83, 2 (1989).

Pomeranz, K. and Topic, S. *The World That Trade Created: Society, Culture, and the World Economy, 1400–The Present* (Armonk: M. E. Sharpe, 1999).

Porter, B. *War and the Rise of the State: The Military Foundations of Modern Politics* (New York: Free Press, 1994).

Price, R. 'A Genealogy of the Chemical Weapons Taboo', *International Organization*, 49, 1 (1995), pp. 73–103.

Price, R. 'Reversing the Gun Sights: Transnational Civil Society Targets Land Mines', *International Organization*, 52, 3 (1998), pp. 613–44.

Prins, G. and Tromp, H. (eds) *The Future of War* (The Hague: Kluwer Law International, 2000).

Przetacznik, F. 'The Illegality of the Concept of Just War under Contemporary International Law', *Revue de Droit International*, 70, 4 (1993), pp. 245–94.

Rabin, M. 'Psychology and Economics', *Journal of Economic Literature*, 36 (1998), pp. 11–46.

Rapoport, A. 'Editor's Introduction', in C. von Clausewitz, *On War* (Harmondsworth: Pelican Books, 1968 [1832]).

Rasler, K. and Thompson, W. 'War Making and State Making', *American Political Science Review*, 79, 2 (1985), pp. 491–507.

Rauf, T. 'Disarmament and Non-Proliferation Treaties', in G. A. Wood and L. S. Leland Jr (eds), *State and Sovereignty: Is the State in Retreat?* (Dunedin: University of Otago Press, 1997), pp. 142–88.

Rauschning, H. *Hitler Speaks: A Series of Conversations with Adolf Hitler on his Real Aims* (London: Thornton Butterworth, 1939).

Ray, J. L. 'The Abolition of Slavery and the End of International War', *International Organization*, 43, 3 (1989), pp. 405–39.

Raymond, G. A. 'International Norms: Normative Orders and Peace', in J. A. Vasquez (ed.), *What Do We Know About War?* (Lanham: Roman & Littlefield, 2000), pp. 281–97.

Record, J. 'Collapsed Countries, Casualty Dread, and the New American Way of War', *Parameters*, summer (2002), pp. 4–23.

Reid, B. H. *J. F. C. Fuller: The Military Thinker* (London: Macmillan, 1987).

Reiter, D. and Stam, A. C. *Democracies at War* (Princeton: Princeton University Press, 2002).

Reynolds, R. L. *Europe Emerges: Transition Towards an Industrial World-wide Society 600–1750* (Madison: University of Wisconsin Press, 1982 [1961]).

Rhodes, E. 'Constructing Peace and War: An Analysis of the Power of Ideas to Shape American Military Power', *Millennium*, 24, 1 (1995).

Rich, N. *Friedrich von Holstein: Politics and Diplomacy in the Era of Bismarck and Wilhelm II*, 2 vols (Cambridge: Cambridge University Press, 1965).

Rich, N. and M. H. Fisher (eds) *The Holstein Papers IV* (Cambridge: Cambridge University Press, 1955–63).

Richardson, J. L. *Crisis Diplomacy: The Great Powers since the Mid-Nineteenth Century* (Cambridge: Cambridge University Press, 1994).

Ricks, T. E. 'U.S. Faces Defense Choices: Terminator, Peacekeeping Globocop or Combination', *The Wall Street Journal*, 12 November 1999.

Riley, J. C. *The Seven Years War and the Old Regime in France: The Economic and Financial Toll* (Princeton: Princeton University Press, 1986).

Ritcher, P. 'U.S. Weighs Tactical Nuclear Strike on Iraq', www.latimes.com, 26 January 2003.

Roberts, A. 'The Crisis in UN Peacekeeping', in C. A. Crocker, F. O. Hampson and P. Aalt (eds), *Managing Global Chaos: Sources of and Responses to International Conflict* (Washington DC: US Institute of Peace Press, 1996), pp. 297–319.

Roberts, A. 'The United Nations: A System for Collective International Security?' in G. A. S. C. Wilson (ed.), *British Security 2010* (Camberley: Camberley Staff College, Strategic and Combat Studies Institute, 1996), pp. 65–8.

Robinson, E. V. D. 'War and Economics in History and in Theory', *Political Science Quarterly*, 15, 4 (1900), pp. 581–627.

Robinson, R. and Gallagher, J. *Africa and the Victorian Mind: The Official Mind of Imperialism* (London: Macmillan, 1965).

Rogers, C. J. 'The Age of Hundred Years War', in M. Keen (ed.), *Medieval Warfare: A History* (Oxford: Oxford University Press, 1999).

Roppe, T. *War in the Modern World* (London: Collier Macmillan, 1962).

Rosecrance, R. *The Rise of the Trading State: Commerce and Conquest in the Modern World* (New York: Basic Books, 1986).

Rosecrance, R. *The Rise of the Virtual State: Wealth and Power in the Coming Century* (New York: Basic Books, 1999).

Rosenau, J. 'New Dimensions of Security: The Interaction of Globalizing and Localizing Dynamics', *Security Dialogue*, 25, 3 (1994), pp. 255–81.

Rosenberg, H. *Bureaucracy, Aristocracy and Autocracy: The Prussian Experience 1660–1815* (Boston: Beacon Press, 1958).

Rosenthal, J.-L. 'The Political Economy of Absolutism Reconsidered', in R. H. Bates *et al.* (eds), *Analytic Narratives* (Princeton: Princeton University Press, 1998).

Rotberg, R. 'New Breed of African Leader', *Christian Science Monitor*, 9 January 2002, p. 9.

Rothenberg, G. 'Maurice of Nassau, Gustavus Adolphus, Raimondo Montecuccoli, and the "Military Revolution" of the Seventeenth Century', in P. Paret (ed.), *Makers of Modern Strategy from Machiavelli to the Nuclear Era* (Princeton: Princeton University Press, 1986), pp. 34–45.

Ruggie, J. G. 'Multilateralism: The Anatomy of an Institution', in J. G. Ruggie (ed.), *Multilateralism Matters: The Theory and Praxis of an Institutional Form* (New York: Columbia University Press, 1993), pp. 1–47.

Rumsfeld, D. H. 'Transforming the Military', *Foreign Affairs*, 81, 3 (2002), pp. 20–32.

Russett, B. *Controlling the Sword: The Democratic Governance of National Security* (Cambridge, Mass.: Harvard University Press, 1990).

Russett, B. *Grasping the Democratic Peace: Principles for a Post-Cold War World* (Princeton: Princeton University Press, 1993).

Russett, B. and Oneal, J. R. *Triangulating Peace: Democracy, Interdependence, and International Organizations* (New York: W. W. Norton, 2001).

Russett, B., Oneal, J. and Davis, D. R. 'The Third Leg of the Kantian Tripod for Peace: International Organizations and Militarized Disputes, 1950–85', *International Organization*, 52, 3 (1998), pp. 441–67.

Sabrosky, A. N. (ed.) *Polarity and War: The Changing Structure of International Conflict* (Boulder: Westview, 1985).

Sagan, S. D. *Moving Targets* (Princeton: Princeton University Press, 1989).

Sagan, S. D. *The Limits of Safety: Organizations, Accidents and Nuclear Weapons* (Princeton: Princeton University Press, 1993).

Saita, A. 'Un Riformatore pacifista Contemporaneo de Richelieu: E. Cruce', *Rivista Storica Italiana*, 64 (1951), pp. 183–92.

Sarkees, M. R., Wayman, F. and Singer, J. D. 'Inter-State, Intra-State, and Extra-State Wars: A Comprehensive Look at their Distribution over Time', *International Studies Quarterly*, 47, 1 (2003), pp. 49–70.

Sarkees, M. R. and Singer, J. D. 'The Correlates of War Warsets: The Totality of War', Paper presented at the annual meeting of the International Studies Association, Chicago, 21–24 February 2001.

Schama, S. *The Embarrassment of Riches* (New York: Alfred A. Knopf, 1987).

Schelling, T. C. *The Strategy of Conflict* (Cambridge, Mass.: Harvard University Press, 1960).

Schelling, T. S. *Arms and Influence* (New Haven: Yale University Press, 1966).

Schöllgen, G. *Imperialismus und Gleichgewicht: Deutschland, England und die orientalische Frage 1871–1914* (Munich: R. Oldenbourg, 1984).

Schottelius, H. and Deist, W. (eds) *Marine und Marinepolitik im kaiserlichen Deutschland, 1871–1914* (Düsseldorf: Droste, 1972).

Schreker, O. 'Leibnitz, ses idées sur l'organisation des Relations Internationales', *Proceedings of the British Academy*, 23 (1937), pp. 218–19.

Schroeder, P. W. 'Alliances, 1815–1945: Weapons of War and Tools of Management', in K. Knorr (ed.), *Historical Dimensions of National Security Problems* (Lawrence: University Press of Kansas, 1976), pp. 227–62.

Schroeder, P. W. 'A Pointless Enduring Rivalry: France and the Habsburg Monarchy, 1715–1918', in W. R. Thompson (ed.), *Great Power Rivalries* (Columbia: University of South Carolina Press, 1999).

Schulte, B. F. *Vor dem Kriegsbruch 1914: Deutschland, die Türkei und der Balkan* (Düsseldorf: Droste, 1980).

Schulze, H. *States, Nations, and Nationalism: From the Middle Ages to the Present* (tr. by William E. Yuill), (Oxford: Basil Blackwell, 1996).

Schumpeter, J. A. 'The Sociology of Imperialisms', reprinted in R. Swedberg (ed.), *The Economics and Sociology of Capitalism* (Princeton: Princeton University Press, 1991 [1919]).

Schwartz, H. M. *States versus Markets: The Emergence of a Global Economy*, 2nd edn (New York: St Martin's Press, 2000).

Schweller, R. L. 'The Problem of International Order Revisited: A Review Essay', *International Security*, 26, 1 (2001), pp. 161–86.

Schweller, R. L. 'Correspondence', *International Security*, 27, 1 (2002), pp. 181–85.

Senghaas, D. 'Zivilisierung und Gewalt: Wie den Frieden gewinnen?', in W. R. Vogt (ed.), *Frieden als Zivilisierungsprojekt – Neue Herausforderungen an die Friedens- und Konfliktforschung* (Baden-Baden: Nomos, 1995), pp. 37–55.

Shambaugh, D. 'Facing Reality in China Policy', *Foreign Affairs*, 80, January/February (2001), pp. 50–64.

Shaw, M. *Post-Military Society: Militarism, Demilitarization and War at the End of the Twentieth Century* (Philadelphia: Temple University Press, 1991).

Sidorenko, A. A. *The Offensive* (Washington DC: Government Printing Office, 1970).

Siegelberg, J. *Kapitalismus und Krieg: Eine Theorie des Krieges in der Weltgesellschaft* (LIT Verlag, 1994).

Sigal, L. V. 'No First Use and NATO's Nuclear Posture', in J. D. Steinbruner and L. V. Sigal (eds), *Alliance Security: NATO and the No-First Use Question* (Washington DC: The Brookings Institution, 1983).

Sikkink, K. 'The Power of Principled Ideas: Human Rights Policies in the United States and Western Europe', in J. Goldstein and R. Keohane (eds), *Ideas and Foreign Policy* (Ithaca: Cornell University Press, 1993), pp. 139–70.

Simai, M. *The Future of Global Governance* (Washington DC: US Institute of Peace Press, 1994).

Simmons, B. A. 'Compliance With International Agreements', in N. W. Polsby (ed.), *Annual Review of Political Science, Volume I 1998* (Palo Alto: Annual Reviews, 1998), pp. 75–93.

Simpkin, R. *Race to the Swift* (London: Pergamon Press, 1985).

Singer, J. D. 'Peace in the Global System: Displacement, Interregnum, or Transformation?', in C. W. Kegley Jr (ed.), *The Long Postwar Peace:Contending Explanations and Projections* (New York: HarperCollins, 1991).

Singer, J. D., Bremer, S. and Stuckey, J. 'Capability Distribution, Uncertainty, and Major Power War', in B. Russett (ed.), *Peace, War, and Numbers* (Beverly Hills: Sage, 1972), pp. 19–48.

Singer, M. and Wildawsky, A. *The Real World Order: Zones of Peace/Zones of Turmoil* (Chatham: Chatham House, 1993).

Small, M. and Singer, J. D. *Resort to Arms: International Civil Wars, 1816–1980* (Beverly Hills: Sage, 1982).

Smalldone, W. *Rudolf Hilferding: The Tragedy of a German Social Democrat* (Dekalb: Northern Illinois University Press, 1998).

Smith, A. *An Inquiry into the Nature and Causes of the Wealth of Nations* (ed. by E. Cannan), (Chicago: University of Chicago Press, 1976 [1776]).

Smith, R. J. 'Clinton Directive Changes Strategy on Nuclear Arms', *The Washington Post*, 7 December 1997, p. A01.

Smith, T. *The Pattern of Imperialism* (New York: Cambridge University Press, 1981).

Snider, D. M. 'The Coming Defense Train Wreck', *Washington Quarterly*, 19, 1 (1996), p. 92.

Snyder, G. 'The Balance of Power and the Balance of Terror', in P. Seabury (ed.), *The Balance of Power* (San Francisco: Chandler, 1965), pp. 184–205.

Snyder, J. *Ideology of the Offensive: Military Decision Making and the Disasters of 1914* (Ithaca: Cornell University Press, 1984).

Snyder, J. *Myths of Empire* (Ithaca: Cornell University Press, 1991).

Snyder, J. and Ballentine, K. 'Nationalism and the Marketplace of Ideas', *International Security*, 21, 2 (1996), pp. 5–40.

Solingen, E. *Regional Orders at Century's Dawn: Global and Domestic Influences on Grand Strategy* (Princeton: Princeton University Press, 1998).

Sombart, W. *Krieg und Kapitalismus* (München: Verlag von Duncker & Humboldt, 1913).

Sowards, S. W. *Austria's Policy of Macedonian Reform* (Boulder: East European Monographs, 1989).

Spinney, F. *Defense Facts of Life* (Boulder: Westview, 1986).

Spruyt, H. *The Sovereign State and Its Competitors: An Analysis of Systems Change* (Princeton: Princeton University Press, 1994).

Spruyt, H. 'The End of Empire and the Extension of the Westphalian System: The Normative Basis of the Modern State Order', *International Studies Review*, 2, 2 (2000), pp. 65–92.

Stein, A. A. *Why Nations Cooperate: Circumstances and Choice in International Relations* (Ithaca: Cornell University Press, 1990).

Steinbruner, J. D. and Segal, L. V. (eds) *Alliance Security: NATO and the No-First Use Question* (Washington DC: The Brookings Institution, 1983).

Stevenson, D. *Armaments and the Coming of War: Europe, 1904–1914* (Oxford: Oxford University Press, 1996).

Stevenson, D. 'Militarization and Diplomacy in Europe before 1914', *International Security* 22, 1 (1997), pp. 125–61.

Strachan, H. *European Armies and the Conduct of War* (London: Allen & Unwin, 1983).

Strunk, M. 'The Quarter's Polls', *Public Opinion Quarterly*, 14, 1 (1950), p. 182.

Tallett, F. *War and Society in Early-Modern Europe, 1495–1715* (London: Routledge, 1992).

Tammen, R. L. *et al. Power Transitions: Strategies for the 21st Century* (New York: Chatham House, 2000).

Tannenwald, N. 'The Nuclear Taboo: The United States and the Normative Basis of Nuclear Non-Use', *International Organization*, 53, 3 (1999), pp. 433–68.

Teschke, B. 'Geopolitical Relations in the European Middle Ages: History and Theory', *International Organization*, 52, 2 (1998), pp. 339–41.

Thompson, J. E. *Mercenaries, Pirates, and Sovereigns: State-building and Extraterritorial Violence in Early Modern Europe* (Princeton: Princeton University Press, 1994).

Thompson, K. W. *Toynbee's Philosophy of World History and Politics* (Baton Rouge: Louisiana State University Press, 1985).

Thompson, W. R. *On Global War: Historical–Structural Approaches to World Politics* (Columbia: University of South Carolina Press, 1988).

Thompson, W. R. 'Long Cycles and Global War', in M. Midlarsky (ed.), *Handbook of War Studies* (Ann Arbor: University of Michigan Press, 1989).

Thompson, W. R. and Tucker, R. 'A Tale of Two Democratic Peace Critiques', *Journal of Conflict Resolution*, 41, 3 (1997), pp. 428–54.

Thomson, J. 'State Practices, International Norms, and the Decline of Mercenarism', *International Studies Quarterly*, 34, 1 (1990), pp. 23–48.

Tilly, C. *Coercion, Capital, and European States, AD 990–1990* (Oxford: Basil Blackwell, 1990).

Tilly, C. *The Politics of Collective Violence* (New York: Cambridge University Press, 2003).

Toumanoff, P. 'Economic Reform and Industrial Performance in the Soviet Union: 1950–1984', *Comparative Economic Studies*, 29, 4 (1987), pp. 128–49.

Trebilcock, C. 'War and the Failure of Industrial Mobilization: 1899 and 1914', in J. M. Winter (ed.), *War and Economic Development* (Cambridge: Cambridge University Press, 1975), pp. 139–64.

Trumpener, U. *Germany and the Ottoman Empire, 1914–1918* (Princeton: Princeton University Press, 1968).

Tuck, R. *The Rights of War and Peace: Political Thought and the International Order from Grotius to Kant* (Oxford: Oxford University Press, 1999).

Turner, S. *Caging the Nuclear Genie: An American Challenge for Global Security* (Boulder: Westview Press, 1997).

Tyler, P. E. 'Russia and U.S. Optimistic on Defense Issues', www.nytimes.com, 19 October 2001.

Unger, R. *Plasticity into Power* (New York: Cambridge University Press, 1987).

U.S. President, 'The National Security Strategy of the United States of America', www.whitehouse.gov/nsc/nss.pdf, September 2002.

329

U.S. White House, 'National Strategy to Combat Weapons of Mass Destruction', www.whitehouse.gov/news/releases/2002/12/WMDStrategy.pdf, December 2002.

Valentino, B. *Final Solutions* (Ithaca: Cornell University Press, 2004).

Valleau, J. 'The Final Frontier', *Globe and Mail* (Toronto), 15 January 2001, p. A9.

Van Cleave, R. and Barnett, R. W. 'Strategic Adaptability', *Orbis*, 18, 3 (1974), pp. 655–76.

Van Creveld, M. *Technology and War from 2000 B.C. to the Present* (New York: Free Press, 1989).

Van Creveld, M. *The Transformation of War* (New York: Free Press, 1991).

Van Creveld, M. *The Rise and Decline of the State* (Cambridge: Cambridge University Press, 1999).

Van Creveld, M. 'The Future of War', in R. G. Patman (ed.), *Security in a Post-Cold War World* (New York: St Martin's Press, 1999), pp. 22–36.

Van den Doel, H. W. *Het Rijk van Insulinde* (Amsterdam: Prometheus, 1996).

Van Doorn, J. A. 'The Dutch–Indonesian Conflict and the Persistence of the Colonial Pattern', *The Netherlands Journal of Social Sciences*, 31, 2 (1995), pp. 153–71.

Van Doorn, J. A. *Indische lessen* (Amsterdam: Uitgeverij Bert Bakker, 1995).

Van Evera, S. 'Offense, Defense, and the Causes of War', *International Security*, 22, 4 (1998), pp. 5–43.

Van Evera, S. *Causes of War: Power and the Roots of Conflict* (Ithaca: Cornell University Press, 1999).

Vasquez, J. A. *The Power of Power Politics: A Critique* (New Brunswick: Rutgers University Press, 1983).

Vasquez, J. A. 'The Deterrence Myth: Nuclear Weapons and the Prevention of Nuclear War', in C. W. Kegley Jr (ed.), *The Long Postwar Peace: Contending Explanations and Projections* (New York: HarperCollins, 1991).

Vasquez, J. A. *The War Puzzle* (Cambridge: Cambridge University Press, 1993).

Vasquez, J. A. 'What Do We Know About War?', in J. A. Vasquez (ed.), *What Do We Know About War?* (Lanham: Rowman & Littlefield, 2000), pp. 366–8.

Vasquez, J. A. 'Mapping the Probability of War and Analyzing the Possibility of Peace: The Role of Territorial Disputes', Presidential Address to the Peace Science Society (International), *Conflict Management and Peace Science*, 18 (2001), pp. 145–73.

Vasquez, J. A. and Henehan, M. 'Territorial Disputes and the Probability of War, 1815–1992', *Journal of Peace Research*, 38, 2 (2001), pp. 123–38.

Vaughan, C. E. *The Political Writings of J. J. Rousseau* (Cambridge: Cambridge University Press, 1915).

Väyrynen, R. 'Joseph A. Schumpeter on Imperialism and War: A Historical and Conceptual Inquiry', in Pauli Kettunen (ed.), *Jäljillä: Kirjoituksia historian ongelmista*, Vol. 2 (Turku: Aurora Books, 2000), pp. 91–122.

Veblen, T. *Imperial Germany and the Industrial Revolution* (New York: Viking Press, 1939 [1915]).

Veblen, T. *The Nature of Peace*, with a new introduction by W. J. Samuels (New Brunswick: Transaction Publishers, 1998 [1917]).

Virilio, P. 'Military Space', in J. D. Derian (ed.), *The Virilio Reader* (Oxford: Blackwell, 1998), pp. 22–8.

Von Bismarck, O. *Reflections and Reminiscences*, Vol. 2 (London: Smith, 1898).

Von Treitschke, H. *Politics* (New York: Macmillan, 1916).

Wallensteen, P. 'Incompatibility, Confrontation, and War: Four Models and Three Historical Systems, 1816–1976', *Journal of Peace Research*, 18, 1 (1981), pp. 57–90.

Wallensteen, P. 'Universalism vs. Particularism: On the Limits of Major Power Order', *Journal of Peace Research*, 21, 3 (1984), pp. 243–57.

Wallerstein, I. *The Modern World System I. Capitalist Agriculture and the Origins of the World-Economy in the Sixteenth Century* (New York: Academic Publishers, 1974).

Wallerstein, I. *The Modern World System II. Mercantilism and the Consolidation of the European World-Economy, 1600–1750* (New York: Academic Press, 1980).

Wallerstein, I. 'The West, Capitalism, and the Modern World-System', in T. Brook and G. Blue (eds), *China and Historical Capitalism: Genealogies of Sinological Knowledge* (Cambridge: Cambridge University Press, 1999).

Waltz, K. N. 'Kant, Liberalism, and War', *American Political Science Review*, 56, 2 (1962), pp. 331–40.

Waltz, K. N. *The Spread of Nuclear Weapons: More May Be Better*, Adelphi Paper No. 171 (London: Institute for Strategic Studies, 1981).

Waltz, K. N. 'The Origins of War in Neorealist Theory', in R. I. Rotberg and T. K. Rabb (eds), *The Origin and Prevention of Major War* (Cambridge: Cambridge University Press, 1989), pp. 39–52.

Waltz, K. N. 'The Emerging Structure of International Politics', *International Security*, 18, 2 (1993), pp. 44–79.

Waltz, K. N. 'Structural Realism after the Cold War', *International Security*, 25, 1 (2000), pp. 5–41.

Warden III, J. A. 'Air Theory for the Twenty-First Century', in K. P. Magyar (ed.), *Challenge and Response: Anticipating US Military Security Concerns* (Maxwell: Air Force University Press, 1994).

Wayman, F. W. and Morgan, T. C. 'Measuring Polarity in the International System', in J. D. Singer and P. F. Diehl (eds), *Measuring the Correlates of War* (Ann Arbor: University of Michigan Press, 1990).

Weart, S. R. *Never at War: Why Democracies Will Not Fight Each Other* (New Haven: Yale University Press, 1998).

Weber, F. G. *Eagles on the Crescent: Germany, Austria, and the Diplomacy of the Turkish Alliance, 1914–1918* (Ithaca: Cornell University Press, 1970).

Webster, P. and Watson, R. 'Bin Laden's Nuclear Threat', *The Times* (London), 26 October 2001.

Wedgwood, C. V. *The Thirty Years War* (London: Jonathan Cape, 1938).

Wedgwood, R. 'Regional and Subregional Organizations in International Conflict Management', in C. A. Crocker, F. O. Hampson and P. Aall (eds), *Managing Global Chaos: Sources of and Responses to International Conflict* (Washington DC: US Institute of Peace Press, 1996), pp. 275–85.

Weeks, T. E. *Nation and State in Late Imperial Russia: Nationalism and Russification on the Western Frontier, 1863–1914* (DeKalb, 1996).

Welch, D. A. 'The Politics and Psychology of Restraint: Israeli Decision-making in the Gulf War', in J. G. Stein and L. W. Pauly (eds), *Choosing to Cooperate: How States Avoid Loss* (Baltimore: Johns Hopkins University Press, 1993), pp. 128–69.

Weltman, J. J. *World Politics and the Evolution of War* (Baltimore: Johns Hopkins University Press, 1995).

Wendt, A. *Social Theory of International Relations* (New York: Cambridge University Press, 1999).

Wendt, A. *Social Theory of World Politics* (Cambridge: Cambridge University Press, 1999).

White, J. A. *The Diplomacy of the Russo-Japanese War* (Princeton: Princeton University Press, 1964).

Wight, M. *Power Politics* (ed. by H. Bull and C. Holbraad), (Harmondsworth: Penguin, 1978).

Wilson, P. 'European Warfare 1450–1815', in J. Black (ed.), *War in the Early Modern World 1450–1815* (Boulder: Westview Press, 1999), pp. 192–6.

Wippich, R.-H. *Japan und die deutsche Fernostpolitik 1894–1898* (Stuttgart: F. Steiner, 1987).

Wirsing, A. S. 'The Siachen Glacier Dispute, part 1', *Strategic Studies*, x, 1 (1987), pp. 49–66.

Wirsing, A. S. 'The Siachen Glacier Dispute, part 2', *Strategic Studies*, xi, 3 (1988), pp. 75–94.

Wirsing, A. S. 'The Siachen Glacier Dispute, part 3', *Strategic Studies*, xii, 1 (1988), pp. 38–54.

Wirtz, J. J. 'Counterproliferation, Conventional Counterforce and Nuclear War', *Journal of Strategic Studies*, 23, 1 (2000), pp. 5–23.

Wirtz, J. J. and Russell, J. A. 'U.S. Policy on Preventive War and Preemption', *The Nonproliferation Review*, spring (2003), pp. 113–23.

Wohlfort, W. C. 'The Stability of a Unipolar World', *International Security*, 24, 1 (1999), pp. 5–41.

Woolf, S. *Napoleon's Integration of Europe* (New York: Routledge, 1991).

Wright, R. 'What Was War? In the Next Millennium, Peace Will Have a Chance', *The New York Times Magazine*, 15 December 1999, pp. 98–100.

Yardeni, E. 'The Economic Consequences of the Peace', in J. Mueller (ed.), *Peace, Prosperity, and Politics* (New York: Westview, 2000), pp. 91–110.

Zacher, M. W. 'The Territorial Integrity Norm: International Boundaries and the Use of Force', *International Organization*, 55, 2 (2001), pp. 215–50.

Zolberg, A. 'Origins of the Modern World System: A Missing Link', *World Politics*, 33, 2 (1981), pp. 253–81.

Websites

'Escalating Space Race', www.stratfor.com, 5 January 2001.

'NATO in the 21st Century', Millennium Year Lord Mayor's Lecture by the NATO Secretary General, 20 July 2000. Distributed at iipmag@hq.nato.int

'NATO: What Have You Done For Me Lately?' Earl Grey Memorial Lecture by the NATO Secretary General, 16 February 2001. Distributed at iipmag@hq.nato.int

'U.S. Warns Iraq over Using Mass Destruction Arms', www.reuters.com, 26 January 2003.

NAME INDEX

SUBJECT INDEX